A TEXT BOOK OF

FUNDAMENTALS OF CIVIL ENGINEERING

FIRST YEAR (F.E.) DEGREE COURSE IN B.TECH.

STRICTLY ACCORDING TO SYLLABUS OF BHARATI VIDYAPEETH UNIVERSITY, PUNE

(COMMON FOR ALL DEGREE ENGINEERING BRANCHES)

V. R. Phadke

M. E. (Civil)
Assistant Professor of Civil Engg.,
J.S.P.M.'s Rajshri Shahu College of Engineering,
Tathwade, **PUNE**.

U. S. Patil

B.E. Civil, M. Tech (Construction Management),
Associate Professor, Civil Engg. Deptt.,
Bharati Vidyapeeth's Group of Institutes Technical Campus,
College of Engineering,
Lavale, PUNE - 43

FUNDAMENTALS OF CIVIL ENGINEERING (BHARATI VIDYAPEETH UNIVERSITY)

First Edition	: August 2014	ISBN 978-93-5164-102-5
©	: Authors	

The text of this publication, or any part thereof, should not be reproduced or transmitted in any form or stored in any computer storage system or device for distribution including photocopy, recording, taping or information retrieval system or reproduced on any disc, tape, perforated media or other information storage device etc., without the written permission of Authors with whom the rights are reserved. Breach of this condition is liable for legal action.

Every effort has been made to avoid errors or omissions in this publication. In spite of this, errors may have crept in. Any mistake, error or discrepancy so noted and shall be brought to our notice shall be taken care of in the next edition. It is notified that neither the publisher nor the authors or seller shall be responsible for any damage or loss of action to any one, of any kind, in any manner, therefrom.

Published By :
NIRALI PRAKASHAN
Abhyudaya Pragati, 1312, Shivaji Nagar,
Off J.M. Road, PUNE – 411005
Tel - (020) 25512336/37/39, Fax - (020) 25511379
Email : niralipune@pragationline.com

Printed By :
Repro Knowledgecast Limited
Thane

DISTRIBUTION CENTRES
PUNE

Nirali Prakashan
119, Budhwar Peth, Jogeshwari Mandir Lane
Pune 411002, Maharashtra
Tel : (020) 2445 2044, 66022708, Fax : (020) 2445 1538
Email : bookorder@pragationline.com

Nirali Prakashan
S. No. 28/25, Dhyari,
Near Pari Company, Pune 411041
Tel : (020) 24690204 Fax : (020) 24690316
Email : dhyari@pragationline.com
bookorder@pragationline.com

MUMBAI
Nirali Prakashan
385, S.V.P. Road, Rasdhara Co-op. Hsg. Society Ltd.,
Girgaum, Mumbai 400004, Maharashtra
Tel : (022) 2385 6339 / 2386 9976, Fax : (022) 2386 9976
Email : niralimumbai@pragationline.com

DISTRIBUTION BRANCHES

NAGPUR
Pratibha Book Distributors
Above Maratha Mandir, Shop No. 3, First Floor,
Rani Jhanshi Square, Sitabuldi, Nagpur 440012,
Maharashtra, Tel : (0712) 254 7129

BENGALURU
Pragati Book House
House No. 1, Sanjeevappa Lane, Avenue Road Cross,
Opp. Rice Church, Bengaluru – 560002.
Tel : (080) 64513344, 64513355,
Mob : 9880582331, 9845021552
Email:bharatsavla@yahoo.com

JALGAON
Nirali Prakashan
34, V. V. Golani Market, Navi Peth, Jalgaon 425001,
Maharashtra, Tel : (0257) 222 0395
Mob : 94234 91860

KOLHAPUR
Nirali Prakashan
New Mahadvar Road,
Kedar Plaza, 1st Floor Opp. IDBI Bank
Kolhapur 416 012, Maharashtra. Mob : 9850046155

CHENNAI
Pragati Books
9/1, Montieth Road, Behind Taas Mahal, Egmore,
Chennai 600008 Tamil Nadu, Tel : (044) 6518 3535,
Mob : 94440 01782 / 98450 21552 / 98805 82331, Email : bharatsavla@yahoo.com

RETAIL OUTLETS
PUNE

Pragati Book Centre
157, Budhwar Peth, Opp. Ratan Talkies,
Pune 411002, Maharashtra
Tel : (020) 2445 8887 / 6602 2707, Fax : (020) 2445 8887

Pragati Book Centre
Amber Chamber, 28/A, Budhwar Peth,
Appa Balwant Chowk, Pune : 411002, Maharashtra,
Tel : (020) 20240335 / 66281669
Email : pbcpune@pragationline.com

Pragati Book Centre
676/B, Budhwar Peth, Opp. Jogeshwari Mandir,
Pune 411002, Maharashtra
Tel : (020) 6601 7784 / 6602 0855

PBC Book Sellers & Stationers
152, Budhwar Peth, Pune 411002, Maharashtra
Tel : (020) 2445 2254 / 6609 2463

MUMBAI
Pragati Book Corner
Indira Niwas, 111 - A, Bhavani Shankar Road, Dadar (W), Mumbai 400028, Maharashtra
Tel : (022) 2422 3526 / 6662 5254, Email : pbcmumbai@pragationline.com

www.pragationline.com info@pragationline.com

PREFACE

We are very glad to present this text book "**Fundamentals of Civil Engineering**" to the students of First Year (F.E.) Degree in Engineering of Bharati Vidyapeeth University, Pune.

The authors are well aware of the Syllabus of Civil Engineering for First Year Engineering. The relevant matter from the text book of "Fundamentals of Civil Engineering" has been incorporated in this text book which was very popular in the student community. Wherever necessary additional figures with proper illustrations have been added. The text has been revised at many places for clarity and new problems have been added. The authors hope that the book will be warmly received by the student community since they get the subject matter in concise form at one place instead of requiring them to search many reference books. Any suggestions to improve the utility of the book will be highly appreciated.

Our sincere thanks are due to **Shri. Dineshbhai Furia, Shri. Jignesh Furia, Shri. M. P. Munde** and whole staff of Nirali Prakashan who are responsible in bringing out this book in time.

PUNE **Authors**

SYLLABUS

UNIT I : CIVIL ENGINEERING SCOPE AND APPLICATIONS　　　(06 Hours)

Civil engineering scope, Importance and applications to other disciplines of engineering, Civil engineering construction process and role of civil engineer, Government authorities related to civil engineering, Types of structures based on loading, material and configuration, Building components and their functions, Civil engineering materials : Concrete, Construction - Steel, Bricks, Flooring materials and tiles, Plaints, Plywood, Glass and Aluminium.

UNIT II : SURVEYING　　　(06 Hours)

Objectives, Principles and Classification of Surveying, Linear, Angular, Vertical and Area measurements and related instruments.

UNIT III : BUILDING PLANNING AND BYE-LAWS　　　(06 Hours)

Site selection for residential building, Principles of building planning, Building bye-laws : Necessity, Floor space index, Heights, Open space requirements, Set back distance, Ventilation and lighting, Concept of carpet and built-up area, Minimum areas and sizes for residential buildings, Concept of eco-friendly structures and intelligent buildings.

UNIT IV : FOUNDATIONS AND EARTHQUAKES　　　(06 Hours)

Function of foundation, Concept of bearing capacity and its estimation, Types of foundation and its suitability, Causes of failure of foundation.

Earthquakes : Causes, Effects and Guidelines for earthquake resistant design, Earthquake zones.

UNIT V : IRRIGATION AND WATER SUPPLY　　　(06 Hours)

Rainfall measurement and its use in design of damps, Types of dams, Canals, Methods of irrigation and their merits and demerits, Hydropower structures, Water supply, Drinking water requirements and its quality, Water and sewage treatment flow chart.

UNIT VI : INFRASTRUCTURE　　　(06 Hours)

Roads : Types of roads and their suitability, Cross-section of roads, Meaning of terms : Width of roads, Super elevation, Camber, Gradient, Sight distance, Materials used for construction of roads.

Railways : Types of gauges, Section of railway track, Components of railway track, Advantages.

Bridges : Components – Foundation, Piers, Bearings, Deck.

Airways : Components – Runway, Taxiway and Hangers.

CONTENTS

Unit I

1. Civil Engineering Scope and Applications — 1.1 – 1.76

Unit II

2. Surveying — 2.1 – 2.36

3. Angular Measurements — 3.1 – 3.42

4. Vertical Measurements — 4.1 – 4.36

5. Area Measurements and Related Instruments — 5.1 – 5.20

Unit III

6. Building Planning and Bye-Laws — 6.1 – 6.22

Unit IV

7. Foundation — 7.1 – 7.12

8. Earthquake — 8.1 – 8.8

Unit V

9. Irrigation and Water Supply — 9.1 – 9.24

Unit VI

10. Infrastructure — 10.1 – 10.32

❑❑❑

UNIT I

Chapter 1
CIVIL ENGINEERING SCOPE AND APPLICATIONS

1.1 SCOPE OF CIVIL ENGINEERING

Civil Engineering is a broad based term which contains allied subjects such as Surveying, Construction Engineering, Transportation Engineering, Fluid Mechanics, Irrigation Engineering, Structural Engineering, Geotechnical and Foundation Engineering, Environmental Engineering, etc. All these subjects are interrelated to each other and study of these subjects is complimentary in nature. The subject of civil engineering encompasses wide variety of topics such as civil engineering applications to different disciplines including linear and angular measurements using traditional as well as modern electronic equipments, planning and construction of buildings and plants required for manufacture of machine components, electrical and electronic components, chemicals, etc. Similarly, acts concerned with Acquisition of land required either for construction of houses and factories and protection of environment are also included in Civil Engineering. First five chapters of the book cover the syllabii related with the branch 'surveying' of Civil Engineering, which involves measurements in horizontal as well as in vertical plane. Chapters 6 to 8 are dealing with the planning and constructional aspects of buildings. With the industrialisation of cities, setting up of industrial townships and movement of number of vehicles i.e. automobiles on road, there has been a lot of atmospheric pollution. This has an adverse effect on the clean natural environment. Chapter 9 of the book deals only with the conventional and non-conventional sources of energy and their impact on environment, sources, causes and effects of different types of pollution and remedial measures to control pollution.

1.2 IMPORTANCE AND APPLICATIONS TO OTHER DISCIPLINES OF ENGINEERING

The basic areas in Civil Engineering can be classified depending on the needs of the mankind which can be broadly stated as under.

1. Housing : The people need houses as a shelter. Similarly, certain structures such as bridges, dams, multistoreyed buildings are needed to accomplish other needs. The engineering sciences dealing with the different aspects of housing, and construction of structures are listed below :

(a) Surveying.
(b) Construction engineering.
(c) Structural engineering.
(d) Geotechnical and foundation engineering.
(e) Earthquake engineering.
(f) Quantity surveying.

2. Water : Water is the basic need which is required not only for supplying water through pipelines for drinking purposes but for cultivation of crops, cleaning purposes i.e. maintaining the clean environment and in some manufacturing processes. The areas in Civil Engineering which cater to this need are

(a) Irrigation engineering.
(b) Fluid mechanics.
(c) Environmental engineering which includes water supply and sanitary engineering.

3. Communication : This is achieved by providing different means of communication such as surface or land transport, water transport and air transport. The discipline in engineering (with reference to land transport) which covers this aspect is known as.

(a) Transportation engineering : In this we consider mainly road transport and railway transport.

The different branches of Civil Engineering can be summarised as shown below :

Basic Areas in Civil Engineering

Housing	Water	Surface communication
(i) Surveying	(i) Irrigation Engg.	Transportation Engg.
(ii) Construction Engg.	(ii) Fluid Mechanics	Road transport / Railway Transport
(iii) Construction Magt.	(iii) Environmental Engg.	
(iv) Structural Engg.		
(v) Geotechnical and Foundation Engg.		
(vi) Earthquake Engg.		
(vii) Quantity surveying		

1.2.1 Surveying

It is a branch of civil engineering which enables the engineer

(i) To prepare maps and plans of the existing features of ground from the field observations taken in the horizontal plane.

(ii) To determine or to establish relative positions of the points on the surface of earth.

The relative positions of points in the vertical plane are shown by sections with the help of measurements in the vertical plane. Such measurements are covered in the topic of Levelling.

Before the construction of any structure is undertaken, surveying of the land on which the construction is to come up i.e. linear and angular measurements and vertical measurements are always necessary.

Applications :

1. To determine the horizontal distances between different points by methods of survey and to prepare plan of an area.
2. To find the levels or elevations of various points along the proposed road, railway track, canal or earthen dam. From this data, it is possible to determine the quantity of earthwork beforehand.
3. To determine the positions of inaccessible points.
4. To fix the alignment of road, railway line, tunnel, bridges and marine structures.
5. To lay the water supply, drainage, oil and gas pipe-lines having a particular slope i.e. gradient.
6. To determine the nature of bed surface i.e. profile of a lake, river or sea. (The data collected is useful for navigational purpose i.e. water transport.)

1.2.2 Construction Engineering

This subject includes the construction of residential buildings, industrial structures; such as workshop buildings for housing different types of machines, plants for manufacturing of automobiles or machine components or chemicals and storage sheds. The study of this subject enables the engineer to know about different materials of construction and different techniques of construction or erection of these structures efficiently and economically.

Applications :

1. To make use of modern materials of construction for special types of structures such as Concrete dams, Buildings for housing the explosives, Atomic power plants, T.V. Towers, Transmitting and Receiving stations, Tunnels, Viaducts (i.e. bridges constructed in Valleys, etc.)
2. To make use of the knowledge of this subject for planning a big project and decide the sequence of stages of construction.
3. To apply modern techniques and machinery for safe and speedy construction of special types of structures for different disciplines of engineering.

Construction Management :

This is a branch of Civil Engineering in which the management of men and materials is done in such a way that the construction project is completed in the stipulated time and in the economical way. To achieve this, special techniques such as C.P.M. and PERT are employed. In any construction project, the different activities required to be done are listed from the beginning to the end of the project and then these special techniques are applied to achieve the desired result.

Applications :

1. This is useful in the planning of big projects.
2. The application of techniques of construction management helps in completing the project in the stipulated period of time.
3. The study of this branch helps in achieving economy in the project.
4. The construction activities can be planned in a symmetric way.

1.2.3 Structural Engineering

The structures are broadly classified as Steel Structures and Reinforced Cement Concrete structures. In a framed structure, the supporting members of the frame are stanchion or column, girders and trusses in Steel Structures, columns and footing, beams and R.C.C. slab in case of R.C.C. structures. The study of the structural engineering includes the design of the supporting members of the frame to ensure stability and safety of structures. Engineering mechanics, strength of materials, theory of structures form the basis for structural engineering.

Applications :

1. To enable the engineer to design the structural steel members as well as the structures itself, for given loads to ensure safety of structures.

2. To make the economical designs of the structural steel members or R.C.C. framed structures.

3. To decide the procedure for the execution of work for special type of steel or R.C.C. constructions.

4. To ensure desired factor of safety for members of structures and connections like rivets, bolts, etc.

1.2.4 Geotechnical and Foundation Engineering

1.2.4.1 Geotechnical Engineering

This is also called as soil mechanics. It is a discipline of civil engineering in which study of soil, its behaviour on application of load and its application as an engineering material in the construction work such as construction of earth dams, embankments for roads, is done.

The subject is useful for

1. Determining properties and strength characteristics of different types of soils.

2. Classifying the soils to predict their usefulness for different purposes.

3. Determining intensity of stresses on soil strata at different depths under varying loads.

4. Assessing capability of a subgrade of a road and to determine thickness of various layers of pavement.

5. Designing earthen embankments.

1.2.4.2 Foundation Engineering

Foundation Engineering is a branch of civil engineering which deals with the application of knowledge of Geotechnical Engineering in the design and construction of different types of foundations for buildings, bridges, marine structures, light and heavy machine foundations, etc.

Applications :

1. Carrying out soil exploration to know the nature of soil strata and to determine suitable depth of foundation.

2. Determining safe bearing capacity of soil for a given type of foundation and to predict probable settlement of a structure.

3. Choosing a suitable type of foundation for safety and stability of the structure.

1.2.5 Earthquake Engineering

Earthquake is a deadly and devastating natural phenomenon, which is considered for design of structures. Destructions caused by earthquakes at Killari i.e. in Maharashtra and at Bhuj in Western part of Gujarat in the recent past underline the need of such design. In the subject of earthquake engineering, the effect of earthquakes on the structures is studied. i.e. magnitude and direction of earthquake force is calculated and the factor of safety is calculated for this purpose. The country is divided into different earthquake zones to find the location of structure in a particular zone from earthquake point of view. (See the map of India for earthquake zones.)

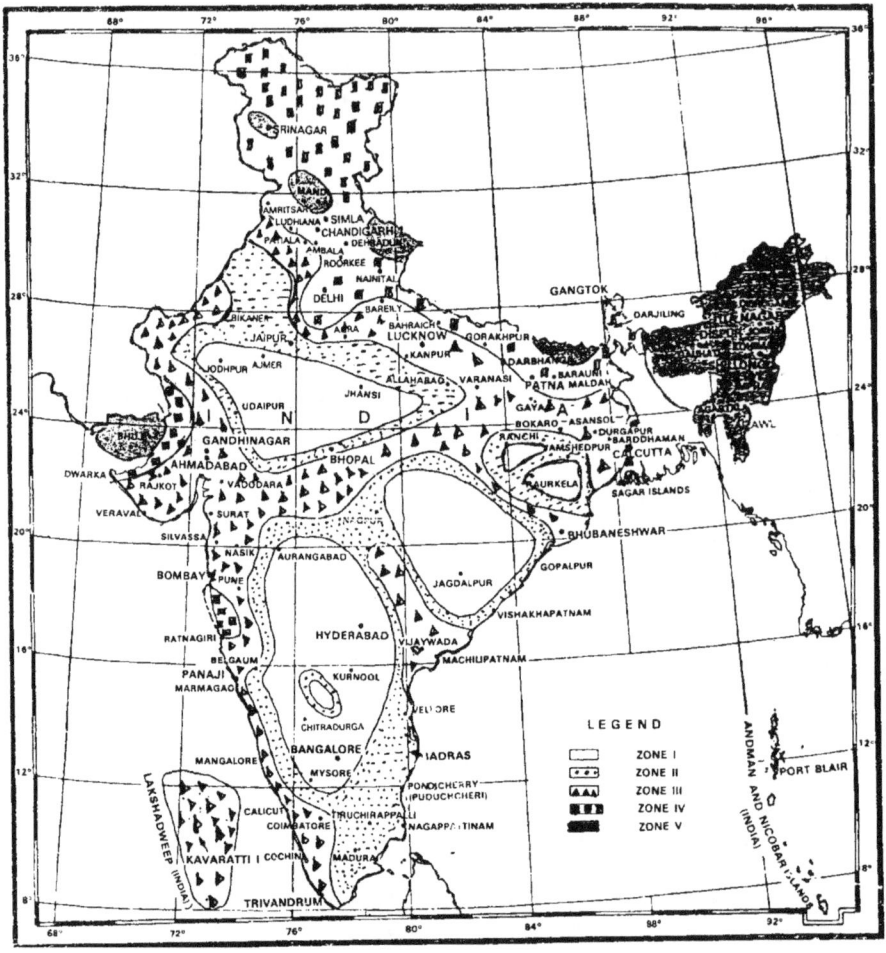

Fig. 1.1 : Map of India showing Earthquake Zones

Applications :

1. The knowledge of earthquake engineering helps in the design of important structures such as dams, high rise buildings, towers, etc. to withstand normal expected earthquakes.

2. To strengthen the existing structures if the earthquake force was not accounted for in the original design. After the Koyna earthquake, different dams in Maharashtra have been strengthened by suitable measures.

1.2.6 Quantity Surveying

The study of this enables the engineer to estimate in advance the quantities of various materials and different items in a project. The estimation is useful in knowing the approximate cost of the work to be taken up in hand at a later date.

Applications : Knowing the quantities of different items in a project

1. Enables the engineer to plan the execution of work in phases according to the modern techniques of management.

2. The owner in case of buildings or the Government in case of large projects, can allocate the finances looking to the stages in which the whole work is contemplated to be finished.

3. This knowledge of quantity surveying is useful to decide the feasibility of project in advance.

Quantity Surveying also includes the valuation of an existing building or an old property. Hence it would be interesting to note the difference between the estimation and valuation of a building.

	Estimation		Valuation
1.	It aims at determining approximate cost of building or other services in a project.	1.	It aims at determining value of a property (usually old property).
2.	Estimated quantities and cost are determined.	2.	Market value of property to be sold or purchased is determined.
3.	It only involves quantities, rate analysis and cost as per detailed drawings/plans.	3.	It involves quantities, present value of structure and other techniques for valuation.

1.2.7 Irrigation Engineering

This is a branch of civil engineering in which supply of water is done to the areas scanty of rainfall either for purposes of cultivation of crops or for supplying drinking water. The storage of water is done by construction of dams or weirs and supplying water to fields through open canals or closed pipes.

Applications :

1. To study the application of water to fields in accordance with the requirement of water for crops by new techniques such as sprinkler irrigation and drip irrigation.
2. To determine the capacity of a reservoir.
3. To design and construct different types of dams for storage of water.
4. To design different allied structures such as spillways, weirs and canals.
5. To design the flood control devices.

1.2.8 Fluid Mechanics

Scope : Fluid Mechanics is a branch of civil engineering which deals with the behaviour of fluids i.e. liquids and gases when at rest or in motion and subjected to a system of forces. The subject includes three subdivisions.

- (i) **Fluid statics :** The study of fluids at rest and force exerted by liquid on immersed areas.
- (ii) **Fluid kinematics :** The study which deals with velocity, acceleration, displacement of fluid mass.
- (iii) **Fluid dynamics :** The study of fluids in motion concerning forces, acceleration, etc.

Applications : Knowledge of fluid mechanics is useful in

1. Design of gates used to control the flood water in case of dams.
2. Design of water retaining structures such as dams, elevated water reservoirs, etc.
3. Design of pipe lines carrying liquids or water under pressure from storage reservoirs upto desired location.
4. Design of hydraulic machines such as reciprocating pumps, centrifugal pumps, turbines, etc.
5. Design of structures subjected to water pressure as in the case of piers or abutments of bridges, gate valves, etc.
6. Knowledge of fluid mechanics is also useful in other fields such as irrigation engineering, environmental engineering, chemical engineering, ocean engineering, aeronautical engineering, etc.

1.2.9 Environmental Engineering

This is an important branch of civil engineering which was previously known as Public Health Engineering. It includes water supply engineering and waste water engineering. The quality of life is affected due to various factors like :

(i) Increase in population and urbanisation i.e. concentration of population in urban areas.

(ii) Phenomenal growth of industries, thereby requiring more water, fuel, energy, transport facilities and human resources.

The above factors have also adversely affected human life due to various types of pollution such as (a) Air pollution, (b) Land pollution, (c) Water pollution, (d) Noise pollution, (e) Thermal pollution, (f) Radioactive pollution.

Environmental engineering deals with

(i) Tapping water from different sources, treating the raw water and purifying it, testing its quality and distributing it to the consumers.

(ii) Receiving waste water from different sources such as residential colonies, different industries, treating the same upto safe acceptable standards and its disposal in a suitable manner.

(iii) To study the causes and effects of other types of pollutions such as air, land, water, noise, thermal and radioactive and methods to control the same.

The central and state governments have enacted various laws for the protection of environment such as

(i) The water act 1974.

(ii) Maharashtra preservation of trees act 1975.

(iii) Environmental protection act 1986.

(Refer chapter 8 for details of the above act.)

Applications :

1. To study interrelationship between biotic and abiotic factors of the environment.
2. To test quality of water used for drinking and industrial purposes.
3. To design, construct and maintain water treatment plants and sewage treatment plants.
4. To control and reduce different types of pollution by various methods.
5. To quantify (measure) the parameters of pollution like B.O.D., S.P.M., etc.

1.2.10 Transportation Engineering

This subject deals with the transport of men and materials through different communication routes such as land, water and air. The Railways and Roads are the important modes of communication by land. The water transport is feasible only where the rivers, canals are navigable or sea coast is available. Transportation by air routes is increasing day by day. The transportation of men and goods for short distances can be speedily done by Road transport, whereas Railway transport is considered safe, convenient for long distances. The knowledge of surveying and levelling is very useful before deciding the alignments of Roads or Railways. The preparation of contour plan of a hilly region obtained from levelling operation is useful in deciding the alignment of hill roads. The knowledge of surveying and levelling enables the engineer to decide alignment of tunnels, which becomes necessary when the road or railway transportation is to be done through the hilly region.

Roads and railways form the major means of land transport, hence it will be worthwhile to see the comparative aspects of Road and Railway transport.

Comparison of Road and Railway transport

	Road Transport		Railway Transport
1.	Door to door service is possible.	1.	Service is from station to station.
2.	Safety of cargo due to careful handling and direct accountability of driver and cleaner.	2.	There is breakage and pilferage in handling.
3.	Suitable for any distance.	3.	Suitable for long distance hauls.
4.	Tractive resistance of pneumatic wheels is greater than steel wheels.	4.	Tractive resistance of steel wheels on rails is lesser than pneumatic wheel tyres.
5.	Steeper gradients are possible.	5.	There is limitation on the steeper gradients.
6.	Services can be customer tailored.	6.	Only specified services are provided.
7.	Octroi holdups affect the delivery of goods.	7.	No such octroi holdups.
8.	More employment potential.	8.	Less employment potential.
9.	Packaging economies are possible.	9.	No other economies.

Applications :

1. To design and construct safe as well as efficient transportation routes.
2. To select proper construction materials for transportation routes.
3. To repair and maintain working of transportation routes and to maintain safe conditions of travel.

1.2.10.1 Railway Track

It is also called as the Permanent Way. It consists of rails, fixed to sleepers and sleepers in turn resting on ballast (crushed stone metal) and subgrade. Fig. 1.2 shows the typical cross-section of a Railway track.

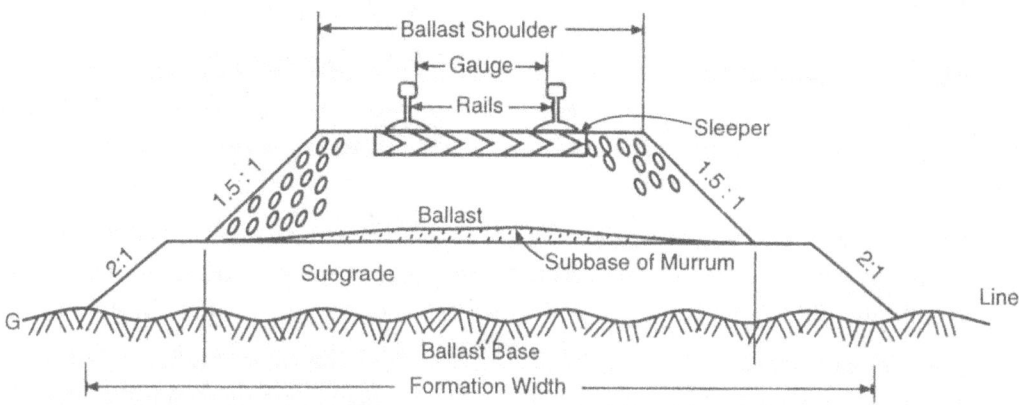

Fig. 1.2 : Typical cross-section of a Permanent Way or Railway Track

Gauge of the railway track : The clear distance between the inner faces of rails is called gauge of the track. The following three gauges are used on Indian railways.

Gauge	Distance between the inner faces
1. Broad gauge	1.676 m
2. Meter gauge	1.000 m
3. Narrow gauge	0.762 m

The present policy of the government is to convert meter gauge and narrow gauge section to broad gauge and thus to have a uniform gauge throughout the country. Indian railways are divided into different zones for convenience of operation and maintenance :

(i) Northern railway (ii) Central railway
(iii) Southern railway (iv) Eastern railway
(v) Western railway (vi) Northeastern railway.
(vii) South eastern railway (viii) South Central railway.

1.2.10.2 Types of Roads

Roads can be classified in two ways.

(a) **According to materials of construction**, roads are classified into four categories as follows :

(i)   Earth Roads : These are kutcha roads where earth is the main constituent of road and usually provided in villages.

(ii) Water bound Macadam roads : In this type, broken stones of size varying from 2.5 cm to 7.5 cm are laid in three layers, on prepared subgrade with bigger pieces of stones laid in the bottom course. This has become the method of road construction today.

(iii) Bituminous roads : On the water bound mecadam surface, smaller chips of stone size varying from 16 mm to 20 mm with bitumen as binder are laid in the form of 30 mm to 40 mm thick carpet. This provides a smooth wearing course at top of the road. (Fig. 1.3)

(iv) Concrete roads : In this the binding agent is cement. Cement concrete is used to lay the top course of road slab. This forms a rigid wearing surface on the top and has got good durability. (Fig. 1.4)

Flexible pavements : Bituminous pavements, W. B. Macadam roads, Stabilized soil bases are the examples of flexible pavements. The pavement assumes the shape of underlying base course layers on application of load. The strength and rigidity of flexible pavement is much less than that of rigid pavement. See Fig. 1.3 for flexible pavement.

Rigid pavements : It is a concrete slab laid on subgrade. It has considerable strength and rigidity. Rigid pavement is not deformed to the shape of lower surface as it can bridge the gaps in the lower layer. See Fig. 1.4 i.e. section of a concrete road which is the example of rigid pavement.

The following figures show the section of a Bituminous road and a concrete road.

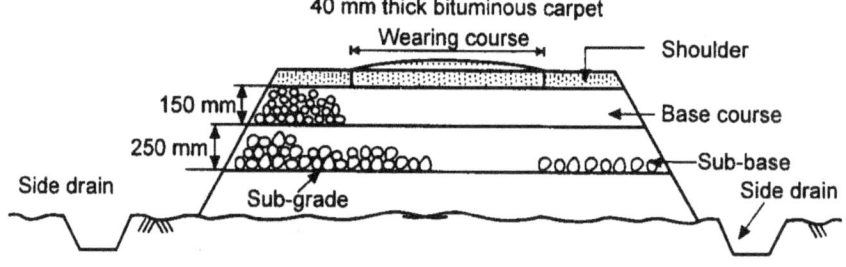

Fig. 1.3 : Section of a Bituminous road (i.e. Flexible Pavement)

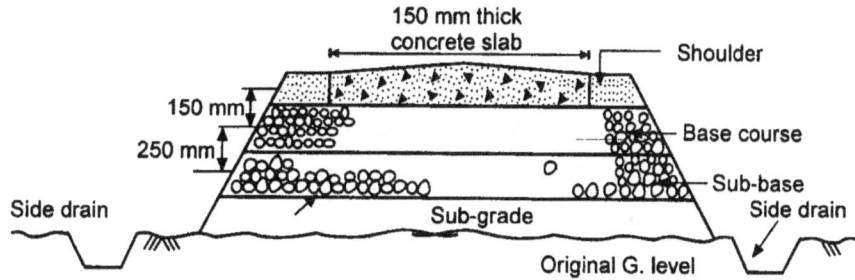

Fig. 1.4 : Section of a concrete road (i.e. Rigid Pavement)

(b) According to **Nagpur Road Plan**, roads have been classified into four categories considering the significance of towns.

(i) **National highways :** These roads connect capital cities or large cities in different states.

(ii) **State highways :** These roads form the main trunk or arterial roads connecting the district headquarters and important cities within a state. These roads are connected with the National Highways of adjacent states.

(iii) **District roads :** These roads are constructed to serve areas of production and markets and are capable of taking road traffic into the rural areas. These are further subdivided into Major District Roads (M.D.R.) and Other District Roads (O.D.R.).

(iv) **Village roads :** These roads connect villages within a district headquarters and carry the traffic into the heart of rural areas.

1.2.11 Infrastructure Development

Infrastructure facilities include

(1) good surface communication links such as Tar or Concrete roads,

(2) provision of water supply distribution systems i.e. construction of water storage reservoirs or sumps, laying of underground pipes, etc.

(3) supply of electrical power for which construction of switch yards, construction of transmission line towers, construction of electrical substations,

(4) provision of drainage systems which may include construction of surface drains or subsurface drains for the disposal of waste water,

(5) providing inland communication lines i.e. telephone lines, etc.

The knowledge of basic areas of civil engineering can be of great use in providing the infrastructural facilities where constructional aspect is involved for development of regions/towns. Hence, it will not be an exaggeration to make a statement "good infrastructural facilities help rapid growth of a particular area". In Maharashtra State, Maharashtra Industrial Development Corporation has provided the infrastructural facilities at many places where industrial townships were thought of. To cite few examples where rapid growth of a particular area has taken place are :

(i) Industrial area near Sinnar, a Taluka in Nasik district.

(ii) Pimpri-Chinchwad township in Pune district, where many industries are located. The development of Pimpri-Chinchwad area was so enormous that Pimpri-Chinchwad township have got their own Municipal Corporation.

(iii) Waluj industrial area near the city of Aurangabad.

(iv) The development of Vashi town near Mumbai due to provision of infrastructural facilities which has helped to reduce the burden of providing civic amenities to populous city of Mumbai.

1.3 CIVIL ENGINEERING CONSTRUCTION PROCESS

Although the requirements of buildings falling under the mechanical engineering, chemical engineering, electrical engineering constructions may vary in each type of constructions, the role of civil engineer is more or less same in the execution of a project.

The role of civil engineer starts from the stage when the project is conceived. In the completion of any project, the work is to be broadly divided in the following stages.

1. Preparation of drawings as per the user's requirements.

2. Estimation of the quantities of items pertaining to civil engineering structures.

3. Preparation of tender documents and inviting quotations from the contractors.

4. After the tenders are accepted, execution of work as per the specifications.

Earlier we have seen the different types of constructions which the civil engineer will be required to execute. Usually the part of civil engineer in each of the stage described above will be explained in the following paragraphs.

1. Preparation of drawings : Usually the drawings are prepared by the Architect considering the user's requirements; however the civil engineer can prepare drawings if the work is of a smaller extent and to decide about the specifications of work. In that case the role of civil engineer is that of an Architect/Designer.

2. Estimation of the quantities : The civil engineer has to estimate the quantities pertaining to civil engineering items and to prepare approximate estimates of work. The civil engineer works as a quantity surveyor.

3. Preparation of tender documents : After the approximate cost of the work is known, the agency who will do the construction is to be fixed. Preparation of tender documents and inviting quotations from reputed contractors is either done by an architect or civil engineer himself. After the scrutiny of tenders, the agency who will execute the work is decided. Here the role of civil engineer is that of a consultant/consulting engineer.

4. Execution of work : After the tender is accepted, the work pertaining to civil engineering construction is supervised and executed as per the specifications of the contract.

5. Maintenance of buildings : Finally after the work is completed during the life of building, the civil engineer has to look after the maintenance of buildings. In this case the role of civil engineers is that of a maintenance engineer.

1.3.1 Adverse Conditions

Under which the civil engineer has to work :

There are certain situations where the civil engineer is required to work under adverse conditions. The few examples can be listed as below :

(i) In the concreting operations such as concreting of footings, concreting of R.C.C. slab or beams, columns, there may be intermittent rains. Due to this, the strength of concrete is affected. The civil engineer has to see that the ingredients of concrete are properly proportioned so the strength of concrete is not affected.

(ii) If the bridge is to be constructed across the river which is flowing, the foundation work is to be necessarily done under water. The construction of foundation under water poses a problem to the civil engineer. This is one of the adverse conditions which the civil engineer has to tackle.

(iii) When the tunneling work is to be done through a soft strata which is unstable, this poses a challenge to the civil engineer; in making the tunnel.

(iv) When a railway line or road is to be constructed in a marshy soil, the laying of road or railway becomes difficult. Some special techniques are necessary to stabilize the soil so that the soil will bear the load of railway or road.

1.4 ROLE OF CIVIL ENGINEER IN SPECIFIC FIELDS

Different types of constructions coming under different disciplines are listed below :

1.4.1 Civil Engineering Constructions

The type of constructions covered under this category include (i) Residential building, (ii) Factory sheds, (iii) Roads, (iv) Railways, (v) Bridges, (vi) Tunnels, (vii) Dams, (viii) Reservoirs, (ix) Harbours, (x) Jetties, (xi) Silos and Bunkers, etc. The ancillary services which the civil engineer has to cater are laying of water supply pipes, drainage lines, air ducts etc. The civil engineer has to execute the different types of works as per the drawings and to see that the work is done as per the specifications of work.

1.4.2 Mechanical Engineering Constructions

(i) Industrial sheds for the manufacture of automobiles, (ii) Sheds for manufacture of compressors, (iii) Sheds for manufacture of pipes, diesel engines, heavy vessels, etc. (iv) Storage tanks for oil, etc. (v) Forging shops, (vi) Construction of ducting for air, telephone cable, water pipe lines, etc. (vii) Foundations for heavy machines, (viii) Conveyor system, (ix) Material handling systems.

1.4.3 Electrical Engineering Constructions

Construction of Power Houses, Substations, Transmission line towers, underground power houses, construction of switch yards, etc. including design and construction of machine foundations.

1.4.4 Chemical Engineering Constructions

Sheds for chemicals, storage of chemicals (such as sulphuric acid, hydrochloric acid) in tanks, petrochemical plants. Design of thin and thick shells for storage of chemicals.

1.4.5 Special Type of Works

Construction of atomic power stations, construction of heavy water plants, Refineries, construction of Transmitting and Receiving stations, TV Towers, M.S. structures holding dish Antennas, Aeroplane Hangers, Earth Satellite Stations (such as at Arvi near Pune) etc.

The above list gives an idea about the type of constructions of different nature which the civil engineer may be required to execute.

1.5 CONSTRUCTION OF INDUSTRIAL BUILDINGS

1.5.1 Role of Civil Engineer in the Construction of Buildings for Mechanical Engineering

There are three basic types of industrial buildings : (i) Light Duty, (ii) Medium Duty, (iii) Heavy Duty.

(i) Light Duty Buildings : These buildings include packaging industry, light metal work, clothing, consumer durable small printers etc. Sub-Depots for retail distribution of electrical goods, builder's hardware and similar such items are covered under this category.

(ii) Medium Duty Buildings : The buildings where the batch production of machine components or machines is done, can be classified in this category.

(iii) Heavy Duty Buildings : These buildings are designed such that they accept large scale batch or mass production systems, environmental and other ancillary services and have material handling systems and have overhead gantry cranes for lifting and movement of machinery.

1.5.2 Buildings Housing Different Types of Machines and Equipments

Usually in a plant layout, the following points are considered : (i) Present and future requirement of production. (ii) Quantity of product to be produced. (iii) Flow of materials. (iv) Machinery required. (v) Whether there is batch production or mass production. (vi) Plant facilities etc.

In the transfer line concept where the raw material passes from one machine to other, the operation time in each machine is fixed. Taking into account the above requirements, the sizes of different sheds are fixed. Depending on whether the overhead travelling cranes of different capacities are to be provided, height of sheds is decided. Similarly there are statutory requirements laid down by Government in Factory Act regarding height of sheds, floor areas required for the movement of workers in a shop, water supply and toilet facilities, canteen facilities etc. We will take a typical example of factory manufacturing gears. The operations involved are in Turning section, Milling section, (Hobbing) Gear teeth cutting section, Drilling section, Grinding section and Heat treatment section. **Civil Engineer has to see the following points during execution of work while carrying out the supervision** :

I. (i) If the shed is long and provided with North light roofing on steel trusses, the alignment of steel columns is to be seen.

(ii) The foundation of columns, concrete blocks/pedestals for erection of machines are properly provided. The necessary foundation bolts are provided on the RCC foundation of machines at proper spacing.

(iii) If the heavy machines are provided then the flooring must be hard and durable. Accordingly reinforced concrete floor or Granolithic floor is provided.

(iv) Proper ducting for air, water, telephone and electric cables are provided during the execution of work.

(v) For receiving the gantry girders carrying over-head travelling cranes, the brackets are fixed (welded) to steel columns at proper height.

(vi) The roof drainage and surface drainage are provided in the big sheds.

(vii) To provide the supporting structures for conveyor belts or material handling systems.

(viii) In a 'Standard Room' where sensitive equipments are provided and where calibration of gauges is an important activity, Airconditioning of the room is done and flooring constructed in such a way that it is free from vibrations.

(ix) The alignment of different machines is also required to be checked in transfer line concept of production by civil engineer.

(x) To provide proper foundation for impact and Reciprocating type of machines.

An interesting application where civil engineer is required to see minutely certain constructional details can be cited in respect of Components Plant of General Motors Corporation of U.S.A. A racking system was to be installed covering 1400 sq. met and 30,000 pallet locations with fully automated material handling. This required very precise flooring and positioning of racking uprights (within ± 5 mm tolerance for uprights and ± 3 mm for floors). This precision in flooring was achieved using modern equipments like laser levels.

II. Importance of Civil Engineering in laying a foundation for a big machine.

The different steps involved in laying a foundation for a big machine are indicated below :

(1) The plan of the foundation of the machine is studied first and the important centre lines to be marked on ground are decided first.

(2) The centre lines of the machine are accurately marked on the ground, as well as the size of the foundation pit.

(3) The excavation of the foundation pit is done knowing the depth of foundation.

(4) Making a proper mixture of concrete is absolutely essential to obtain the desired strength of concrete.

(5) If it is a R.C.C. foundation, lowering of the steel bars at proper place is necessary before the concrete is laid.

(6) Leaving proper spaces for the foundation bolts is absolutely important while the concreting of foundation block is done.

The above steps will show how important it is for a civil engineer to know the proper sequence of operations while laying a foundation for a big machine.

1.5.3 Role of Civil Engineer in the Construction of Chemical Plants Required for Chemical Engineering

In the case of plants which manufacture chemicals, which may be acidic in nature or having explosive properties, certain special **points are to be seen by a civil engineer** during the construction. These are as listed below :

(i) Generally the manufacture (production) of acids or hazardous chemicals is done in open sheds.

(ii) The statutory provisions regarding storage of raw chemicals in liquid, gaseous or solid state should be strictly adhered to.

(iii) In chemical plants where the storage of chemical liquids is done, acid proof floor using **acid proof tiles** should be provided.

(iv) Provision **of sand in** the open spaces and surrounding areas of chemical plants is done. Adequate ducts for water pipe lines and provision **of fire hydrants** should be provided during execution of work.

(v) In case of chemicals explosive in nature or actual explosives stored in sheds, precautionary measures such as construction of blast walls, earth traverses alround the building are necessary.

(vi) Provision of earthing and electrical conductors for each shed is necessary.

(vii) Steel work in roof or the frame work and shed needs to be painted with **rust proof** paint periodically.

(viii) The norms regarding industrial safety of buildings should be strictly adhered to.

Refractory linings for Furnaces

In certain plants where manufacture of glass ware or ceramic products is done, the construction of furnaces is of special type. The construction of furnaces is done by ceramic bricks or fire resistant lining in furnace. During the construction of furnaces as in the manufacture of iron, aluminium, copper, etc. where resistance of material to very high temperature is required, a special type of lining is provided for such furnaces by using fire clay bricks. Similarly, the flooring to be provided is also of fire resistant type.

Thus we can conclude that the type of construction may vary in industrial plants constructed under different disciplines but the civil engineer has to cater to the specific requirement of different plants during the execution of works.

1.5.4 Role of Civil Engineer in the Constructions Required for Electrical Engineering

1.5.4.1 Transmission Line Towers

In case of transmission line towers carrying H.T. cables, the following points are to be seen from civil engineering point of view :

(i) Fixing the alignment of towers and the location of towers.

(ii) Checking the centre to distance between the towers by modern equipments such as electronic distance meter.

(iii) Construction of plain cement/reinforced cement concrete foundations for structural frame of tower.

(iv) Actual erection of structural steel members of tower.

1.5.4.2 Power Houses

In the conventional methods of generation of Electricity, the Civil Engineering branches involved are Surveying, Fluid Mechanics, Geotechnical and Foundation Engineering, Irrigation Engineering.

There are different methods of generation of electric power such as (i) Hydroelectric power stations, (ii) Thermal power stations, (iii) Atomic power stations.

In case of hydroelectric power, the location of power stations may be underground or above the ground. The specifications for each type of power station vary depending on the type of generation of power. In case of hydroelectric power and thermal power stations, the civil engineer has to look after the construction of power house buildings mainly and supervise the construction of cooling water tanks in certain cases. In case of super thermal power stations which consist of number of other units, the work of civil engineer starts from siting and locating different units on grid lines of the project land and then to execute the construction of individual structures such as Electrostatic precipitator, Turbo generator house, coal handling plant, cooling towers, etc.

For big size hydroelectric power stations located underground like the one at Koyna, the civil engineering part consists of following components :

- (i) Construction of intake structure at Reservoir.
- (ii) Construction of Head Race Tunnel (a tunnel carrying water under pressure).
- (iii) Construction of penstock (pressure pipes) underground.
- (iv) Construction of power house underground.
- (v) Construction of tail race tunnel.

In case of generation of Atomic power, the construction of power house is of special type involving the use of special materials to prevent the radiation hazards. Hence the civil engineer has to meticulously do the execution of such works.

1.5.5 Role of Civil Engineer in the Constructions required for Instrumentation Engineering and Electronics and Telecommunication Engineering

The civil engineer has to ascertain the specific needs of the buildings required for these branches; which may fall into following broad categories.

1. Some buildings or rooms may need sound proofing as in the case of Broadcasting stations or where recording of music is done.
2. Certain buildings/rooms may require air-conditioning as in the case of television studios.
3. There may be requirement of special type of floorings (e.g. in the case of buildings where work with explosives/ammunition is carried out i.e. Lead sheet flooring).
4. It may be necessary to provide special type of electrical fittings in certain rooms.
5. Sometimes housing or installation of an instrument/gadget, proper or special foundation may be needed.

Knowing the specific requirements of these buildings, or rooms, these are catered for by making special provisions in the Tender documents and executing the same as desired.

1.5.6 Foundation for Antenna Towers

Civil engineering part will include the following :
(i)   Selecting proper site for the location of Antenna towers.
(ii) Construction of plain cement/reinforced cement concrete foundation for the tower.
(iii) Fabrication and Erection of tower on the foundation.

1.6 TYPES OF SUPERSTRUCTURES

The methods used for the construction of superstructures depend on various factors such as loading pattern, purpose, area covered, economy or cost criteria, stability, expected life span of the structure, sub-soil conditions, availability of materials, etc.

There are mainly three types of superstructures :
(A) Load bearing wall structure, (B) Framed structures, (C) Composite structures.

1.6.1 Load Bearing Wall Construction

In load bearing wall construction, the entire load of the superstructure is transmitted through walls to the firm soil below the ground. Thus, the walls are supported on continuous foundations that are resting on hard strata (soil). Usually, this type of construction is adopted at places where hard strata is available at shallow depths. This type of construction can be adopted maximum upto four storeyes but usually two storeyes are constructed. If the number of storeyes are increased, the dead load and thickness and size of foundation increase.

All these factors not only reduce the carpet area but also increase the cost. This type of construction cannot be used for multistoreyed construction as it poses many practical difficulties in construction.

In this type of construction, the structural elements such as beams, trusses, etc. rest directly on the walls. The floors rest on the walls. A typical load bearing structure is shown in Fig. 1.5.

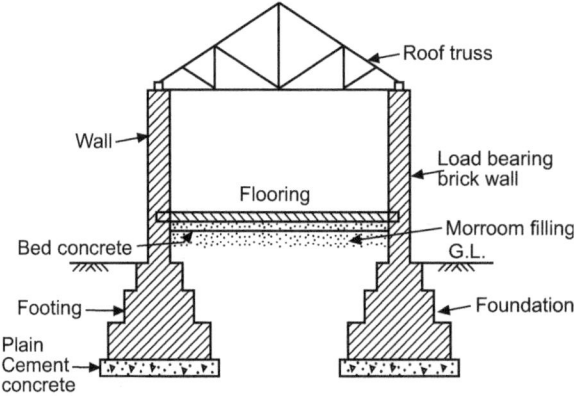

Fig. 1.5 : Load Bearing structure

1.6.2 Framed Structures

Framed structure comprises of a frame made up of beams and columns. Beams are the horizontal members of the frame. All the loads on a floor as well as those of walls are supported by beams. The beams transmit loads to vertical members of the frame known as columns. Columns rest on the footing or foundation on hard soil below the ground. Thus, the loads of the structure are transmitted through the columns to the foundation.

Beams are provided at floor levels. The columns may be erected on separate foundations or on the combined or raft foundations. In general, the partition walls or the external walls of room rest on beams. The cost of the structural frame is about 30 % of the total cost of construction. Fig. 1.6 shows details of a framed structure.

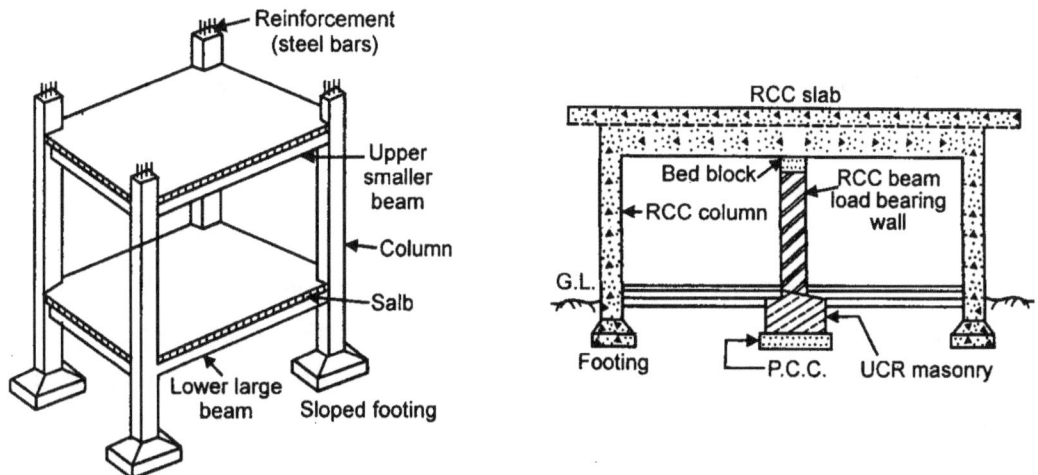

Fig. 1.6 : Framed structure   Fig. 1.7 : Composite structure

The different materials like timber, steel, reinforced cement concrete (R.C.C.). are used for construction of a frame.

1.6.3 Composite Structures

When the superstructure is composed of load bearing as well as framed construction, it is known as *composite structure*. In this type, outer walls are load bearing type and the intermediate supports are in the form of columns. Thus, the floors and the roofs are supported by load bearing walls as well as the inner columns. Composite structures are preferred for buildings, which are not multistoreyed and have larger spans such as workshops, warehouses. Composite structure, thus, has advantages of framed and load bearing structure. Fig. 1.7 shows all essential details of this type of construction.

1.6.4 Comparison of Load Bearing and Framed Structures

The load bearing and framed structures can be compared considering the various aspects in building planning and construction such as, sub-soil conditions, floor space, time required for construction, height of structure, economy, flexibility in planning, etc.

(i) Sub-soil conditions : The load bearing structures can be constructed where the hard soil is available at shallow depth; otherwise the cost of construction increases on account of deep foundations. Thus, on black cotton soil or reclaimed soil, load bearing structures prove to be uneconomical. However, on the same soil framed structure proves to be economical and safe, too.

(ii) Floor space : The external as well as internal walls of load bearing structures are thicker as compared to the thickness of walls of framed structures. Therefore less floor area is available for use in load bearing structures compared to framed structures.

(iii) Height : The load bearing structures can be built at the most upto four storeys, but the framed structures are suitable for any number of floors.

(iv) Time of construction : For the same number of storeys, the load bearing construction requires more time. In case of framed structure, different construction activities can be carried out simultaneously and hence there is reduction in the time required for the completion of framed construction as compared to load bearing structure.

Further, if prefabricated building elements such as floor panels, beams, etc., are used in the framed structure then the time for construction reduces.

(v) Economy : In general, load bearing structure works out to be cheaper upto 2 storeyes, whereas framed structure becomes necessary and economical for multistoreyed construction.

(vi) Flexibility in planning : In case of the framed structure, the panel walls can be shifted and new work place can be created, which is not possible for the load bearing structures.

(vii) Resistance to vibrations : The load bearing structures are susceptible to vibrations due to machines and earthquakes; whereas the framed structure can be designed to withstand these vibrations effectively.

The points of difference can be better understood in the following tabular chart.

Table 1.1 : Comparison of L.B. and Framed structure

Point	Load bearing structure	Framed structure
1. Sub soil conditions	Can be constructed where hard strata is available.	Constructed in case of weak soils i.e. black cotton soil or reclaimed soil.
2. Floor space	Less floor area is available due to thicker walls.	More floor area is available due to thinner section of columns.
3. Height	Construction can be upto four storeys.	No restriction on number of floors.
4. Time of construction	Requires more time as construction activities can not be carried out simultaneously.	Requires less time as activities can be carried out simultaneously.
5. Economy	Cheaper for two storeyed construction.	Cheaper for multistoreyed construction.
6. Flexibility in planning	Changes in the location of panel walls is not possible.	Changes in the location of panel walls is possible.
7. Resistance to vibrations.	Susceptible to vibrations due to machines and earthquakes. Hence becomes weaker and cracks are seen in walls.	Design takes care of the effect of vibrations and earthquake forces.

1.6.5 Components of Superstructure

The superstructure of a building consists of different components such as (1) Walls, (2) Doors and windows, (3) Roofs, (4) Floors, etc. Some of these components are discussed in the following articles.

1.6.5.1 Walls

Wall is one of the basic components of a building. It encloses or divides the space of a building rendering it as useful. The walls serve as protection against weather conditions (such as heat, cold, rains, wind, etc.). Walls provide privacy, security too.

A wall may be defined as a vertical load-bearing member whose length exceeds four times its thickness. It is constructed of brick or stone masonry.

These are two types of walls :

(A) Load bearing and

(B) Non-load bearing walls.

Both these types can be further classified as external and internal walls.

[A] Load bearing walls

These walls are designed to support the superimposed loads including the self-weight.

Masonry may be classified as :

(A) Stone masonry (B) Brick masonry and

(C) Composite masonry

(A) Stone Masonry

Since primitive age, man has identified stone as a building material. Stone masonry is used for the construction of walls, columns, lintels, arches, footings, etc. of a building. The materials used for stone masonry are (i) stones and (ii) mortar (i.e. binding material).

The binding materials may be lime or cement while the inert material is sand. Sand serves as a filler along with the binder and reduces shrinkage of the mortar.

(i) Stones : Strength and durability are the two important properties of stones for construction work. Economy and appearance of the stones are the additional requirements. Table 1.2 gives the suitability of various stones for different construction purposes.

Table 1.2 : Suitability of stones for construction

Sr. No.	Type of stone	Colour	Purpose of construction
1.	Granite	White to green	Walls, steps, sills, facing works.
2.	Sand stone	Various colours	Walls, columns, facings, steps, flooring etc. (architectural treatment)
3.	Lime stone	Various colours	Walls, floors, steps etc.
4.	Marble	Various colours	Flooring monumental structures.
5.	Slate	Black	Roofing work.

(ii) Mortar : Generally lime and cement mortars are used for stone masonry. Cement mortar of 1 : 6 proportion is used.

Types of stone masonry

Broadly speaking, there are two types of stone masonry, namely

(a) Rubble masonry and (b) Ashlar masonry.

(a) Rubble masonry : It consists of blocks of stones either undressed or roughly dressed and having wider joints. Dressing of stone is the operation of giving it proper size and shape with the help of hammer. The rubble masonry is of various types.

(b) Ashlar masonry : This class of masonry consists of accurately dressed rectangular or square stone blocks. The thickness of joints between stone blocks is only about 3 mm. The height of stone varies from 25 to 30 cm. The length of stones should not exceed three times the height. This is the highest grade of masonry and is very costly.

[B] Brick Masonry

Brick masonry is constructed of brick units bonded together with mortar. Brick masonry has the following advantages over stone masonry and hence it is preferred over other types of masonry.

(i) Bricks are available in uniform shape and size; so they can be laid in definite pattern.

(ii) Bricks are comparatively small in size and therefore can be easily handled.

(iii) Bricks do not need any dressing.

(iv) Construction of brick masonry is simpler and easier than stone masonry.

(v) Architectural beauty can be achieved by ornamental construction in brick masonry.

(vi) Brick masonry can be used to provide thin and light partitions, filler walls.

(vii) In general, brick masonry is economical and when laid in good mortar forms durable construction.

(C) Composite Masonry :

Composite masonry is constructed with different types of building materials such as stone, brick-stone, cement concrete, reinforced brick, etc. Use of composite masonry improves the appearance of masonry and also achieves economy by using available materials.

1. Stone composite masonry : This type consists of a combination of rubble and ashlar masonry as shown in Fig. 1.8 (b).

2. Brick-stone composite masonry : In this type, ashlar masonry is constructed at the facing and the backing is of brick masonry. For uniform course the height of stone should be a multiple of brick thickness plus masonry joint. See Fig. 1.8 (a).

 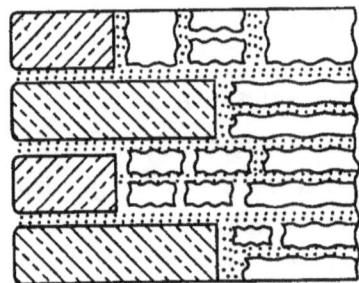

(a) Brick-stone composite masonry   (b) Stone composite masonry

Fig. 1.8 : Composite masonry

1.6.6 Fundamental Requirements of Masonry

Strong masonry can be constructed by taking following precautions :

(i) Good quality bricks or stones should be used so that the masonry will not fail in crushing.

(ii) Vertical joints in the brickwork or stonework should break to distribute load.

(iii) In order to avoid rupture, joints should have uniform thickness and should be as thin as possible.

(iv) Strength of mortar should be in conformity with the strength of brick or stone.

(v) Bricks should be soaked in water for 24 hours before use.

(vi) In case of stone masonry through stones should be provided to increase stability.

1.6.7 Openings

Openings are provided in building to serve the following purposes :

(i) To have an access to room.

(ii) To provide daylight, vision (prospect) and ventilation.

(iii) Allowing air and light, but concealing the view for the outsiders (as in case of louvered windows.)

The requirements of a good opening are :

(i) Opening should be of such a size and shape that the purpose providing it is efficiently served.

(ii) They should be rainwater, fire and heat resistant, when closed.

(iii) They should be economical, with low maintenance costs too.

(iv) They should have single or multiple shutters either opening inside or outside as per the requirement (or sliding).

The openings may be in the form of doors and windows.

1.6.8 Doors

These are provided as an access to a room. The doors can be made of timber, steel, aluminium or plastics and these can be coupled with glass panels. Following types of doors are used (See Fig. 1.9) :

(1) *Battened door :* long wooden planks are joined as single or double shutter.
(2) *Panelled door :* wooden panels are used.
(3) *Glazed and panelled door :* wooden panels and glass are used.
(4) *Sliding door :* very little space is required.
(5) *Folding door :* hinged portions can be folded.
(6) *Revolving door :* for heavy traffic in markets, shops, etc.

Also there are other types like collapsible door, rolling door (shutter), etc.

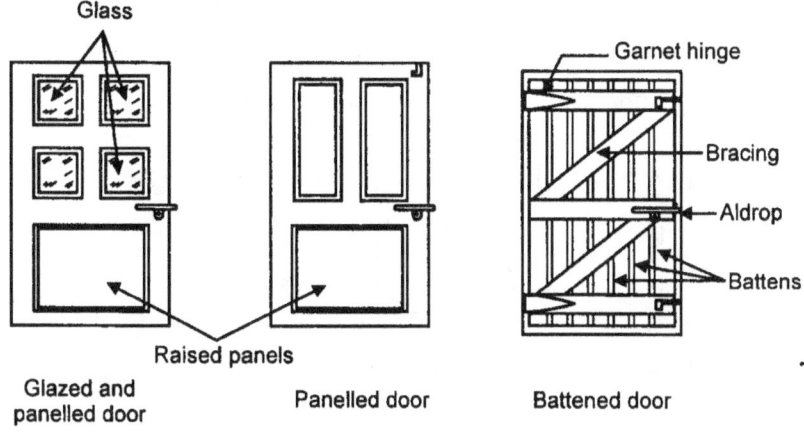

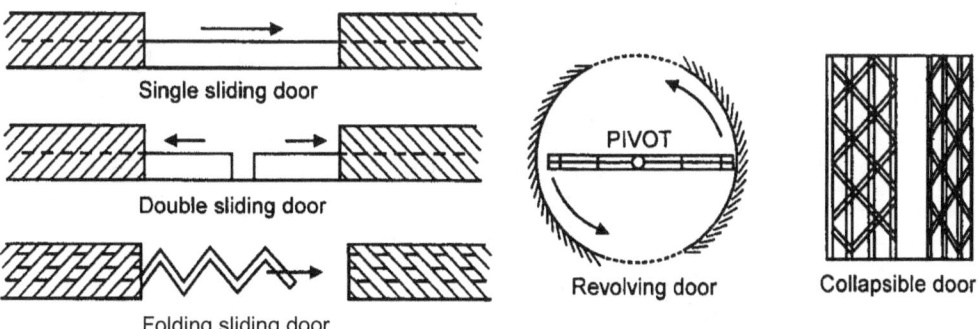

Fig. 1.9 : Types of doors

1.6.9 Windows

These are provided in the wall for providing daylight, vision (prospect) and ventilation, windows have frame and shutter as two main parts. Frame invariably is same, but single or multiple type depending on size and location of the window.

Main types of windows generally used are : (See Fig. 1.10).

1. *Fixed window* : Fixed at a position to allow entry of natural light.
2. *Casement window* : Similar to the doors.
3. *Pivoted window* : Shutter is pivoted and usually is self-closing.
4. *Dormer window* : Provided on sloping roofs.
5. *Corner window* : Placed in the corner of room for better prospects.
6. *Louvered window* : To allow fresh air and light from outside, without possibility of view to the outsiders.

Various types of doors and windows are shown in Fig. 1.9 and 1.10.

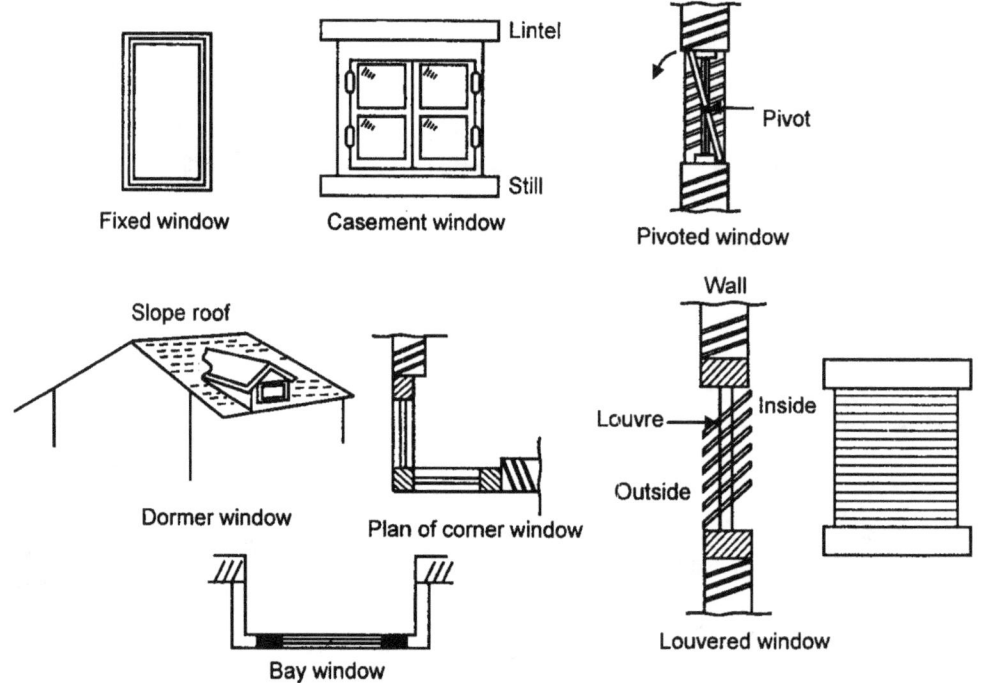

Fig. 1.10 : Types of windows

1.6.10 Floors

The horizontal members of the building which divide vertical space into different parts at different level are called as floors. Floor supports the occupants, furniture and equipments. A building may be single storeyed or multi storeyed. Single storeyed building has only one floor which is called as ground floor. In multi storeyed structures, there are additional floors which are called as upper floors. The floors which are constructed below ground floor are called as basement floor. A floor consists of two components [1] sub floor or base course or sub-grade which imparts strength, stability and support floor covering and all other super imposed loads. [2] Floor covering which provides a hard, durable, clean, smooth, impervious and beautiful surface to the floor.

1.6.10.1 Construction Requirements of Floor

While constructing the floors following requirements are required to be considered.

1. **Durability :** The floor should be clean, smooth, impervious and durable.
2. **Damp proofness :** The floor should be damp proof.
3. **Fire resistance :** While selecting material for upper floors, care should be taken to make the floor fire resistant.
4. **Heat insulation :** In case of basement or ground floors, insulation against heat should be provided especially when suspended and ventilated timber floors are used.
5. **Sound insulation :** The insulation against sound should be provided in case of upper floors as they act as horizontal barriers for the passage of sound in vertical direction.

1.6.10.2 Selection of Floorings

The different types of floors are constructed to serve different types of purposes. Each type of flooring material has got its own merits and demerits. No single type of material is suitable for all purposes under all circumstances. Therefore, it is necessary to study properties of various materials used for flooring and the material selection criteria. Following are the factors which affect selection of flooring materials.

1. Initial cost
2. Appearance
3. Cleanliness
4. Durability
5. Damp prevention
6. Sound insulation
7. Thermal insulation
8. Smoothness
9. Hardness
10. Comfort
11. Fire resistance
12. Maintenance
13. Slipperiness.

Floors are named after the covering materials used in them. If covering material is brick it is called as brick flooring, if it is cement concrete, it is called as cement concrete flooring. There are so many types of flooring materials. Each type of material has got its own advantages and disadvantages and it is suitable under specific conditions. Following are the commonly used ground floors.

1. Mud flooring
2. Murum flooring
3. Flag stone flooring
4. Brick flooring
5. Cement concrete flooring
6. Granolithic flooring
7. Tiled flooring
8. Terrazzo flooring
9. Mosaic flooring
10. Timber flooring
11. Asphalt flooring
12. Linoleum flooring
13. Rubber flooring
14. Magnetic flooring
15. Cork tile flooring
16. Glass flooring
17. Marble flooring
18. Plastic or PVC flooring

Table 1.3 : Showing flooring materials normally used for various purposes

Sr. No.	Location	Selection criteria	Type of flooring material
1.	Recreational hall of first class hotel	Appearance, cleanliness, smoothness, fire resistance, maintenance, durability	Terrazzo, marble
2.	Warehousing	Initial cost, smoothness, fire resistance, damp proofing slipperiness	Concrete, shahabad stone
3.	Chemical laboratory	Resistance to chemical, cleanliness, durability	Glazed tiles, plastic sheet, concrete
4.	Toilets	Initial cost cleanliness, durability, damp proofing, slipperiness	Polished shahabad, marble, glazed tiles
5.	Railway platform	Initial cost, cleanliness, durability, slipperiness	Concrete, tiles, rough shahabad.

1.7 ROOFS AND ROOF COVERINGS

A 'Roof' is the uppermost part of a building which is supported on structural members and is covered with a roofing material. The main function of a roof is to enclose the space or building and to protect the same from the damaging effects of weather elements such as rain, wind, heat, snow, etc.

Pitched roofs or sloping roofs are very suitable to coastal regions where rainfall is heavy

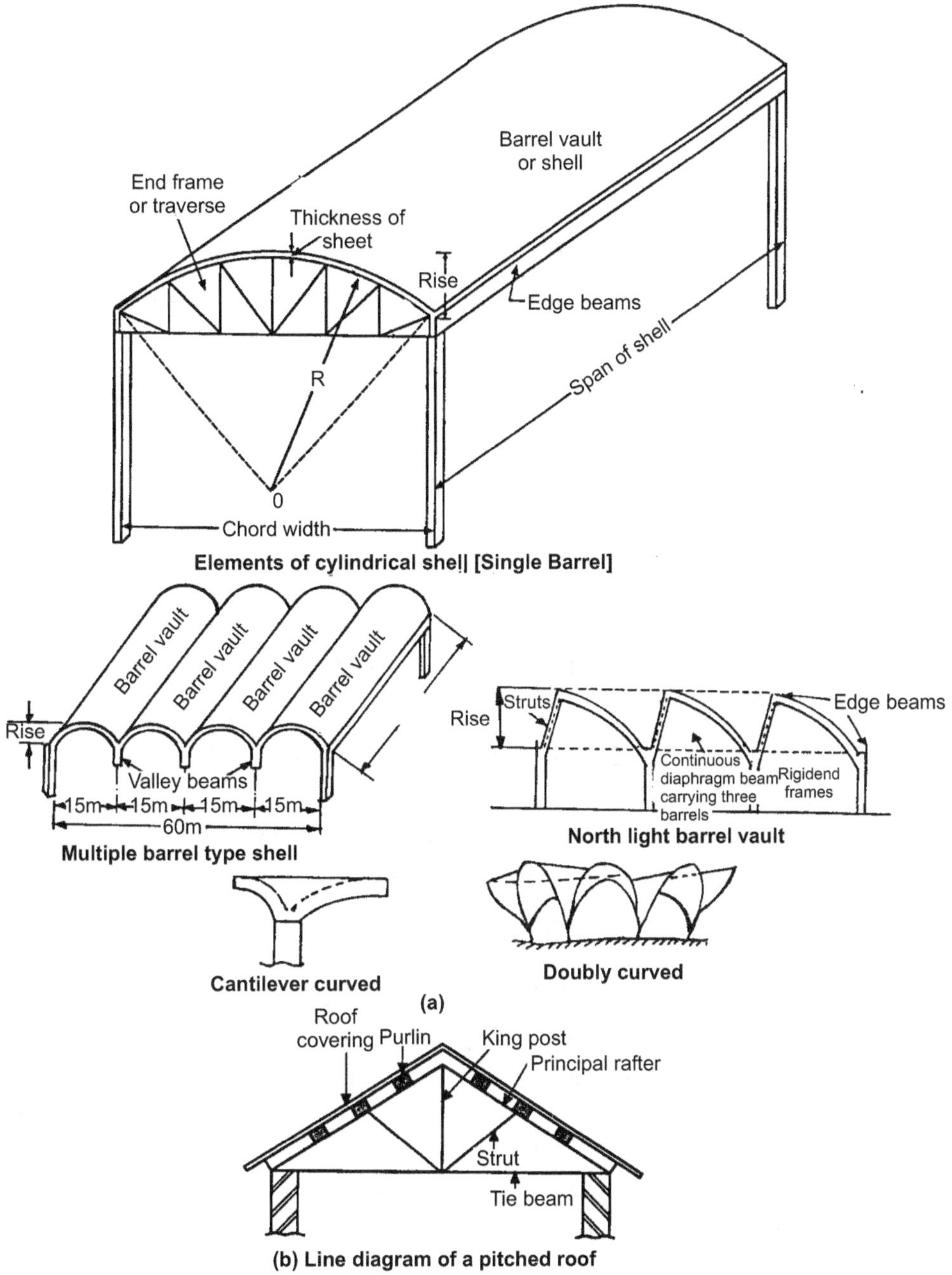

Fig. 1.11 : (a) Types of curved (shell) roofs, (b) Diagram of a pitched roof

but the temperature is more or less equal. Flat roofs are considered suitable in plains where rainfall is meagre and heat is great, and hence greater protection is required from the Sun. Many other types of roofs are constructed for different types of buildings in view of their specific functional requirements. For instance, shell roofs and folded plate North light roofs are being employed for buildings such as factories, workshops, assembly halls, theatres, recreation centres, libraries, etc., where either large areas are required to be covered without obstruction or for the purposes of natural lighting, ventilation, etc. Similarly, a dome, which is a special type of shell roof, is used for covering large circular areas for assembly halls, gymnasiums, monumental structures, etc. Fig. 1.11 shows few types of curved (shell) roofs.

1.7.1 Sloping Roof Trusses

In olden days, timber roof trusses were quite common. However, now-a-days, mild steel trusses have proved to be more popular, especially for greater spans.

The relative advantages of steel roof trusses over timber sloping roofs are as follows :

1. They are light in weight and can be fabricated in different shapes and sizes to suit the structural as well as architectural requirements.

2. They are free from the attack of white ants and dry rot.

3. They are much stronger than timber trusses and they are equally strong in tension and compression.

4. These trusses have a greater resistance against fire and hence especially suited where fire-proof construction is desired.

5. Steel roof trusses are used for structures requiring large spans such as industrial buildings, large sheds, assembly halls, hangers, auditorium, etc.

6. The erection of steel trusses is very easy, rapid and economical.

1.7.2 Roof Covering for Pitched Roofs

Roof covering is a material covering provided over the form-work of roof structure, to safeguard the roof against the weather elements such as rain, Sun rays, wind action, snowfall, etc., and sometimes to give it a decorative appearance also. **The roof covering does not share the loads in the building**.

There are several types of roof-coverings, but only those which are commonly adopted in India for pitched roofs are given below :

(1) Thatch covering, (2) Tiles, (3) Asbestos cement sheets, (4) CGI sheet (corrugated galvanised iron sheet).

1.8 SUPERSTRUCTURE
1.8.1 Introduction

It is that part of the structure which is constructed above the plinth level or ground floor level. The various components of superstructure are walls, floors, doors and windows, roofs, stairs, sill, lintel, weather sheds, finishes for wall, utility fixtures, etc. The functions of various components of superstructure are as follows:

1. **Walls:** The vertical components of the building, which are constructed to enclose the space, are called walls. They are also constructed to divide the space into various rooms and small compartments as per the requirement of the building.

2. **Floors:** Floors are the horizontal elements of a building structure which divide the building into different levels for the purpose of creating more accommodation within the restricted space one above the other and to provide support for the occupants, their furniture and requirements in the building.

3. **Doors:** The openings provided in the walls of the building to connect the internal rooms, to be used as a means of free movement inside and outside the building.

4. **Windows**: The openings provided in the outer walls of the building for the purpose of light and air.

5. **Roofs:** The uppermost horizontal or inclined part of a building provided to cover the space enclosed by the walls is called the roof. Roofs protect living spaces from direct sun, rain or snow and wind.

6. **Stairs:** The component of the building which is provided for climbing from one floor to another floor is called stairs.

7. **Lintel:** Lintel is the component of the building provided over the openings i.e. doors and windows. It supports the load of the brick or stone masonry above the opening and transfers the same on either side of the supporting walls.

8. **Sill:** Sill is the component of the building provided between the bottom of a window frame and the wall below it. It protects the top of the wall from wear and tear. Window sill are usually weathered and throated to throw the rain water off the face of the wall.

9. **Weather sheds:** The horizontal slabs projecting from the external wall just above the doors, windows, verandas, etc. are called weather sheds or sun shades or chhajjas. They are monolithically constructed with the lintels. They protect the doors, windows, etc. from direct effects of the sun and rain.

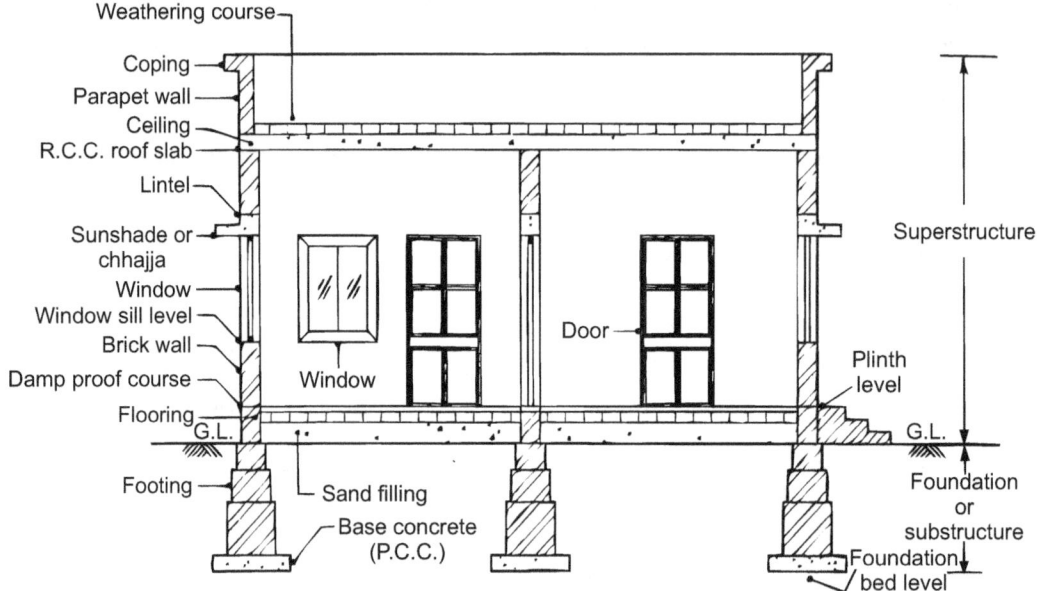

Fig. 1.12: Components of a Building

10. **Finishes of Wall:** Finishes are of several types such as pointing, plastering, distempering, decorative colour washing, etc. that are applied on the walls. The main functions of these finishes are as follows:
    (i) They provide an even and smooth finished surface and also improve the aesthetic appearance of the structure as a whole.
    (ii) They rectify, rather cover to some extent, the poor or defective workmanship.
    (iii) They protect the structure from the effects of weather, such as rain, sun.

11. **Utility Fixtures:** These are built-in items of immovable nature, which add to the utility of a building and hence, are termed as utility fixtures. The most common of such built-in fixtures are: cupboards, shelves, smokeless chulas, etc.

1.9 BRICKS

Bricks are of regular shape, hence do not require any dressing, speed of construction is high, require less mortar. As thin as 10 cm thick wall can be constructed, lifting is easy and structures of beautiful shapes can be constructed with ease. Bricks can be manufactured by moulding clay, whereas stones are usually required to be 'quarried' and dressed.

1.9.1 Size of Bricks

Bricks may be made in various sizes, but usually it is rectangular in shape with

length = 2 times width + one mortar joint.

Depth is less or equal to width.

I.S. 1077 - 1976 specifies size of bricks as $19 \times 9 \times 9$ or $19 \times 9 \times 4$ cm. The size of brick with mortar joint becomes modular size of 20 cm $\times$ 10 cm $\times$ 10 cm. However, bricks of size $9" \times 4\frac{1"}{4} \times 2\frac{3"}{4}$ are still being manufactured in many places.

1.9.2 Requirements of a Good Brick

1. It should be well burnt, should have uniform texture and red colour.

2. Edges should be sharp, and at right angles to each other.

3. It should not absorb water more than 20 % of its dry weight when immersed in water for 24 hours.

4. When two bricks are struck against each other, should give metallic ringing sound and should not break when dropped on a hard surface from a height of 1 metre.

5. Alkalies present in bricks, are responsible for efflorescence. Efflorescence should not be more than moderate upto 'class 125' and not more than 'slight' for higher classes; when bricks are dried after soaking in water.

6. Freshly fractured surface should not show pebbles or lime stone.

1.9.3 Uses of Bricks

1. Bricks are used in the construction of buildings, bridge piers, culverts, construction of sewers for sewage disposal, chimneys, etc.

2. First class bricks are used for pleasing appearance in the face work, arches, domes.

3. Bricks with lesser water percentage of absorption are used in water proofing of terraces.

4. Refractory bricks are used to resist high temperature for larger time like furnace.

5. Second class bricks are used in construction of compound walls, temporary quarters.

6. As aggregate for foundation concrete, base course of road parement.

1.10 STONES

Stone as a construction material has many advantages like higher strength, resistance to weather, less absorption of water, and usually stone work is not plastered. However, as stones are required to be "dressed", speed of construction is less, walls are thick and more mortar is required.

1.10.1 Properties of Good Building Stones

Stone used in building construction should have following properties : -

(a) Strength : The stone should be strong enough to withstand all external loads coming over it. Crushing strength of various stones is sufficiently high, however, crushing strength of sedimentary and metamorphic rocks along the plane of stratification is very less. Hence while laying such stones, it should be ensured that, the load is acting perpendicular to the plane of stratification as shown in Fig. 1.13 (a) and not as in Fig. 1.13 (b).

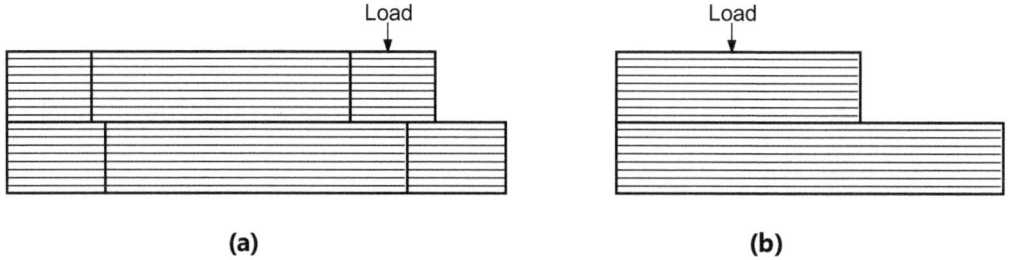

Fig. 1.13

(b) Durability : Durability of stone depends upon its chemical composition, homogeneity and cementing material. A stone having high strength may not be durable, if various granular particles of stone are not held together by equally strong cementing material. (To check durability, stone chips of size 2 to 3 cm are placed in a beaker containing clean water, and stirred for about 30 minutes. If stone contains soluble minerals, then water will become dirty, indicating lesser durability).

(c) Resistance to Weathering : Through various industrial and chemical wastes, fumes of acid are emitted. These fumes are dissolved in rain water, which attack stone masonry gradually.

Sand stone, gneiss have higher weathering resistance, whereas lime stone, laterite rocks are less weather resistant.

(d) Colour/Appearance : The exposed surface of stone masonry should have pleasing appearance/colour and should be in conformity with the desired effect of building.

(e) It should be easy to work with and should be able to take polish.

Marble, sand stone are easy to work with for ornamental purposes. Granite is not easy to work with ornamental purposes, but can take very high polish.

(f) Resistance to fire : The fire resistance of stone depends upon percentage of calcium carbonate and iron oxide present in the stone. Lesser the percentage of the same, higher is the fire resistance. Relatively, sedimentary rocks have higher resistance to fire than igneous or metamorphic rocks.

1.10.2 Characteristics of Some Familiar Stones

1. Sand Stone : This is a sedimentary rock in which sand grains are cemented together by

(i) Calcium or magnesium carbonate.

(ii) By Silicic acid, Alumina and Oxide of Iron.

Sand stone is strong, hard, non-absorbent and can be worked with ease. Therefore, this stone is used for carving ashlar stone masonry. It is available in many colours like red, grey brown, yellowish, bluish etc. However, if it contains mica, then it becomes flaky.

It is found at Burdwan in Bengal, at Ranchi in Bihar, at Cuttack in Orissa, at Bharatpur, Bikaner in Rajasthan and at Agra and Allahabad. Famous Red Fort, Rashtrapathi Bhavan, the Secreteriate Building at Delhi, are built with sand stone.

2. Deccan Trap : This igneous rock consists of fine grained crystals of Feldspar, and Hornblende. Feldspar is a silicate of Aluminium with Silicate of Sodium and/or Potassium.

Hornblende is a silicate of Calcium and Magnesium. It is hard, tough, and greenish black or black in colour. It is suitable for pavement and stone masonry work.

3. Granite : It is an igneous rock containing about 55 % Quartz; 35 % Feldspar and about 10 % Mica and is superior as regards durability. As it possesses high strength, it is suitable for heavily loaded structures like piers, marine structures. Granite is very hard to work with, hence in general, is not used for ornamental works. Fine grained polished granite is used for columns and coarse granite is used in steps. If variations in temperature are very high, then, minute cracks are likely to be developed.

4. Lime Stone : This is a sedimentary rock in which grains of

Calcium Carbonate	are cemented together by	Matrix of silica, magnesium carbonate, iron and clay	leading to stones of	White, grey, blue, brown and pink colour.

Lime stones are soft, liable to be affected by acids and are not suitable for building purposes.

Dolomite is a Magnesium lime stone containing higher percentage of Magnesia and is therefore more durable. However, if percentage of sillica increases then, stone will have poor weathering qualities.

Lime stone when metamorphised by heat and pressure, gets converted into dense, compact Marble having crystalline structure. Marble takes good polish and can be used in ornamental carvings. Marble is used for columns, stair cases, steps, table tops, floors, tiles, kitchen otta, etc.

Marble is available at Chittor, Jaisalmer, Alwar, Jaipur in Rajasthan, green marble is available near Baroda.

5. Laterite : It is porous, cellular structured sandy clay stone. It takes its red colour due to higher percentage of oxides of iron present in it, which protects rock from decay.

6. Murum : It is decomposed laterite rock and acts as fine blindage for roads. It is used in embankment, filling behind retaining wall, filling below plinth and around foundations.

1.11 NATURAL AND ARTIFICIAL SAND

1.11.1 Natural Sand

Natural sand is formed by weathering and wearing of pebbles, boulders, etc. in river bed for a number of years and is not replenished at the rate at which it is being consumed.

Environmental pressures, costs and shortage of natural sand has necessitated manufacture of artificial sand. Normally, river sand is only used for constructional purposes after washing. Although large quantity of sand is available on the sea shore, it is not used for construction since it contains salts and deleterious material.

Due to various constraints, many times, it is not economically possible to get natural sand of desired quality and quantity, e.g. if construction site of National Express way may be far off from the river (where from natural sand is obtained.)

1.11.2 Artificial Sand

In naturally available sand, often undesirable materials (like chlorides, harmful chemicals which adversely affect the concrete) are present in clayey material adhered to sand. On the contrary, the same are absent in manufactured sand. Thus manufactured sand is clean and does not contain harmful or deleterious materials as it is produced from clean parent rock.

Due to advances in technology, now it is possible to manufacture sand which has following advantages :

1. Well graded.
2. Superior surface texture.
3. It can be compacted properly to produce low voids.
4. Lesser quantity of coating material (such as cement) is required.
5. Required quantity and quality of sand can be produced in a short time.
6. Wastage of sand is less.

If economy at large is considered, artificial sand, many times, proves to be economical.

1.11.3 Uses of Sand

1. Sand forms a major constituent in cement concrete. Roughly 45 to 50% of volume of concrete is occupied by sand.
2. Sand is also required for making mortar used in brick work, stone masonry.
3. Sand is required in plastering to give a smooth surface to walls.
4. Sand serves as a draining material and is therefore used in filteration plants, filling behind retaining wall, around foundation, filling well foundations, as a filter to drain seepage water from Earthen dams.

1.12 STEEL FOR REINFROCEMENT

PCC (Plain Cement Concrete) is able to take higher compressive stresses, i.e. PCC is strong in compression, but it is weak in tension. As a result, in any structural concrete, where tensile stresses are developed, steel reinforcement is provided, to take care of tensile stresses. The steel reinforcement can be provided in the form of

   (i)   Plain mild steel bars,
   (ii) Ribbed tor steel bars,
   (iii) High tensile strength bars,
   (iv) TMT (Thermo Mechanically Treated Bars).

1. Plain mild steel bars : It possesses all properties required for normal structural steel work for residential and industrial buildings, bridges, etc. Manufacturing cost of mild steel is less that that of wrought iron. Bars may be round, flat or square in cross-section.

2. Ribbed tor steel bars : These are deformed cold twisted steel bars. The bars have projections or recesses on the surface due to which there is better bond between concrete and reinforcement. These bars can take relatively higher strains before failure.

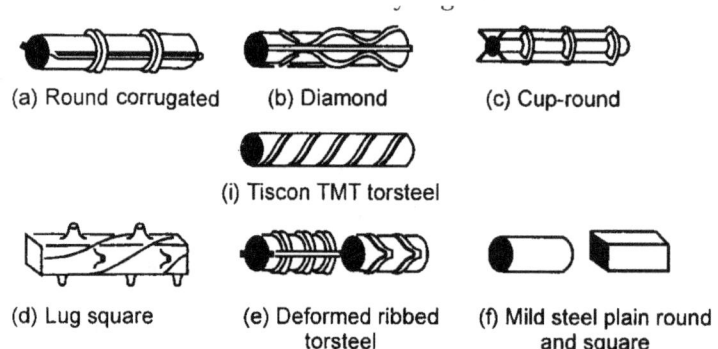

(a) Round corrugated   (b) Diamond   (c) Cup-round

(i) Tiscon TMT torsteel

(d) Lug square   (e) Deformed ribbed torsteel   (f) Mild steel plain round and square

Fig. 1.14 : Reinforcement bars

Different grades of tor steel bars such as FE 415, FE 500, FE 550 are available. The grade indicates strength in N/mm^2. e.g. Grade FE 415 indicates stress of 415 N/mm^2 (minimum). These bars have following advantages over mild steel round bars :

   (i)   Better bond strength and lesser crack width due to improved bar geometry.
   (ii) Fully weldable.
   (iii) Better fatigue strength.
   (iv) 20 to 25% higher factor of safety due to hyper resistance to plastic flow.

TMT bars : Thermo Mechanically Treated (TMT) Bars is a recent technological advancement for production of high strength deformed steel bars for concrete reinforcement. In this process higher strength is obtained by thermo mechanical treatment, wherein the steel bars get intensive cooling immediately after rolling. Sudden reduction in temperature creates a hardened surface layer with the internal core still being hot. While further cooling in atmosphere, tempering takes place by the heat from the core. This process of thermo mechanical treatment improves the properties of strength and ductility of the bars.

Advantages :

So far, in India, cold twisting of bars is still being used extensively for production of high strength bars. In the case of TMT bars, besides thermo mechanical treatment, the Carbon content also has been brought down leading to following advantages :

- Higher strength
- Superior ductility
- Weldability
- Bendability
- Higher corrosion resistance.

1.12.1 Uses of Steel

Uses of Mild Steel : It is the most commonly used steel, because it possesses all requisite properties required for normal structural steel work for Residential, as well as industrial buildings, bridges, rails etc. because it is easy to manufacture mild steel at less cost than wrought iron. It is used in :

1. It is used in making structural steel like various angles iron selections, channels, beams, tees, etc.
2. In refrigerators, air conditioners, pipes, industrial buildings.
3. Ships, boiler plants, ropes.
4. As a reinforcement in R.C.C. works, in manufacture of nuts, bolts, tubes, et.

Uses of High tensile steel :

1. It is used for making gears, ball mills, crushers, wheel tyres.
2. Making high speed cutting tools like drills, files, chisels, finest cutlary, knives, surgical instruments.
3. As a reinforcement in prestressed concrete works.
4. Springs to absorb shocks.

Uses of Cast Iron :

1. A large quantity of C.I. is used for manufacture of wrought iron and steel.
2. Due to low melting point, it is used for manufacture of Flywheels, weights, bed plates etc.

3. It does not rust easily, hence it is used for manufacture of water pipes, gas pipes, manhole covers.

4. It is easily fusible and shrinks on cooling, but can not absorb shocks. Hence, it is used for ornamental castings, gates, and supports of heavy machinery parts subjected to heavy compressive static loads only.

Uses of wrought from : Now a days, wrought is seldom used due to higher manufacturing cost and also because, desired properties can be obtained by using mildsteel at lesser cost.

1.13 CEMENT CONCRETE

1.13.1 Plain Cement Concrete (P.C.C.)

It is a homogeneous mixture of inert materials like aggregate (crushed or natural stone) and fine aggregate (sand) which are cemented together by chemical action of cement paste. Properties of concrete depend upon each of the following ingredients : -

(a) Coarse aggregate, (b) Fine aggregate (sand), (c) Cement, (d) Water.

Plain cement concrete is produced by mixing the different ingredients mentioned above in certain proportion either on volumetric basis or on weight basis.

Concrete has high strength in compression with bricks. But if it is subjected to tensile stresses, it fails at low loads. Tensile strength of concrete is only about $\frac{1}{10}$ th of its strength in compression. Hence plain cement concrete has limited uses. Following Table 1.4 gives mix proportion used in various situations.

Table 1.4

Sr. No.	Nature of Construction	Mix proportion of plain concrete
1.	Levelling course below the base of foundation footings, mass concrete for heavy walls.	(1 : 4 : 8) or (1 : 5 : 10)
2.	In concrete flooring, compound walls, foundation walls, parapet, ordinary machine bases.	1 : 3 : 6
3.	Damp proof course (DPC) at plinth level.	1 : 2 : 4

1.13.2 Reinforced Cement Concrete (RCC)

As stated above, plain cement concrete is strong in compression but weak in tension. Reinforced cement concrete (RCC) is defined as cement concrete strengthened by providing steel reinforcement is such a way that all tensile stresses are taken care of/resisted by the steel reinforcement. (Refer Fig. 1.15)

FUNDAMENTALS OF CIVIL ENGINEERING — CIVIL ENGINEERING SCOPE AND APPLICATIONS

Reinforced Cement Concrete (RCC) is being used extensively in the construction of multistoreyed buildings, water tanks, bridges, marine structures, roads, dams, pipes, machine foundations etc.

In RCC proper use of compressive strength of concrete and tensile strength of steel is made and economy is achieved. As proper bond is developed between concrete and reinforcement steel both act together monolithically.

Following are the advantages of Reinforced Cement Concrete :

(i) It can be cast at site to the desired shape and size.

(ii) Comparatively it is fire resistant, durable, maintenance free and is not attacked by termites.

(iii) It can be made water proof and proves to be economical in long run.

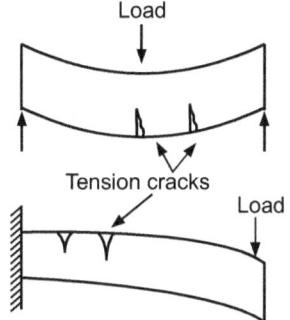

(a) Cracks are developed due to tension in plain cement concrete

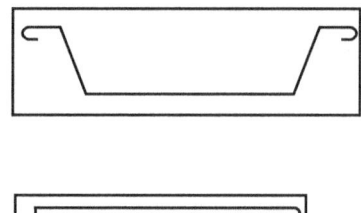

(b) Steel reinforcement is provided the region where tension is likely to be developed

Fig. 1.15

1.13.3 Prestressed Concrete

Prestressed concrete is cement concrete in which high tensile steel is provided and the same is initially stretched and released to induce permanent high compressive stresses in concrete. These induced opposite compressive stresses in concrete nullify the likely tensile stresses caused by superimposed load on the structure.

For long span beams such as those in bridges, use of RCC beams becomes uneconomical due to heavy dead load of beams. In such cases, prestressed concrete is used. In prestressed concrete, permanent opposite stresses to those which super imposed load will cause, are induced in concrete.

If we wish to carry a number of books, in two hands we apply compressive force at the ends i.e. a force direction and of opposite nature, as a result of which books will not fall.

Same principle is applied in prestressed concrete. Steel cables of high tensile strength are stretched and when stresses are removed, the cable gets shortened and induces compressive stresses in concrete. As a result, even small beam is in a position to take heavier load.

Prestressed concrete beams are free from cracks and considerable reduction in quantity of steel, concrete and hence reduction in dead weight can be made.

Prestressed Cement Concrete

The principle of prestressed concrete is to induce stresses in the concrete of the opposite to those induced by the imposed load. The concrete member which is subjected to bending be kept in a state of compression. Fig. 1.16 (a) (i) and (ii) show the comparison of pre-stressed concrete with that of normal reinforced concrete.

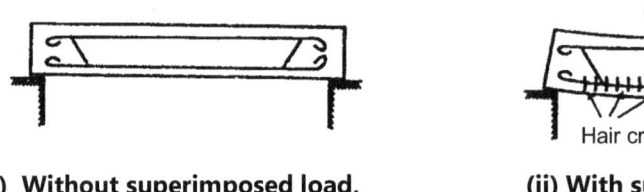

(i) **Without superimposed load, only dead weight**

(ii) **With superimposed load**

Fig. 1.16 (a) : Normal reinforced concrete

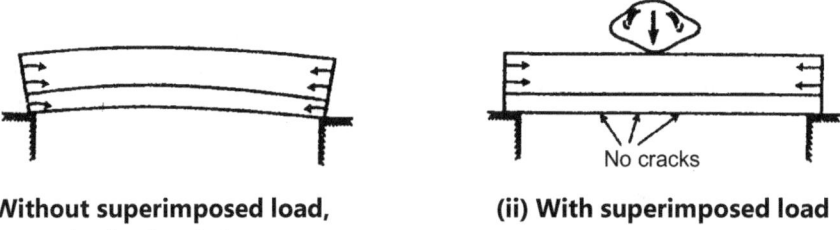

(i) **Without superimposed load, only dead weight**

(ii) **With superimposed load**

Fig. 1.16 (b) : Prestressed concrete

Material : Prestressed concrete is reinforced by mean of steel with a very high tensile strength. Frequently the steel bars used are not thicker than 2 mm, and have higher strength than normal reinforcing steel. The concrete must be composed and fabricated in such a way that concrete of high strength is ensured (e.g. 600 kg/cm^2 or 60 N/mm^2).

Methods of manufacture : There are two principle methods of manufacture of prestressed concrete such as (i) 'pre-tensioned method' and (ii) 'post-tensioned method'.

(i) Pre-tensioned method : Here the steel bars are stretched (tensioned) by means of tensioning devices (presses) before concrete is placed around them. The pull on the bars is released when concrete is so hardened as not to cause any slip of steel bars in concrete zone. As soon as the tension is removed in the steel bars, they tend to contract, by virtue of elasticity, in order to regain the original length and in doing so, they impose compressive force and keep the member in state of compression. See beam 4 in Fig. 1.16 (c). When the load is applied the internal stresses set up by pre-stressing are neutralised. See beam in Fig. 1.16 (b). Then pre-stressed beam will carry extra load in addition to its own weight. This evidently ensures that the load bearing capacity is considerably increased by mere application of compression.

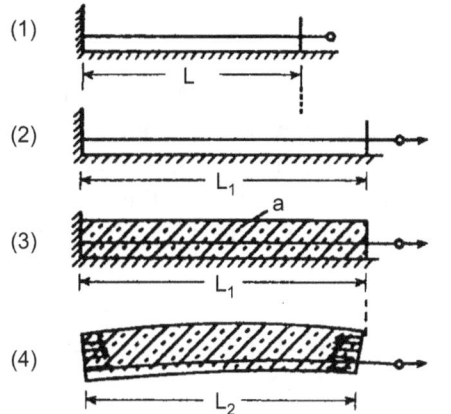

Manufacturing method used in the concrete block plant.

1. Placing the pre-stressing steel,
   L = Length
2. Tensioning the steel :
   L_1 = Length
3. Bending the tensioned steel in concrete,
   a = concrete.
4. Removing the pre-stressed device after the concrete has hardened. The concrete unit is reduced to the length L_2.

Fig. 1.16 (c) : Pre-tensioned method

Manufacturing method used at the site

1. Fabrication of concrete units (l = length) and allowing them to harden
   a = concrete,
   b = pre-stressing steel, it is arranged in a sheath and has no firm connection with the concrete as yet.
   c = anchorage of the pre-stressing steel.
2. Tensioning the steel against the concrete. In this way, the concrete is compressed and reduced to the length = L.
3. Clamping the pre-stressed steel (d) and removing the pre-stressing device.
   e = fine grained mortar.

Fig. 1.16 (d) : Post-tensioned method

(ii) Post-tensioned method : In this method, the steel bars are prevented from bonding with the concrete. They are therefore, enclosed in metal sheath. First concrete is placed and allowed to harden. Then the steel bars are stretched by means of press-stressing head. When steel bars try to regain the original length, they exert a pull on the concrete and keep the concrete in state of compression. See Fig. 1.16 (d).

Before the press is removed, the press-stressing head must be firmly anchored to the concrete. Finally, fine-grained mortar is grouted into the sheath so that the bars inside the sheath are fully embedded in mortar. This helps the bars to make firm connection with the concrete. This also protects the bars from rusting.

Uses of Prestressed Concrete :

Prestressed concrete though a recent innovation in field of concrete world, has now been widely applied to many engineering structures. It is now widely used for building structures, long span girder bridges on account of their increased weight bearing capacity. It is widely used for pavement because no cracks are seen to develop nor the construction joints open. As pre-stressed concrete helps to avoid too many expansion joints now it is possible to construct run-ways of longer length.

Advantages of prestressed concrete :

There is a lot of saving in concrete and steel in prestressed concrete, because smaller sections can be safely used. There is also saving in material, labour and time.

Disadvantages of prestressed concrete :

- It requires high strength concrete and high tension steel.
- It requires high technical skill.
- Construction cost is very high.

1.13.4 Precast Concrete

Precast concrete is a concrete cast at a convenient place in moulds and later on after curing lifted, shifted and placed in its final position of use.

When a large number of light weight units of same or similar dimensions such as fencing posts, pipes, concrete blocks, lintels, slabs etc. are to be manufactured, an effort is always made to precast the units in factory, instead of casting at site. This has many advantages :

(i) Work can be done under close supervision in factory and is of better quality.

(ii) Lot of time and material which otherwise is required for centering, shuttering etc. can be saved. It is very difficult to provide cast-in-situ concrete in situations like high sea, heavy wind, places where it is difficult to provide centering and shuttering such as jetties in sea, bridges across deep valley, river, lining to tunnels, RCC trusses for factories, etc. In such cases, the elements are precast on shore / casting yard then transported and placed in position.

However, proper precaution is required to be taken during transportation, erection etc.

1.13.5 Prefabricated Concrete

In precast technique of production of concrete elements, large number of units are manufactured. Thus, it is nothing but industrialization of concrete elements, which are of utmost importance in any construction activity.

1.13.5.1 Precast Concrete - Applications

Precasting techniques are adopted in production of following elements :

1. Mass housing : Building components like beams, columns, slabs, stairs, water tanks, partition walls [panels], balusters, septic tanks, step units, cladding panels, manholes, pipes viz., water supply and drainage, fencing posts.

2. Industrial elements : Viz. girders, columns, trusses [funicular etc.], portal frames, shells, domes, louvres, pressure vessels.

3. Miscellaneous : Bridge deck [segments or girders as a whole], electric poles, prestressed concrete pipes, sleepers, fencing posts, piles, caissons, retaining walls, traffic barriers, road dividers, shaft lining, tunnel segments, wharfs, jetty components, dry dock and harbour wall elements, sea defence blocks [tetrapods] etc.

1.13.5.2 Advantages of Precast Concrete Products

1. Due to close supervision, the quality of each product can be controlled.
2. Due to repeated use of moulds, economy can be achieved.
3. Due to quality products, the prefabricated units can be erected speedily; resulting in economy.
4. Prefabricated units have smooth, good finish, and do not need any finishing. In respect of cast-in-situ construction, usually, members are required to be plastered/pointed. This results in substantial saving in time and cost.
5. The principle of modular co-ordination if adopted in design, results in further overall economy.

1.13.5.3 Disadvantages of Precast Concrete Products

The following are the disadvantages of precast products :

1. Extra cost is involved in handling, transporting, unloading and erecting prefabricated units.
2. More storage space is required for storing prefabricated product due to :
    (a) Until the product attains desired strength to take handling and other stresses, the product is required to be stored in casting yard.
    (b) If time lag between construction and erection increase, more storage space is required.
3. Skilled labour and costly equipments are required to handle and erect prefabricated units. Thus, it involves high initial investment.
4. If adequate care is not taken, then there is a danger of "progressive collapse" of entire structure.

1.14 SIPOREX CONCRETE BLOCKS

These are light weight concrete blocks which can be easily drilled, cut or nailed with wood working tools, thus simplifying plumbing, electrical wiring, fixing of wooden joinery etc. These blocks have uniform and accurate surfaces, edges and corners being wire cut before autoclaving. The blocks are available in thicknesses of 200, 150, 125 and 100 mm for load bearing walling, partitions and cladding. The masonry construction by these units is very fast as compared to burnt brick construction because, a block of size 200 × 200 × 400 mm is equal to about 8 bricks. Consequently lesser mortar is required for construction.

The blocks are made of cellular concrete and are steam cured. Density of the blocks is 640 kg/m^3 which is less than 1/4th the density of dense cement concrete. Due to this light weight, dead load of walls decrease, and supporting frame work can be designed economically. Handling, hoisting and transportation becomes easier.

In addition to light weight, the blocks have following advantages :

(i) Siporex blocks offer far better fire protection than concrete and is ideal for fire protection.

(ii) As regards compressive strength, it compares well with cement concrete.

(iii) Due to lesser widths of walling, more carpet area is available.

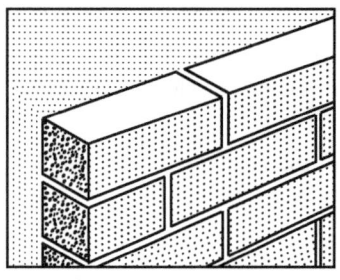

(a) Siporex buidling blocks

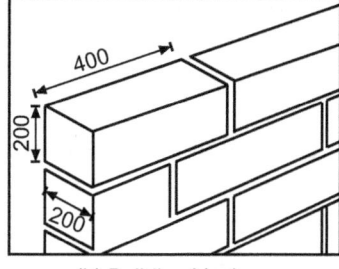

(b) Building blocks

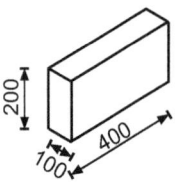

(c) Partition blocks

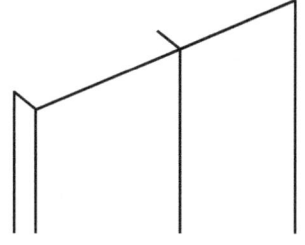

(d) Partition walls

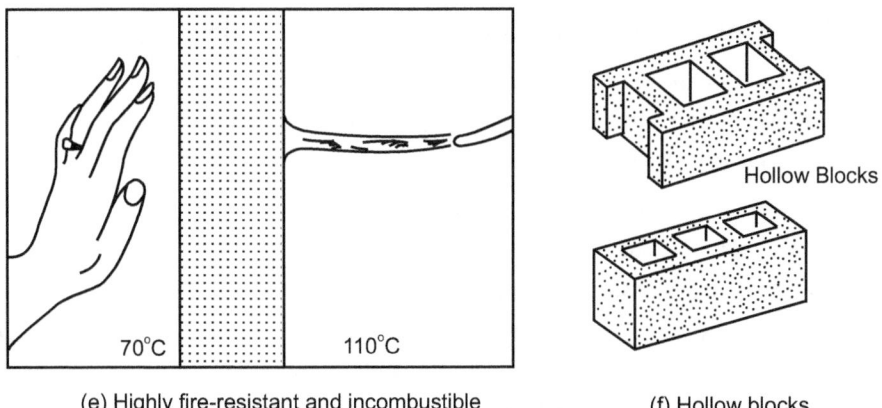

(e) Highly fire-resistant and incombustible   (f) Hollow blocks

Fig. 1.17 : Siporex Concrete Blocks

1.15 FLOORING MATERIALS

The horizontal members of the building which divide vertical space into different parts at different level are called as **floors**. Floor supports the occupants, furniture and equipments. A building may be single storeyed or multi storeyed. Single storeyed building has only one floor which is called as ground floor. In multi-storeyed structures, there are additional floors which are called as upper floors. The floors which are constructed below ground floor are called as **basement floor**. A floor consists of two components :

(1) Sub-floor or base course or sub-grade which imparts strength, stability and support floor covering and all other super imposed loads.
(2) Floor covering which provides a hard, durable, clean, smooth, impervious and beautiful surface to the floor.

1.15.1 Functional Requirements of Flooring Material

The floor is intended to serve the following functions :

1. It should be strong though to sustain safely the intended to the applied.
2. It should resist wear and tear.
3. It should sustain impact load.
4. It should be easy to clean and maintain.
5. It should have pleasing appearance.
6. It should be impermeable.
7. It should take polish.
8. It should not be slippery.
9. It should be easily available and economical.

1.15.2 Varieties of Floor Finishes and Their Suitability

Flooring materials can be broadly classified as :

(i) Hard Floor : Natural stone, clay/ceramic tiles and cement/cement based floors.

(ii) Wooden Floors : Hardwood, softwood.

(iii) Soft Floors : PVC (vinyl), coir, cork, linoleum.

(iv) Floor Coverings : Carpets, rugs and other floor furnishings.

(v) Specialised Floors : Mild steel/iron tiles, plastics, seamless, aluminium.

Note : "All purpose" referes to the human activities confined to domestic houses, flats etc. commercial offices, shops, schools and public buildings.

Light Foot Traffic : Seldom used areas i.e. floors in houses, executive cabins etc.

Medium Foot Traffic : Moderately used areas i.e. floors in commercial establishments.

Heavy Foot Traffic : Much used areas i.e. floors in public buildings and reception room of offices.

Table 1.5 : Different types of flooring materials and their applications

Sr. No.	Material	Usage	Remarks
(1)	**Hard floors**		
1.	**Natural stone**		
	(a) Cuddapah	All purpose	Economical, available only in black. Not commonly used in bathroom, main room.
	(b) Granite	All purpose	Expensive, elegant and durable.
	(c) Marble	All purpose	Expensive, elegant and durable.
	(d) Quartzite	All purpose	Economical
	(e) Slate	All purpose	Economical
	(f) Sand stone	Light traffic areas	Economical
	(g) Shahabad	All purpose	Economical
	(h) Kotah, limestone	All purpose	Available in black colour only.
2.	**Clay/ceramic tiles**		
	(a) Sintered clay/ceramic glazed tiles	All purpose	
	(b) Unglazed or quarry tiles	All purpose	

... (Contd....)

Sr. No.	Material	Usage	Remarks
3.	**Cement/cement based**		
	(a) Cement concrete (in-situ)	All purpose includes industrial floor	End use governs mix properties.
	(b) Terrazzo floors (in-situ)	All purpose	Frequently laid where a high standard of appearance and cleanliness is required.
	(c) Mosaic tiles	All purpose	Used where high cleanliness is not required.
	(d) Other cement based tiles	All purpose	Available in various designs and shapes.
(2)	**Wooden floors (Timber flooring)**		
1.	Hard wood	Heavy foot traffic areas	It can be painted with polyurethane points. It is often covered by carpet. Durability can be improved by good seal.
2.	Parquet	Light medium foot traffic areas	It is not used in damped areas.
3.	Softwood	Light foot traffic areas	Painted with polyurethane paint. It is covered by carpet.
(3)	**Soft floors**		
1.	Coir tiles	Light medium foot traffic areas	
2.	Cork tiles	Light-heavy foot traffic areas	Avoid its use in damp areas.
3.	Linoleum	Light-heavy foot traffic areas	Available with anti-static properties.
4.	PVC (vinyl) with Asbestos	Light-heavy foot traffic areas	Available with anti-static properties.

1.16 MATERIAL, TESTS AND IS SPECIFICATION

Various types of tiles are available. The following are types of tiles:

1. Clay Flooring Tiles - IS 1478 – 1969.
2. Flat Burnt Clay Tiles for Terracing – IS 2690 Part I and II.
3. Flat Burnt Clay Tiles for Irrigation, Drainage Work - IS 3367 – 1975.
4. Manglore Tiles - IS 654 – 1972.
5. Roofing Slate Tiles - IS 6250 – 1981.
6. Tiles of Lime Stone - IS 1128 – 1974.
7. Tiles of Sand Stone - IS 6250 – 1981.
8. Tiles of Marble - IS 3622 – 1977.
9. Glazed Earthen Ware Tiles - IS 777 – 1970.
10. Cement Concrete Flooring Tile - IS 1237 – 1980.

1.16.1 Clay Flooring Tiles

These tiles are flat, square and are available in many colours. These should be uniform in size, shape and free from irregularities and foreign materials either on the surface or on the fractured surface.

Dimensions and permissible tolerances are :

Length	Width	Minimum thickness
150 mm	150 mm	15 / 20
200	200	20 / 25
250	250	30
Tolerances ± 5 mm	± 5 mm	± 2 mm

The tiles are classified in three classes, the physical requirements of which are as under :

Characteristics of Clay Flooring Tile	Class I	Class II	Class III
1. Water Absorption (maximum)	10%	19%	24%
2. Flexural strength kg/cm^2	6	3.5	2.5
3. Impact Test : Maximum height (in mm) drop of steel ball of 35 mm diameter and mass 170 gm.			
Thickness of tile 15 mm	25	20	15
20 mm	60	50	40
25 mm	75	65	50
30 mm	80	70	60

1.16.2 Flat Burnt Clay Tiles

Usually, these are available in rectangular shape in various sizes available for terracing. These may be hand made or machine made.

Burnt clay tiles are also used for lining irrigation and drainage work. However, these tiles differ from those used in roofing, as detailed in the following table.

Table 1.6

Type of Tiles	IS No.	Dimensions with tolerances	Physical properties			
			Compressive strength kgf/cm^2 min	Water Absorption % (max.)	Transverse strength kgf/cm^2	Wrap Max (mm)
1. Tiles for lining irrigation and drainage works.	3367 – 1975	l = 300 ± 10 mm b = 150 ± 5 mm t = 50 mm ± 1.5 mm	105 75	15% (for class 105) 20	15 12	3 mm 3
	2690 Part II (Hand made)	l = 150 to 250 in stages of 25 mm. b = 100 to 200 mm in stages of 25 mm	75	20% by weight	–	2%
2. Burnt clay flat terracing tiles.	2690 Part I (machine made)	Thickness = 25 to 50				
		l and b same as above t = 15 and 20 mm		15% by weight	15	

1.16.3 Cement Concrete Flooring Tile

According to IS : 1237 – 1980 followings are definitions of some types of tiles :

(1) Plain Cement Tiles : Tiles in the manufacture of which no pigments and stone chips are used in the wearing surface.

(2) Plain Coloured Tiles : Tiles having a plain wearing surface where pigments are used but no stone chips.

(3) Terrazo Tiles : Tiles at least 25% of whose wearing surface is composed of stone chips in a matrix of ordinary or coloured portland cement mixed with or without pigments and mechanically ground and filled.

Materials :

(1) Cement : Cement used in the manufacture of tiles shall be ordinary portland cement conforming to IS : 269 – 1976 or rapid hardening portland cement conforming to IS : 8041 – 1978 or white portland cement conforming to IS : 8041 – 1978 or Port land cement conforming to IS : 1489 – 1976.

(2) Aggregate : Aggregate used in the backing layer of tiles shall conform to the requirements of IS 383 – 1970.

For the wearing layer aggregates shall consist of marble chips or any other natural stone chips of singular characteristics of hardness, marble powder or dolomite powder, or mixture of two.

(3) Pigments : Pigments, synthetic or otherwise, used for colouring tiles shall have durable colour. It shall not contain any detrimental matter.

The pigments should not contain zinc compounds or organic dyes. Lead pigments should not be used unless otherwise specified by the purchaser.

Pigments	I.S.
(i) Black/red/brown	IS : 44 – 1969
(ii) Green	IS : 54 – 1975
(iii) Blue	IS : 55 – 1970
	IS : 56 – 1975
(iv) White	IS : 411 – 1968
(v) Yellow	IS : 50 – 1979

Dimensions :

The size of cement concrete tiles are as follows :

Length (mm)	Breadth (mm)	Thickness (mm)
200	200	20
250	250	22
300	300	25

Physical Requirements :

(i) **Flatness of the Tile Surface :** It can be tested by means of a metal ruler. The length of it is not less than the tile diagonal. The amount of concavity convexity should not exceed 1 mm.

(ii) **Perpendicularity :** It can be tested by square. The longest gap between the arm of the square and the edge of the tile shall not exceed 2% of the length of the edge.

(iii) **Wet Transverse Strength :** According to IS : 1237 – 1980, for this test the span between the supports shall be follows :

Size of tile (mm)	Span (mm)
200 × 200	150
250 × 250	200
300 × 300	250

The load shall be applied gradually and at a uniform rate not exceeding 2000 N per minute, until the tile breaks.

The average wet transverse strength shall not be less than 3 N/mm^2.

(iv) **Straightness :** The gap between the fine thread and the plane of the tile cannot exceed 1% of the length of the edge.

(v) **Water absorption :** The average percentage of water absorption shall not exceed 10%.

(vi) **Resistance to Wear :** The wear shall not exceed the following value :

(a) For general purpose tiles :
   (i) Average wear 3.5 mm
   (ii) Wear on individual specimen 4 mm.

(b) For heavy duty floor tiles :
   (i) Average wear 2 mm
   (ii) Wear on individual specimen 2.5 mm.

Other than cement concrete flooring tiles, based upon purpose and materials, followings are types of tiles :

   (i) **Common Tiles :** These are having different shapes and sizes. They are used for paving, flooring etc.

   (ii) **Encaustic Tiles :** These tiles are mainly used for decorative purposes in floors, walls ceilings etc.

   (iii) **Clay Flooring Tile (CBRI) :** It is based upon type of raw material used for it's preparation. It contains alluvial soil mainly. It represents high water absorption but poor impact and abrasion resistance. It possess uniform texture and colour, a metallic sound and good finish. It is available in three sizes $15 \times 15 \times 1.5$ cm, $20 \times 20 \times 2$ cm, $25 \times 25 \times 2.5$ cm etc.

   (iv) **Cinder Flooring Tiles :** Cinder i.e. coal ash is an industrial waste. It is effectively used to manufacture semi-vitreous unglazed tiles. It is economical and cheaper. It can be used in school, hospital, public buildings, industrial sheds, railway platforms, roads etc.

   (v) **Terracota Flooring Tiles :** It is unglazed clay flooring tiles of semi-vitreous type. It is widely used in various public buildings.

   (vi) **Matt Glazed Flooring Ceramic Tiles :** It was manufactured traditionally by use of twice fired earthenware body glazed tiles. Due to advanced technology it is available in various types of shades. It has a strength of 44 N/mm^2, 0.5 – 1% water absorption.

In the market various companies like NITCO etc. offering tiles in various shapes, sizes, categories. Tiles are generally available in 30 cm $\times$ 30 cm, 40 $\times$ 40 cm, 10 $\times$ 40 cm. These are categorised as exotica, elegant, prime plus, super exclusive, rustic etc.

1.17 PAINTS

Paints are thick fluid materials which are applied over the surfaces of wood work, metal work etc. to provide a thin coating. The process of application of paints is called as painting.

Objects of Paintings :

1. To protect wood from decaying effects.
2. To prevent corrosion in metals.
3. To protect the surface from harmful effects of atmospheric agencies.
4. To give decorative and attractive appearance to the surfaces and to make it pleasant.
5. To render surfaces hygienically safe and clean.
6. To provide healthy condition to live in.

Requirements of Good Paint :

1. It should have good spreading or covering power i.e. it should cover maximum area with minimum paint. The cost of painting depends upon covering power of the paint.
2. It should have good consistency so that it can be applied easily and freely on the surface with the help of brush.
3. It should be harmless to the user.
4. The paint should be cheap.
5. It should form a thin uniform film on the painted surface. The film should be hard and durable.
6. It should adhere properly to the surface.
7. The paint should dry within 24 hrs. after application, but should not dry too rapidly.
8. The painted surface should not get affected by atmospheric agencies such as rain, heat, wind etc.
9. The paint should give attractive, decorative and pleasant appearance to the surface.
10. The colour of the paint should be retained for long time.
11. After painting, paint should not show signs of brush marks, shrinkage marks or cracks on the painted surface.
12. It should have good fire and moisture resistance.

Ingredients of a Paint :

Following are the ingredients of a paint :

1. A base
2. An inert extender or filler
3. A vehicle or carrier
4. A drier
5. A solvent or thinner
6. A colouring pigment.

1. **Base :** A base is a solid substance of a metallic oxide in a fine state of division. It forms the main body of the paint and performs following functions.
   (i) To provide opaque coating which hides the surface to be painted.
   (ii) To make a coating film of paint resistant against abrasion and prevent formation of shrinkage cracks.

Table 1.7

Sr. No.	Type of base	Properties and Uses
1.	White lead	Cheapest base and commonly used for ordinary painting work, forms base for lead paint, has great covering power, protective qualities and workability, very poisonous, available in powder and paste form, suitable for wood work painting but not recommended for painting iron work as it does not provide resistance against rusting
2.	Red lead	It is a oxide of lead which is base for lead paints, got excellent properties of rust prevention, toughness and durability. It is available in powder and paste form. Dries very fast and can be used as drier. Used for steel work and as a priming coat for wood work.
3.	Zinc white or Zinc oxide or Zinc sulphate	It is a base for zinc paint. It is non-poisonous transparent, smooth and does not get affected by sulphur fumes. It has got good binding and spreading properties. It is costlier than white lead and less durable and workable. The zinc white film is very hard, brittle and has tendency to crack.
4.	Iron oxide	It is the base for all iron paints. The tink of this base varies from yellowish to brown to black. It is used for the priming coat on structural steel work. It is very effective in preventing rusting of steel. It is cheap and durable and mixes rapidly with the vehicle oil.
5.	Titanium white	It is a oxide of titanium which is bright white in colour. It is non-poisonous and not affected by heat, light or chemicals. It forms opaque coating. It has high oil absorption capacity, high elasticity and great covering properties. It is used as under coat in case of enamel paints.
6.	Aluminium powder	It is the base for all aluminium paints. It is impervious and maintain moisture in the wood which reduces warping and cracking of wood. It is used as priming coat to new wood work.
7.	Lithopone	It is a white substance attained by mixing in equal quantities zinc sulphide and barium sulphate and processing under controlled condition. It is cheap and has good covering capacity. Since it changes colour when exposed to sunlight it is used as a priming coat for interior work.

2. **Vehicles :** It is a liquid substance which is used to keep solid ingredients in suspensions. It performs the following functions :
   (a) It imparts adhesive property to paint by acting as a binder for solid ingredients.
   (b) It helps the ingredients to spread evenly on the surface to be painted.
   (c) Because of vehicles, paint develops an elastic and protective film on the surface after drying.

Following are commonly used vehicles and their properties and uses.

Table 1.8

Sr. No.	Type of vehicle	Properties and Uses
1.	Linseed oil	It is commonly used as a vehicle in all oil paints and is extracted from flax seeds. After oxidizing it gets thicker. Linseed oil is clear, pale, transparent, brilliant odourless. It is used in different forms as follows.
	(a) Raw linseed oil	It is thin, odourless, transparent and brilliant. It dries very slowly and therefore used for interior painting work.
	(b) Boiled linseed oil	It is obtained by boiling the mixture of 10% drier like red lead or litharge and raw linseed oil. It is thicker and darker as compared to raw oil and dries rapidly. But has got lesser penetration power and elasticity. It is basically used for exterior painting work.
	(c) Pale boiled linseed oil	It has got properties similar to boiled oil but it is not dark in colour. It can be used for light or white coloured paints. It is suitable for painting plastered surface and metal work.
	(d) Double boiled linseed oil	It has quick drying properties but it is very thick and requires turpentine for thinning purpose. It is colourless and transparent. It is used for painting external work.
	(e) Stand oil	It is obtained by heating linseed oil. It dries slowly, and gives clean, durable and shining finish.
2.	Tung oil	It is used for superior work as it has got properties superior than linseed oil.
3.	Poppy oil	It is obtained from poppy seeds. It dries very slowly. It is expensive. The colour lasts for longer period. Its raw quality is not suitable for painting work and is mixed with some other materials. It is used for making delicate, light coloured paints.
4.	Nut oil	It is obtained from ordinary walnuts. It is colourless, cheap, quick drying. But less durable. Hence, it is used for temporary painting work for white or light coloured paints.

3. **Extenders or Inert Filler or Adulterants :** These are the cheap inert materials used to alter properties of paints. Their functions are as follows :

   (a) They reduce cost of the base and the cost of painting work.

   (b) They keep other ingredients in suspension.

   (c) They change weight of the paint and reduce rapid setting of paint.

   (d) They increase durability of the paint.

   (e) They reduce shrinkage and cracking of paint.

   The commonly used extenders are Baryte (barium sulphate), Silica, Lithopone, Whiting, Charcoal, Gypsum, Silicate of magnesia, Alumina etc. They should not be used in excess because in that case paint looses its original character and becomes weak.

4. **Drier :** It is a metallic compound and acts as a catalyte and accelerates the process of drying of the paint. It absorbs oxygen from atmosphere and oxidizes the vehicle to become thicker. It adversely affects colour and elasticity of the paints. It is not used in final coat of paints. Various patented driers are available in the market. They are either oil driers or paste driers. Types of oil driers are litharge, magnesium dioxide, magnesium borates. Paste driers are compounds of lead, cobalt, manganese which are mixed in inert fillers and ground with linseed oil.

5. **Thinner or Solvent :** It is liquid which is added to the paint to obtain derived consistency so that the paint can be applied easily on the surface. It helps the paint to penetrate through the porous surface. It improves spreading properties of paint. It evaporates after application and surface becomes more even and smooth. For oil paints Turpentine is generally used as a thinner. It is inflammable, volatile and colourless liquid. It gets affected by weather and should be used for interior work. White spirit and naptha are also used as thinner in place of turpentine.

6. **Colouring Pigments :** It is added in white paints to get different shades of colour when the desired colour of paint is different from the colour of base. For white, black and other dark shades of paints are obtained by selecting base of specific colours. The other desired shade may be obtained by using single or combination of colouring pigments.

Table 1.9 : Colouring pigments for paints

Sr. No.	Desired colour of paint	Pigment used
1.	Blue	Indigo blue, pursian blue, cobalt blue, ultramarine blue
2.	Brown	Burnt umber, raw umber, burnt sienna
3.	Black	Lamp black, ivory black, graphite, vegetable black
4.	Green	Chrome green, copper sulphate, emerald green, green earth
5.	Yellow	Chrome yellow, raw sienna, yellow ochre, zinc chromate, barium chromate
6.	Red	Cormine, red lead, vermilion red, venetian red, Indian red.

1.18 GLASS

It is an important engineering material and it has many applications in construction industry.

Manufacturing Process : It is an amorphous, transparent or translucent, coloured or colourless material which is obtained by fusing a mixture of pure sand (SiO_2), soda (NaOH or KOH) and chalk ($CaCO_3$) with some quantity of broken glass. These ingredients are grounded to fine powder and are melted and fused in a furnace known as Tank Furnace at about 800 to 950°C. The molten mass is poured into moulds of required shape.

Many varieties of glass have been developed so far and it is possible to make glass lighter than cork, softer than cotton or stronger than steel.

1.18.1 Types of Glasses

1. Crown Glass (Soda Ash Glass) : Major constituents are 75 parts silica, 12.5 parts soda, alumina and cullet (pieces of glass). It represents cheapest quality and used for window panes, bottles, bulbs etc.

2. Sheet Glass (Window Glass) : Transparent, thin (2 to 6 mm), glossy, apparently smooth surface (with some wavy texture visible at an acute angle or in reflected rays). Transmits light rays of visible portion (85 to 90%) and blocks ultraviolet rays. Properties like density, strength, thermal conductivity are similar to that of soda - lime - silica glass. Used for glazing, interior doors, skylights and if thickness > 3 mm then employed for multiple glass units, exterior doors, shop windows, showcases etc.

3. Flint Glass : Major constituents are 100 parts (by weight) of sand or silica, 70 parts of lead, 33 parts of potash, 100 parts of cullet. It is a very fine variety of glass and is used for making glassware, art glass, radio valves. Very fine polished surface can be obtained for this variety.

4. Ground Glass : It is semi-transparent or translucent variety, hence to be used in situations where light transmission without transparency is essential. One of the surface is made rough either by grinding or by melting powdered glass over it.

5. Pyrex Glass : Very much heat resistant variety. Sand 90 parts, lime 36, borax 0.5, feldspar 0.5 and cullet 90 parts by weight. Used for laboratory apparatus, cooking utensils, electric insulators etc.

6. Plate Glass : Thickness ranges within 5 mm to 25 mm and is available in larger sheets (upto 4.5 m × 3.5 m). There is no distortion of vision at any angle of observation. It is obtained by mechanical grinding and polishing or by floating molten glass on surface of molten tin contained in tank. Manufactured glass is usually flat. It has very high compressive strength (about 1200 MPa). Bending and impact strength can be improved by tempering, ion exchange or alike methods.

As light transmission is good (around 87%), it is used for shopping glass window, showcases, mirrors, furniture etc. Also in case of public building fenestration it is employed.

7. Tempered Glass : Tempering dates back to 17th century but commercial production began in 1930s. It has high mechanical strength and heat resistance. Manufactured by heating thick sheets (thickness > 5 mm) to a temperature of 700 to 900°C and then subjected to rapid but uniform cooling with a stream of air or a liquid (By immersion, spraying or hosing).

Glass products to be tempered are fully shaped in advance as tempered glass cannot be cut, ground, drilled etc. Bending strength is 5 to 6 times and resistance to heat is twice as that of ordinary annealed glass.

Used for shop windows, public building fenestrations, flush doors etc. and where impact load is predominantly to be resisted.

8. Wired Glass : It is an ordinary plate glass 5 to 6 mm thick with wire mesh reinforcement. Like tempered glass, it constitutes no hazard when shattered. It is more heat resistant as steel wires are good conductors of heat.

9. Glass Blocks : These are hollow or solid, translucent masonry units made from structural glass annealed to withstand the stresses. Available in various sizes 140 × 140 × 100, 190 × 190 × 100 or 194 × 194 × 98, 244 × 244 × 98 mm (depending upon the partition wall thickness appropriate use is expected). Block units are formed by fusing two sections at a high temperature which are casted separately. They may have one or two air cells. Partial vacuum in the interior improves heat insulation capacity. The joining edges are painted internally and sanded externally to form a key to mortar and front and back faces are decorative or plain. Blocks are laid in cement lime mortar 1 : 1 : 4. If the height is upto 150 mm then expanded metal strip reinforcement is placed in every third or fourth course, however if the height is more than 250, it is to be provided in every course. Provision for thermal expansion is made along jambs and heads of each panel. Glass bricks are also casted with joggles and end grooves to form glass wall, glass claddings.

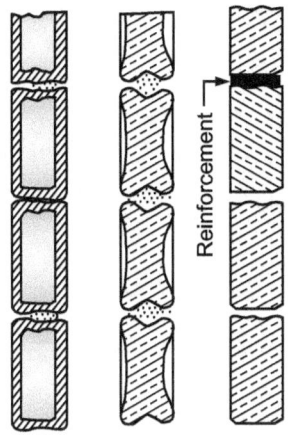

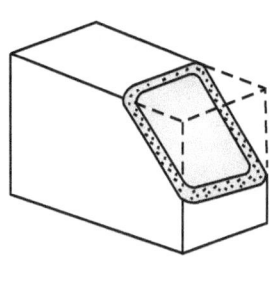

(a) Glass block walls

(b) Hollow glass block

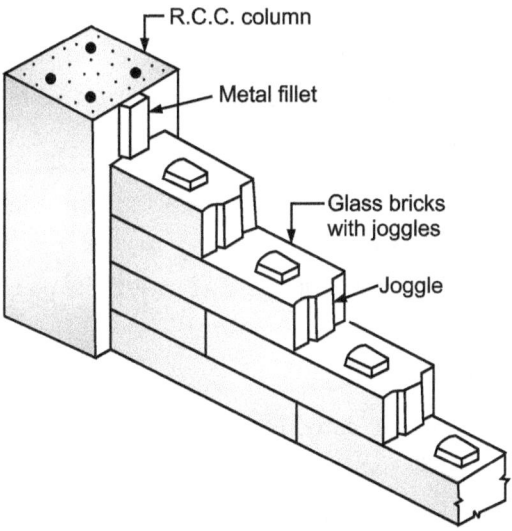

(c) Glass brick wall

Fig. 1.18 : Glass block and glass brick

Properties :

    Compressive strength – 1.5 MPa (min)

    Toughness – 0.8 joule

    Light transmission – 30 to 50%

    Thermal conductivity – 0.5 W/machine

    Fire resistance – upto 2.4 hrs.

Uses : Exterior claddings, external walls, partitions, windows or in combination with concrete, masonry work, roofing where concrete members serve as a skeleton.

Advantages :

1. Non-porous, impervious, non-absorbent of moisture.
2. Diffused light admittance, at desired tinge of colour, pleasing to eye.
3. As the surface is smooth, less catch to dirt/dust.
4. Does not allow condensation on the internal surface.
5. Provides good architectural effect.
6. Sound proof, fire proof, heat proof to some extent.
7. If used as external cladding, no necessity to provide windows, at the same time admittance is less and diffused, hence partial privacy is maintained.

1.18.2 Glass and Aluminium Cladding

All the mega cities in the world are adopting a modern international look, for their residential and commercial projects. For improving the exterior facades of any building whether old or new; techniques like cladding are adopted. The material used for cladding is glass, aluminium, tiles etc.

Aluminium Composite Panel Cladding

It is basically a typical metal curtain wall system. Its application include Exterior claddings, Column covers, In-fill panels, Fascias-Canopies, Clean rooms, Interior walls and partition panels, Sunshades, Cornices etc.

Characteristics : Light in weight, modern finish, available in many colours, ease in installation, weather proof coats, colour consistency, flatness, can take various forms of bends and curves, recyclable, non-toxic etc.

1.19 ALUMINIUM AND ALLOYS

The most popular non-ferrous metal is Aluminium. Other non-ferrous metals are lead, copper magnesium nickel, tin, zinc etc.

Main ore for aluminium is bauxite. Bluish-silver white lustrous metal i.e. aluminium is obtained from it. The necessary provision for extracting aluminium from its ore is continuous abundant electric supply. This is the main drawback in commercial exploitation of rich bauxite deposits in India.

Aluminium Plants	States in India (With Hydroelectric Power Supply)
Belgaum	Karnataka
Mettur	Tamil Nadu
Koyana	Maharashtra
Renukoot	U.P.

Procedure : Crushed ore is treated with caustic soda forming sodium aluminate. This is separated by filteration and converted into Aluminate hydrate by precipitation. Finally, after calcination what is obtained is aluminium oxide called alumina. Alumina thus obtained is deoxidised by electrolysis of molten solution. Further, subjected to purification which give 99.5% pure aluminium.

Properties of Aluminium :

1. It is soft, ductile, light in weight (specific gravity 2.7), malleable metal with high luster, corrosion resistant (due to formation of tough adherent oxide film when exposed to air).
2. It melts at 658°C and is a good conductor of heat and electricity.
3. The tensile strength of aluminium is about 100 N/mm^2 for pure metal but for alloys it can reach to 500 N/mm^2.
4. During cold work strength goes to 150 N/mm^2 but there is considerable loss of ductility.

Uses :

1. Production of utensils, electric wires, machine parts etc.
2. Structural load bearing members.
3. Construction of aeroplanes.
4. Roofing sheets.
5. Post-panels-balustrade formation.
6. Door-window frames etc.

7. Aluminium paints, glazing bars, rods etc.
8. Bathroom fittings, surgical instruments, explosive manufacturing, precession survey etc.
9. Flash bulbs for photography.
10. Self lubricated sintered aluminium bearing (improved corrosion resistance, high thermal conductivity, greater oil retention and stability, less frictional coefficient).

EXERCISE

1. (a) Name various areas of civil engineering and applications of any one.
   (b) State importance of any two disciplines.
2. (a) State the importance of Structural and Earthquake Engineering.
   (b) Differentiate between estimation and valuation. (any 3 points)
3. (a) Give the objectives of surveying, fluid mechanics, quantity surveying and Transportation engineering.
   (b) How a quantity surveying decides the feasibility and economic viability of a project ?
4. (a) Write two applications of each of the following :
   Irrigation Engineering, Geotechnical Engineering.
   (b) Explain the importance of Environmental Engineering in day-to-day life.
5. (a) State different types of constructions attributable to Mechanical Engineering Discipline.
   (b) Enumerate the basic role of civil engineer in any kind of construction work.
6. Describe the role of civil engineer in the activities involved in the construction of a big factory building producing automobiles.
7. (a) Describe different points to be borne in mind in the construction of chemical plants.
   (b) State the points which a civil engineer has to keep in mind in the construction of transmission line towers.
8. (a) What are the different types of civil engineering constructions ?
   (b) What are the stages in the completion of any project ?
9. Write a note on the role of civil engineer in the construction of power houses generating hydroelectric power.
10. (a) What are the civil engineering aspects of thermal power stations ?
    (b) Write a note on the type of construction where the material has to withstand high temperature.
11. (a) How is the classification of roads done ?
    (b) Draw a typical cross-section of a concrete road.

12. (a) State any four merits of road transport.
    (b) Draw a typical cross-section of a Broad gauge railway track.
13. Write any four uses of the following branches :
    (a) Geotechnical Engineering, (b) Environmental Engineering.
14. What is infrastructure development ? State the basic facilities required to be provided for rapid development of a region.
15. Enlist and briefly explain the infrastructural facilities that are to be provided in a locality for its development.

(A) Foundation :
1. Explain the term foundation. Why it is necessary ?
   State different function of foundation.
2. (a) Explain with the help of load settlement curve ultimate bearing capacity.
   (b) What is safe bearing capacity ?

Settlement :
3. (a) What is differential settlement ? How it is expressed ? Explain with sketch.
   (b) State allowable limits for total settlement and differential settlement as per I.S.
   (c) State causes of settlement and differential settlement.
   (d) State the max. settlement that can be allowed for
       (i) Raft foundation (ii) Spread footing on clays.
   (e) State effects of differential settlement.
   (f) Write short note on :
       (i) Differential settlement
       (ii) Settlement of foundation.

Types of foundation :
4. (a) Explain with sketches the circumstances under which following types of foundation are adopted.
       (1) Combined footing. (2) Isolated footing. (3) Raft foundation.
       (4) Pile foundation.
   (b) Distinguish between the following :
       (1) Isolated footing and combined footing :
       (2) Bearing pile and friction pile.
       Name different types of combined footings.
       Draw sketch of (i) Cantilever footing, (ii) Trapezoidal footing when they are provided.

5. What do you understand by raft foundation ? Explain with a neat sketch. When you will adopt raft foundation ?
6. Explain the suitability of each of the following : -
   (i) Stepped footing (ii) Raft foundation (iii) Pile foundation
   (iv) Isolated RCC column footing.
   Explain the following with suitable examples : -
   (i) Choice of foundation and bearing capacity of soil.
   (ii) Bearing capacity of soil and failure of foundation.
7. State functions of foundation. State the causes of failure of foundation.
8. State the permissible amount of settlement in clayey and sandy soil.
9. Differentiate between ultimate and safe bearing capacity of soil.
10. When it is necessary to provide combined footing ?
11. What are the remedial measures adopted in case of failure of foundation ?
12. List out different types of footings and explain in one sentence their specific importance.

(B) Superstructure

13. What are the different types of loads on a superstructure ?
14. What is 'live load' ? How is it considered in the design of a structural member ? What live load would you consider for
    (i) Residential buildings (ii) Class room (iii) Assembly hall (iv) Workshop ?
15. Differentiate clearly between 'framed structure' and 'load bearing structure' OR State the advantages of 'framed structure' over a load bearing structure.
16. (a) What are the different components of a superstructure ?
    (b) Distinguish clearly between substructure and superstructure.
17. State why would you prefer brick masonry to stone masonry ?
18. State the requirements of good brick.
19. Write short notes on :
    (a) Composite structures, (b) R.C.C. and steel framed structure, (c) Stone masonry,
    (d) Dead load and live load.
20. Explain difference between PCC and RCC. State the conditions underwhich each is used. Give examples.
21. What is precast cement concrete ? State its advantages. State any two commonly used precast products.
22. What are the properties of good building stones ?
23. Explain the term pre-stressed concrete and state the advantages of pre-stressed concrete.

FUNDAMENTALS OF CIVIL ENGINEERING   CIVIL ENGINEERING SCOPE AND APPLICATIONS

24. Differentiate between "load bearing" and framed structure.
    (a) State the advantages of stone masonry over brick masonry.
    (b) How you will detect the adulteration in cement ?
    (c) What is precast concrete ? What are the advantages of precast units ?
25. Explain with the help of sketches laying of stratified stones of a building.
26. Explain the use of various grades of concrete mixes, along with their mix proportions.
27. State the differences between end bearing piles and friction piles.

Cement

1. Why cement is used in preference to lime ?
2. State a few physical properties of ordinary portland cement.
3. How you will check quality of cement in field ?
4. Under what circumstances, use of
    (a) Bricks is preferred to that of stones.
    (b) Stones is preferred to that of bricks.
    (c) Natural sand is preferred to that of artificial sand.
    (d) Artificial sand is preferred to natural sand.
5. State the requirements of good quality bricks.
6. State simple test that you may carry to check quality of bricks at site.
7. Explain with sketch, the correct method of laying of stones in (a) arches, (b) columns with reference to plane of stratification.
8. What are advantages and disadvantages of prefabricated products ?
9. What are the advantages of artificial sand ?
10. Name a few types of Indian stones, useful for building construction. State the place where the same are available in large quantities.
11. Explain difference between :
    (a) PCC and RCC   (b) RCC and pre-stressed concrete.
12. Give the examples where the following types of concrete are used :
    (a) PCC, (b) RCC, (c) Pre-stressed concrete.
13. Compare the advantages of :
    (a) Tor steel over mild steel.
    (b) TMT (Thermo Mechanically Treated) bars over TOR steel bars.

FUNDAMENTALS OF CIVIL ENGINEERING CIVIL ENGINEERING SCOPE AND APPLICATIONS

Bricks, Stones etc.

(a) Enlist any four basic materials used in construction. Give 2 uses of each.

(b) State any two uses of each of following stones, cement, bricks.

UNIVERSITY QUESTIONS

Type A : Role of Civil Engineer

1. State clearly the four basic roles of a Civil Engineer in any type of construction work.
   (May 2005, May 2006) (4)

2. Briefly describe the role of civil engineering during the construction of (i) power houses, (ii) erection of electrical transmission towers. **(Dec. 2005, May 2006) (4)**

3. Enumerate the basic role of civil engineer in any kind of construction work.
   (Dec. 03) (4)

4. In what way the civil engineering will be helpful for the construction of
   (i) power houses, (ii) erection of electrical tower. **(Dec. 2003) (2 + 2 = 4)**

5. During the construction of an industrial shed, what is the role of civil engineer other than the basic role ? Explain with the help of a line sketch. **(Dec. 2003) (4)**

6. Enlist the various allied disciplines in which the role of civil engineer is very very essential and hence point out the role of civil engineer in any one discipline, starting from location of site till its completion of work. You may also draw line sketches if found necessary. **(Dec. 2004) (2 + 4 = 6)**

7. State and briefly explain any two adverse conditions under which the civil engineer has to execute the work. **(May 2004) (3)**

8. Explain with the examples role of civil engineering in : **(Dec. 2004, May 06) (6)**
   (i) Mechanical engineering.
   (ii) Chemical engineering.

9. Explain role of civil engineering in transportation engineering in the 21st century.
   (Dec. 2004) (5)

10. Describe at least in four steps, how a civil engineer will be useful in erection of an electrical tower. **(Dec. 2004) (4)**

11. State any four points that are to be necessarily considered by the civil engineer in the following construction works : **(May 2004) (2 M each = 6)**
    (i) Laying foundation for big machine.
    (ii) Erection of transmission tower.
    (iii) Chemical plant.

Type B : Applications in the field of

1. State any two practical applications of each of the following :
   - (i) Structural engineering.
   - (ii) Environmental engineering.
   - (iii) Geotechnical engineering. **(Dec. 2004, May 2006) (2 × 3 = 6)**

2. State any two applications of
   - (i) Quantity surveying **(Dec. 2004)**
   - (ii) Construction management.

3. State any two practical applications of the following : **(2 + 2 = 4)**
   - (i) Transportation engineering. **(May 2004 and 2006)**
   - (ii) Irrigation engineering.

4. State any two practical applications of each of the following : **(May 2004) (4)**
   - (i) Irrigation engineering.
   - (ii) Foundation engineering.

5. Briefly explain three applications of each of the following : **(6)**
   - (i) Earthquake engineering. **(Dec. 204, May 2006)**
   - (ii) Environmental engineering.

6. Explain in brief any two practical applications associated with the following :
   - (i) Foundation engineering. **(Dec. 2003)**
   - (ii) Fluid mechanics. **(2 + 2 = 4)**

7. Briefly explain any two practical applications of
   - (i) Fluid mechanics,
   - (ii) Environmental engineering. **(Dec. 2005) (3 + 3 = 6)**

8. Write short notes on the following :
   - (i) Earthquake engineering. **(Dec. 2003, May 2006) (2 + 2 = 4)**
   - (ii) Quantity surveying.

9. State any four uses of each of following branches of civil engineering.
   - (i) Geotechnical engineering. **(Dec. 2003)**
   - (ii) Environmental engineering. **(2 + 2 = 4)**

10. Explain with examples the necessity of the subject 'fluid mechanics'. **(4)**
    - (a) Enlist any eight areas in civil engineering and explain any two in brief.
      (May 2004) (2 + 2 + 2 = 6)

Type C : Infrastrutural Facilities

1. Enlist any six infrastructural facilities that are needed to be provided for the development of any new locality. **(Dec. 2004, May 2006) (1/2 × 6 = 3)**
2. Explain the need of infrastructure development with example. Also state activities in such development. **(Dec. 2004) (5)**
3. Enlist and briefly explain the infrastructural facilities that are to be provided in a locality for its development. **(Dec. 2003)**

Type D : Difference

1. Draw a neat labelled sketch to show the permanent way of a railway track. Also state clearly where you will use narrow gauge track. **(Dec. 2004) (3 + 1 = 4)**
2. Bring out the difference between road ways and railway w.r.t. any four characteristic points. **(Dec. 2004) (1 each = 4)**
3. Define the term "GAUGE" and show this with the help of a sketch. Also state the various types with their dimensions. **(May 2004) (1 + 1 + 3 = 5)**

    Define the term "GAUGE" and state the types of gauges. Also give their values.

    (May 2005) (5)

4. Differentiate between the following w.r.t. any three points. **(3 + 3 = 6)**
    (i) Estimation and valuation.
    (ii) Flexible pavement and rigid pavement. **(May 2004)**
5. Bring out the difference between Roadways and railways in respect of any 4 points.

    (May 2005) (4)
6. Compare roadways and railways w.r.t. any four points. **(4)**
7. Give only the names of the types of roads based upon. **(May 2004) (2 + 2 = 4)**
    (i) Material used for construction.
    (ii) Function and location.

Foundation

1. State any three functions of foundations. **(Dec. 2003)**
2. Write short note on causes of settlement. **(Dec. 2003)**
3. Explain terms : **(Dec. 2003)**
    (i) Safe bearing capacity.
    (ii) Differential settlement.

4. Differentiate between shallow foundation and deep foundation. Give two examples of each. **(May 2004)**
5. Explain four causes of failure of foundation. **(May 2006)**
6. Draw sketches of following types of foundation :
   (i) Simple strap footing. **(Dec. 2003)**
   (ii) Isolated rectangular footing. **(Dec. 2003)**
   (iii) Sloped column footing. **(May 2006)**
   (iv) Trapezoidal combined footing. **(May 2006)**

Components of Building

1. Enlist various components of a building/superstructure and state their functions. **(Dec. 2004, 2005, May 2006)**
2. Explain difference between formed structure and load bearing structure. **(Dec 03)**
3. State advantages and disadvantages of framed structure and load bearing structure. **(May 2005)**
4. Write a short note on various types of loads on a building. **(Dec. 2003)**

Doors and Windows etc.

1. Name any two types of doors and two types of window. State their necessary in building. **(Dec. 2004)**
2. Write a short note on doors and windows. **(May 2004)**
3. Point out necessity of doors and windows in building. Name types of doors used in residential building and college building. **(May 2005)**
4. State purpose of following : **(Dec. 2003)**
   (i) Floors, (ii) Openings in a building.

Bricks

1. Write a short note on :
   (i) Classification of bricks. **(May 2004, 2005)**
   (ii) Classification of stones **(Dec. 2004, May 2004)**
   (iii) Requirements in good brick masonry work. **(May 2004)**
   (iv) Requirements of good quality bricks. **(May 2005)**
   (v) Types of steel reinforcement. **(May 2006)**
   (vi) Sand as construction material. **(May 2006)**
2. Draw sketch of frog in conventional brick. State its importance. **(Dec. 2005)**

Cement and Concrete

1. Explain following terms and give uses of :
   (i) PCC, (ii) PSC, (iii) RCC, (iv) PC. **(Dec. 2003, May 2005)**
2. Explain difference between the following and give examples of uses of same :
   (a) Cement mortar and cement concrete. **(May and Dec. 2005)**
   (b) Pretensioning and post tensioning. **(May 2004, Dec. 2005)**
3. State advantages of following as compared with cast-in-situ concrete.
   (a) Prestressed concrete.
   (b) Aerated light weight concrete.
   (c) Precast blocks. **(Dec. 2003, May 2005)**
1. State any four flooring materials. State the advantages and limitations of each. **[Dec. 2004]**
2. State step-by-step procedure to construct concrete flooring for an industrial building. **[Dec. 2004]**
3. Explain the construction of flat slab floor for commercial buildings. State the advantages of it. State recent technology used to reduce thickness of it. **[Dec. 2004]**
4. A hall of size 7.50 m and 10.0 m is to be provided with two way ribbed floor construction. Explain process of construction with the help of neat sketches. State the grade of concrete and steel used for the construction. **[May 2005]**
5. State with reason, most suitable type of flooring material for the following situations :
   (a) A drawing room of a high specification bungalow.
   (b) Car parking of a residential flat building.
   (c) Ware house where heavy articles are stored.
   (d) Kitchen flooring for middle income group housing. **[May 2005]**
6. State step-by-step procedure of providing vacuum processed concrete flooring for industrial sheds. What type of coating is provided to make floor more resistant to abrasion and avoid dusting ? **[May 2005]**
7. Draw a labelled sketch of flat slab floor and show the following :
   (a) Capital, (b) Drop panel, (c) Flat slab.
   State two important advantages of the flat slab flooring. **[May 2005]**
8. Name the type of flooring materials available in the market. State advantages and limitations of each. **[Dec. 2005, 06]**

UNIT II

Chapter 2
SURVEYING

2.1 INTRODUCTION

Surveying is an important branch of Civil Engineering which includes Linear and Angular measurements.

Linear and angular measurements are carried out to obtain information about the piece of land or a plot or features in a particular locality. These measurements enable the surveyor to locate the boundaries of the plot or features of an area and to show them on paper by drawing a plan of these features. Angular measurements include the measurement of bearings or angles using some instruments. Linear measurements are the measurements carried out for measurement of horizontal distances in horizontal plane and vertical distances in vertical plane. In this chapter, it is proposed to deal with the objects, purposes and principles of Surveying and Linear Measurements in chapter 2 and Angular measurements in chapter 3. Vertical measurements are dealt within a separate chapter.

2.2 SURVEYING : OBJECT, PURPOSES AND PRINCIPLES

2.2.1 Object of Surveying

The object of surveying is to make a representation on paper to some scale, of the earth's surface including the natural and manmade features upon or under it. This object is achieved by preparing a map or plan of the area surveyed.

The map or plan is the horizontal projection of the area surveyed. It indicates horizontal distances. The vertical distances between the points on earth's surface are shown by vertical sections obtained by taking measurements in vertical plane i.e. by levelling operation. Thus levelling helps to prepare sections of features of ground.

A map is a drawing where scale is small e.g. map of India. When the scale of drawing is large, it is called a plan e.g. plan of a building.

2.2.2 Purposes of Surveying

The purposes of surveying are :

1. To determine the relative positions and sizes of natural features on earth's surface such as mountains, hills, lakes, seas, rivers, etc. and also artificial features such as roads, railways, buildings, structures, fences, etc.

2. To find relative heights of various points on the surface of the earth. These are measured vertically above some horizontal plane called datum. These are known as elevations or levels.

FUNDAMENTALS OF CIVIL ENGINEERING   SURVEYING

2.2.3 Principles of Surveying

Surveying involves different operations and techniques, but all these are based on the following principles such as :
1. **To work from whole to part.**
2. **To locate a point by at least two independent processes :**
    (a) Linear measurements, (b) Angular measurements or
    (c) Both linear and angular measurements.

1. **To work from whole to part :**

For any particular survey, whether it is of an entire town or field, the main framework for the entire area to be surveyed consists of polygons or triangles and is set out by fixing control points. The main framework is then divided suitably for detailed surveying. This principle prevents accumulation of errors in the surveying. The principle can be illustrated as follows :

Suppose a big piece of land PQRST is to be surveyed. Then control points i.e. stations P, Q, R, S and T are established at each of the corners of land. Then the rectangular area is subdivided into two triangles PQR and RPT by joining stations P and R. Further subdivision of △ PQR can be done by selecting another station M on the line PR and forming triangles PQM and QMR. For surveying purposes by selecting stations N, O, U and V on different sides, the bigger area can be divided into smaller triangles as shown in Fig. 2.1. This process is called as working from whole to part. This will localise the errors of measurement.

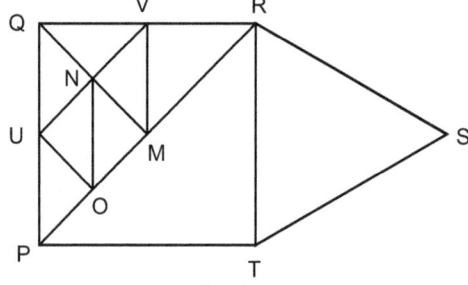

Fig. 2.1

However, if the work is started from part to whole i.e. from △ MNO and survey is completed by extending the sides of the △ MNO, then the errors in the measurement of length will accumulate and will result in the wrong calculation of area. Thus it can be stated that if we adopt the method of working from part to whole, small errors increase and thus become uncontrollable at the end. This will have adverse effect on the precision of survey.

Comparing the two methods, it can be said that in the first method, i.e. working from whole to the part the errors are minimised and will prove to be of great advantage. However, in the second method of working from part to whole, the errors are accumulated and will give inaccurate results in the end.

Adopting the principle of working from whole to part, various localities of a town can be surveyed with high precision and plotted to scale. Here first the whole boundary of the town is fixed by system of horizontal control points and plotted on map. Then the town can be divided into large triangles which are surveyed and plotted with greatest accuracy. They are further divided into smaller triangles and surveyed. Thus the errors are controlled and localised to corresponding triangles only.

2. **To locate a point by at least two independent measurements (Fig. 2.2) :**

Here, two points are selected in the field and distance between them is measured. The relative positions of other points in the field can be located from these two reference points.

To locate a point d with respect to given points of reference, A and B, the following methods can be employed.

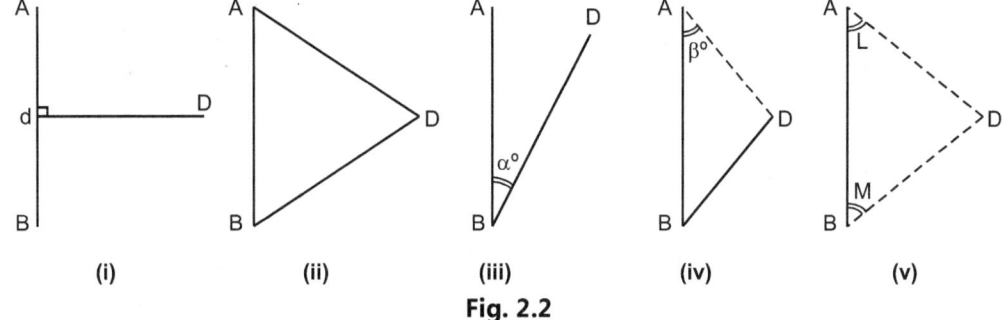

Fig. 2.2

(i) Distance Ad and perpendicular dD;
(ii) Lengths AD and BD;
(iii) Length BD and angle α°;
(iv) Length BD and angle β°;
(v) Angles L and M (∠ DAB and ∠ DBA).

Similarly position of new point with reference to three known points can also be fixed up.

2.2.4 Classification of Surveying

Surveying is classified into two broad categories :
1. Plane surveying and
2. Geodetic surveying.

1. Plane surveying : In this type of surveying, the effect of curvature of surface of earth is not taken into account. The surface of earth is taken to be plane surface. The extent of area upto which this assumption of plane surface holds good is 260 sq. km. Therefore, plane surveying is adopted for small areas. The degree of accuracy of plane survey is relatively low.

2. Geodetic surveying : In Geodetic surveying, the curvature of earth's surface is taken into account. Geodetic surveys are carried out for large distances and areas with a high degree of precision. In India, Survey of India, a Government department undertakes the work of Geodetic surveying.

2.3 LINEAR MEASUREMENTS

The distances on the ground are measured either with a metric chain or tape.

Different methods can be adopted for making linear measurements depending on the degree of precision required. These methods can be broadly divided into three groups :
1. Direct measurement.
2. Measurement by optical distance measuring instrument.
3. Electronic devices.

In direct measurement, distances are actually measured on the ground with the help of a tape. Measurements by optical instruments means which involve the use of instruments like tacheometer, subtence bar, telemeter, etc. The electronic distance measuring instruments rely on propagation, reflection and reception of radio or light waves. These include instruments like Geodimeter, Tellurometer, and Distomat. i.e. Electronic Distance meter or Total station.

2.3.1 Direct Measurement of Distances

The most commonly adopted method for measurement of distances is by using chain or tape known as 'chaining' or 'taping'.

2.3.2 Instruments for Chaining

Following instruments are used for determining the length of a given line.
- A. (i) Chain or (ii) tape
- B. Arrows
- C. Pegs
- D. Ranging rods.
- E. Offset rods
- F. Plumb bob
- G. Line ranger

A. (i) Chain :

The chains are available in lengths of 20 m and 30 m. The chain consists of 100 links for 20 m. chain and 150 links for 30 m chain. Link is made of galvanised mild steel wire 4 mm in diameter. Length of each link is the distance between the centres of two consecutive middle rings. Each link is bent into loop at the ends and joined to each other by three small circular or oval shaped rings. These rings offer flexibility to the chain. The ends of the chain are provided with brass handle at each end with a swivel joint, so that the chain can be turned without twisting. A semicircular groove is provided in the centre on the outer periphery of handle for fixing the m.s. arrow at the end of one chain length. Brass tags or tallies are inserted at every 5 m. length to make out the part length of chain. The length of chain is measured from the outside of one handle to the outside of the other handle.

The commonly used chain is the metric chain.

FUNDAMENTALS OF CIVIL ENGINEERING

(i) Metric chain : These are available in lengths of 20 m and 30 m. The details for 30 m chain are shown in Fig. 2.3.

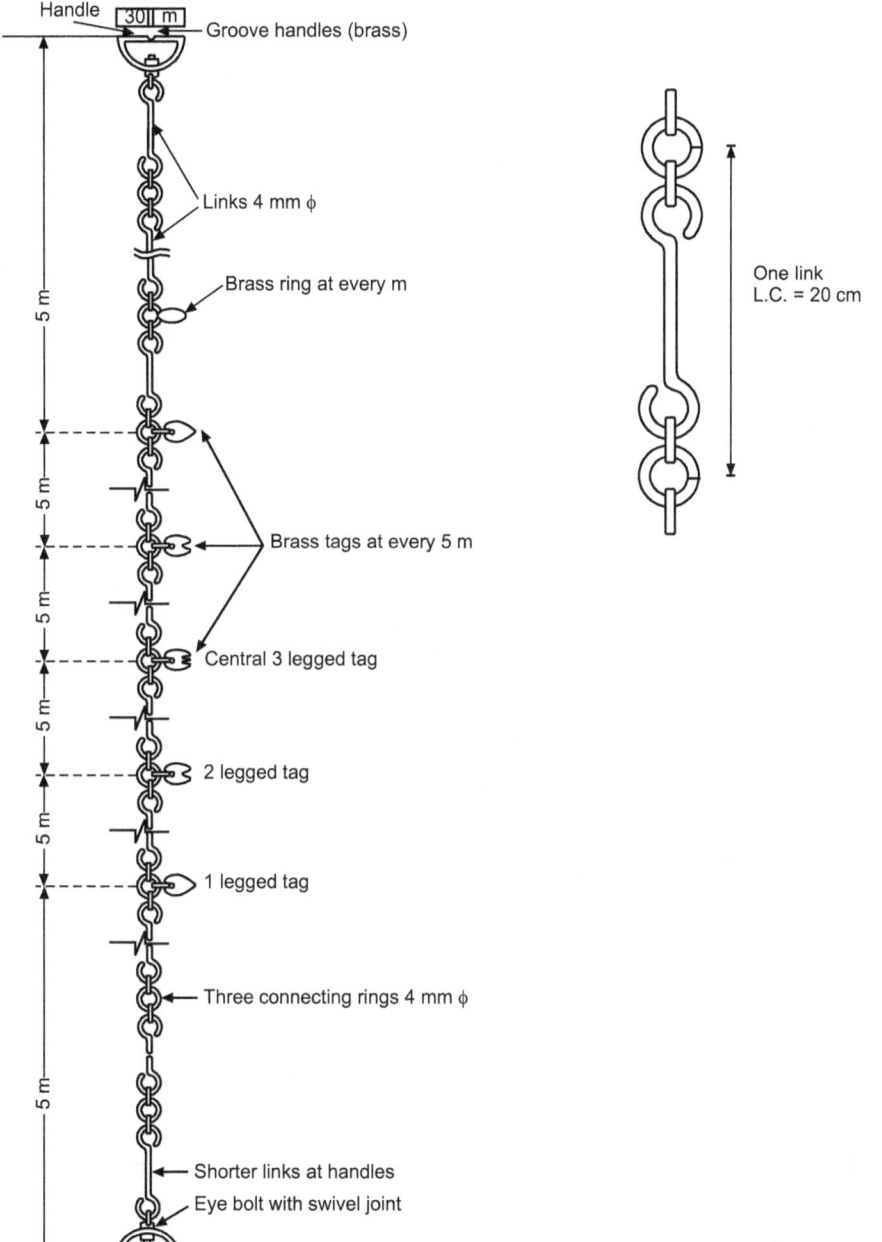

Fig. 2.3

FUNDAMENTALS OF CIVIL ENGINEERING   SURVEYING

(ii) Tapes :

Tapes are used for more accurate measurements of length and are classified as per the material of which they are made.

1. Cloth or linen tape,
2. Metallic tape,
3. Steel tape,
4. Invar tape and
5. Fibre glass tape.

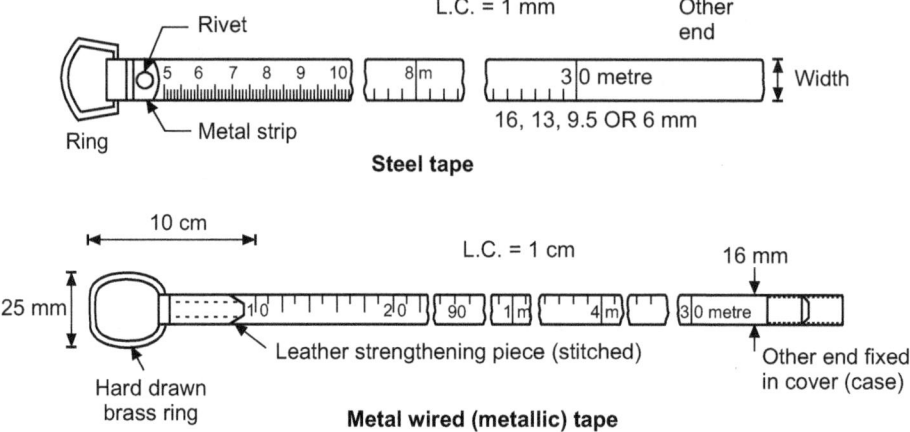

Fig. 2.4 : Types of tape

1. Cloth or Linen Tape : It is made up of closely woven linen, 12 to 15 mm wide and varnished to resist moisture. It is light and flexible. It is commonly available in lengths of 10 m, 20 m, 25 m and 30 m. This tape is rarely used for accurate measurements due to its shrinkage when wet, twisting and weakness.

2. Metallic Tape : It is made up of varnished strip of waterproof linen interwoven with small brass, copper or bronze wires and does not stretch as easily as cloth tapes. It is available in lengths of 2, 5, 10, 20, 30 and 50 m. Tapes of 10, 20, 30 and 50 m lengths are supplied in metal or leather case fitted with winding device.

3. Steel Tape : A steel tape consists of a light strip of steel of width 6 to 10 mm and is more accurately graduated. Steel tape is available in lengths of 2, 10, 30, 50 metres. It is delicate and very light type and therefore it's rough use should be avoided. The tape should be wiped clean and dry after using, to avoid rusting.

4. Invar Tape : Invar tape is made up of an alloy of nickel (36%) and steel and has very low coefficient of thermal expansion. It is used mainly for linear measurements of a very high degree of precision. It is more expensive, and more easily deformed than steel tapes.

5. Fibre-glass Tape : Fibre glass tape is now-a-days extensively used in the field. This tape has very low coefficient of thermal expansion, and it is strong and durable. It is cheap and gives fairly good degree of precision. The tape is available in 5 m, 10 m, 20 m and 30 m lengths. The least count of measurement may be 1 cm or 1 mm.

Precautions in using the tape for measurement of distance :

1. While laying the tape on the ground, it should be laid straight (without twist).
2. The tape should not be allowed to get wet and smeared with soil.
3. While winding back in the case, it should be wound dry (if wetted) and straight after cleaning or wiping out properly.

B. Arrows :

Arrows or chain pins are made of stout steel wire, 4 mm in diameter and 10 arrows are supplied with a chain. These are black ennameled. Length is approximately 400 to 405 mm. Arrow is used to mark the end of each chain length.

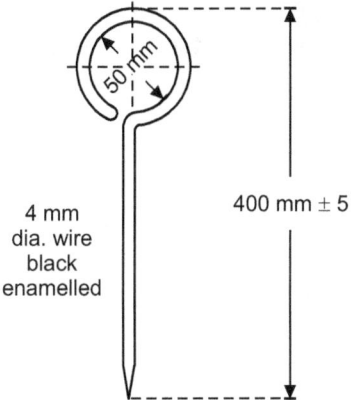

Fig. 2.5 : Arrow

C. Pegs :

Wooden pegs are used to mark the positions of the stations. They are made of stout timber, generally 2.5 cm or 3 cm square and 15 cm long, tapered at the end. They are driven in the ground with a hammer and kept about 4 cm projecting above the ground.

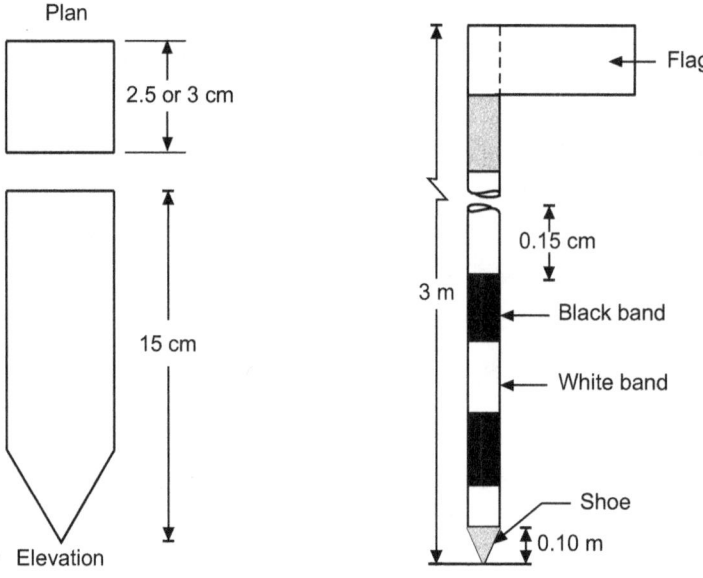

Fig. 2.6 : Wooden Peg   Fig. 2.7 : Ranging Rods

D. Ranging Rods :

These are generally 2 to 3 m in length and are painted with alternate bands of black and white or red and white, 3 m length being more common. They are octagonal or circular in cross section with an iron shoe provided at the lower end. The pointed shoe enables the rod to be planted in ground firmly. They may be used with flag on top. They may be made of timber or hollow steel pipe.

E. Offset Rods :

An offset rod is similar to a ranging rod, having a length of 3 m. It is graduated in metres and one-tenth of metre and it is used for measurement of short offsets in chain surveying. A hook or notch is provided at the top to facilitate pulling and pushing the chain through hedges and other obstructions.

F. Plumb Bob :

It is used to transfer points to the ground. It is specially useful for measurement of distance on sloping ground as in the method of stepping. It is also used to centre the theodolite over the station point accurately.

G. Line Ranger :

It is an optical instrument to obtain an intermediate point on a given line.

2.3.3 Chaining or Taping

Measurement of distance on ground with the help of chain is known as *"Chaining"* and done with the help of tape is called 'Taping'. Chaining/taping involves following operations :

1. Marking the stations.
2. Unfolding the chain/unwinding the tape.
3. Ranging.
4. Measurement of distance.
5. Folding the chain/winding the tape.

1. Marking the stations : The stations along the direction of survey line are marked with ranging rods so that these are distinctly visible.

2. Unfolding the chain : Two persons are required for measuring the length of a line which is greater than a chain length. The person staying at the zero end of chain or starting station is called *'follower'*, while the other person holding the forward handle is called 'leader'. The leader also carries few arrows and a ranging rod. To unfold the chain, both handles are kept in one hand and the rest of the bundle of chain is thrown in the forward direction with the other hand. The chain is laid straight.

3. Ranging : If the distance between two stations is less than one chain/tape length, then after stretching the chain/tape, the distance can be directly measured. When the length of a survey line is more than one chain length, intermediate points are to be located in order that the chain/tape is pulled along the proper survey line in a straight direction. This operation is known as Ranging a Line, discussed in detail in section 2.2.4.

4. Measurement of distance : After setting up of each intermediate point and stretching the chain/tape between two points, the leader fixes up arrow at the end of one chain/tape length, touching the groove of handle. The chain is dragged forward upto the last station point. The follower goes on collecting the arrows. The length of the line is determined from the arrows collected by the follower. Each arrow represents one chain/tape length. Any fractional distance at the end is measured by stretching the chain/tape and counting the length upto the end station. The total length of line is, thus, determined.

5. Folding the chain : Starting from the middle of the chain, it is folded, holding pair of links at a time. If a metallic tape is used for measurement of distance, winding back in the case is very simple.

2.3.4 Ranging

It is the process of establishing some intermediate points on a survey line, between the two terminal stations; when the length of line exceeds the length of chain. There are two methods of ranging : (a) Direct ranging, (b) Indirect ranging.

(a) Direct ranging :

Direct ranging is possible when the ends of survey line i.e. end survey stations are intervisible. It can be done by eye or by an instrument called line ranger.

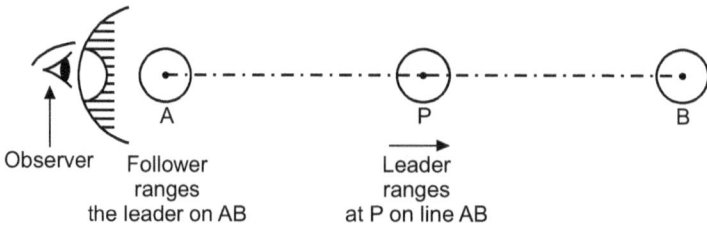

Observer | Follower ranges the leader on AB | Leader ranges at P on line AB

Fig. 2.8 : Ranging by eye

(i) Ranging by eye : After the chain/tape is stretched and laid approximately on line AB, the follower stands behind ranging rod at A and the leader stands at such a distance not greater than one chain/tape length from A, with ranging rod in his hand at an arm's length sideways from his body. The follower positions himself behind A in line with AB. Then he directs the leader by means of signals, to move his ranging rod to the desired direction so that the leader is brought in line with AB at point P. The code of signals used for this purpose are tabulated as follows :

Code for Ranging by hand signals

Signal by Follower	Action of Leader
1. Rapid sweep with right/left hand.	1. Move considerably to right/left.
2. Slow sweep with right/left hand.	2. Move slowly to right/left.
3. Right/left arm extended.	3. Continue to move to right/left.
4. Right/left arm up and moved to right/left.	4. Plumb the rod to right/left.
5. Both hands above head and brought down.	5. Correct position; no movement.
6. Both arms extended forward horizontally and depressed briskly.	6. Fix the rod.

(ii) Ranging by Line Ranger : The line ranger consists of either two plane mirrors or two right-angled isosceles prisms, placed one above the other, as shown in Fig. 2.9. In case the prisms are used, the diagonals of both prisms are silvered so as to reflect the incident rays.

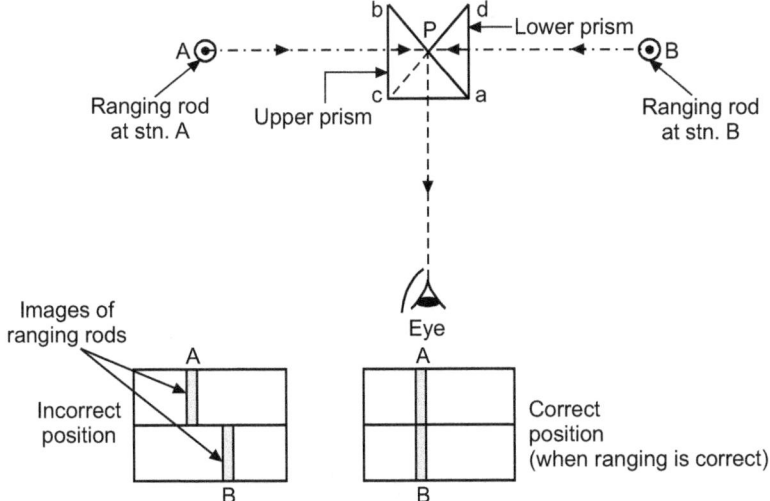

Fig. 2.9 : Line Ranger

Line ranger is provided with a handle at the bottom, to hold the instrument in hand. From the handle, required point can be transferred to the ground.

Two ranging rods are fixed at A and B. To obtain a point P on survey line AB, the surveyor holds the line ranger approximately very near to the line AB. Upper prism abc receives rays from A which are reflected by diagonal ab towards the observer. The lower prism cda receives rays from B that are reflected by diagonal cd to the observer. Thus, observer can see both ranging rods at A and B. The images of these two ranging rods may not be coinciding indicating that the instrument is not on line AB [as shown in Fig. 2.9 (b)]. To remove the parallax, the observer moves the instrument sideways till the two images are in the same vertical line, as shown in Fig. 2.9 (c). Now the point P is transferred to the ground.

Thus use of line ranger proves to be advantageous from the point of view of requirement of only one person to do the ranging. Line ranger can also be used for setting out right angle.

(b) Indirect Ranging or Reciprocal Ranging :

This process of ranging is adopted when both the ends of survey line are not visible either due to high intervening ground or due to long distance between them. In such a case, ranging is done indirectly. Two intermediate points M_1 and N_1 are selected approximately in line such that from M_1, both N_1 and B are visible and from N_1 both M_1 and A are visible.

Two persons stand at M_1 and N_1 with ranging rods. Person at M_1 directs person at N_1 to move to N_2 in line with M_1 B. Then person at N_2 directs person at M_2 to move to a new position M_2 in line with N_2 A. Thus, the two persons continue to range each other alternately till both of them at M and N are on line AB. From M and N, other points can be established by direct ranging.

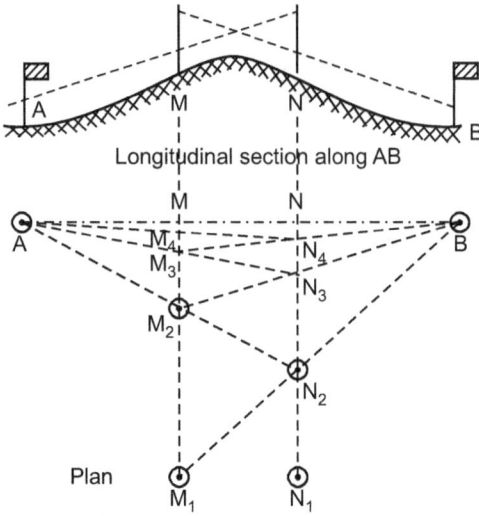

Fig. 2.10 : Reciprocal Ranging

2.3.5 Errors in Chaining/Taping

There are two types of errors which occur while chaining :

1. Systematic errors (cumulative errors).
2. Accidental errors (compensating errors).
3. Mistakes.

The errors that make the result too great are termed as 'Positive errors'; and when the result is too small, errors are 'Negative'.

2.3.5.1 Systematic Errors (Cumulative Errors)

A cumulative error is that which occurs in the same direction and tends to accumulate. These affect the accuracy considerably. Cumulative errors are due to –

1. Erroneous length of chain or tape (+ ve or - ve)
2. Bad ranging (+ve)
3. Bad straightening (+ve)
4. Non-horizontality of chain (+ve)
5. Sag in chain or tape (+ve)
6. Variations in temperature (+ve or -ve)

2.3.5.2 Accidental Errors (Compensating Errors)

These are the errors that are liable to compensate. The compensating errors may occur in either direction and hence tend to compensate. Thus, these are not serious in nature. These are due to :

1. Careless holding of chain/tape with arrow and marking.
2. The variation in pull applied for straightening the chain.

2.3.5.3 Mistakes

Mistakes occur mainly due to carelessness on the part of a surveyor. These can be avoided by taking suitable precautions and alertness on the part of the surveyor while chaining/taping. Mistakes may be due to :

1. Displacement or loss of arrows.
2. Reading the chain in wrong manner.
3. Wrong booking of measurements in the record book i.e. field book.

2.3.6 Obtaining True Distances of Lines

A chain may be found to be too long or too short than its designated length before or after the distance measurements are taken. If the chain is found to be too long, it will measure less distance than the true distance. Similarly, if the chain is too short more than true distance will be measured.

Hence, if the incorrect length of chain (or error in chain length) is known, correction can be applied to the measured distance, so the true distance is known.

True or correct distance = $\frac{L'}{L}$ × Measured distance

where L' = Incorrect or actual length of the chain
L = Designated length of the chain

Similarly,

True or Correct area of field = $\left(\frac{L'}{L}\right)^2$ × Measured area

2.3.7 Degree of Accuracy in Chaining

In practice, the following limits of errors are followed :

1. Ordinary measurements with steel band on flat ground.   1 in 2000
2. Ordinary measurements with tested chain on a fairly level ground.   1 in 1000
3. All other average conditions.   1 in 500
4. Measurements on an uneven or hilly ground.   1 in 250

FUNDAMENTALS OF CIVIL ENGINEERING   SURVEYING

2.3.8 Chain Surveying

It is a simple method of surveying in which the area is divided into triangles and the sides of triangles are measured directly in the field. Since a triangle can be formed by knowing lengths of three sides, without even knowing any of the angles; therefore, in chain surveying, no angular measurements are taken.

Chain surveying is suitable for small areas with fairly level and open ground, having simple details. It is unsuitable for area which are large, uneven and crowded with many details. The chain surveying is adopted for :

(i) determining the area of a given piece of land; (ii) locating exact boundaries of land; (iii) securing data for making a plan.

2.3.9 Principle of Chain Surveying

Chain surveying is based on the principle of 'triangulation'. In triangulation, the whole area is divided into a framework of triangles, since a triangle is the only simple plane figure which can be plotted by measuring its sides in the field.

The framework should consist of triangles, the sides of which are as nearly equal as possible, from the point of view of obtaining accurate results. Such triangles are known as well-shaped or well conditioned triangles. In a **well-conditioned triangle**, all angles should be selected between 30° and 120°.

Triangles with angles less than 30° or greater than 120° are known as **'ill-conditioned' triangles**, which must be avoided in chain surveying. If at all, ill-conditioned triangles cannot be avoided, great care should be taken in chaining and plotting.

2.3.10 Survey Stations

A survey station is an important and prominent point on the ground at the beginning and end of survey line. These stations serve as the control points of survey. Survey stations can be marked on the ground by :

(i) driving pegs, if the ground is soft; or

(ii) marking on roads and streets on hard ground.

The survey stations are of two kinds :

(1) **Main stations** which are at the ends of a chainline and command the boundaries of the survey.

(2) **Subsidiary or tie stations** are the points selected on the main chainlines to run subsidiary lines to locate interior details.

Main stations are denoted by a small circle round the station point i.e. Capital letters A, B, C etc. are used for main stations. Small letters a, b, c or letters like t_1, t_2 are used to denote the tie stations.

2.3.10.1 Selection of Survey Stations

The survey stations on which the survey lines are fixed should be selected so that a good skeleton of survey lines is obtained. This can be achieved by observing following points :

1. Main survey stations must be mutually visible.
2. The survey lines should run through as level ground as possible, and should run close to the boundaries.
3. The framework must have one or two base lines. In case, one base line is chosen, it must run roughly through the middle of the area.
4. Survey lines should be as few as possible and should be so arranged as to avoid obstacles in ranging and chaining.
5. The main lines should form well-conditioned triangles.
6. The tie lines should be run so as to locate the details and to avoid long offsets.
7. Each triangle should be provided with at least one check line.

2.3.11 Survey Lines

The survey lines joining the main survey stations are called **Main Survey Lines** or **Chain lines**. The longest of main survey lines is called the **'Base Line'**.

Base Line : It should run roughly through the middle of the area to be surveyed. It should be laid on a fairly level ground. The framework of survey is built on the base line. It fixes up the directions of all the survey lines. It should be measured very accurately.

Tie Line : A line which joins the tie or subsidiary stations on main line is known as **Tie line**. Tie lines are run to locate the interior details such as buildings, fences, hedges, etc., when they are distant from the main survey lines. A framework may have one or more tie lines, depending on the field requirements.

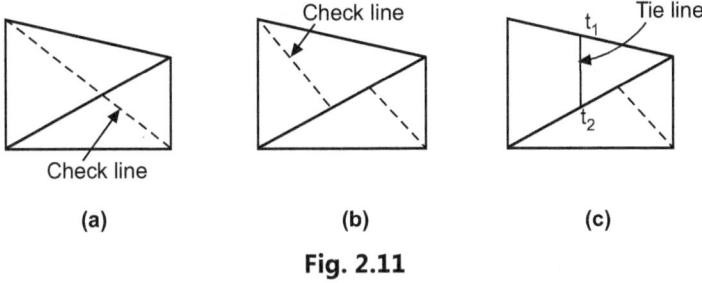

Fig. 2.11

Check Line : Apart from subsidiary lines, other types of lines are run in the field to check the accuracy of the work. Such lines which are laid in the field to check the accuracy of the framework are known as **check lines** or **proof lines**. The length of check line measured in the field should agree with its length on the plan. A check line may join the apex of triangle to any point on the opposite side or join two points on two sides of a triangle. Each triangle must have a check line. Fig. 2.11 shows various arrangements of check lines for the framework.

2.3.12 Equipments for Chain Surveying

The equipments required for carrying out chain survey are as follows :

1. One chain or tape (20 m or 30 m.)
2. Ten arrows.
3. Metallic tape.
4. Ranging rods and offset rod.
5. Instruments for setting out right angles-cross staff, optical square, Indian optical square.
6. Plumb bob.
7. Pegs, hammer, axe, etc.
8. Survey field book, pencil, eraser, set square, chalks, etc.

2.3.13 Steps in Chain Surveying

As has been explained earlier, chain surveying is carried out by following the principle of working from whole to the part. The chain surveying is conducted in the following steps :

1. Reconnaissance.
2. Marking the stations.
3. Preparing location sketches.
4. Running the survey lines.

1. Reconnaissance

It is the preliminary inspection of the area to be surveyed. In reconnaissance, the area that is to be surveyed, is observed by walking to every nook and corner. The main features and the boundaries of the area are observed from the point of view of choosing the best locations of survey stations and thus fixing the positions of survey lines. The survey stations selected should be intervisible among each other.

An index sketch or key plan is prepared, showing the plan of ground, boundaries of the land and prominent features such as buildings, roads, nallas, poles, trees, etc.

A thoughtfully carried out reconnaissance gives the surveyor a fair idea of the shape and extent of the area, difficulties in the work and also the time required for the completion of survey.

2. **Marking the Stations**

The positions of stations determined in reconnaissance, are marked on the ground in such a way that these can be readily located if required in future. The survey stations can be marked by adopting following methods :

(a) By driving a wooden peg in the ground with 8 small projection of 2.5 cm to 4 cm above ground.

(b) By fixing a ranging rod temporarily.

(c) In case of hard surfaces such as roads, pavement or rocks, by using nails or spikes or by cutting a cross on the surface.

(d) For permanent marking, a stone can be embedded in the ground and a cross-mark made on its top.

3. **Preparation of Location Sketches (Reference sketch) :**

The location sketch of a station indicates the position of the station with reference to two or three permanent and prominent features in the vicinity of the station. These features may be a building corner, tree, electric pole, etc. The location sketches of the stations are necessary to retrace the positions of stations if required in future.

The location sketch is drawn, facing the North at every station. North-line has to be shown on the location sketch as shown in Fig. 2.12 (b).

4. **Running the Survey Lines**

Chaining operation is started from the base line and carried through all the lines of the framework. The work consists of :

(i) Laying the chain line/tape line.

(ii) Locating the adjacent details along the chain line by means of offsets.

The record of chaining and offsetting is made in the field-book.

The details of chain lines in chain surveying are shown in Fig. 2.12 (a).

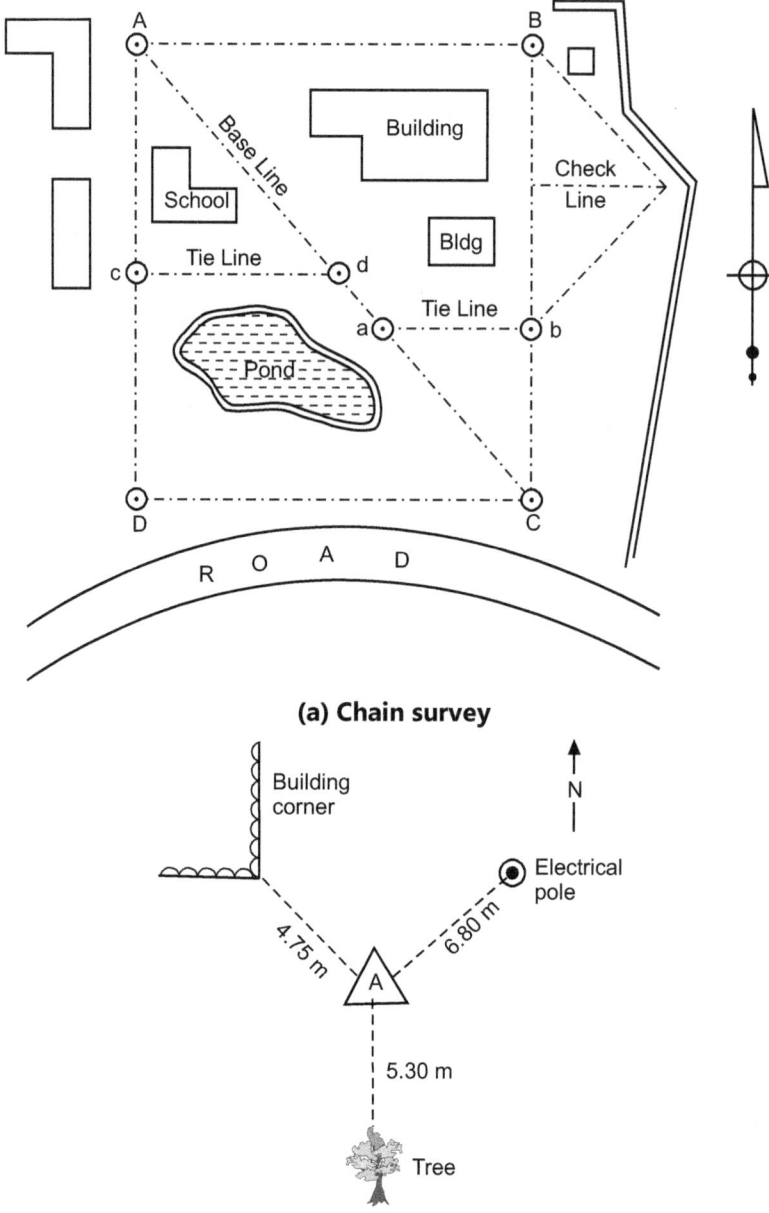

(a) Chain survey

(b) Typical location sketch of station A

Fig. 2.12

2.3.14 Offsets

For locating the details on ground, with reference to survey lines, it is necessary to measure lateral distance of the features or ground points from survey lines. Such lateral distances which are measured from the chain line to the objects are called **offsets**.

The offsets can be measured either to the right or left of chain line.

Thus, there are two **types** of offsets :

(1) Perpendicular offsets, and (2) Oblique offsets.

Perpendicular offsets are the lateral distances taken at right angles (90°) to the chain line. These are also known as offsets.

Lateral distances measured at any angle other than 90° to the chain line are called oblique offsets.

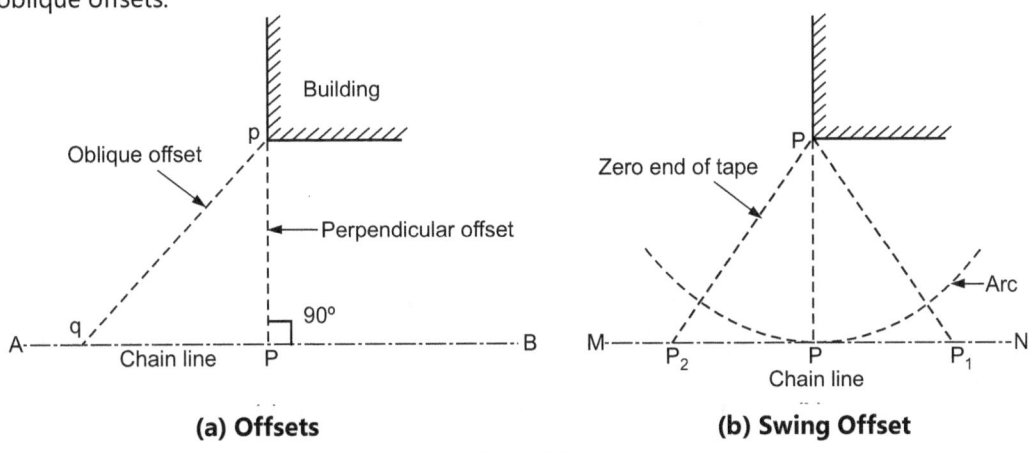

(a) Offsets   (b) Swing Offset

Fig. 2.13

Generally, metallic tape is used for measuring offset distance. For greater accuracy, steel tape is also used.

Every offset is characterised by two measurements :

1. Chainage of chain/tape line at which the offset is taken (Ap), and
2. Length of the offset (Pp), as shown in Fig. 2.13 (a).

2.3.14.1 Offset Measurements-Types

(i) Short and Long offsets : Offsets upto a distance of 15 m are called short offsets and those longer than 15 m are called long offsets.

(ii) Swing offset : A swing offset is the one which is obtained by swinging the tape from outside point along a chain line. Short offset can be set out and measured by swinging the tape along the chain line as shown in Fig. 2.13 (b). The position of the offset on chain line MN is located by swinging the tape from P and the point where the arc is tangential to the chain line, is the required foot of offset. In the figure, Pp is the swing offset.

2.3.14.2 Instruments for Setting out Perpendicular Offsets

Offsets may be taken by using the instruments such as cross staff, optical square, Indian optical square and prism square.

I. Open Cross Staff

It is the simplest instrument used for setting out right angles. It consists of a head in the form of wooden block or metallic frame with two pairs of vertical slits and is mounted on a pole.

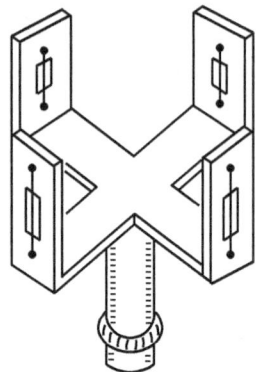

Fig. 2.14 : Open cross staff

It is provided with two pairs of vertical slits. Each pair of slits forms a line of sight. Thus two lines of sight at right angles to each other are formed. The frame or head is mounted on a pole. [Refer Fig. 2.14]. The height of the open cross staff can be adjusted to suit the observer's eye level.

Procedure

(i) **To set out a right angle to a chain/tape line :** For this, the open cross staff is held at the required chainage say M' on the chain line PQ. The instrument is turned till one of the lines of sight passes through the ranging rod at the other end of the line i.e. Q. The line of sight through the other pair of slits will be a line at right angles to the survey line PQ. A ranging rod is erected at say M in the direction of other line of sight. Thus MM' is a perpendicular to the chain line at M'. Refer Fig. 2.15 (a).

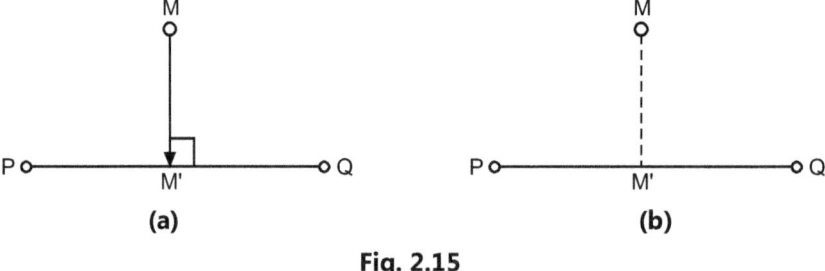

Fig. 2.15

(ii) To find the foot of perpendicular on the chain/tape line : In case a perpendicular offset is to be laid from a given object say M to the chain line PQ, then open cross staff is held vertically on the chain line at a point where the foot of perpendicular offset is likely to occur. It is then turned so that one line of sight passes through the ranging rod, fixed at the end of survey line i.e. Q. Looking through the other pair of slits, it is seen if the point from which the offset is to be laid is bisected. If not, the cross staff is moved forward or backward on the chain line, till the line of sight also passes through the point M'. M' is the foot of perpendicular offset. Refer Fig. 2.15 (b). Thus for laying perpendicular offset by open cross staff, two persons are required simultaneously at the instrument; which is rather a disadvantage.

II. Optical Square

Optical square is an instrument based on the principles of optics. The perpendicular offsets can be set to the chain line with this instrument. It consists of a circular box about 50 mm in diameter and 12.5 mm in depth, with a sight or eye hole (E), a horizon sight [window H] and an index sight [window I]. The box is provided with a small rod at the bottom. Inside the circular box as shown in Fig. 2.16, aa' is horizon mirror, which is half silvered and half unsilvered, bb' is the index mirror fixed opposite to index sight and makes an angle of 45° with mirror aa'.

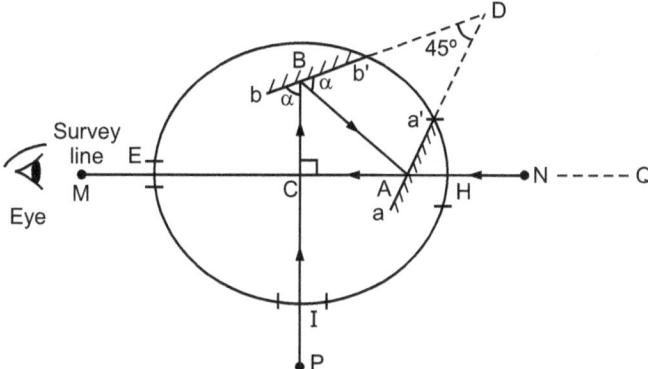

Fig. 2.16 : Optical square

(i) Principle

For a reflecting instrument, the angle between the first incident ray and the last reflected ray is twice the angle between the two mirrors. Thus, in the case of optical square, the angle between two mirrors aa' and bb' is 45°, and therefore the angle between the first incident ray PB and the last reflected ray AM is 90°. Thus, a perpendicular offset can be set out with optical square.

Explanation

MQ is the chain line.

Let ray PB make an angle α with bb' i.e. mirror at B.

$$\angle BDA = 45°$$

$\therefore \quad \angle BAD = 180° - (45° + \alpha) = 135° - \alpha$

By the law of reflection,

$$\angle CAa = \angle BAD = 135° - \alpha$$

$\therefore \quad \angle BAC = 180° - 2(135° - \alpha) = 2\alpha - 90° \quad \ldots (1)$

Also $\angle CBA = 180° - 2\alpha$

From $\triangle$ BAC, $\angle BCA = 180° - (\angle CBA + \angle BAC)$

$\therefore \quad \angle BCA = 180° - (180° - 2\alpha + 2\alpha - 90°) \quad \ldots (2)$

$\quad = 90°$

Therefore, if the images of rods at P and Q are in the same vertical line (parallax removed), then lines PB and MQ are at right angles to each other.

(ii) Uses of Optical Square

Optical square can be used :

1. To set out perpendicular from a given point on the chain line.
2. To find the foot of perpendicular to the chain line.

(1) Let the point 'C' be given on the chain line MQ. If the object lies on right hand side of the observer, the optical square is held in the left hand, and in the right hand in case of left hand side object. It is necessary to take precaution, to hold the instrument exactly over the point i.e. C on the chain line from which right angle is to be laid out. This can be achieved by holding a plumb-bob from the small rod of instrument or by dropping a pebble from the instrument centre. The instrument should be held horizontal. It should be remembered that optical square is to be used only on a fairly level ground.

Observing the end station ranging rod at Q through opening H, the lateral ranging rod is moved sideways till the images of both ranging rods coincide with each other as shown in Fig. 2.17.

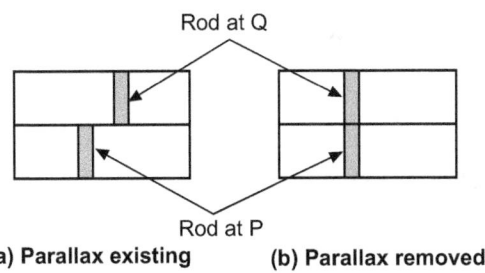

(a) Parallax existing   (b) Parallax removed

Fig. 2.17

Thus the perpendicular offset can be set out with the help of optical square.

(2) In order to find the foot of perpendicular from a lateral object to the chain line, the observer moves on the chain line, with optical square, backward or forward, till the ranging rod at the other end and the image of the object as seen in Horizon glass coincides with each other. The point at which the foot of perpendicular lies on the chain line is transferred to the ground by dropping a small pebble or suspending a plumb-bob from the centre of the instrument.

(iii) Testing and Adjusting the Optical Square

Test : From an intermediate point P on survey line AB, sight the ranging rod at A with optical square and mark point a.

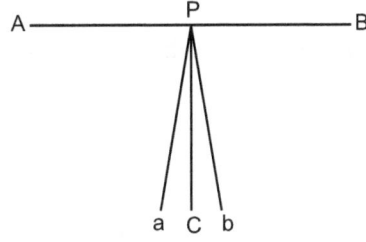

Fig. 2.18

Now standing at P, turn round and sight the ranging rod at B through optical square. If the optical square is in adjustment, the image of rod at 'a' will coincide with the ranging rod at B. If not, mark 'b' as the new position of 'B'. Bisect distance ab at C. Now PC is the true perpendicular at P to survey line AB as shown in Fig. 2.18.

Adjustment : Rotate the mirror bb' with a small milled head till ranging rod at B and the image of C are coincident.

2.3.14.3 Locating Irregular Boundaries of Objects

An offset from an object to chain line is necessary wherever the outline of the object changes. In case of an object having straight boundary, offset at each corner is sufficient. In order to locate irregular boundaries, sufficient number of offsets should be taken at suitable intervals, particularly where the direction changes.

Figs. 2.19, 2.20 and 2.21 indicate the method of locating objects having irregular boundaries.

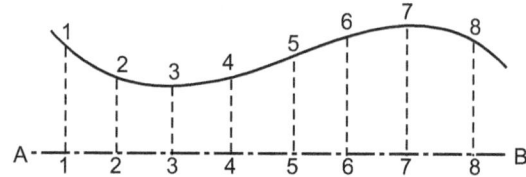

Fig. 2.19 : Offsets to curved boundary

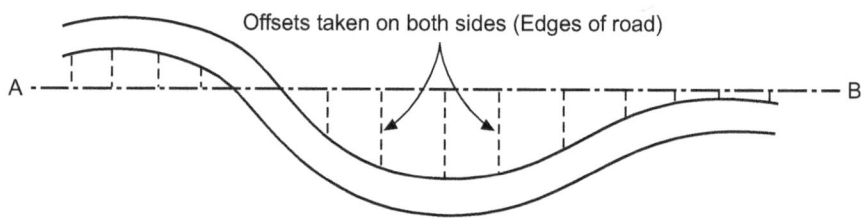

Fig. 2.20 : Offsets to smooth curved boundary such as Road or Railway

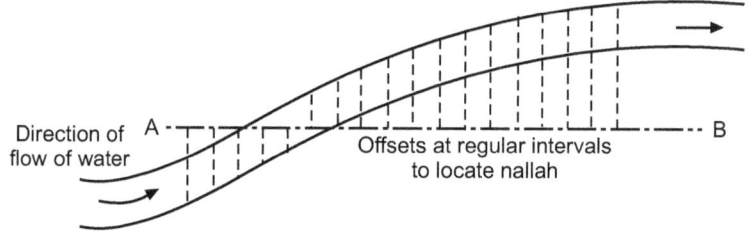

Fig. 2.21 : Offsets to a Nallah

2.3.15 Field Book

It is a note-book of about 20 cm × 12 cm to 20 cm × 15 cm size. In the field book the measurements in the field are recorded properly and sketches drawn where necessary.

FUNDAMENTALS OF CIVIL ENGINEERING   SURVEYING

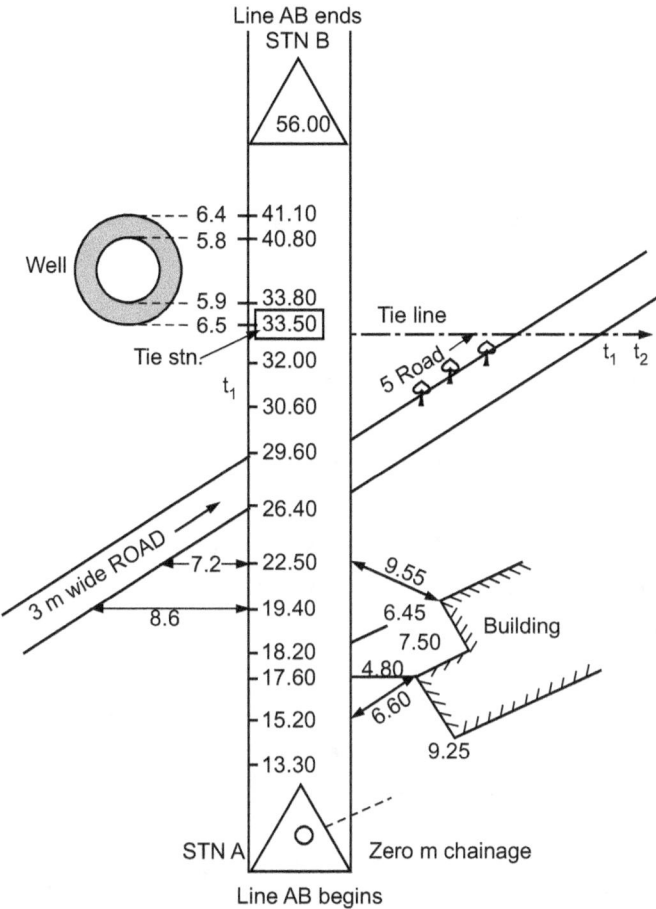

Fig. 2.22 : Recording measurements in the field book

The chain line is represented by a ruled double line at the centre of each page and the distances along the chain line are written between the two lines. The following steps indicate the method to record the measurements of chain survey :

1. Recording of chainage i.e. distances along chain line, is started from the bottom of page and continued upwards.

2. At the beginning and the end of chain line, the survey station is indicated by triangle and its chainage written inside the triangle.

3. As the surveyor moves along the chain line, the chainages at which offsets to the right or left hand side are taken, are written along the centre of ruled lines.

FUNDAMENTALS OF CIVIL ENGINEERING   SURVEYING

4. The oblique or perpendicular offsets are noted nearer the object from the appropriate chainage.

5. The objects or features are not drawn to scale, but are shown proportionately. The features are named.

6. The sketch of the object should not cross the blank space between the two centrally ruled lines.

7. Each chain line should be recorded on a separate page.

The above steps have been shown in detail in Fig. 2.22.

2.3.16 Cross Staff Survey

In case of locating boundaries of a field and determining its area, the cross-staff survey is carried out. The instruments used for cross staff survey are chain, tape, arrows, ranging rods and cross-staff. In this survey, a chain line is run through the centre of the field. The field is divided into a number of triangles and trapezoids as shown in Fig. 2.23 (b). From the central chain line perpendicular offsets are taken, on both sides to the boundaries of the field. Knowing the chainages and offset lengths, the survey can be plotted. As the whole field is divided into a number of regular figures and numbered as shown, areas of all figures when added give the total area of the field.

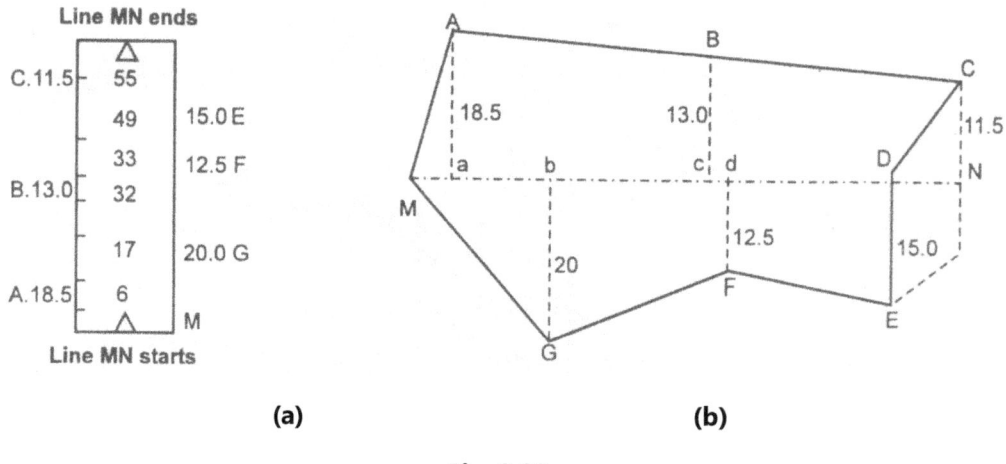

Fig. 2.23

The observations are recorded as shown.

The area of the field ABCDEFGMA can be found out as follows:

Sr. No.	Figure	Chainage (m)	Base (m)	Offsets (m)	Mean offset (m)	Area (sq.m)
1.	MaA	0 & 6	6	0 & 18.5	9.25	55.5
2.	MbG	0 & 17	17	0 & 20	10	170.0
3.	acBA	6 & 32	26	18.5 & 13.0	15.75	409.5
4.	bdFG	17 & 33	16	20 & 12.5	16.25	260.0
5.	CNcB	32 & 55	23	13 & 11.5	12.25	281.75
6.	DNC	49 & 55	6	0 & 11.5	5.75	– 34.5 (Negative area)
7.	dFED	33 & 49	16	12.5 & 15.0	13.75	220.0
					Total area	**1362.25 m²**

Note: Here, it is observed that due to typical configuration of the field, area of the figure DNC works out to be *negative*.

SOLVED EXAMPLES

Example 2.1 A 30 m chain was found to be 2 cm too long after chaining 1500 m. The same chain was found to be 4 cm too long after chaining the total distance of 3000 m. Find the correct length of the total distance chained, assuming the chain was correct at the commencement of the work. **(P.U. May 96)**

Solution: (1) Mean error in the chain length during measurement of first 1500 m.

$$= \frac{\text{Initial error + Final Error}}{2} = \frac{0.02}{2}$$

$$= 0.01 \text{ m (too long)}.$$

∴ True distance $= \frac{L'}{L} \times$ measured distance

$$= \frac{30.01}{30} \times 1500$$

$$= 1500.50 \text{ m}.$$

(2) For the remaining distance of (3000 – 1500) = 1500 m. The chain was 0.04 m too long.

∴ Mean elongation or error of chain in second measurement

$$= \frac{0.02 + 0.04}{2} = 0.03 \text{ m}$$

∴ True distance = $\frac{L'}{L}$ × measured distance

$= \frac{30.03}{30} \times 1500$

$= 1501.50$ m

∴ Total True distance = 1500.50 + 1501.50 = 3002 m   ... **Ans.**

Example 2.2 : The distance between two points was measured with 30 m chain which was correct at the beginning of work and found to be 6000 m. At the end of first 1500 m, the chain was tested and found to be 3 cm too long. The work was continued with the same chain and remaining distance was completed. At the end of work, the chain was 6 cm too long. Find the correct distance.   **(P. U. Nov. 1988)**

Solution : (1) Mean elongation of the chain during measurement of first 1500 m.

$= \frac{\text{Initial error + Final error}}{2}$

$= \frac{0 + 0.03}{2} = 0.015$ m

∴ Actual incorrect chain length

$= L' = 30 + 0.015 = 30.015$

$= \frac{30.015}{30} \times 1500 = 1500.75$ m.

(2) Mean elongation of the chain during measurement of remaining (6000 − 1500) = 4500 m distance

$= \frac{0.03 + 0.06}{2} = 0.045$ m.

∴ Actual incorrect chain length

$= 30 + 0.045 = 30.045$ m.

∴ True distance $= \frac{L'}{L}$ × measured distance

$= \frac{30.045}{30} \times 4500 = 4506.75$ m

∴ The total true or correct distance

$= 1500.75 + 4506.75$

$= 6007.50$

FUNDAMENTALS OF CIVIL ENGINEERING   SURVEYING

Example 2.3 : A line was measured with a 20 m chain and found to be 235.80 m. When measured with a 30 m chain, it was found to be 235.00 m. If the 20 m chain was half decimetre too short, what was the error in 30 m chain ?

Solution : 20 m chain was 0.05 m too short.

∴ Incorrect length of 20 m chain = 20 − 0.05 = 19.95 m.

∴ True or correct length of line

$$= \frac{L'}{L} \times \text{measured length}$$

$$= \frac{19.95}{20} \times 235.80 = 235.21 \text{ m.}$$

Now the same length was measured by 30 m chain.

∴ Correct length $= \dfrac{L'_{30}}{L_{30}} \times$ measured length with 30 m chain

∴ $235.21 = \dfrac{L'_{30}}{30} \times 235$

∴ L'_{30} i.e. incorrect chain length of 30 m chain

$$= \frac{235.21 \times 30}{235} = 30.02 \text{ m.}$$

Hence, 30 m chain was 2 cm (i.e. 0.02 m) too long.   ... **Ans.**

Example 2.4 : A chain was tested before starting the survey of a field and was found to be exactly 20 m. At the end of survey, it was tested again and was found to measure 20.15 m. The area of plan drawn to scale of 1 cm = 50 m was 120 sq. cm. Find true area of the field in hectares.

Solution : Measured area of the field :

(1)   Scale of plan 1 cm = 50 m
∴   1 cm² on paper = (50 × 50) m² on ground.
i.e.   1 sq. cm. = 2500 sq. m.
∴   Measured area of the field = (120 × 2500) = 3,00,000 sq. m.

(2) The chain was found to be 20.15 m at the end.

Mean elongation of chain $= \dfrac{0 + 0.15}{2} = 0.075$ m.

FUNDAMENTALS OF CIVIL ENGINEERING   SURVEYING

∴   Incorrect chain length = 20.075 m.

∴   True area of field = $\left(\dfrac{L'}{L}\right)^2$ × measured area of field.

$= \left(\dfrac{20.075}{20}\right)^2 \times 300000$

= 301125 sq. m.

(3)   1 hectare = 10,000 sq. m.

∴   True area of field $= \dfrac{301125}{10000}$

= 30.1125 Hectares   … **Ans.**

Example 2.5 : A chain was admeasuring exactly 20 m at the beginning of survey. At the end of the survey, it was found to be 20 cm longer. The area surveyed and drawn to a scale of 1 cm = 100 m was found to be 100 cm², find the true area in hectares.   **(P.U. May 98)**

Solution :   The area surveyed = 100 cm² on paper

= (100 × 100) × 100 = 10^6 sq.m on ground

Now, Mean elongation of chain $= \dfrac{0 + 0.20}{2} = 0.10$ m

Incorrect chain length = 20.10 m

True area $= \left(\dfrac{20.10}{20}\right)^2 \times 10^6$

= 10,10,025 sq. met.

True area in hectares $= \dfrac{1010025}{10^4}$

= 101.0025 ha   … **Ans.**

Example 2.6 : To find the horizontal distance between two stations on a sloping ground with a 8° slope, the chaining was carried out. The chain having a length of 20 m which was correct in the beginning was used. The measured distance along the sloping ground was recorded to be 1200 m. At the end of chaining, the chain was tested and was found to be one link too long. Find the true horizontal distance.

Solution : For a 20 m chain, length of one link is 0.20 m. The chain was correct at the beginning of survey. See Fig. 2.24.

∴ Mean elongation of chain = $\dfrac{0 + 0.20}{2}$ = 0.10 m

Incorrect chain length = 20.10 m

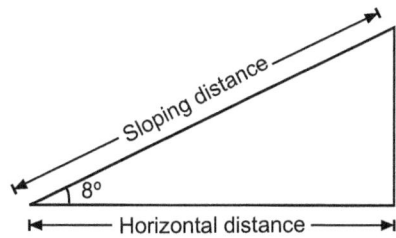

Fig. 2.24

∴ True sloping distance = $\dfrac{L'}{L}$ × measured sloping distance

= $\dfrac{20.10}{20}$ × 1200 = 1206 m.

∴ True horizontal distance = 1206 × cos 8° = 1194.26 m ... **Ans.**

Example 2.7 : Line AB was measured along a falling gradient of 1 in 15 with a 30 m chain, which was 20 cm short throughout the work. If the measured distance was 405 m, find the correct horizontal distance.

Solution : Falling gradient of 1 in 15 means 1 metre drop in a horizontal distance of 15 metres. The angle of the slope i.e. θ can be found out as follows.

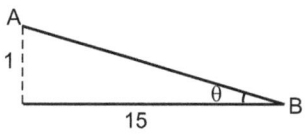

Fig. 2.25

$\tan \theta = \dfrac{1}{15}$ ∴ θ = $\tan^{-1} \dfrac{1}{15}$. Hence θ = 3°48'50".

It is given that the chain was 20 cm short throughout.

Incorrect chain length = 30.00 − 0.20 = 29.80 m

True sloping distance = $\dfrac{29.80}{30}$ × 405 = 402.30 m

Now, True horizontal distance = 402.30 cos (3°48'50") = 401.408 m

Example 2.8 : A line ABC was measured with a 20 m chain along the ground. The ground had an upward slope of 1 in 20 from A to B and downward slope of 1 in 25 from B to C. Chainage of B was 444 m and chainage of C was 1021 m. The chain was 2 cm too short at A, 4 cm too long at B and half a link too long at C. What would be the correct length of AC on plan if plotted to a scale of 1 cm = 20 m ?

Solution :

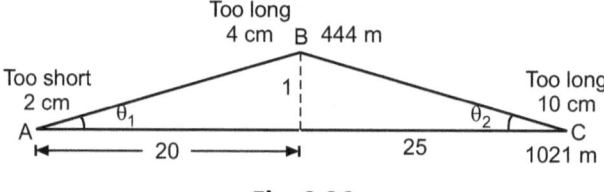

Fig. 2.26

$\tan \theta_1 = \dfrac{1}{20}$ ∴ $\theta_1 = 2° 51' 44'' = 2.862°$, $\tan \theta_2 = \dfrac{1}{25}$ ∴ $\theta_2 = 2°17'26'' = 2.29°$

To find the correct length of AC on plan (scale 1 cm = 20 m)

I. Length AB :

$$\text{The average elongation of chain in AB} = \dfrac{-2 + 4}{2 \times 100} = 0.01 \text{ m}$$

$$\text{True inclined distance AB} = \dfrac{20.01}{20} \times 444$$

$$= 444.22 \text{ m}$$

$$\text{True horizontal distance AB} = 444.22 \cos (2.862°)$$

$$= 444.22 \times 0.998$$

$$= 443.66 \text{ m}$$

II. Length BC :

$$\text{The average elongation of chain in BC} = \dfrac{4 + 10}{2} = 7 \text{ cm}$$

$$= 0.07 \text{ m}$$

$$\text{True inclined distance BC} = \dfrac{20.07}{20} \times (1021 - 444)$$

$$= \dfrac{20.07}{20} \times 577$$

$$= 579.019 \text{ m}$$

True horizontal distance BC = 579.019 cos (2.29°)

= 578.557 m

Total horizontal distance ABC = 1022.217 m

Correct length of AC on plan = 51.11 cm

with a scale of 1 cm = 20 m

EXERCISE

(A) Surveying

1. What is surveying ? Mention how the knowledge of surveying is useful for various civil engineering purposes ?
2. What are the objects and purpose of surveying ?
3. What are the different types of survey ?
4. Differentiate clearly between 'plane surveying' and 'geodetic surveying.'
5. What is 'scale' ? What do you mean by R.F. ? Differentiate between the two.
6. (a) Write short notes on :
   (i) Topographical survey, (ii) Cadastral survey.
   (b) Distinguish between a 'Plan and Map'.
7. A road of length 2.5 km is represented on a map by 5 cm line. What is the scale of map and its R.F. ? (**Ans.** Scale : 1 cm = 500 m; R.F. = $\frac{1}{50000}$)
8. An area on map is represented by 600 sq. cm. If the R.F. of map is 1 : 200, what is the area on ground in sq. m. ? (**Ans.** 2400 sq. m.)
9. (a) Explain the principle 'to work from whole to part'.
   (b) Explain how will you locate position of a point with reference to two given objects.

(B) Linear Measurements

10. Enlist the various methods of measurement of horizontal distances.
11. Explain in brief the procedure of chaining/taping.
12. What is direct ranging ? Explain the use of line ranger for ranging.
13. What is the code of signals for direct ranging by eye ?
14. Explain how will you continue chaining past an intervening hillock. (Hint : Reciprocal Ranging or Indirect Ranging).

FUNDAMENTALS OF CIVIL ENGINEERING   SURVEYING

15. What is chain surveying ? Where is it suitable ?
16. Differentiate between well-conditioned and ill-conditioned triangles.
17. Explain with neat sketches : (i) Base line, (ii) Tie line and (iii) Check line.
18. What is the difference between errors and mistakes ?
19. What are the different errors in chaining ? Classify them and give example of each one of them.
20. What are the different mistakes in chaining ?
21. What is the method of correcting the distances measured with an incorrect chain or tape ?
22. What is an offset ? What are the different types of offsets that are required to be measured in chain surveying ?
23. (a) Explain the principle, use and construction of 'Optical Square'.
    (b) Explain the test and adjustment of optical square.
24. What are the different instruments used for laying perpendicular offsets in the field ?
25. What is a location sketch ? Why is a location sketch drawn for a survey station ? Draw a typical location sketch.
26. Give conventional signs for the following :
    Road, road in cutting, single line railway, bridge, level crossing, barbed wire fencing.
27. Explain the procedure of carrying out survey of an open field in the form of a polygon for finding out area of the field.   (**Hint :** Cross-staff survey)
28. A chain was tested before starting survey of a field and was found to be exactly 20 m. At the end of survey, it was tested again and was found to measure 20.15 m. The area of the plan drawn to scale 1 cm = 50 m, was 120 sq cm. Find the true area of the field.   (**Ans.** 302254.2 sqm Or 30.225 Hectares)
29. A line AB measured on a gradient of 1 in 12 was found to be 375.8 m. It was found afterwards that the 30 m chain used was 5 cm too short. Find the correct horizontal distance between A and B.
    (Note: The incorrect length of chain is 19.95 m as the initial error in the chain is not mentioned).   (**Ans.** 373.615 m).
30. Chaining work was carried with a 30 m chain for a total length of 255.60 m on a ground sloping at 10°. The chain was correct at the beginning. When the chain was tested after completion of first 150 m, it was found to be 1 cm too long. At the end of work the measured length of chain was 30.02 m. Find the true horizontal distance measured.   (**Ans.** 251.794 m)

FUNDAMENTALS OF CIVIL ENGINEERING   SURVEYING

UNIVERSITY QUESTIONS

1. Define surveying and state the principle of surveying.   **(Dec. 03; May 05)**

2. Define the following terms.   **(Dec. 03)**
   (i) Scale
   (ii) Map
   (iii) R.F.

3. Sketch any ten sign convections used in surveying giving their names also.
    (Dec. 03, 04, 05; May 06)

4. State the principle of surveying and explain any one with the aid of neat sketches.
    (Dec. 03; May 04, 05, 06)

5. Differentiate between the following :
   (i) Geodetic surveying and plane surveying.   **(May 04)**
   (ii) Scale and Map.   **(May 04)**
   (iii) Tie line 4 check line.   **(Dec. 04; May 05)**

6. Define the following with the aid of sketches.
   (i) Base line.   **(May 04, 05; Dec. 04; May 06)**
   (ii) Tie line.   **(Dec. 04, 05; May 04, 05, 06)**
   (iii) Check line.   **(May 05)**
   (iv) Survey station.   **(Dec. 04)**

7. State clearly the meaning of offset and also state their types with sketches.
    (May 04; Dec. 04, 05)

8. Differentiate between the following :
   (i) Scale and R.F.   **(Dec. 04)**
   (ii) Base line and check line.   **(May 05)**

9. State the importance of Location sketch.   **(Dec. 04, 05; May 06)**

10. Mention two types of tapes used for measurements. State their specific characteristics and applications.   **(May 04)**

11. Draw neat sketch of open cross staff and explain its use with relevant sketch.

(May 04; Dec. 05)

12. Differentiate between the following :
    (i) Plan and Map. **(May 05)**
    (ii) Cloth tape and steel tap. **(May 05; Dec. 05)**
    (iii) Offset rod and ranging rod. **(May 05)**

13. State the importance of the following :
    (i) Arrow
    (ii) Ranging rod.
    (iii) Open crossstaff.

14. Define surveying. State the classification of surveying and differentiate them w.r. to any 3 points. **(Dec. 05)**

Chapter 3
ANGULAR MEASUREMENTS

3.1 INTRODUCTION

Angular measurements mean measurement of angles made either directly or indirectly by using some instruments. In chain surveying, the linear measurements are taken by chain or tape. However, if the area to be surveyed is large, measuring the length of survey lines becomes tedious and inconvenient. Hence, it becomes necessary to fix directions of survey lines. Similarly, if chaining cannot be done due to certain obstructions then fixing directions of survey lines by some angle measuring instruments becomes essential. These instruments are prismatic compass, theodolite etc. The survey work carried out using chain and prismatic compass is called as chain and compass survey.

3.2 CHAIN/TAPE AND COMPASS SURVEY

In this type of survey, survey is carried out along a series of lines either forming a closed polygon or along a series of lines connected to each other. The survey done in this manner is said to be done along a traverse. The lengths of survey lines are measured by chain or tape and the directions of survey lines are fixed by angle measuring instruments such as prismatic compass and theodolite.

3.3 CLOSED TRAVERSE

A traverse is said to be a closed traverse when the starting point and the end point of polygon i.e. traverse, meet at the same point P. The survey is carried out for locating boundaries of fields, small irrigation tanks and survey of moderately large area. In a closed traverse, the angular measurements can be checked by doing the summation of internal angles of closed traverse as shown in Fig. 3.1.

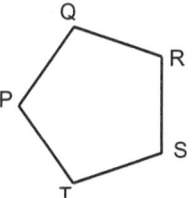

Fig. 3.1 : PQRST is a closed traverse

Sum of internal angles of a closed traverse = (2N − 4) right angles, where N is the number of sides of a traverse. In this case, N = 5.

∴ Sum of internal angles = 6 right angles = 540°.

3.4 OPEN TRAVERSE

A traverse is said to be an open traverse when the starting point and end point of survey lines do not coincide and the progress of survey is generally in the same direction. This type of survey is suitable for fixing the alignment of a new road or a railway line or a canal work. (Refer Fig. 3.2)

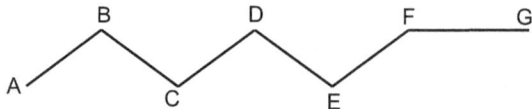

Fig. 3.2 : Open traverse

ABCDEFG is the open traverse. In the angular measurements, compass is the basic instrument in which magnetic needle is used. The needle is enclosed in a box which carries the graduated circle. It is possible to measure the bearings of the lines by using a compass.

3.5 DEFINITION OF BEARING OF A LINE

The magnetic needle points to the Magnetic North. Hence Magnetic North is the reference direction with respect to which the angles made by survey lines are measured. The horizontal angle made by a survey line with reference to Magnetic North in a clockwise direction is called the Bearing of a line.

Types of compass : (i) Prismatic compass, (ii) Surveyor's compass.

3.5.1 Prismatic Compass

Parts of Prismatic Compass

Fig. 3.3 (a) shows the parts of prismatic compass and Fig. 3.3 (b) shows the pictorial view of prismatic compass.

(i) It consists of a circular metal brass box about 100 mm in diameter with a hard steel pivot at the centre.

(ii) A magnetic needle is freely suspended on the pivot and carries a graduated aluminium ring. The graduations are marked from 0° to 360° in clockwise direction. Each degree is subdivided into two parts so that the minimum reading of the scale is 30'. The zero is placed at the south end and 180° at the north end and the graduations are marked in the inverted fashion. The reason for inverted graduations is that when the reading is taken through the reflecting prism, the graduations will be seen erect.

(iii) A reflecting prism carries a sighting slit and the object vane has a vertical horse hair for bisection of the object. The object vane and the reflecting prism are placed diametrically opposite to each other. The prism and the object vane can be folded so as to lie on the glass cover of compass.

(iv) The glass cover at the top prevents the entry of dust inside the compass.

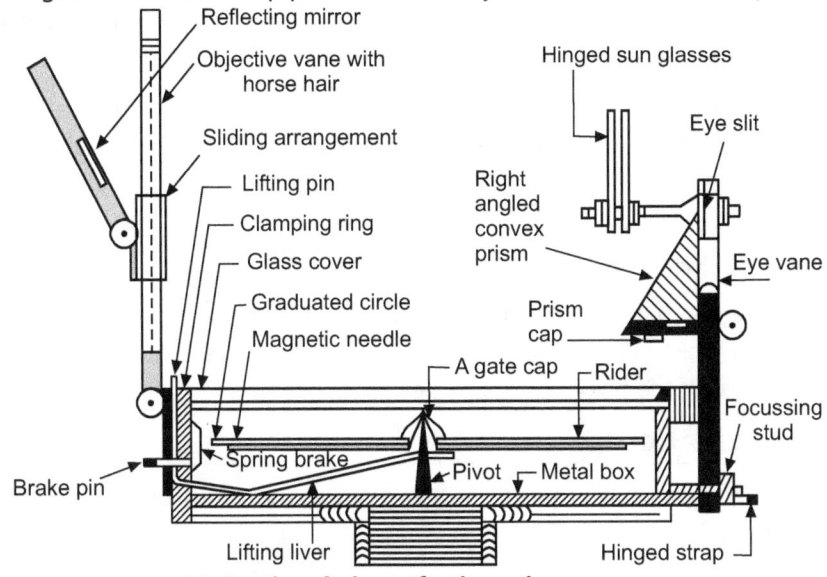

(a) Sectional view of prismatic compass

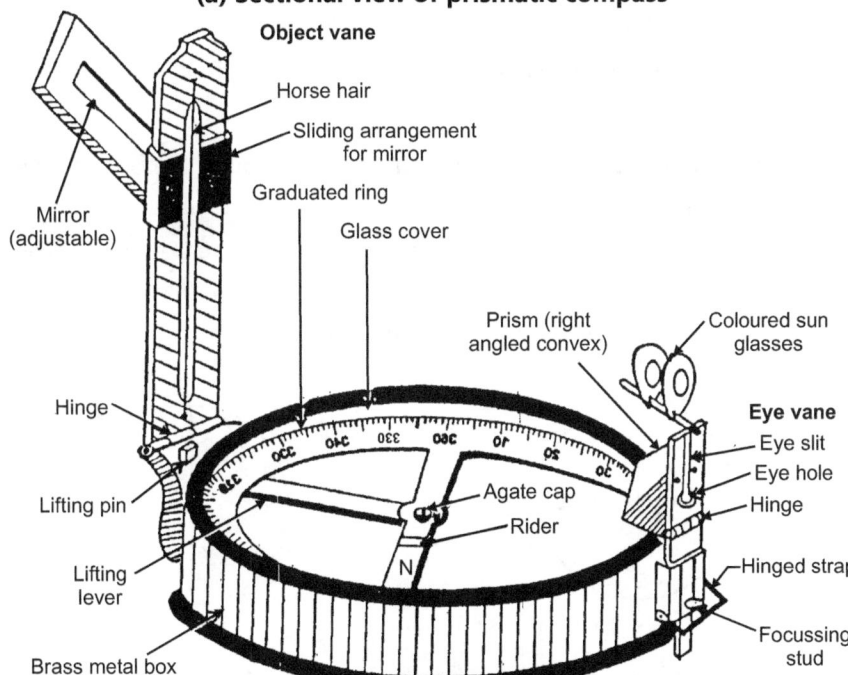

(b) Pictorial view of prismatic compass
Fig. 3.3

(v) The object vane carries an adjustable mirror which can be slided on the object vane. The objects too high or too low can be sighted by reflection by giving suitable inclination to this mirror.

(vi) Hinged sun glasses usually red and blue are attached to the frame of prism. These coloured glasses can be interposed into the line of sight when brighter objects are to be sighted.

(vii) A brake pin is provided on the side of compass box to damp the oscillations of the graduated circle with needle.

(viii) When the compass is not in use, the object vane when folded presses against the lifting pin which lifts the needle from the pivot and holds it against the lid. Thus undue wear of the pivot point is prevented.

3.5.2 Surveyor's Compass

This is another type of compass in which graduations vary from 0 to 90°. The other peculiarities are as follows :

(i) The graduated card is attached inside the box to the bottom and the card moves with the movement of compass.

(ii) The graduations are marked in erect position.

(iii) The magnetic needle is of edge bar type.

(iv) After the object is bisected, the observer has to go round the box to take readings through the top of compass.

(v) Surveyor's compass cannot be held in hand but is mounted on tripod. The bearings obtained are the reduced bearings.

However, this compass has become obsolete now-a-days.

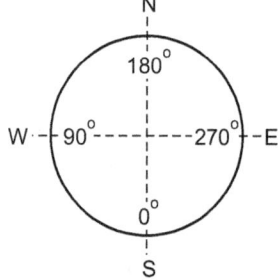
(a) Figure for graduations on prismatic compass

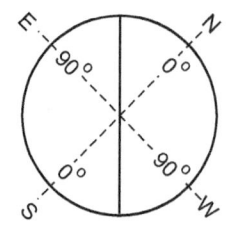
(b) Figure for graduations on surveyor's compass

Fig. 3.4

3.6 REFERENCE MERIDIANS AND BEARINGS OF SURVEY LINES

Earlier, the bearing of a line is defined as the horizontal angle made by a survey line with some reference direction in a clockwise direction. This reference direction is called a Meridian and the meridians are classified as follows.

(i) True Meridian

This is a line obtained by the intersection of a plane passing through a given point and North and South poles of the earth with the surface of the earth. When the reference direction is True Meridian, the horizontal angle made by a survey line with True meridian is called **True bearing** of a line or azimuth. For a given point on the surface of earth, the direction of True Meridian is always same.

(ii) Magnetic Meridian :

A freely suspended and properly balanced magnetic needle will always point to the Magnetic North or Magnetic Meridian. The angle made by a survey line with the magnetic North, in the clockwise direction is called **Magnetic bearing** of a line.

(iii) Arbitrary Meridian :

When it is not possible to measure bearings of lines either with respect to True North or Magnetic North, some convenient line is chosen as Arbitrary Reference direction and angle made by lines with this Arbitrary Meridian is termed as an arbitrary bearing of the line. This Arbitrary Meridian can be chosen as a line joining the survey station with some well defined object on the ground such as an electric pole and flag pole, etc.

3.7 MEASURING BEARINGS WITH PRISMATIC COMPASS

The prismatic compass is fixed to the top of a tripod by a ball and socket arrangement. The compass is required to be centred over a station point before bearings are observed. Hence certain temporary adjustments are carried out at each station where the compass is set up over a station point.

1. Temporary Adjustments

(i) Centering : It is the operation in which the compass is to be set exactly over the station peg. This is checked by dropping a small piece of stone or pebble from the underside of the compass. If the stone falls on the top of peg, then centering is correct. Otherwise the legs of the tripod are adjusted in two positions at right angles to each other.

(ii) Levelling : The levelling is checked by keeping a circular pencil on the glass cover of compass. If the pencil does not roll, the compass is in level. Otherwise, it can be done by ball and socket arrangement till the graduated ring moves freely inside the compass box.

2. Observing the bearing of a line (Fig. 3.5)

Suppose the bearing of line OA is to be observed. The compass is centred over station O as explained in (i) above and levelling is checked as explained in (ii) above. Let the ranging rod be fixed at 'A'. Turn the compass in the direction of line OA. See through the eye vane and bisect the ranging rod at 'A' by the middle hair of object vane. Let the needle i.e. graduated ring come to rest. The reflecting prism is adjusted to the eyesight of observer by raising or lowering the stud. The reading under the vertical hair through prism is taken which gives the bearing of line OA. The bearings obtained in the prismatic compass are **whole circle bearings**. If ON is the magnetic North, then the F.B. of OA observed w.r.t. ON is called the Magnetic Bearing of line OA.

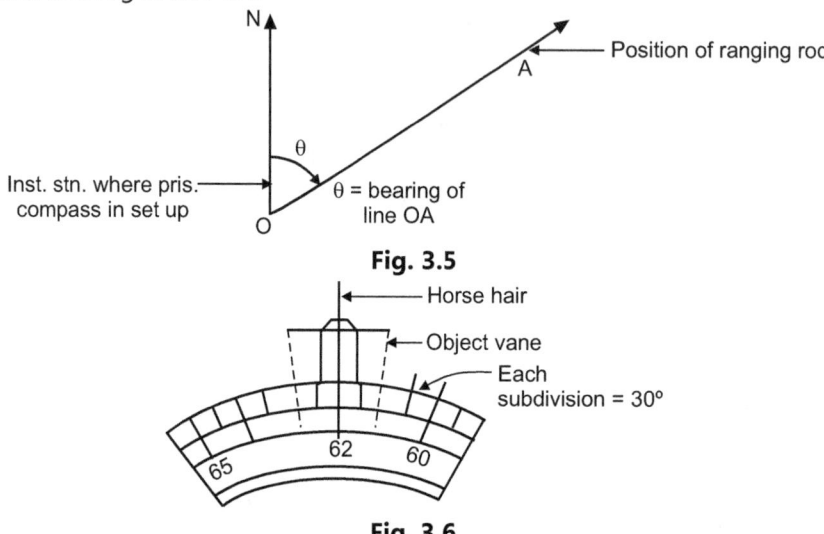

Fig. 3.5

Fig. 3.6

3.8 TYPES OF BEARINGS

The bearings of survey lines are classified in the following systems.

(i) Whole Circle Bearing System :

When the bearing of a line measured in clockwise direction from North varies from 0° to 360°, it is termed as whole circle bearing. The bearings obtained using prismatic compass are the whole circle bearings.

(ii) The Reduced Bearing or Quadrantal Bearing System :

The space is divided into four quadrants and the bearings of survey lines are always measured with respect to North and South line either in clockwise or anticlockwise direction towards East or West. In Fig. 3.7, α_1 is the reduced bearing of line OA and it is written as N α_1^0 E. It is essential to write the directions before and after the value of angle. This helps to identify the quadrant in which the line lies. The maximum value of bearing in the quadrantal system is 90°. It is also called as Reduced bearing of a line. The bearings obtained using Surveyor's compass are Reduced Bearings.

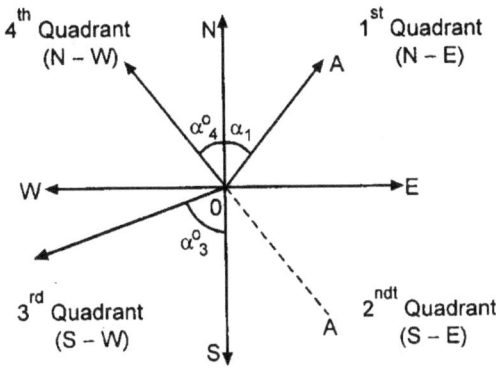

Fig. 3.7

3.8.1 Conversion of Bearings from One System to Other

The whole circle bearings can be converted to quadrantal bearings and quadrantal bearings can be converted to whole circle bearings by referring to the following Table 3.1.

Table 3.1 : Conversion from W.C.B. to R.B.

W.C.B. lying between	Quadrant in which line lies	Rule for conversion to Reduced Bearing	Quadrant
(1) 0° to 90°	I	R.B. = W.C.B.	N – E
(2) 90° to 180°	II	R.B. = 180° – W.C.B.	S – E
(3) 180° to 270°	III	R.B. = W.C.B. – 180°	S – W
(4) 270° to 360°	IV	R.B. = 360° – W.C.B.	N – W

3.9 FORE BEARING AND BACK BEARING

The bearing of a survey line observed in the direction of progress of survey is called fore bearing of the line while the bearing of the same line observed from the other end or observed in the reverse direction is called back bearing of the same line.

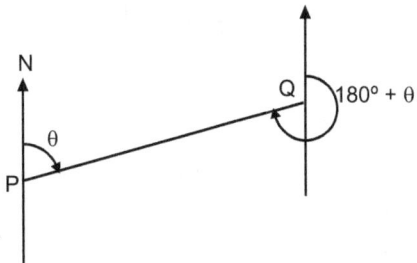

Fig. 3.8

In Fig. 3.8, θ° is the fore-bearing of line PQ observed from P to Q and if the prismatic compass is shifted from P to Q and the bearing of the same line is observed from Q to P i.e. in the reverse direction then (180° + θ°) will be the back bearing of the line PQ. Thus it can be seen that for the same line, **the difference between Fore bearing and Back bearing of the same line is always 180°** or it can be stated as under.

Back Bearing of a line = Fore Bearing ± 180°

The negative sign is to be used when the fore bearing exceeds 180°. The above rule is true for whole circle system.

In the quadrantal system, the fore and back bearings of a line are numerically same but with opposite directional signs.

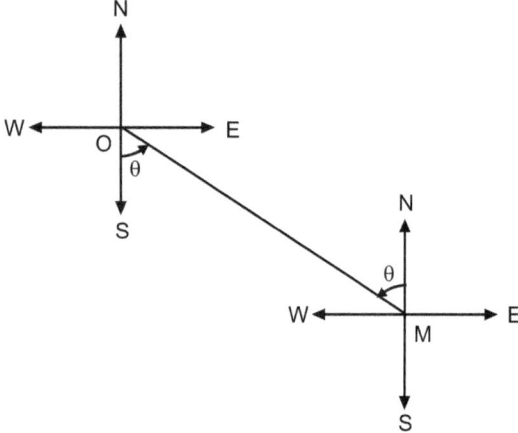

Fig. 3.9 : F.B. of OM and B.B. of OM in quadrantal system

In Fig. 3.9, S θ° E is the fore bearing of line OM and the back bearing of OM is N θ° W. Similarly the fore bearings of lines lying in the other quadrants can be converted to back bearings with change of directional signs knowing that reference meridian in case of quadrantal bearings is North-South line.

SOLVED EXAMPLES

Example 3.1 : Convert the following whole circle bearings to reduced bearings.

(i) 72° 30' (ii) 128° (iii) 248° 30' (iv) 325° 15'

Solution : It is better to draw figures for such problems and knowing the quadrant in which the line lies, the conversion to quadrantal system will be easier.

(i) In the first quadrant, Whole circle Bearing = Reduced Bearing

∴ Reduced Bearing = N 72° 30' E as shown in Fig. 3.10.

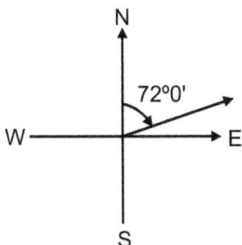

Fig. 3.10

(ii) In the Second Quadrant (making use of Table 3.1)

Reduced bearing = 180° − 128° = S 52° E as shown in Fig. 3.11.

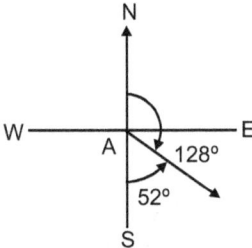

Fig. 3.11

(iii)   Reduced Bearing = (248° 30') − (180°) = S 68 30' W

(iv)   Reducing Bearing = (360°) − (325° 15') = N 34° 45' W

Using Table 3.1.

Example 3.2 : Convert the following reduced bearings to whole circle bearings.

(i) N 23° W (ii) S 37° 30' E (iii) S 52° W (iv) N 44° 30' E

Solution : (i)

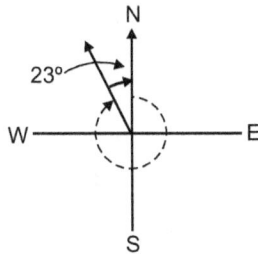

Fig. 3.12

N 23° W = W.C. Bearing 360° − 23°

W.C. Bearing = 337°

(ii) S 37° 30' E

W.C. Bearing = 180° − 37° 30'

= 142° 30'

(iii) S 52° W

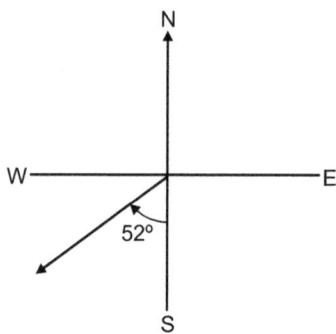

Fig. 3.13

Whole Circle Bearing = 180° + 52°

∴ W.C.B. = 232°

This will be clear from Fig. 3.13.

(iv) N 44° 30' E

Whole Circle Bearing = 44° 30' (being the first quadrant)

Example 3.3 : Find the back bearings of the following lines.

(i) AB − S 37° W (ii) CD − N 21° 15' E (iii) EF − 301° 30' (iv) GH − 117°

Solution : (i) F.B. of AB = S 37° W

B.B. of AB = N 37° E

(ii) F.B. of CD = N 21° 15' E

B.B. of CD = S 21° 15' W

(iii) F.B. of EF = 301° 30'

B.B. of EF = (301° 30') − (180°) = 121° 30'

(iv) F.B. of GH = 117°

B.B. of GH = 117° + 180° = 297°

3.10 CALCULATION OF ANGLES FROM BEARINGS

(i) The included angle between two consecutive lines can be calculated from their observed bearings. It can be interior or exterior angle.

(a) When the whole circle bearings of two lines measured from their point of intersection are known :

The included angle = Difference between the W.C. bearing of two lines provided the difference is less than 180°.

To illustrate the above rule, let the lines PQ and QR meet at Q as shown in Fig. 3.14 (a).

The included ∠ PQR =

(142° 30') – (60°) = 82° 30'

i.e.   F.B. of QR – F.B. of QP = ∠ PQR

(ii) If the difference exceeds 180°, it is the exterior angle between the two lines.

The included angle = 360° – (Difference of the W.C. bearings between the two lines).

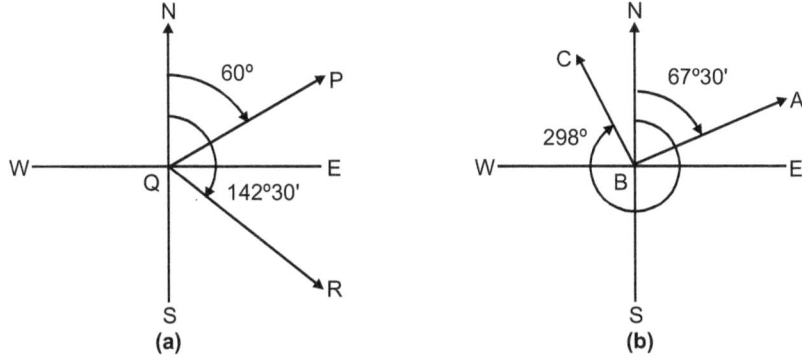

Fig. 3.14

In Fig. 3.14 (b), F.B. of BC is 298° and F.B. of BA = 67° 30'.

∠ ABC = (298°) – (67° 30')

= 230° 30'

Since the difference between the bearings is greater than 180°, it is the exterior angle.

∴   Included ∠ CBA = 360° – (230° 30')

= 129° 30'

(b) When the whole circle bearings of two lines are given :

The rule given in (a) can be applied only when the bearings are expressed as if measured from the point where the lines meet.

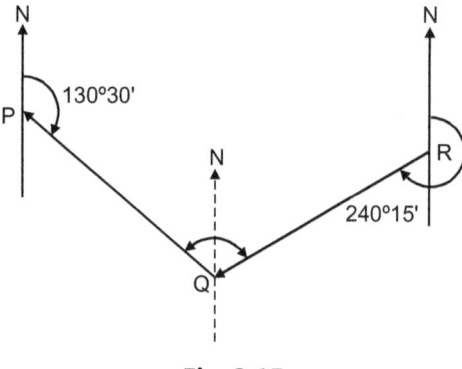

Fig. 3.15

The following example illustrates the calculation of included angle when the fore bearings of two lines are given.

Given : F.B. of PQ is 130° 30' and F.B. of RQ is 240° 15' as shown in Fig. 3.15. Looking at Fig. 3.15.

$$\text{To calculate } \angle PQR = \text{F.B. of QR} - \text{F.B. of QP}$$

$$\text{Now F.B. of QP} = \text{B.B. of PQ}$$

$$= 130° 30' + 180°$$

$$= 310° 30'$$

$$\text{F.B. of QR} = \text{B.B. of RQ}$$

$$= (240° 15') - (180°)$$

$$= 60° 15'$$

$$\therefore \quad \angle PQR = (60° - 15') - (310° - 30')$$

$$= -250° 15'$$

Since the difference between the fore bearings of QP and QR exceeds 180° and is negative, it is the exterior angle PQR.

$$\text{Included } \angle PQR = (360°) - (250° 15')$$

$$= 109° 45'$$

(ii) When the reduced bearings of the lines are given, the included angles between the lines can be calculated as described below. The calculation work is simplified by showing the two lines in proper quadrant and calling the upper half of quadrant as North Meridian and the lower half of the quadrant of South Meridian.

(a) If the lines are lying on the same side of the same meridian.

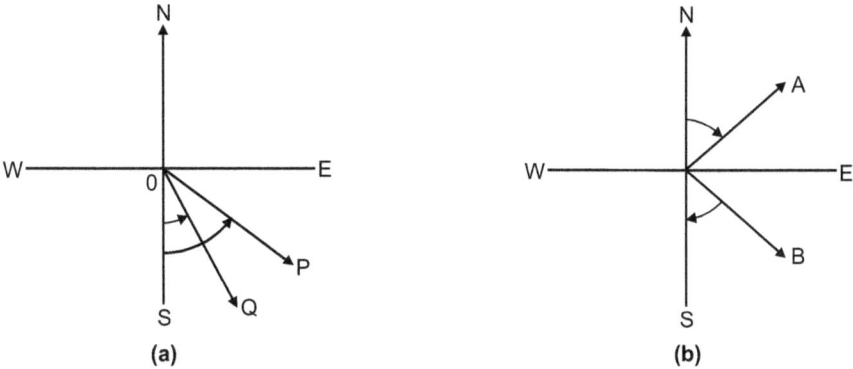

Fig. 3.16

In Fig. 3.16 (a), ∠ POQ = Difference of reduced bearings between OP and OQ.

(b) If the lines lie on the same side of different meridian as shown in Fig. 3.16 (b), the included ∠ POQ

= 180° − (Sum of the reduced bearings of OP and OQ)

(c) If the lines lie on the different sides of the different meridians as shown in Fig. 3.17 (a), included ∠ POQ = 180° − (Difference of the reduced bearings of OQ and OP).

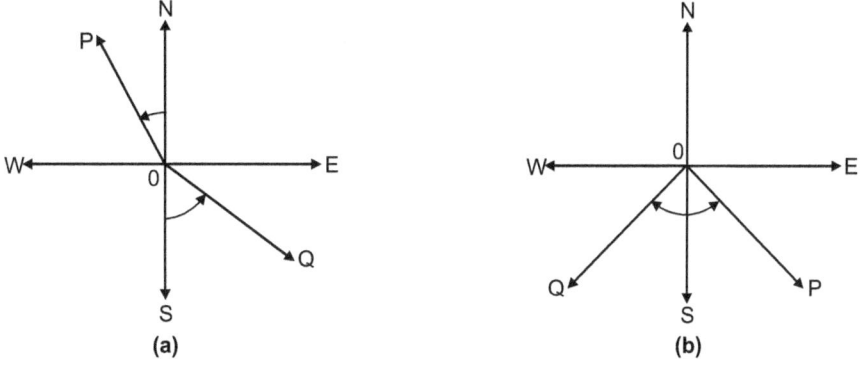

Fig. 3.17

(d) If the lines are on the opposite sides of the same meridian as shown in Fig. 3.17 (b), included ∠ POQ = Sum of the reduced bearings of OP and OQ.

3.11 CALCULATION OF BEARINGS FROM ANGLES

The bearings of lines can be calculated from the observed bearing of any one line and the included angle measured clockwise between the different lines.

Thus bearing of a line = Given bearing + Included angle

In Fig. 3.18 (a), let F.B. of OP be 65° 30' and let ∠ POQ be 77° 45'

Fore Bearing of OQ = 65° 30' + 77° 45' = 143° 15'

(i.e. in the whole circle bearing system)

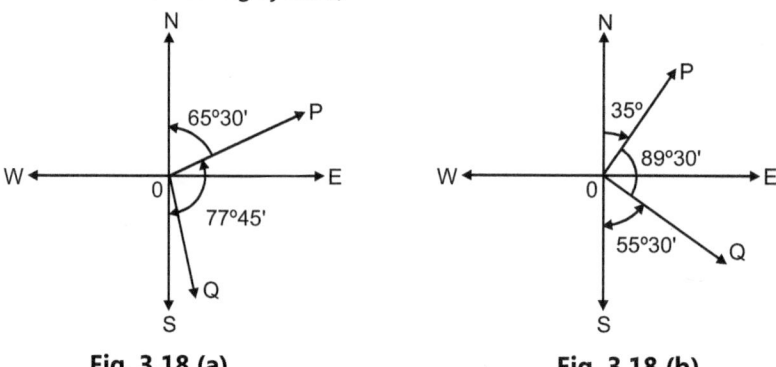

Fig. 3.18 (a)   **Fig. 3.18 (b)**

In Fig. 3.18 (b), let F.B. of OP be 330° 30' and let ∠ POQ = 135° 0'

∴ Fore Bearings of OQ = (330° 30') + (135°) = (465 30') – 360°

F.B. of OQ = 105° 30' (i.e. WCB of OQ)

In Fig. 3.19,

If F.B. of OP = N 35° E and ∠ POQ = 89° 30'

From Fig. 3.19,

Fore bearing of OQ = 35° + 89° 30' = 124° 30' in the WCB system

F.B. of OQ = 180° – 124° 30' = S 55° 30' E

(i.e. in the Quadrantal system)

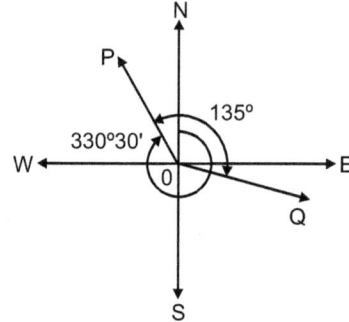

Fig. 3.19

Example 3.4 : The fore bearing of AB = 106° and F.B. of BC = 296° 30'. Calculate the ∠ ABC.

Solution : From Fig. 3.20,

$$\angle ABC = \text{F.B. of BC} - \text{Back bearing of AB}$$
$$= 296° 30' - (106° + 180°) = 296° 30' - 286° 0'$$
$$\angle ABC = 10° 30'$$

Fig. 3.20

Example 3.5 : Find the included angles between the lines OP and OQ whose reduced bearings are as given below :

(i) N 21° 30' E and S 65° W

(ii) N 32° W and S 51° 45' W

Solution : (i) Referring to Fig. 3.21,

$$\angle QOP = 180° - (65° - 21° 30') = 180° - (43° 30')$$
$$= 136° 30'$$

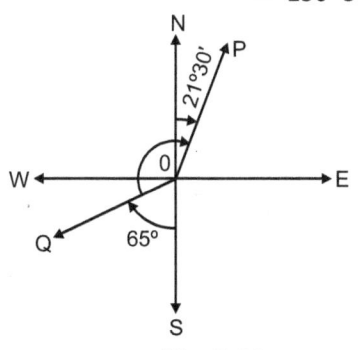 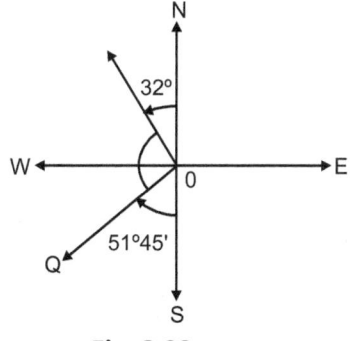

Fig. 3.21   **Fig. 3.22**

(ii) From Fig. 3.22,

$$\angle QOP = 180° - (32° + 51° 45')$$
$$= 180° - (83° 45')$$
$$\angle QOP = 96° 15'$$

Example 3.6 : The following bearings were observed in running a closed traverse PQR in clockwise direction. Calculate the included angles of traverse.

Line	Observed	
	Fore bearing	Back bearing
PQ	115°	295°
QR	260°	80°
RP	35°	215°

Solution : Draw the sketch of closed traverse as shown in Fig. 3.23. It shows the closed traverse PQR with the marking of fore bearings as observed in the field.

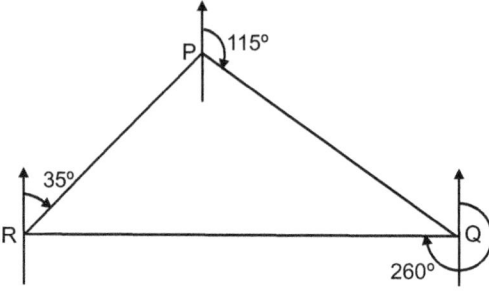

Fig. 3.23

Calculation of included angles :

$\angle Q$ = Back bearing of PQ − Fore bearing of QR
      = 295° − 260° = 35°

$\angle R$ = B.B. of QR − F.B. of RP = 80° − 35° = 45°

$\angle P$ = B.B. of RP − F.B. of PQ = 215° − 115° = 100°

Summation of Internal Angles = $\angle Q + \angle R + \angle P$
              = 35° + 45° + 100° = 180°

Example 3.7 Following bearings were observed while running a closed traverse in the clockwise direction.

Line	Fore bearing	Back bearing
AB	285° 30'	105° 30'
BC	32° 0'	212° 0'
CD	151° 0'	331° 0'
DA	198° 0'	18° 0'

Calculate the included angles at different stations and check their sum.

Solution :

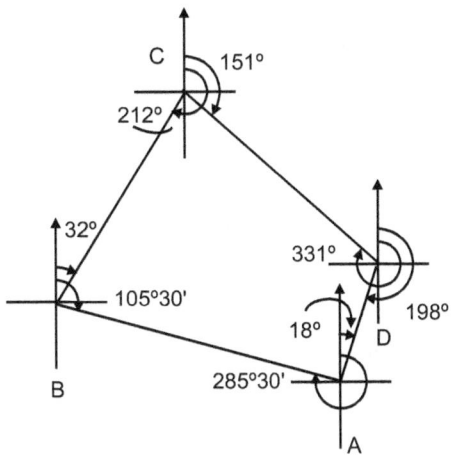

Fig. 3.24

Draw the sketch of the traverse ABCD from the given data. Also check whether the back bearings and fore bearings differ by 180°.

∠ A = B.B. of DA – F.B. of AB
= 18° – 285° 30'
= – 267° 30'

The negative sign shows that it is an exterior angle.

∴ ∠ A = 360° – 267° 30' = 92°30'

∠ B = B.B. of AB – F.B. of BC
= 105° 30' – 32° 0' = 73° 30'

∠ C = B.B. of BC – F.B. of CD
= 212° 0' – 151° 0' = 61° 0'

∠ D = B.B. of CD – F.B. of DA
= 331° – 198° = 133°

Sum of Internal Angles = 92° 30' + 73° 30' + 61° 0' + 133° 0'
= 360° 0'

Example 3.8 : F.B. of Line AB was measured to be 30° 15' in a closed traverse ABC which is an anticlockwise equilateral triangle. Assuming no L.A., calculate F.B. and B.B. of all lines. Tabulate your result in usual format. **(P.U. Dec. 95)**

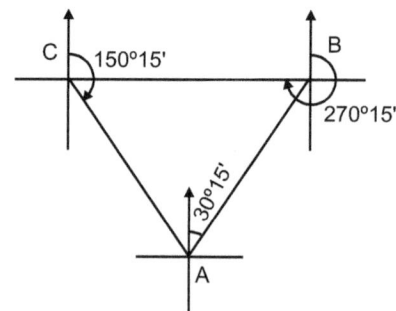

Fig. 3.25

Solution : For an anticlockwise traverse,
Included angle = F.B. of next line − B.B. of previous line
From Fig. 3.25,

$$\text{B.B. of AB} = 30°\ 15' + 180°\ 0'$$
$$= 210°\ 15'$$

∴ F.B. of BC − 210° 15' (BB of AB) = 60° = ∠ B.
∴   F.B. of BC = 270° 15'
             B.B. of BC = 270° 15' − 180° = 90° 15;
   F.B. of CA − 90° 15' = 60°   ∴ F.B. of CA = 150° 15'

Results are tabulated as under

Line	Fore Bearing	Back Bearing
AB	30° 15'	210° 15'
BC	270° 15'	90° 15'
CA	150° 15'	330° 15'

Example 3.9 : A square ABCD was surveyed from starting station A, in a counter clockwise direction. The fore bearing of AB was observed as 130° 30'. Find out the bearings of the other sides of traverse.   **(P.U. May 89)**

Solution :

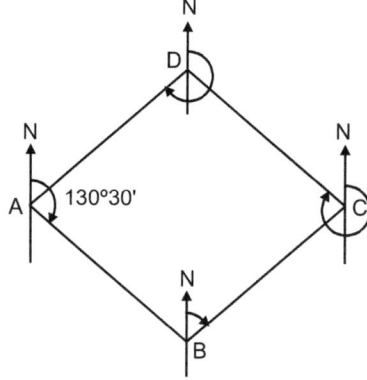

Fig. 3.26

The direction of North will be as shown in the figure since the traverse is run in counter-clockwise direction.

$$\text{F.B. of AB} = 130° 30'$$
$$+ 180° 0'$$
$$\overline{\text{B.B. of AB} = 310° 30'}$$

From Fig. 3.26,
F.B. of BC = B.B. of AB − Ext. angle at B
F.B. of BC = 310° 30' − 270° = 40° 30'
B.B. of BC = 40° 30' + 180° = 220° 30'
F.B. of CD = B.B. of BC + ∠ C
F.B. of CD = 220° 30' + 90° = 310° 30'
B.B. of CD = 310° 30' − 180° = 130° 30'
F.B. of DA = B.B. of CD + ∠ D
= 130° 30' + 90° = 220° 30'

As a check,
F.B. of AB = B.B. of DA + ∠ A
= (220° 30' − 180°) + 90°
= 40° 30' + 90° = 130° 30'

The results are tabulated in a tabular form in Table 3.2.

Table 3.2

Line	Fore bearing	Back bearing
AB	130° 30'	310° 30'
BC	40° 30'	220° 30'
CD	310° 30'	130° 30'
DA	220° 30'	40° 30'

3.12 LOCAL ATTRACTION

When the prismatic compass is set up at a station, a freely suspended and properly balanced magnetic needle will point to the 0° mark i.e. magnetic north. However when a compass is set up in the vicinity of iron or steel structures, or under the cables carrying electric current, the magnetic needle does not point to the magnetic north and is seriously deflected from its normal position. This deviation of the needle from its normal position (North direction) due to external disturbing sources (steel structures etc.) is called **Local attraction**. In cities, its effect is felt more. The external disturbing source can be the articles of steel such as lamp posts, iron pipes, rails, steel chains etc. Hence while selecting stations for compass survey, proximity of such objects should be avoided as far as possible.

3.12.1 Detecting Local Attraction

The presence of local attraction can be detected by observing the fore bearing and back bearing of each survey line from both the ends. A line is said to be free from local attraction if the fore bearing and back bearing of the same line differs by 180°. Hence the stations at the ends of the survey line are said to be free from local attraction provided there are no observational errors and instrumental errors.

The local attraction is the same for the bearings taken at the affected station. Hence it should be noted that the difference between the bearings of lines observed at the station gives the correct values of included angles even though the station is affected by local attraction.

3.12.2 Methods of Correcting Bearings of Lines Affected by Local Attraction

There are two methods of applying corrections to observed bearings of lines affected by local attraction.

Method - I : In this method, the fore bearing and back bearing of survey lines are examined. The line in which the difference between the fore bearing and back bearing is exactly equal to 180° is selected. Starting from this unaffected line, the magnitude and direction of error due to local attraction at other station is found out and then corrections are applied to the observed bearings of other lines. If the observed bearing is less than the corrected bearing, the error is negative and the correction to observed bearing will be positive and vice versa. This method is mostly used.

Steps : To be followed while solving examples :

(1) Draw the sketch of traverse from known Fore bearings and Back bearings.
(2) Find out the line which is not affected by L. A. (where the difference between B.B. and F.B. is 180°).
(3) Calculate the correction to be applied to each station.
(4) Obtain the corrected values of F.B. and B.B. by applying corrections.
(5) Tabulate the correced bearings.

Method - II : In this method, the included angles are calculated from the observed fore bearing and back bearing of the lines and in case of closed traverse if the summation of internal angles of traverse is not equal to (2 N – 4) right angles, the error is distributed equally in all the angles. Starting from the line which is not affected by local attraction, and from the values of included angles, the corrected bearings of other lines can be calculated.

Steps : To be followed in solving problems :
(1) Draw the figure of traverse and find the included angles from the observed bearings of lines.
(2) Check the sum of internal angles of a closed traverse which should be (2N – 4) right angles. Find the error if any.
(3) Distribute the error equally in all the angles.
(4) Starting from the bearing of unaffected line, and using the corrected values of angles, the corrected bearings of other lines can be calculated.

Note : When the fore bearing and back bearing of none of the lines differs by 180°, then the survey line where the discrepancy between the fore bearing and back bearing is the least is selected and by allocating the error equally to both F.B. and B.B. the difference between F.B. and B.B. is made equal to 180° and then the bearings of the other lines are corrected as usual i.e. as per method - II.

Example 3.10 : The following bearings were taken in traversing with a compass in a place where local attraction was suspected. At what stations do you suspect local attraction ? Find the corrected bearings of the lines and also calculate included angles.

Line	Fore Bearing	Back Bearing
PQ	124° 30'	304° 30'
QR	68° 15'	246° 0'
RS	310° 30'	135° 15'
SP	200° 15'	17° 45'

Solution : From the observed fore bearing and back bearings of lines, it will be seen that only in case of line PQ the fore bearing and back bearing differs by 180°. Hence stations P and Q are not affected and observations taken from stations P and Q will be correct.

∴ Fore bearing of QR 68° 15' is correct.

Add 180° to F.B. of QR to get B.B. of QR = 248° 15'. This does not tally with observed B.B. of QR.

Hence, station R is affected and local attraction at R will be 248° 15' (–) 246° 0' = + 2° 15' and this correction will have to be applied to observations taken from R.

∴ Corrected F.B. of RS = 310° 30' + 2° 15' = 312° 45'
∴ Corrected B.B. of RS = 312° 45' – 180° = 132° 45'

which is less than the observed B.B. of RS.

∴ Local attraction at S = 132° 45' – 135° 15' = – 2° 30'.

Hence correction to observed F.B. of SP will be – 2° 30'.

The corrected F.B. of SP will be 200° 15' – 2° 30° = 197° 45'.

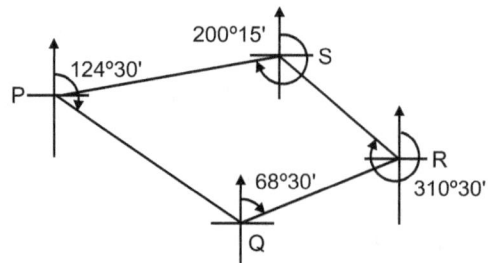

Fig. 3.27

Now observed B.B. of SP 17° – 45' is correct since it differs exactly by 180° from the corrected F.B. of SP. The observed and corrected bearings in tabular form will be as follows.

Line	Observed		Local attraction at	Corrected	
	F.B.	B.B.		F.B.	B.B.
PQ	124° 30'	304° 30'	P and Q are not affected. At stn. R L.A. = + 2° 15' At stn. S, L.A. = – 2° 30'	124° 30'	304° 30'
QR	68° 15'	246° 00'		68° 15'	248° 15'
RS	310° 30'	135° 15'		312° 45'	132° 45'
SP	200° 15'	17° 45'		197° 45'	17°45'

Calculation of Angles

$\angle P$ = F.B. of PQ – B.B. of SP = 106° 45'

$\angle Q$ = F.B. of QR – B.B. of PQ = 68° 15' (–) 304° 30'

= – 236° – 15' – ve sign indicates exterior angle

∴ Internal angle = 360° – 236° 15' = 123° 45'

$\angle R$ = F.B. of RS – B.B. of QR = 312° 45' – 248° 15'

= 64° 30'

$\angle S$ = F.B. of SP – B.B. of RS = 197° 45' – 132° 45' = 65° 0'

Sum of $\angle P + \angle Q + \angle R + \angle S$ = 360° 0'

Example 3.11 : Following bearings were taken with a prismatic compass at the closed traverse.

Line	F.B.	B.B.
AB	120° 30'	300° 00'
BC	30° 00'	209° 00'
CD	330° 30'	150° 30'
DE	260° 30'	80° 00'
EA	210° 00'	31° 00'

Find corrected bearings and record them in a tabular form.

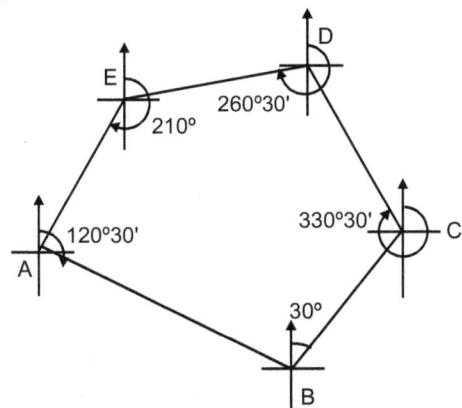

Fig. 3.28

Solution : If the first method of applying corrections to observed bearings of lines is adopted starting from the unaffected line CD, it will be observed that the calculated back bearing of BC and observed back bearing of BC does not tally. Hence the second method of applying corrections to observed bearings of lines by calculating included angles first will be used here. First the included angles at each station will be calculated and check for summation of internal angles will be applied.

Line	Observed bearings		Included angles		Correction to angles	Corrected Incl. Angles
	F.B.	B.B.	Stn.	Angle		
AB	120° 30'	300° 00'	∠A	89° 30'	– 12'	89° 18'
BC	30° 00'	209° 00'	∠B	90° 00'	– 12'	89° 48'
CD	330° 30'	150° 30'	∠C	121° 30'	– 12'	121° 18'
DE	260° 30'	80° 00'	∠D	110° 00'	– 12'	109° 48'
EA	210° 00'	31° 00'	∠E	130° 00'	– 12'	129° 48'
		Total		541° 00'	– 1°	540° 00'

Now starting from the line which is not affected due to local attraction, the bearings of other lines can be calculated. From Fig. 3.28.

$$\text{F.B. of DE} = \text{B.B. of CD} + \text{corrected } \angle D$$
$$= 150° 30' + 109° 48' = 260° 18'$$
$$\text{B.B. of DE} = 260° 18' – 180° = 80° 18'$$
∴ $$\text{F.B. of EA} = \text{B.B. of DE} + \text{Corr. } \angle E$$
$$= 80° 18' + 129° 48' = 210° 06'$$

FUNDAMENTALS OF CIVIL ENGINEERING ANGULAR MEASUREMENTS

$\therefore$ F.B. of AB = B.B. of EA + Corr. $\angle$ A
= (210° 06' − 180°) + 89° 18'
= 30° 06' + 89° 18' = 119° 24'

F.B. of BC = B.B. of AB + Corrected $\angle$ B
= (119° 24' + 180° 0') + 89° 48'
= (299° 24') + (89° 48') = 389° 12'

$\therefore$ F.B. of BC = 389° 12' − 360° = 29° 12'

F.B. of CD = B.B. of BC + Corrected $\angle$ C
= (29° 12' + 180°) + 121° 18'
= 209° 12' + 121° 18' = 330° 30'

which tallies with the observed F.B. of CD. Results are tabulated as under.

Line	Observed		Included Angles	Corrected Incl. Angle	Corrected	
	F.B.	B.B.			F. B.	B.B.
AB	120° 30'	300° 00'	$\angle$ A	89° 18'	119° 24'	299° 24'
BC	30° 00'	209° 00'	$\angle$ B	89° 48'	29° 12'	209° 12'
CD	330° 30'	150° 30'	$\angle$ C	121° 18'	330° 30'	150° 30'
DE	260° 30'	80° 00'	$\angle$ D	109° 48'	260° 18'	80° 18'
EA	210° 00'	31° 00'	$\angle$ E	129° 48'	210° 06'	30° 06'
			Total 540° 00'			

Example 3.12 : Following observations were made in running a compass traverse survey.

Line	Fore Bearing	Back bearing
PQ	242° 0'	63° 0'
QR	89° 45'	270° 15'
RS	70° 0'	250° 0'
ST	292° 45'	112° 45'
TP	20° 0'	198° 30'

Calculate the included angles and apply usual check.   **(P.U. May 88)**

Solution : First the figure of traverse PQRST should be drawn from the observed values of bearings.

FUNDAMENTALS OF CIVIL ENGINEERING   ANGULAR MEASUREMENTS

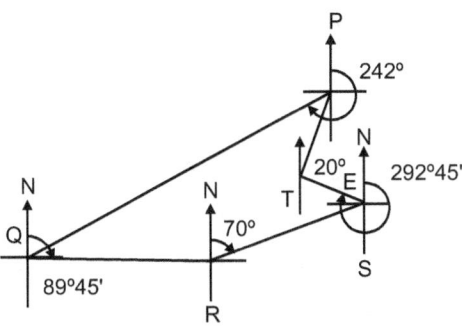

Fig. 3.29

The fore bearings and back bearings of all lines will be checked to find whether stations are affected by local attraction. It will be seen that stations R, S and T are free from Local Attraction. Hence corrected bearings of other lines of traverse will be found by applying corrections for local attraction and then included angles will be found out.

Line	Observed Bearings		Correction due to L.A.	Corrected Bearings		Remarks
	F.B.	B.B.		F.B.	B.B.	
PQ	242° 00'	63° 00'	+ 30' at Stn. Q	243° 30'	63° 30'	Stns R, S, and T are free from L.A.
QR	89° 45'	270° 15'		90° 15'	270° 15'	
RS	70° 00'	250° 00'		70° 00'	250° 00'	
ST	292° 45'	112° 45'	+ 1° 30' at stn. P	292° 45'	112° 45'	
TP	20° 00'	198° 30'		20° 00'	200° 00'	

Calculation of angles :

From Fig. 3.29, $\angle Q$ = F.B. of QR – B.B. of PQ
                        = 90° 15' – 63° 30'
                        = 26° 45'
              $\angle R$ = F.B. of RS – B.B. of QR
                        = 70° 0' – 270° 15' = – 200° 15'

Negative sign indicates that it is an exterior angle.

∴ $\angle R$ = 360° – (200° 15') = 159° 45'
              $\angle S$ = F.B. of ST – B.B. of RS
                        = 292° 45' – 250° 0' = 42° 45'
              $\angle T$ = F.B. of TP – B.B. of ST
                        = 20° – 112° 45' = – 92° 45'

– ve sign indicates that it is an exterior angle.

$$360° - 92° 45' = 267° 15'$$

$$\angle P = \text{F.B. of PQ} - \text{B.B. of TP}$$

$$= 243° 30' - 200° 0' = 43° 30'$$

Check : $\angle P + \angle Q + \angle R + \angle S + \angle T = 43° 30' + 26° 45' + 159° 45' + 42° 45' + 267° 15'$

$$= 540° 00' \text{ which tallies with } (2N - 4) \times 90°$$

where N = No. of sides of traverse

Example 3.13 : In a closed clockwise compass traverse ABCD, no station was affected by local attraction. Fore bearing of line DA was observed to be 120°, and $\angle A = \angle C = 60° - 30'$ and $\angle B = \angle D = 119° - 30'$. Draw rough sketch of the traverse and find fore and back bearings of all lines. Enter the readings in usual tabular form.

(P.U. May 94)

Solution : Sum of angles = $\angle A + \angle B + \angle C + \angle D = 360°$

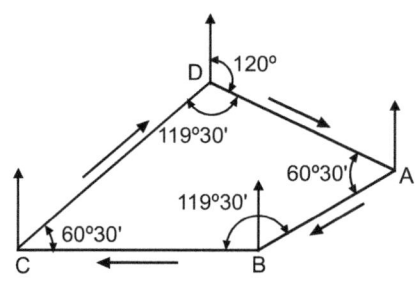

Fig. 3.30

B.B. of line DA = $120° + 180° = 300° 0'$

F.B. of AB = $300° 0' - 60° 30' = 239° 30'$

B.B. of AB = $239° 30' - 180° 0' = 59° 30'$

Now, included $\angle B$ = $360° - (\text{F.B. of BC} - \text{B.B. of AB})$

or $119° 30' = 360° - (\text{F.B. of BC} - 59° 30')$

or F.B. of BC = $300° 0'$

∴ B.B. of BC = $300° 0' - 180° 0' = 120°$

F.B. of CD = $120° - 60° 30' = 59° 30'$

B.B. of CD = $59° 30' + 180° = 239° 30'$

∴ F.B. of DA = $239° 30' - 119° 30'$

$$= 120° \text{ which is correct}$$

Line	F.B.	B.B.	Difference	Angle	Remarks
AB	239° 30'	59° 30'	180° 0'	∠A = 60° 30'	No station
BC	300° 0'	120° 0'	180° 0'	∠B = 119° 30'	is affected by
					Local attraction
CD	59° 30'	239° 30'	180° 0'	∠C = 60° 30'	
DA	120° 0'	300° 0'	180° 0'	∠D = 119°30'	
			Sum	360° 0'	

Example 3.14 : The following data is for a closed traverse PQRS taken in clockwise direction :

(i) F.B. and B.B. at P = 45° and 143° resp.
(ii) F.B. and B.B. of line RS = 211° and 31° resp.
(iii) Included angles ∠ Q = 100° and ∠ R = 110°.
(iv) Local attraction at station R = 2° W

Find local attraction if any at other station and hence correct F.B. and B.B. in tabular form for each line. **(P.U. Dec. 96)**

Solution : F.B. of PQ = 45°
B.B. of SP = 143°

Although the difference between F.B. and B.B. of RS is 180°, there is local attraction at station R = 2° W i.e. – 2° and same L.A. must be present at S.

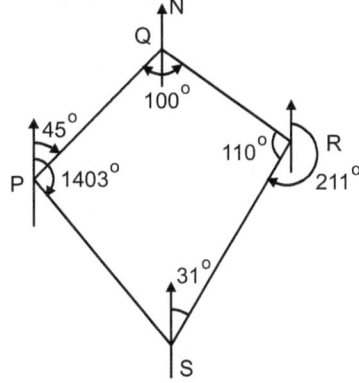

Fig. 3.31

∴ Corrected F.B. of RS = 211° – 2° = 209°
Corrected B.B. of RS = 31° – 2 = 29°
From the figure, B.B. of QR = 209° + 110° = 319°
F.B. of QR = 319° – 180° = 139°
B.B. of PQ = F.B. of QR + 100° = 239°
∴ F.B. of PQ = 59°

FUNDAMENTALS OF CIVIL ENGINEERING   ANGULAR MEASUREMENTS

∴   Station P is affected.

       Now ∠P = B.B. of SP – F.B. of PQ = 143° – 45° = 98°

∴   ∠S = 360° – [∠98° + ∠100° + ∠110°] = 52°

       F.B. of SP = (360° – 52°) + B.B. of RS = 308° + 29° = 337°

       B.B. of SP = 337° – 180° = 157°

       Check B.B. of RS = F.B. of SP – Ext. angle 'S' = 337° – (360° – 52°) = 29°

Example 3.15 : Following bearings were observed in running a closed compass traverse ABCDA.

Line	Observed Bearings	
	F.B.	B.B.
AB	S 40° 30' W	N 41° 15' E
BC	S 80° 45' W	N 79° 30' E
CD	N 19° 30' E	S 20° 0' W
DA	S 80° 0' E	N 80° 0' W

Local attraction at station D was known to be 1° E. Calculate the corrected bearings of all the lines and tabulate the same in usual form. State the amount of local attraction at stations A, B and C.   **(P.U. May 2000)**

Solution : This is an example on Reduced Bearings. (See Fig. 3.32)

The local attraction at station D is given. Hence to obtain corrected reduced bearings, the following rule should be followed.

Rule : "Corrections are positive when bearings are measured in clockwise sense and corrections are negative when bearings are taken in anticlockwise sense".

Although the F.B. and B.B. of DA differ by 180° but the numerical values of F.B. and B.B. of DA will be changed due to local attraction at station D.

Since the line DA is in IInd quadrant, the sense of measurement is anticlockwise. Hence,

       Corrected F.B. of DA will be 80° 0' – 1° = S 79° 0' E.

∴   Corrected B.B. of DA will be N 79° 0' W.

Similarly, F.B. of AB will be 40° 30' + 1° = S 41° 30' W.

Figure for the problem :

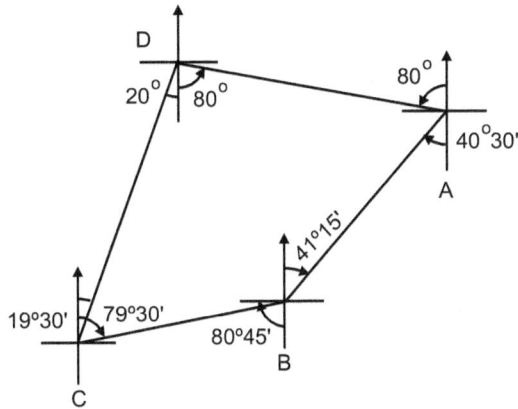

Fig. 3.32 : Traverse ABCDA

Since, the line AB lies in IIIrd quadrant and the sense of measurement is clockwise.
∴ Corrected B.B. of AB = N 41° 30' E. Now observed B.B. of AB is N 41° 15' E.

Thus station B is affected and L.A. at station B is 15' to E. Corrected F.B. of BC will be 80° 45' + 15' = S 81° 0' W (Since line BC lies in IIIrd quadrant and sense of measurement is positive).

Corrected B.B. of BC will be N 81° 0' E.

Now observed B.B. of BC is N 79° 30' E. i.e. station C is affected and L.A. at station C is 1° 30' to East.

∴ Corrected F.B. of CD will be 19° 30' + 1° 30' = N 21° 0' E. (Since line CD lies in 1st quadrant and sence of measurement is clockwise.)

Corrected B.B. of CD will be S 21° 0' W which tallies when correction for L.A. at station D will be applied to the observed B.B. of CD.

∴ Corrected B.B. of CD will be 20° 0' + 1° 0' = S 21° 0' W since sense of measurement is clockwise.

The corrected reduced bearings are tabulated as under.

Line	Corrected		Remarks
	F.B.	B.B.	L.A.
AB	S 41° 30' W	N 41° 30' E	1° to East at A
BC	S 81° 0' W	N 81° 0' E	1° to East at D
CD	N 21° 0' E	S 21° 0' W	15' to East at B
DA	S 79° 0' E	N 79° 0' W	1° 30' to East at C

FUNDAMENTALS OF CIVIL ENGINEERING ANGULAR MEASUREMENTS

Example 3.16 : The following bearings were observed where local attraction was suspected. Calculate the correct bearings.   **(P.U. May 2002)**

Line	Fore bearing	Back bearing
AB	S 40° 30' W	N 41° 15' E
BC	S 80° 45' W	N 79° 30' E
CD	N 19° 30' E	S 20° 00' W
DA	S 80° 00' E	N 80° 00' W

Solution : On examination of Reduced Bearings, it is observed that there is no local attraction at stations D and A since the Reduced Fore and Back Bearings of DA are same but with opposite directional signs.

∴ Observed F.B. of AB must be correct = S 40° 30' W.

Corrected B.B. of AB will be N 40° 30' E but

The observed B.B. of AB = N 41° 15' E.

∴ Local attraction at station B = 41° 15'– 40° 30' = 45' to West.

Now, corrected F.B. of BC will be 80° 45' – 45' = S 80° 0' W.

∴ Corrected B.B. of BC will be N 80° 0' E.

However, observed B.B. of BC is N 79° 30' E.

∴ Local attraction at station C = 80° 0' – 79° 30' = 0° 30' to East.

Corrected F.B. of CD will be 19° 30' + 00° 30' = N 20° 0' E.

Now, corrected B.B. of CD should be S 20° 0' W, which tallies with the observed B.B. of CD.

The corrected bearings are tabulated below :

Line	Corrected F.B.	Corrected B.B.	Remarks
AB	S 40° 30' W	N 40° 30' E	L.A. at station B 45' to West
BC	S 80° 00' W	N 80° 0' E	
CD	N 20° 0' E	S 20° 0' W	L.A. at station C 30' to East
DA	S 80° 0' E	N 80° 0' W	No L.A. at D and A

Example 3.17 : Find F.B. and B.B. of all lines of a regular pentagon ABCDEA run in clockwise direction where local attraction is not suspected. F.B. of line CD was observed to be 80° 45'. Tabulate your answer in the usual form. Draw sketch of traverse. **(P.U. Dec. 2003)**

Solution : Plot by F.B. of CD as shown.

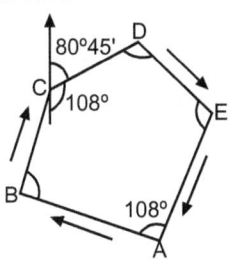

Fig. 3.33

Each angle of the pentagon is 108°.

∴   B.B. of BC = 80° 45' + 108'
             = 188° 45'
∴   F.B. of BC = 188° 45' – 180
             = 8° 45'
∴   B.B. of AB = 8° 45' + 108° = 116° 45'
∴   F.B. of AB = 116° 45' + 180° = 296° 45'
Now, B.B. of EA = 296° 45' – (360° – 108°) = 44° 45'
∴   F.B. of EA = 44° 45' + 180 = 224° 45'
∴   B.B. of DE = 224° 45' + 108° = 332° 45'
∴   F.B. of DE = 152° 45'
∴   B.B. of CD = 152° 45' + 108° = 260° 45'
∴   F.B. of CD = 260° 45' – 180° = 80° 45'

Hence, check O.K. and tabulate.

Lines	F B	B B
AB	296° 45'	116° 45'
BC	8° 45'	188° 45'
CD	80° 45'	260° 45'
DE	152° 45'	332° 45'
EA	224° 45'	44° 45'

Example 3.18 : The following bearings were taken with a prismatic compass in a place where local attraction is suspected. Determine the stations affected by L.A. and correct the bearings for the same. Also find the included angles of the traverse and draw the sketch of the traverse. Tabulate your answers in the usual tabular form.   **(P.U. May 2004)**

Line	F B	B B
PQ	306° 00'	126° 00'
QR	247° 30'	69° 45'
RS	136° 45'	312° 00'
SP	19° 15'	201° 45'

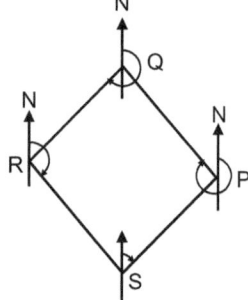

Fig. 3.34

Solution : The traverse is run anticlockwise as it can be seen from Fig. 3.34.

(I) To determine the stations affected by local attraction.

The difference between the B.B. and F.B. of PQ is exactly 180°. Therefore, stations P and Q are free from local attraction.

∴ F.B. of QR i.e. 247° 30' is correct.

The B.B. of QR will be (247° 30') – (180°) = 67° 30'.

As the observed B.B. of QR is 69° 45', the station R' is affected and L.A. at station R = –2° 15'.

The corrected F.B. of RS = 136° 45' – 2° 15' = 134° 30'
The corrected B.B. of RS = 134° 30' + 180° = 314° 30'

As the observed B.B. of RS is 312° 0', the station 'S' is affected.

L.A. at station S = 314° 30' – 312° 0' = + 2° 30'
The corrected F.B. of SP = 19°15' + L.A. at station S
Corrected F.B. of SP = 19° 15' + 2° 30' = 21° 45'

B.B. of SP should be 21° 45' + 180° = 201° 45'. This tallies with observed B.B. of SP.

The observed and corrected F.B. and B.B. are tabulated as under :

Line	Observed F.B.	Observed B.B.	Corrected F.B.	Corrected B.B.	Remark
PQ	306° 00'	126° 00'	306° 00'	126° 00'	L.A. at
QR	247° 30'	69° 45'	247° 30'	67° 30'	Stn. R = –2° 15
RS	136° 45'	312° 00'	134° 30'	314° 30'	L.A. at
SP	19° 15'	201° 45'	21° 45'	201° 45'	Stn. S = +2° 30'

FUNDAMENTALS OF CIVIL ENGINEERING — ANGULAR MEASUREMENTS

(II) To find the included angles :

$$\angle P = \text{F.B. of PQ} - \text{B.B. of SP}$$
$$= 306° \, 00' - 201° \, 45' = 104° \, 15'$$

$$\angle Q = \text{F.B. of QR} - \text{B.B. of PQ}$$
$$= 247° \, 30' - 126° \, 00' = 121° \, 30'$$

$$\angle R = \text{F.B. of RS} - \text{B.B. of QR}$$
$$= 134° \, 30' - 67° \, 30' = 67° \, 00'$$

$$\angle S = \text{F.B. of SP} - \text{B.B. of RS}$$
$$= 21° \, 45' - 314° \, 30' = -292° \, 45'$$

The negative sign indicates that it is an exterior angle.

$$\therefore \quad \angle S = 360° - 292° \, 45' = 67° \, 15'$$

Check for sum of included angles :

$$\angle P + \angle Q + \angle R + \angle S = 104° \, 15' + 121° \, 30' + 67° \, 00' + 67° \, 15' = 360°$$

Example 3.19 : For a closed compass traverse ABCDA, observed fore bearings of lines AB, BC, CD and DA are 93° 00', 37° 30', 260° 00' and 160° 00' respectively. While back bearings of these lines are 268° 00', 220° 00', 80° 00' and 342° 30' respectively. Draw the sketch of the traverse and find interior angles. If required, find corrected bearings of lines and tabulate the answer. **(P.U. May 2006)**

Solution : The figure of the traverse will be as under :

Line	F.B.	B.B.
AB	93° 00'	268° 00'
BC	37° 30'	220° 00'
CD	260° 00'	80° 00'
DA	160° 00'	342° 30'

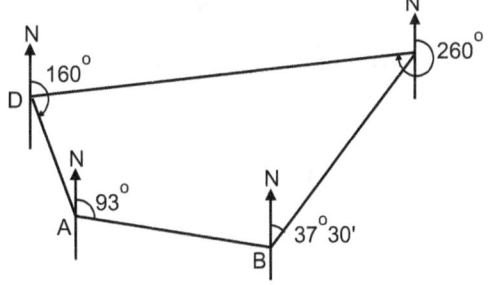

Fig. 3.35

(I) To find the interior angles :

$$\angle D = \text{F.B. of DA} - \text{B.B. of CD}$$
$$= 160° \, 00' - 80° \, 00' = 80° \, 00'$$
$$\angle A = \text{F.B. of AB} - \text{B.B. of DA}$$
$$= 93° - 342° \, 30' = -249° \, 30'$$

The negative sign indicates exterior angle.

$$\therefore \quad \text{Included } \angle A = 360° - 249° \, 30' = 110° \, 30'$$
$$\angle B = \text{F.B. of BC} - \text{B.B. of AB}$$
$$= 37° \, 30' - 268° \, 00' = -230° \, 30'$$

The negative sign indicates that it is an exterior angle.

$$\therefore \quad \text{Included } \angle B = 360° - 230° \, 30' = 129° \, 30'$$
$$\angle C = \text{F.B. of CD} - \text{B.B. of BC}$$
$$= 260° \, 00' - 220° \, 00' = 40° \, 0'$$
$$\therefore \quad \angle A + \angle B + \angle C + \angle D = 110° \, 30' + 129° \, 30' + 40° \, 0' + 80° \, 0'$$
$$= 360° \, 00'$$

The F.B. and B.B. of the lines AB, BC and DA do not differ by 180° but the difference between F.B. and B.B. of CD is 180°. Hence, stations C and D are free from L.A.

F.B. of DA is correct.

$$\therefore \quad \text{B.B. of DA} = 160° \, 0' + 180° \, 0'$$
$$= 340° \, 0'$$

Station A is affected.

$$\text{L.A. at A} = -2° \, 30'$$
$$\therefore \quad \text{Corrected F.B. of AB} = 93° \, 0' - 2° \, 30' = 90° \, 30'$$
$$\therefore \quad \text{Corrected B.B. of AB} = 90° \, 30' + 180° \, 0' = 270° \, 30'$$

Station B is affected.

$$\text{L.A. at B} = +2° \, 30'$$
$$\therefore \quad \text{Corrected F.B. of BC} = 37° \, 30' + 2° \, 30' = 40° \, 00'$$
$$\text{B.B. of BC} = 40° + 180° \, 00' = 220° \, 00' \text{ which tallies with the observed B.B. of BC.}$$

The observed and corrected bearings are tabulated as under :

Line	Observed		Corrected		Remarks
	F.B.	B.B.	F.B.	B.B.	
AB	93° 00'	268° 00'	90° 30'	270° 30'	L.A. at
BC	37° 30'	220° 00'	40° 00'	220° 0'	A = − 2° 30'
CD	260° 00'	80° 00'	260°	80° 0'	B = +2° 30'
DA	160° 00'	342° 30'	160° 00'	340° 00'	

3.13 MAGNETIC DECLINATION

The magnetic meridian at a place does not coincide with the true meridian at that place except in certain places. The horizontal angle made by the magnetic meridian with the true meridian at a place is called magnetic declination at that place. The magnetic meridian may be deflected to the east of True meridian while in other cases the magnetic meridian may be deflected to the west of True meridian.

The declination is different at different places as the magnetic meridian varies from place to place on the surface of earth. To determine declination at a place, astronomical observations are taken to find the true bearing of a line and then the magnetic bearing of the same line is observed. The difference between the true bearing and magnetic bearing of that line will give the magnetic declination at that place. Due to variation in declination, it is beneficial to note the magnitude of declination and the date of survey in order that changes in positions of survey lines can be obtained at a later date.

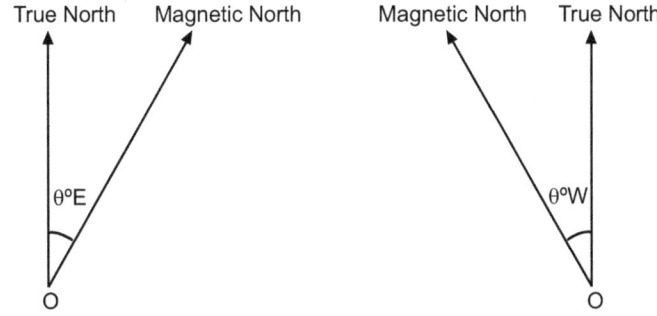

Fig. 3.36

The true bearings of the lines can be obtained from the following rule.

True bearing of a line = Magnetic bearing of a line ± Magnetic declination

Use positive sign if declination is towards east. Use negative sign if declination is towards west. From the above rule, if true bearing of a line and magnetic declination are known, the magnetic bearing of that line can be obtained. After knowing about magnetic declination, it will be interesting to note about the lines showing Magnetic Declination at different places.

(a) Isogonic lines : These are the lines obtained by joining points at which magnetic declination is same at a given time.

(b) Agonic lines : These are the lines obtained by connecting points at which the magnetic declination is zero. Isogonic lines and Agonic lines are represented on charts called as **'Isogonic Charts'** published by the Survey of India.

3.14 DIP OF THE NEEDLE

Due to the magnetic influence of earth, the needle after magnetisation will not remain in horizontal position. But it will be inclined towards the pole. This deflection of the needle with the horizontal is called as the Dip of the needle. The dip is not constant but varies from place to place on the surface of earth. It will be zero degrees at the equator and increases towards the poles. In order to make the needle perfectly horizontal i.e. to nullify the effect of dip of needle, a sliding weight or an aluminium coil is placed on the higher side of the needle.

Example 3.20 : The magnetic bearing of a line PQ is 165° 15'. If the magnetic declination is 4° 30' E, find its true bearing.

Solution : The magnetic meridian is 4° 30' to the East of True meridian referring to Fig. 3.37.

∴ True bearing of PQ = magnetic bearing of PQ + declination

= 165° 15' + 4° 30' = 169° 45'

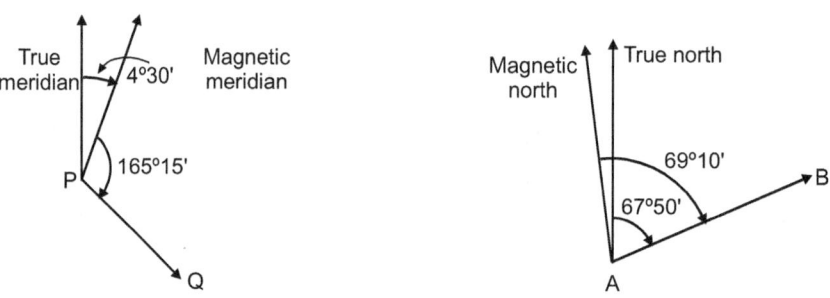

Fig. 3.37 : Deflection of needle to East of True North   Fig. 3.38 : Deflection of needle to West of True North

Example 3.21 : Fill in the blanks at the appropriate places.

Line	True Bearing	Magnetic Bearing	Declination
AB	67° 50'	69° 10'	–
CD	215° 20'	212° 50'	–
EF	–	87° 40'	at E, 2° 20' West
GH	–	174° 35'	at G, 3° 15' East

Solution : Knowing the relation between true bearing, magnetic bearing and declination, the table can be completed as under (see Fig. 3.36)

Line	True Bearing	Magnetic Bearing	Declination
AB	67° 50'	69° 10'	1° 20' West
CD	215° 20'	212° 50'	2° 30' East
EF	85° 20'	87° 40'	at E, 2° 20' West
GH	177° 50'	174° 35'	at G, 3° 15' East

Example 3.22 : If the magnetic bearing of the sun at noon is (a) 183° 30', (b) 357° 40', find the magnetic declination.

Solution : (a) The sun is exactly on the geographical meridian at noon. The magnetic bearing of the sun being 183° 30', it is at the south pole. Hence the magnetic bearing of North pole will be 3° 30'.

Therefore, the magnetic meridian is 3° 30' to the west of the true meridian.

    Magnetic declination = 3° 30' West

(b) The magnetic bearing of the sun at noon is 357° 40'. Therefore the magnetic bearing of the North pole is 357° 40'. The true bearing of the sun is 360° when it is at North pole.

∴   Magnetic declination = 360° – 357° 40' = 2° 20' E

∴ Magnetic declination is 2° 20' E.

Example 3.23 : The following bearings were observed in running a compass traverse in clockwise direction.

Line	Fore Bearing	Back Bearing
AB	52° 30'	229° 30'
BC	127° 15'	309° 15'
CD	186° 00'	6° 00'
DA	295° 00'	116° 00'

Correct the bearings for local attraction and find the true bearings of the lines of traverse if the magnetic declination is 4° 30' W.

Solution : On examining the bearings of lines, it is observed that the line CD is unaffected. It means that stations C and D are free from local attraction. The corrected bearings of other lines are found out as usual and tabulated as under.

Line	Observed		Corrected for L.A.	Corrected	
	F.B.	B.B.		F.B.	B.B.
AB	52° 30'	229° 30'	+ 2° at B	51° 30'	231° 30'
BC	127° 15'	309° 15'		129° 15'	309° 15'
CD	186° 00'	6° 00'		186° 00'	6° 00'
DA	295° 00'	116° 00'	– 1° at A	295° 00'	115° 00'

Now the magnetic declination is given as 4° 30' W. Hence true bearings of all lines will be obtained by subtracting 4° 30' from the corrected bearings of the lines. The true bearings are tabulated as under.

Line	Observed		Magnetic Declination	True Bearings	
	F.B.	B.B.		F.B.	B.B.
AB	51° 30'	231° 30'		47° 00'	227° 00'
BC	129° 15'	309° 15'	4° 30'W	124° 45'	304° 45'
CD	186° 00'	6° 00'		181° 30'	1° 30'
DA	295° 00'	115° 00'		290° 30'	110° 30'

EXERCISE

1. Draw a sectional elevation of a prismatic compass and name all the parts.
2. Differentiate between the following :
   (a) Quadrantal bearing and whole circle bearing.
   (b) Fore bearing and Back bearing.
   (c) Magnetic meridian and True meridian.
3. Explain the temporary adjustments of a prismatic compass.
4. Which compass is used to obtain the Reduced bearings of lines ? Sketch the graduations of dial.
5. (a) Explain how the bearing of a line is measured using prismatic compass.
   (b) Why zero is marked at the south end ?

FUNDAMENTALS OF CIVIL ENGINEERING   ANGULAR MEASUREMENTS

6. (a) Differentiate between a closed traverse and an open traverse.
   (b) List the equipments required for carrying out a chain and compass survey.
7. Convert the following whole circle bearings to reduced bearings :
   (i) 142° 30', (ii) 237°45', (iii) 74° 15', (iv) 304°20', (v) 114º 30'
8. Convert the following reduced bearings to whole circle bearings.
   (i) S 24° 15' E, (ii) N 64° 30' E, (iii) N 55° W, (iv) S 70° 40' W, (v) S 71° 45' E
9. Write a note on local attraction.
10. Calculate the included angle between the following lines from the given data.
    (a) BA – F.B. 34° 30', BC - F.B. 142° 15'
    (b) QP-F.B. 77°15', QR – F.B. 112° 30'
    (c) OA - N 48° 30' E, OB – S 67° 15' E.
    (d) Calculate the ∠ ABC if fore bearing of AB is 75° 30'.
11. Following observations were recorded in running a closed compass traverse.

Line	Fore Bearing	Back Bearing
AB	120° – 30'	300° – 30'
BC	240° – 30'	62° – 0'
CA	32° – 0'	210° – 30'

Mention the stations affected by local attraction. Workout the corrected bearings of all lines and tabulate your results. Calculate included angles.

12. Calculate the included angles of the traverse ABCD and apply the usual check from the following observations.

Line	Fore Bearing	Back Bearing
AB	50° 30'	232° 30'
BC	130°	307° 15'
CD	187° 0'	7° 45'
DA	295° 30'	115° 30'

Ans. ∠ A = 65° 0', ∠ B = 102° 30', ∠ C = 120° 15' and ∠ D = 72° 15'

13. In a closed clockwise compass traverse ABCD, no station was affected by local attraction. Fore bearing of line DA was observed to be 120°, and ∠ A = ∠ C = 60° – 30' and ∠ B = ∠ D = 119° – 30'. Draw rough sketch of the traverse and find fore and back bearings of all lines. Enter the readings in usual tabular form.

(**Ans.** F.B. of AB = 239° 30', F.B. of BC = 300° 0', F.B. of CD = 239° 30')

Ch. 3 | 3.39

14. A square ABCD was surveyed from starting station A, in a counterclockwise direction. The fore bearing of AB was observed as 100° 30'. Find out the bearings of the other sides of traverse.

    Ans. Fore Bearing : BC = 10° 30', CD = 280° 30', DA = 190° 30'

15. Following bearings were recorded while carrying out a closed compass traverse.

Line	Observed Bearing	
	Fore Bearing	Back Bearing
PQ	53° 00'	230° 00'
QR	135° 00'	315° 00'
RS	240° 00'	58° 00'
SP	298° 00'	123° 00'

    (i) Draw a neat sketch of the traverse.

    (ii) Correct the bearings affected by L.A.

    (iii) Calculate the included angles and check for their sum.

    Ans. (ii) Corrected Fore Bearings : PQ = 50°, QR = 135°, RS = 240° and SP = 300°.

    L.A. at station P = – 3°, L.A. at station S = + 2°

    (iii) ∠ P = 70°, ∠ Q = 95°, ∠ R = 75° and ∠ S = 120°

16. (a) What do you understand by the term 'Magnetic declination' ?

    (b) Describe in brief the variations of Magnetic declination.

17. The following bearings were observed in a compass traverse.

Line	Fore Bearing	Back Bearing
PQ	66° 15'	244° 00'
QR	129° 45'	313° 00'
RS	218° 30'	37° 30'
SP	306° 45'	126° 45'

    (a) Find the corrected fore and back bearings.

    (b) Calculate the interior angles of the figure.

    (c) Apply check.

    (d) Calculate the true bearings of the lines if the magnetic declination is 2° 40' East.

Ans. (a) Corrected F.B. : PQ = 66° 15', QR = 132° 00',

RS = 217° 30', SP = 306° 45', L.A. at stn. Q = + 2° 15', L.A. at stn. R = – 1°.

(b) Interior angles – ∠ P = 60° 30', ∠ Q = 114° 15', ∠ R = 94° 30' and ∠ S = 90° 45.

(c) Sum of internal angles = 360°.

(d) True F. Bearings of lines : PQ = 68° 55', QR = 134° 40'

RS = 220° 10' and SP = 309° 25'.

18. Write a note on "Dip of magnetic needle".

19. The following table gives the fore and back bearings of the sides of a closed traverse.

Line	Fore Bearing	Back Bearing
AB	N 55° E	S 54° W
BC	S 67° 30' E	N 66° 00' W
CD	S 25° 00' W	N 25° 00' E
DE	S 77° 00' W	N 75° 30' E
EA	N 64° 30' W	S 63° 30' E

Find the corrected Quadrantal Fore and Back bearings of lines.

Ans. Corrected F.B. of AB = N 55° 30' E,

BC = S 66° 00' E, CD = S 25° 00' W, DE = S 77° 00' W, EA = N 63° 00' W

L.A. at stn. B = + 1° 30', L.A. at stn. A = + 30'

L.A. at stn. E = + 1° 30'.

20. In an anticlockwise traverse ABCA, all the sides were equal. Magnetic fore bearing of line BC was found to be 15° 30'. The bearing of the sun was observed to be 356° 30' at local noon with prismatic compass. Calculate the magnetic bearing and true bearings of all the sides of the traverse. Tabulate the results and sketch a traverse.

Ans.

Line	Fore Bearing	True Fore Bearing
AB	135° – 30'	139° – 0'
BC	15° – 30'	19° – 0'
CA	255° – 30'	259° – 0'

FUNDAMENTALS OF CIVIL ENGINEERING   ANGULAR MEASUREMENTS

UNIVERSITY QUESTIONS

1. Write in a tabular form, how will you convert Q.B. (or R.B.) system into W.C.B. system. **(Dec. 04, 05; May 05)**
2. What do you understand by magnetic declination ? **(Dec. 05)**
3. Define the following with the help of sketches.
   (i) Q.B. **(Dec. 05)**
   (ii) W.C.B. **(Dec. 05)**
4. What is local attraction ? How it can be detected ? **(Dec. 03; May 05)**
5. Differentiate between the following :
   (i) Magnetic bearing and True bearings. **(May 05)**
   (ii) Dip and Declination.
   (iii) Surveyor's compass and Prismatic compass. **(Dec. 04)**
6. Draw sketches to understand the following terms :
   (i) Magnetic bearing of a line. **(Dec. 05)**
   (ii) F.B. and B.B. of a line. **(Dec. 04, 05; May 05)**
   (iii) Magnetic declination. **(Dec. 03, 04)**
7. State the uses of following parts of prismatic compass. **(Dec. 04)**
   (i) Sun glasses.
   (ii) Glass prism.
   (iii) Aluminium ring.
8. Differentiate between the following :
   (i) W.C.B. and R.B. **(May 04)**
9. State the functions of following parts of the prismatic compass. **(May 04)**
   (i) Pivot.
   (ii) Lifting lever.
   (iii) Brake pin.
   (iv) Reflecting mirror.
10. Define various types of meridians with the aid of sketches. **(Dec. 03)**

❐❐❐

UNIT II

Chapter 4
VERTICAL MEASUREMENTS

4.1 INTRODUCTION

Vertical measurements are those measurements which are made in the vertical plane and are grouped under the term 'Levelling'. **Thus Levelling is carried out to determine either the relative heights of points in the vertical plane or to determine elevations of points on the surface of the earth.** The elevations are determined with respect to some reference line called Datum Line. Determination of elevations of points becomes necessary in selecting alignments of highways, railways, water supply and drainage pipelines and in the construction of engineering structures, such as dams, bridges, industrial sheds, etc. Determination of ground levels also helps in locating industrial sheds or different shops of an automobile or chemical industry on a large piece of land. From the ground levels, the undulations of ground could be known by drawing contours. The profile of ground can be plotted in the form of longitudinal and cross-sections from the spot levels. This data can be used to calculate the magnitude of cutting, filling of earthwork involved in the project.

4.2 DEFINITIONS

1. **Level Surface :** A surface which is parallel to the mean spheroidal surface of the earth is called level surface. It is normal to the plumb line at all points.

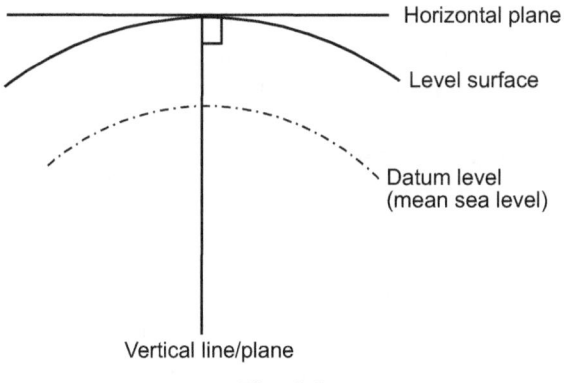

Fig. 4.1

FUNDAMENTALS OF CIVIL ENGINEERING — VERTICAL MEASUREMENTS

2. **Level Line :** A line lying in a level surface is called a level line. It is normal to the plumb line at all points.

3. **Horizontal Plane :** It is a plane through a point which is tangential to the level surface at that point. A horizontal line is a line lying in the horizontal plane.

4. **Datum Surface :** It is an arbitrarily assumed level surface from which vertical distances are measured. The mean sea level at Karachi is taken as the datum surface or datum level from which G.T.S. bench marks are established.

5. **Vertical Line :** It is a line drawn through a point such that it is normal to the level surface. A plane containing a vertical line is a vertical plane.

6. **Reduced Level (R.L.) :** It is the vertical distance of a point measured above or below the datum. It is also called as Elevation of a point. It is abbreviated as R.L.

7. **Bench Mark (B.M.) :** It is a fixed reference point of known elevation. Levelling work is started from the bench mark.

The following terms are used in conjunction with the levelling operation carried out by a levelling instrument called Dumpy level and height measuring device called a levelling staff.

8. **Back Sight (B. S.) Reading :** It is the first staff reading taken on a point of known elevation i.e. bench mark or change point after the level is set up and levelled. It is also called a plus sight since this reading is added to the Reduced Level of the bench mark.

9. **Foresight (F. S.) Reading :** It is a staff reading taken on a point whose Reduced Level is to be determined as in the case of a change point. It is the last reading taken before shifting of the level. It is also called as a minus sight since this reading is subtracted from the reduced level of collimation plane to get the R.L. of the point.

10. **Intermediate Sight (I. S.) Reading :** It is a staff reading taken on a point whose elevation is to be determined from the same set up of level. All readings between backsight and foresight readings are the Intermediate sight readings.

11. **Height of Instrument (H.I.) :** It is the Reduced Level of the plane of collimation, when the instrument is correctly levelled. The Reduced Level or Height of Instrument is obtained by adding Backsight reading to the reduced level of Bench Mark.

12. **Change Point (C.P.) :** It is a point on which foresight and backsight readings are taken. Change point indicates the shifting of the level. Any well defined object whose top surface is level such as boundary stone, manhole cover, kilometer stone can be selected as change point. Sometimes it is also called as "Turning point" **(T.P.)**.

13. **Axis of Telescope :** It is a line joining the optical centre of the eyepiece and the objective.

14. **Vertical Axis :** It is the axis about which the telescope can be rotated in a horizontal plane.

15. **Line of Collimation :** It is a line joining the intersection of the cross hairs of diaphragm to the optical centre of the object glass and its continuation.

16. **Axis of Level Tube :** It is an imaginary line which is tangential to the longitudinal curvature of the bubble tube at its midpoint.

(See Fig. 4.7 for fundamental lines of dumpy level i.e. 13, 14, 15 and 16 defined above).

4.3 TYPES OF BENCH MARKS

There are four types of bench marks in a levelling work.

1. **Great Trigonometrical Survey Bench Marks (G.T.S. B.M.) :**

These bench marks are established throughout the country with high precision by the Government Agency such as Survey of India Department. Their location and reduced levels are shown on the G.T.S. maps published by Survey of India Department elaborate.

2. **Permanent Bench Mark (P.B.M.) :**

These permanent reference points are established between the G.T.S. bench marks on the well defined and permanent objects such as top of parapet of a culvert or a bridge, plinth of some prominent building, etc. by State Government Agency. Its exact location and Reduced level is marked on the top of permanent object.

3. **Arbitrary Bench Mark (A.B.M.) :**

When levelling work is restricted to a small area, any prominent object such as step, plinth of a building is chosen as a bench mark and its elevation is arbitrarily assumed and then this is known as Arbitrary B.M.

4. **Temporary Bench Mark (T.B.M.) :**

When the levelling work cannot be finished in a day, certain prominent and permanent objects are chosen on which the levelling is ended at the end of day's work. These serve as the temporary bench marks from which levelling work is started on the next day. These objects which serve as the reference points should be easily identifiable.

4.4 EQUIPMENTS FOR LEVELLING

Instruments required for levelling are :

1. A level, 2. A levelling staff.

- **Level** is an instrument used to obtain horizontal line of sight while observing the readings on levelling staff.
- **Levelling Staff** is used to measure the vertical distances of points below or above the horizontal line of sight.

Types of Levels :

(1) Dumpy level, (2) Modern tilting level, (3) Automatic level.

Only Dumpy level is described in detail.

4.5 DUMPY LEVEL

The dumpy level is commonly used for levelling work because it is compact and stable type of instrument. The dumpy level or in general a level consists of the following parts :

1. **A Levelling Head :** To bring the bubble in the centre of its run.
2. **The Limb :** Body of the instrument to support the telescope.
3. **Telescope :** To provide the line of sight.
4. **Level Tube :** To make the line of sight horizontal.
5. **A tripod :** To support the level.

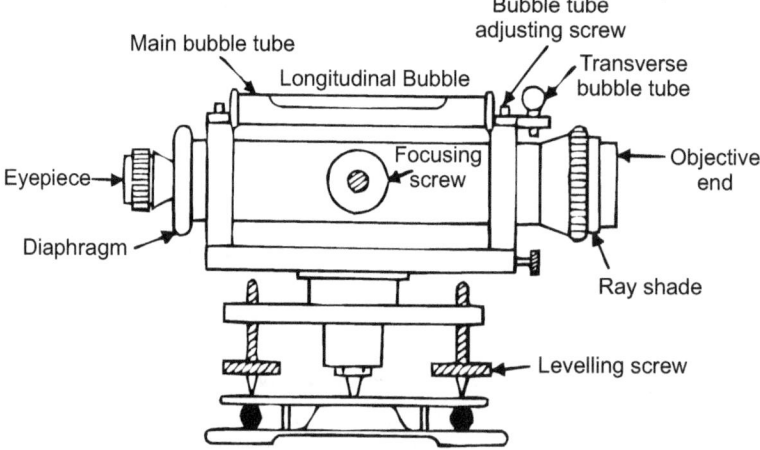

Fig. 4.2 : Dumpy level and its parts

As shown in Fig. 4.2, the dumpy level has a telescope rigidly fixed to its supports and a long bubble tube called Main Bubble Tube attached to the top of the telescope. The axis of the telescope is perpendicular to the vertical axis. The telescope consists of object glass, eyepiece and a diaphragm consisting of a circular ring with cross-wires. A ray shade is provided as a protection to object glass. The levelling head usually consists of two parallel plates with three foot screws, levelling of the instrument can be done by means of these foot screws. In some instruments, a clamp screw is provided to arrest the motion of the spindle about the vertical axis. Also a slow motion screw or a tangent screw is provided for small movement of telescope. A cross bubble tube is also provided perpendicular to the main bubble tube. The telescope has a magnifying power of about thirty diameters. In certain instruments, a compass is provided on the bottom side of telescope to observe bearings of lines. The focussing screw is used to bring the image of the object into the plane of the cross-hairs of the diaphragm. The eyepiece can be rotated in its socket to make the cross-hairs of the diaphragm distinct and clear. The dumpy level has the following advantages :

1. It is stable and compact type of instrument.
2. It is simple in construction with very few movable parts.
3. The adjustments are not easily disturbed.

4.6 LEVELLING STAFF

The levelling staff is a device which enables the surveyor to measure the vertical distance by which the staff station i.e. the foot of the staff is above or below the horizontal line of sight. A levelling staff is a straight rectangular piece of wood or aluminium about 75 mm wide and 25 mm thick. The foot of the staff represents zero reading since graduations are marked from the foot of the staff upwards. A self reading staff is one the reading on which can be directly read by the instrument man sighting through the telescope. In modern levels, the erect image of the staff is seen through the telescope. Hence reading the staff is very easy and convenient.

1. Telescopic Staff (Sopwith pattern) : The telescopic staffs may be made of seasoned timber or aluminium. However, the aluminium staffs are in common use now. It is usually 4 metre long and made in three telescopic lengths. The top solid piece about 1.2 m long slides into the central box of about 1.3 m length. The lower base of 1.5 m length receives the central box. Fig. 4.3 shows a sopwith pattern staff arranged in three lengths.

The inner pieces can be pulled out one after the another and kept in position by metal spring clamps at the back of each piece. On the front face decimetre, markings are neatly painted in black against a white background. The red dot indicates completed metre marking. The least count of the staff is 5 mm. One tenth of a metre is subdivided into twenty equal parts.

FUNDAMENTALS OF CIVIL ENGINEERING   VERTICAL MEASUREMENTS

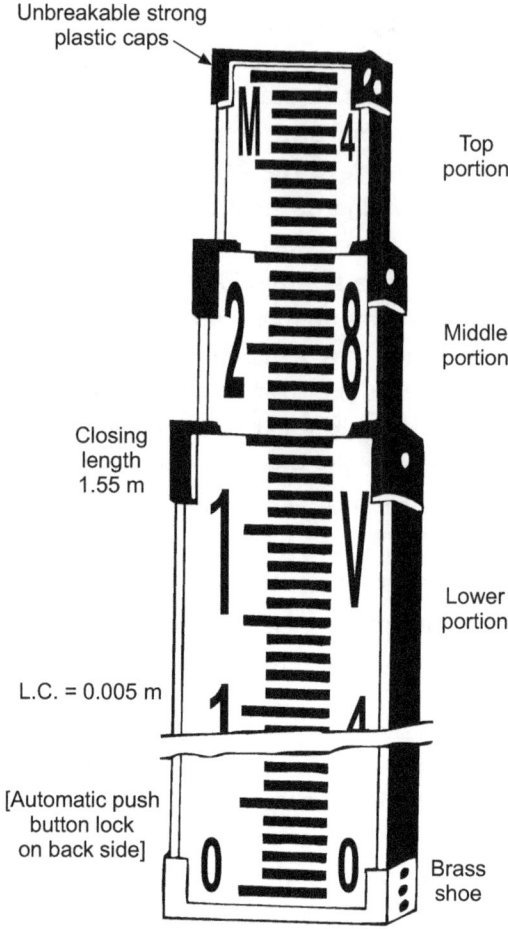

Fig. 4.3 : Telescopic staff

2. Folding Staff : The staff is 4 metre long and consists of two 2 metre wooden pieces with hinged joint in the centre. The width is 75 mm and thickness is about 18 mm. The folding joint has a locking device at the back. When the two pieces are locked together, the two pieces become rigid and straight. The foot of the staff is protected by a brass cap at the bottom. To keep the staff vertical, a circular bubble is fitted at the back. Each metre is subdivided into 200 divisions, the thickness of the graduation being 5 mm. The metre numeral is painted in red and the decimetre numeral is painted in black colour. The decimetre numerals are marked continuously throughout the staff for folding staff.

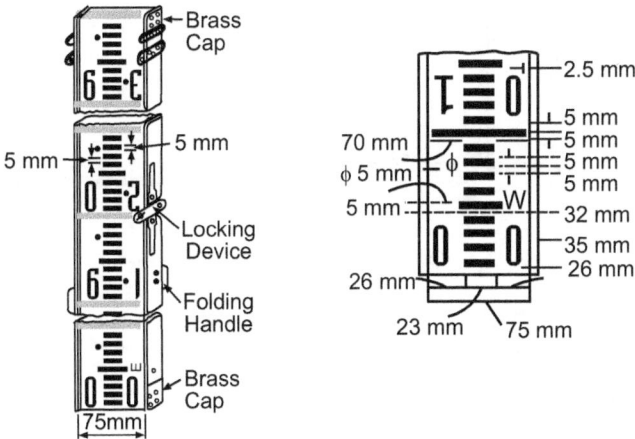

Fig. 4.4 : Folding staff

4.7 TELESCOPE OF DUMPY LEVEL

There are two types of telescope used in the levelling instruments :

1. External focussing type.   2. Internal focussing type.

The telescope consists of the following parts.

(a) Objective or object glass, (b) Body, (c) The eyepiece, (d) Diaphragm, (e) Diaphragm screws to support the diaphragm ring, (f) Ray shade, (g) Focussing screw.

The object glass forms a real inverted image infront of the eyepiece which magnifies the image to produce an inverted virtual image. The cross-hairs are placed infront of the eyepiece where the real inverted image is produced by the objective. However, in modern telescopes, the erect image of the levelling staff is obtained.

The modern levelling instruments are fitted with internal focussing telescope in which a double concave lense is provided along a slide and it is moved by a focussing screw. The internal parts are protected from dust and moisture because it is enclosed in casing. The disadvantage of the internal focussing telescope is the reduction in the brightness of image due to the additional concave lens.

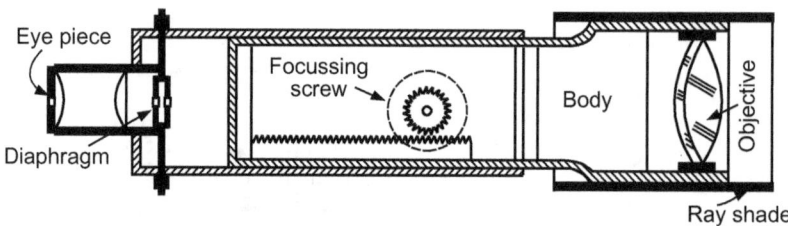

Fig. 4.5 : External Focussing Telescope

4.8 ADJUSTMENTS OF THE DUMPY LEVEL

There are two types of adjustments :

1. Temporary adjustments, 2. Permanent adjustments.

4.8.1 Temporary Adjustments

These adjustments are done at each set up of the level before taking the readings on the staff. These are done in following steps.

(a) Setting up, (b) Levelling up, (c) Focussing the eyepiece, (d) Focussing the object glass.

(a) Setting up : (i) The tripod legs are properly spread on the ground and the dumpy level is fixed to the tripod. If the tripod head is having a circular bubble, see that it is in the centre.

(ii) Leg adjustment : Bring all the foot screws to the centre of their run. Plant any two legs firmly in the ground and move the third leg sideways or radially till the main bubble and the cross bubble are approximately in the centre.

(b) Levelling : (Refer Fig. 4.6)

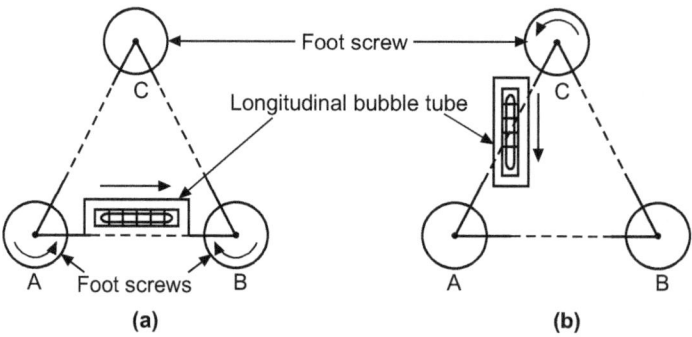

Fig. 4.6

(i) Keep the telescope parallel to any pair of foot screws i.e. say A and B and move the foot screws either inwards or outwards till the bubble comes to the centre.

(ii) Rotate the telescope clockwise through 90° so that it lies over the third foot screw. i.e. C turn this screw till the bubble comes to the centre.

(iii) Bring the level tube back to its original position without changing the positions of eyepiece and objective, check up the centering of bubble. Move the two foot-screws inwards or outward till the bubble traverses in the centre.

(iv) Turn the telescope clockwise through 90° and see whether the bubble remains in the centre.

(v) If not repeat these operations till the bubble remains in the centre in both the positions at right angles to each other.

(vi) Now turn the telescope through 180° and observe the bubble. If it does not remain in the centre, the instrument needs to be corrected for its permanent adjustment.

(c) Focussing the Eyepiece : Hold a piece of white paper infront of the eyepiece and observe the cross-hairs. If the cross-hairs are not clearly seen, move the eyepiece ring in or out till the cross-hairs are distinctly seen. While moving the eyepiece ring, see that the eyepiece does not come out from its socket.

(d) Focussing the object glass : Look through the eyepiece towards the staff and bring the image of the staff in the plane of cross-hairs by moving the focussing screw. Parallax is said to be eliminated when there is no change in the staff reading when the eye is moved up and down. After making the above adjustments, the instrument is ready for taking observations i.e. the line of collimation is horizontal.

4.8.2 Permanent Adjustments

The line of collimation, the axis of bubble tube and the vertical axis are the fundamental axes of the dumpy level which are defined earlier in section 4.2.

There is a fixed relation between these fundamental lines or axes of the dumpy level and it is as follows.

1. The line of collimation should be parallel to the axis of the bubble tube (See Fig. 4.7)
2. The axis of the bubble tube should be perpendicular to the vertical axis (See Fig. 4.7).

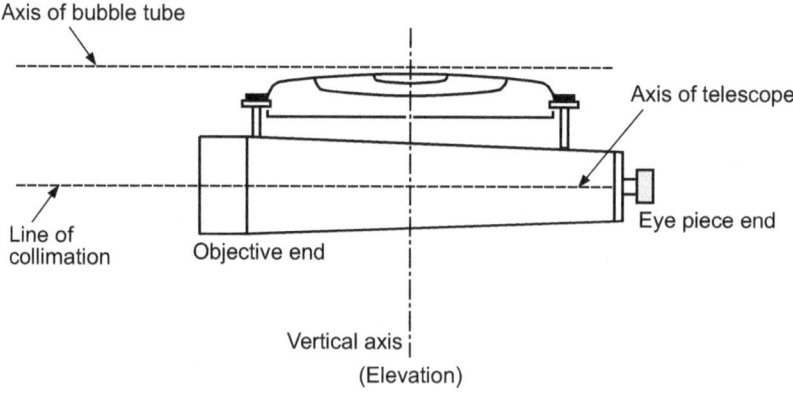

Fig. 4.7 : Relationship between the fundamental axes of Dumpy Level

Normally, these permanent adjustments are done by the manufacturer.

Levelling Procedure :

(a) Holding the Staff : While holding the staff, it should be held truly vertical when the reading is taken. The staffman stands behind the staff and holds it between the palms of his hands. From the figure it will be seen that when the staff is held exactly vertical, minimum reading is obtained. In precise levelling operations, the staff is provided with a circular bubble at the back to hold it in plumb. See Fig. 4.8.

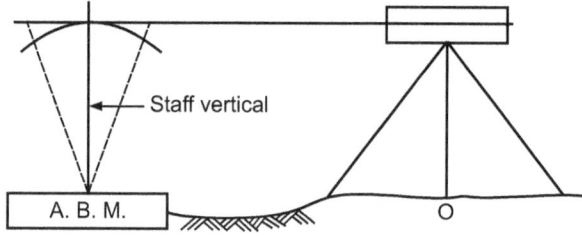

Fig. 4.8

(b) Reading the Staff : (1) After the temporary adjustments are done; the telescope is directed towards the staff and the staff is brought between the two vertical hairs of diaphragm by means of focussing screw.

(2) The reading is taken on the staff where the middle horizontal hair appears to cut the staff. First the red figures of metre are noted. Then the black figures of decimetres and

then the spaces from decimetre marking upto marking on staff where the middle horizontal hair (each of 5 mm thickness) cuts the staff are measured. The sum of all this is the total reading on the staff which is recorded in the field book.

4.9 PRINCIPLES OF LEVELLING

1. Simple Levelling :

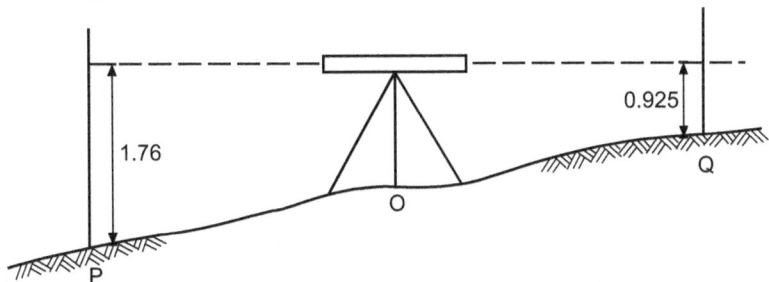

Fig. 4.9 : Simple Levelling

When it is desired to find the difference in elevation between two points which are visible from the same position of the instrument station, this method is adopted. It is called as simple levelling, as shown in Fig. 4.9. Let it be required to find the difference in elevation between points P and Q.

(a) Set up the level approximately midway between P and Q and carry out all the temporary adjustments.

(b) Seeing through the telescope, take the readings on the staff held at P and Q. The reading on the staff is taken at which the central horizontal hair appears to cut the staff. Let the reading at 'P' be 1.760 and that at 'Q' be 0.925.

(c) Let the reduced level of point P be 200.00 m. Then the reading on 'P' will be a backsight reading and the reading on Q will be a foresight reading.

∴ Height of Instrument at 'O' will be R.L. of P + B.S. reading = 200.00 + 1.760 = 201.760.

(d) R.L. of Q = Height of instrument – F.S. reading on Q = 201.760 – 0.925 = 200.835.

Looking to Fig. 4.9, it will be observed that when point P is lower than point Q, the reading on the staff at 'P' is more than the reading at 'Q', due to steepness of ground.

Change point : This is a point selected when shifting of the dumpy level becomes necessary because it becomes difficult to take reading on the levelling staff. This situation arises when the ground is very steep or levelling is to be carried out over large distances.

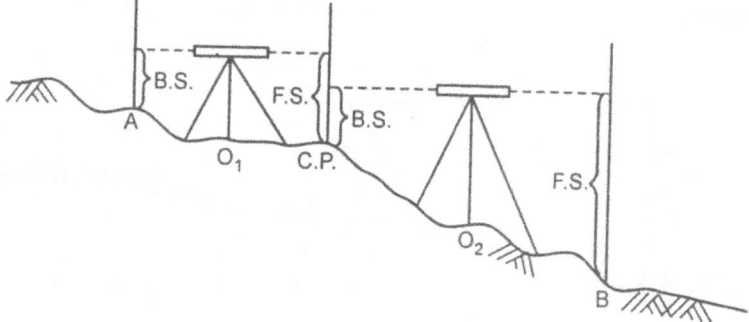

Fig. 4.10

Let us say that difference of elevation between stn. A and stn. B is to be found out. From the position of dumpy level at O_1, it is possible to note the reading on A but it is not possible to take reading on B due to steepness of ground. Hence a suitable point C.P. is selected such that is possible to read the staff from O_1 as well as from O_2 (new position of dumpy level) and also to take reading on stn. B. Thus change point becomes necessary. It should be noted that at C.P. two readings i.e. F.S. reading from previous set up of instrument i.e. O_1 and B.S. reading from new set up of instrument (i.e. O_2) are always taken.

2. Differential Levelling :

Differential levelling is adopted when it is required to find the difference in elevation between the two points spaced at a considerable distance apart. The method is also used when :

(i) The difference in elevation between the two points is much more.

(ii) There are some obstacles coming in the way.

In this case, it becomes necessary to shift the instrument at number of intermediate points and work in stages. Simple levelling is employed in each of the successive stages. This is also known as compound levelling.

As shown in Fig. 4.11, it is required to find the difference in elevation between the points A and B which are situated far apart.

FUNDAMENTALS OF CIVIL ENGINEERING   VERTICAL MEASUREMENTS

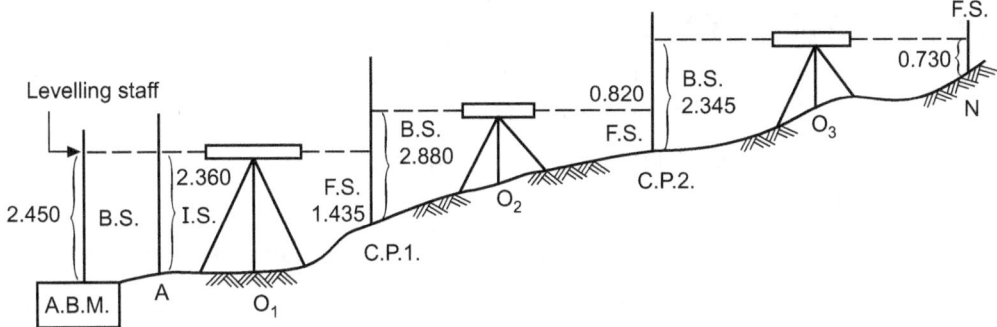

Fig. 4.11 : Differential levelling

The ground is continuously sloping and it is not possible to read the staff at 'B' from the position of dumpy level at 'O_1'. Hence intermediate points such as C.P.1 and C.P.2 are chosen which serve as change points for shifting the dumpy level and reaching nearer to the point B. **On the change point, two readings, foresight from previous set up of level and backsight reading from the new set up of dumpy level are taken** and the work is continued in stages. The levelling work is started from Arbitrary Bench Mark, on which backsight is taken. Then reading on the staff held at A is taken and recorded as intermediate sight reading. Then suitable change point C. P. 1 is chosen and foresight reading is taken on C.P.1 and the level is shifted to O_2 and all the temporary adjustments are done. Again backsight reading on C.P.1 is taken from instrument at 'O_2'. In the same way, second change point C.P. 2 is selected and foresight and backsight readings are taken at C.P. 2. The final reading of foresight is taken on 'B', from the position of instrument at 'O_3'. Then

R.L. of A = R.L. of ABM + B.S. – I.S. reading on A.

R.L. of B = R.L. of ABM + Σ B.S. – Σ F.S.

Thus the difference in elevation between A and B can be found out. The backsight and foresight distances should be kept approximately equal to eliminate the instrumental errors.

While **shifting the level to** a new position after selecting change point C.P.1. or C.P.2 following points should be seen.

(1) The level is planted on a firm ground and is able to cover large distances in the backward and forward directions.

(2) It is possible to take reading on the staff at C.P.1 or C.P.2 (in the backward direction) and the staff position in the forward direction.

(3) The reading is taken as the F.S. reading before shifting the level or stopping the levelling work.

FUNDAMENTALS OF CIVIL ENGINEERING — VERTICAL MEASUREMENTS

4.10 REDUCTION OF LEVELS

There are two methods of working out (calculation of) Reduced Levels or elevations of points from the staff readings observed in the field.

(a) Collimation plane or Height of Instrument method.

(b) Rise and fall method.

(a) Collimation Plane Method or Height of Instrument Method (H.I. Method) :

In this method, the Reduced level of the collimation plane is found out for each set up of dumpy level and then the reduced levels of other points are found out with respect to the respective plane of collimation. The procedure of finding Reduced levels is as given below :

1. First take a reading on bench mark and then find the R.L. of collimation plane by adding backsight reading to the R.L. of bench mark.

   Height of Instrument = R.L. of collimation plane

   = R.L. of bench mark + backsight reading.

2. Calculate the reduced levels of intermediate points or change point by subtracting the I.S. or F.S. readings from the R.L. of Collimation plane.

3. After the instrument is shifted and set up and levelled at new position, take a backsight reading on change point. Determine the R.L. of new collimation plane.

   R.L. of new collimation plane = R. L. of change point + B. S. Reading.

4. Obtain the Reduced levels of the remaining points from the R.L. of new collimation plane.

5. Repeat the procedure till all the levelling work is finished.

On completing the observations, arithmetical check is applied as given below :

Arithmetical check = Summation of Backsights – Summation of foresights

i.e. Σ B.S. – Σ F.S. = Last R.L. – First R.L.

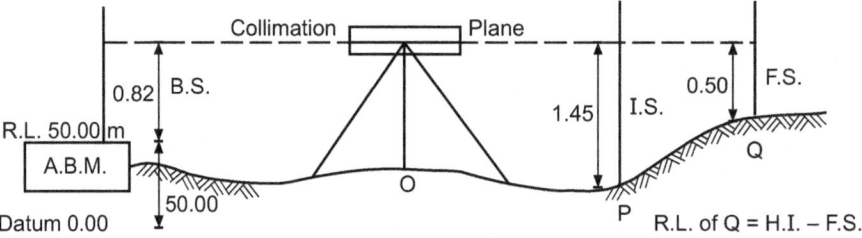

Fig. 4.12 : Sketch illustrating collimation plane or H.I. method

Sketch illustrates collimation plane or H.I. method.

Let the dumpy level be set up at O and all the temporary adjustments are done. The telescope will revolve in a horizontal plane and the readings taken on the staff will indicate the vertical distances measured in the downward direction from this horizontal plane. It is required to find the reduced levels of P and Q. Let the R.L. of Arbitrary Bench mark be 50,000 m. Before the levelling work is started, the observations are first taken on the bench mark. The first step will be to hold the staff on Arbitrary Bench Mark and take the backsight reading. Let the backsight reading be 0.82 m.

∴ Height of Instrument or R.L. of Collimation plane

= R.L. of A.B.M. + B.S. = 50.00 + 0.82 = 50.82 m.

In the second step, staff is held at P and Q and readings will be observed. Let the reading at P be 1.45 m and that at Q be 0.50 m.

R.L. of P = R.L. of collimation plane – I.S.

= 50.82 – 1.45 = 49.37 m

R.L. of Q = H. I. – F.S.

= 50.82 – 0.50 = 50.32 m

The readings will be tabulated as under in the page of a level book.

B.S.	I.S.	F.S.	R.L. of C.P. or H.I.	R.L. in m	Remark
0.820			50.820	50.000	A.B.M.
	1.450			49.370	P
		0.500		50.320	Q

∑ 0.820   0.500

Arithmetical check :

∑ B.S. – ∑ F.S. = 0.320   Last R.L. – First R.L. = 50.320 – 50,000 = 0.320.

FUNDAMENTALS OF CIVIL ENGINEERING   VERTICAL MEASUREMENTS

The following table shows the readings tabulated on the page of a Level Book by H.I. Method (See Fig. 4.12)

Station	B.S.	I.S.	F.S.	H.I.	R. Levels in m	Remarks
	2.450			152.450	150.000	A.B.M.
A		2.360			150.090	
	2.880		1.435	153.895	151.015	C.P.1
	2.345		0.820	155.420	153.075	C.P.2
B			0.730		154.690	
	7.675		2.985	Last R.L.	154.690	
				Minus	–	
Arith. Check	∑ B.S. – ∑ F.S. =	+ 4.690		First R.L.	150.000 = + 4.690	

The check is correct.

(b) Rise and Fall Method :

In this method, the difference of elevation between two consecutive points is determined by comparing each point after the first with that immediately preceding it i.e. two consecutive staff readings. The R.L. of collimation plane is not found out. The difference of readings will indicate a rise or a fall depending on whether the staff reading at the point is smaller or greater than that at the preceding point. The reduced level of each point is then determined by adding the rise to or subtracting the fall from the reduced level of the preceding point. The arithmetical check in the reduction of levels is applied as follows :

Arithmetical Check : Sum of Backsights – Sum of Foresights =

Sum of all rises – Sum of all falls = Last R.L. – First R.L. i.e.

Σ B.S. – Σ F.S. = Σ Rises – Σ Falls = Last R.L. – First R.L.

Thus there is a check on the intermediate reduction of levels i.e. R.L. of intermediate points.

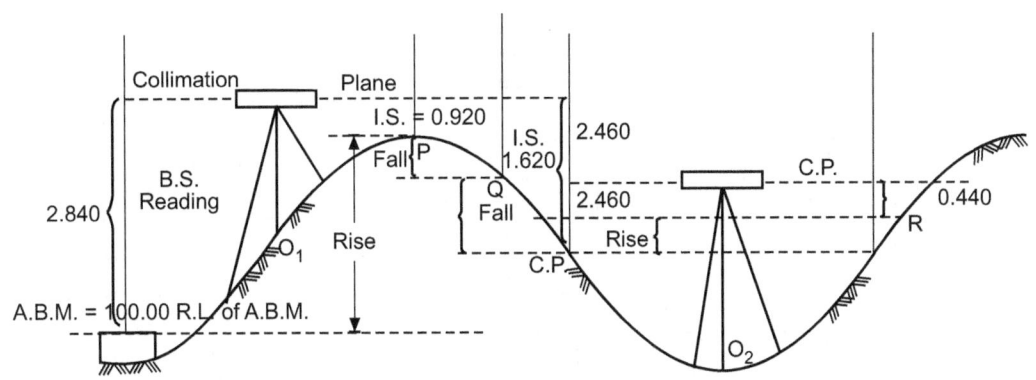

Fig. 4.13 : Illustrative sketch of Rise and Fall method

$$\begin{aligned}
\text{R.L. of P} &= \text{R.L. of A.B.M.} + \text{Rise between ABM and P} \\
&= \text{R.L. of ABM} + \text{B.S.} - \text{I.S.} \\
&= 100.00 + 2.84 - 0.920 \\
&= 101.920
\end{aligned}$$

$$\begin{aligned}
\text{R.L. of Q} &= \text{R.L. of P} - \text{Fall between P and Q} \\
&= \text{R.L. of P} - (\text{I.S. at Q} - \text{I.S. at P}) \\
&= 101.920 - (1.620 - 0.920) \\
&= 101.920 - 0.700 = 101.220
\end{aligned}$$

$$\begin{aligned}
\text{R.L. of CP} &= \text{R.L. of Q} - (\text{Fall between Q and C.P.}) \\
&= \text{R.L. of Q} - (\text{I.S. at C.P.} - \text{I.S. at Q}) \\
&= 101.220 - (2.460 - 1.620) \\
&= 101.220 - 0.840 \\
&= 100.380 \text{ m}
\end{aligned}$$

$$\begin{aligned}
\text{R.L. of R} &= \text{R.L. of C.P.} + \text{Rise between C.P. and R} \\
&= 100.380 + (0.920 - 0.440) \\
&= 100.380 + 0.480 = 100.860 \text{ m}
\end{aligned}$$

The readings are tabulated in the level book as under.

B.S.	I.S.	F.S.	Rise	Fall	R.L. in m	Remarks
2.840					100.00	A.B.M.
	0.920		1.920		101.920	P
	1.620			0.700	101.220	Q
0.920		2.460		0.840	100.380	C.P.
		0.440	0.480		100.860	R.L. of R
∑ 3.760		2.900	2.400	1.540		
∑ B.S. − ∑ F.S. = 0.860 **Arithmetical check :**			∑ Rises − ∑ Falls = 0.860		Last R.L. − First R.L. 100.860 − 100.00 = 0.860 m	

4.11 COMPARISON BETWEEN THE TWO METHODS

Collimation Plane (H.I.) Method	Rise and Fall Method
1. The method is less tedious and it involves less number of calculations.	1. This method is more tedious as it involves more calculations.
2. There is no check on the reduction of levels of intermediate points. Hence mistakes made in the calculation of R.L.'s of intermediate points remain undetected.	2. There is a complete check on the reduction of levels of intermediate points. Mistake made in the calculation of R.L. of intermediate point will be carried forward.
3. The method is used for calculating reduced levels of profile levelling work, constructional work, etc.	3. This method is used for precise levelling, fly levelling and check levelling purposes.

4.12 RECORDING THE STAFF READINGS IN THE LEVEL BOOK

The tabular form of the page of a level book is as shown in the Illustrative examples. The following points should be borne in mind while making entries in the field book.

1. On each page of a level book, the first entry is always a backsight and the last entry is always a foresight.
2. When change point is taken, the foresight and backsight readings should be written in the same line.
3. When transferring the readings from one page to another, if the last entry on previous page happens to be an intermediate sight, it is entered in both Intermediate sight and Foresight column, and on the next page, the foresight reading on previous page is written under **backsight** and intermediate sight column as a first entry.

4. Specific mention of bench marks, change points, prominent features along the alignment of engineering structures such as roads, canals, railway line, etc. should be made in the Remarks column.

The readings shown in Fig. 4.10 i.e. illustrative sketch for differential levelling are recorded in the page of a level book as shown in tabular form. It is to be noted that the readings taken at C.P.1 and C.P.2 are written in the same line.

The Record of Readings and Use of Rise and Fall Method :

B.S.	I.S.	F.S.	Rise	Fall	Reduced levels	Remarks
2.450					150.000	A.B.M.
	2.360		0.090		150.090	A
2.880		1.435	0.925		151.015	C.P.1
2.345		0.820	2.060		153.075	C.P.2
		0.730	1.615		154.690	B
$\sum$ 7.675		2.985	4.690			

Arithmetical check :

$\sum$ B.S. – $\sum$ F.S. $\sum$ Rises – $\sum$ Falls   Last R.L. – First R.L.

= 7.675 – 2.985   = 4.690   = 154.690 – 150.000

= + 4.690   = 4.690

The arithmetical check is O.K.

Note : In the continuously sloping ground, it is to be noted that change point occurs at the point where the reading abruptly changes from smaller value to a bigger value as in the case of rising ground or from bigger value to smaller value abruptly as in the case of a falling ground.

4.12.1 Types of Levelling

(i) **Profile Levelling :** It is the method of levelling in which the elevations of points on the ground along the centre line of a proposed road or railway line are determined at some common interval. Thus, the accurate profile of the ground is obtained along the centre line of proposed railway line, road, water supply or drainage pipe line. It is also called as longitudinal sectioning.

(ii) **Cross-sectioning :** This is the method of levelling which is carried out to determine the outline of ground surface perpendicular to the centre line of proposed road and railway line. This is usually carried out alongwith the longitudinal sectioning.

(iii) Check levelling : This type of levelling is carried out to check the reduced levels of points which have been previously fixed. The temporary bench marks are established at some intermediate points while levelling along a long line. To check the levelling work on a particular day, a line of levels is run returning back to the bench mark to check the work on that day.

SOLVED EXAMPLES

Example 4.1 : The following readings were taken with a level and a 4.00 m staff. The instrument was shifted after 5th and 8th readings.

2.865, 3.345, 2.935, 1.950, 0.855, 2.790, 2.640, 1.540, 0.935, 0.850 and 0.190.

R.L. of the starting station is 150.000 m.

(i) Enter the readings in the form of a level book page and find the R.L.'s by collimation plane method.

(ii) Apply usual checks.

Solution : (i) The readings are entered in a level book page by noting that the instrument was shifted after 5th and 8th readings. Therefore 5th and 8th readings (i.e. 0.855 and 1.540) will be entered in foresight column. Consequently, 6th and 9th readings will be entered in backsight column (i.e. 2.790 and 0.935). The 1st reading is entered in the B.S. column; whereas, the last reading is entered in the foresight column. The remaining readings are entered in intermediate sight column.

It is noted that number of B.S. reading is equal to the number of F.S. readings on a level book page.

Here No. of B.S. = No. of F.S. = 3.

Station No.	B.S.	I.S.	F.S.	H.I. (Collimation Plane level)	R.L. in m	Remarks
1.	2.865			152.865	150.000	Starting stn.
2.		3.345			149.520	
3.		2.935			149.930	
4.		1.950			150.915	
5.	2.790		0.855	154.800	152.010	C.P.1
6.		2.640			152.160	
7.	0.935		1.540	154.195	153.260	C.P.2
8.		0.850			153.345	
9.			0.190		154.005	Last Pt.
Sum ∑	6.590		2.585			

FUNDAMENTALS OF CIVIL ENGINEERING   VERTICAL MEASUREMENTS

The R.Ls. of staff stations are calculated as follows by using collimation plane method :

1. First H.I. = R.L. of starting stn. + B.S. on starting stn.
   = 150.000 + 2.865
   = 152.865 m
2. R.L. of pt. 2 = H. I. – I. S. on point 2.
   = 152.865 – 3.345
   = 149.520 m
3. R.L. of pt. 3 = H.I. – I.S. on point 3.
   = 152.865 – 2.935
   = 149.930 m
4. R.L. of pt. 4 = H.I. – I.S. on point 4.
   = 152.865 – 1.950
   = 150.915 m.
5. R.L. of pt. 5 = H.I. – F.S. on point 5.
   (C.P. 1) = 152.865 – 0.855
   = 152.010 m.

Now the instrument is shifted; hence new H.I. will be calculated.

6. Second H.I. = R.L. of C.P. 1 (point 5) + B.S. on point 5
   (R.L. of colli- = 152.010 + 2.790
   mation plane) = 154.800 m.
7. R.L. of pt. 6 = H.I. – I.S. on point 6.
   = 154.800 – 2.640
   = 152.160 m.
8. R.L. of pt. 7 = H.I. – F.S. on point 7
   (C.P. 2) = 154.800 – 1.540
   = 153.260 m.

As the instrument is shifted, third H.I. is to be found out.

9. Third H.I. = R.L. of C.P. 2 (pt. 7) + B.S. on point 7
   = 153.260 + 0.935
   = 154.195 m

FUNDAMENTALS OF CIVIL ENGINEERING — VERTICAL MEASUREMENTS

10. R.L. of pt. 8 = H.I. – I.S. on point 8.
                    = 154.195 – 0.850
                    = 153.345 m.

11. R.L. of pt. 9 = H.I. – F.S. on point 9.
                    = 154.195 – 0.190
                    = 154.005 m.

Note : It can be noted from above calculations that B.S. is always 'plus' sight and is always added; whereas F.S. and I.S. are 'minus' sights and are always subtracted.

(ii) Check : The arithmetical check on calculations is

Σ B.S. – Σ F.S. = Last R.L. – First R.L.

∴ Σ B.S. – Σ F.S. = 6.590 – 2.585 = + 4.005

and Last R.L. – First R.L. = 154.005 – 150.000
                             = + 4.005 m.

Example 4.2 : Following staff readings were observed successively with a level. Instrument was shifted after third and fifth readings : 1.015, 0.935, 0.625, 2.120, 1.855, 1.705, 0.925, 2.360 m. Enter the above readings in a page of level book and calculate R.L.'s of all points using rise and fall method only. R.L. of first point is 400.000 m. Also apply usual check.

(P.U. Dec. 96)

Solution : From the data, third, fifth and last reading will be entered in the foresight column and first, fourth and sixth reading will be entered in the Backsight Column.

Sr. No.	B.S.	I.S.	F.S.	Rise	Fall	R.L.	Remarks
1.	1.015					400.000	B.M.
2.		0.935		0.080		400.080	
3.	2.120		0.625	0.310		400.390	C.P.1
4.	1.705		1.855	0.265		400.655	C.P.2
5.		0.925		0.780		401.435	
6.			2.360		1.435	400.000	Last reading
Σ	4.840		4.840	1.435	1.435		

Check : Σ B.S. – Σ F.S. = 4.840 – 4.840 = 0

Σ Rises – Σ Falls = 1.435 – 1.435 = 0

Last R.L. – First R.L. = 400.00 – 400.00 = 0

FUNDAMENTALS OF CIVIL ENGINEERING   VERTICAL MEASUREMENTS

Explanation of Calculation : In the rise and fall method, each staff reading is compared with respect to previous one to find out whether it is a rise or fall of next point. This rise or fall is added to or subtracted from the R.L. of previous point to get R.L. of next point.

For point 2, rise will be

$$0.935 - 1.015 = -0.080 \text{ (Rise of pt. 2)}$$

The second reading being smaller than previous one indicates that it is a rise.

1.   RL of pt. 2 $= 400.00 - (-0.080) = 400.080$
2.   C.P.1 $=$ Rise will be $0.625 - 0.935 = -0.310$
   ∴   RL of CP1 $= 400.080 + 0.310 = 400.390$
3.   for CP2 $=$ Rise will be $1.855 - 2.120 = -0.265$
             RL of CP2 $= 400.390 + 0.265 = 400.655$
4. For point 5, rise will be $0.925 - 1.705 = -0.780$
            RL of pt. 5 $= 400.655 + 0.780 = 401.435$
5. For point 6, fall will be $2.360 - 0.925 = 1.435$
            RL of point 6 $= 401.435 - 1.435 = 400.000$

Example 4.3 : The following staff readings were observed by a dumpy level and a 4 m levelling staff : 2.650, 1.650, 4.000, 3.250, 1.555. Level was shifted after third reading. First reading was taken on B.M. of 1000.000 m. **(P.U. May 95)**

(i) Enter the above readings in the page of a level book and calculate the R.L. of points by using rise and fall method.

(ii) Later it was found that, the markings on the staff were erroneous and actually the length of 4.0 m staff was only 3.8 m. Assuming the error to be distributed linearly, find the R.L. of each point.

Solution : Prepare columns for Rise and Fall method to calculate R.L.s. After third reading, level is shifted ∴ 4.000 m is F.S. and also last reading 1.555 m is F.S. reading first reading 2.650 m is B.S. All remaining readings are I.S. Hence fill the table and find R.L.s.

B.S.	I.S.	F.S.	Rise	Fall	R.L.s.	Remarks
2.650					1000.000	B.M. Given
	1.650		1.000		1001.000	
3.250		4.000		2.350	998.650	Change point
		1.555	1.695		1000.345	Last reading
Σ = 5.900		5.555	2.695	2.350		

Arithmetical check is $\sum$ B.S. $-\sum$ F.S. $= \sum$ Rise $- \sum$ Fall $= 2.695 - 2.350$

$\qquad\qquad\qquad\qquad\qquad\quad =$ Last R.L. $-$ First R.L.

(Each value $= + 0.345$)

Now for erroneous staff graduations with error linearly distributed,

$$\text{correct reading} = \left(\frac{L'}{L}\right) \times \text{observed reading}$$

Hence calculate every corrected reading, B.S. reading $= \frac{3.8}{4} \times 2.650 = 2.518$ m

Note that L $= 4$ m and

L' $= 3.800$ m (Given)

All readings will be corrected accordingly.

Corrected readings			Rise	Fall	Corrected R.L.s.	Remarks
B.S.	I.S.	F.S.				
2.518					1000.000	B.M. Given
	1.568			0.950	1000.950	
3.088		3.800		2.232	998.718	C.P.
		1.477	1.611		1000.329	Last reading
$\sum = 5.606$		5.277	2.561	2.232		

Arithmetical Check : $\sum$ B. S. $- \sum$ F. S. $= + 0.329 = \sum$ Rise $- \sum$ Falls.

Example 4.4 : Flying levels are run from a bench mark No. 1 of R.L. 186.415 to a bench mark No. 2 of R. L. 181.160. The sum of the backsights is 25.380 and sum of foresights is 30.645. Find the closing error of levelling work.

Solution : Reduced level of B.M. No. 2

$\qquad = $ R.L. of B.M. No. 1 $+ \sum$ B.S. $- \sum$ F.S.

$\qquad = 186.415 + 25.380 - 30.645$

$\qquad = 186.415 - 5.265$

$\qquad = 181.150$ m

Closing error of levelling work

$\qquad = 181.160 - 181.150$

$\qquad = 0.01$ m

Example 4.5 : A levelling exercise was started from a station 'A' having R.L. = 407.780 m and following readings were taken on a continuously sloping ground successively.

2.220, 2.985, 3.705, 3.905, 0.645, 1.770, 2.815, 3.200, 3.795, 1.220, 1.940 (station 'B').

A levelling staff 4 m long was used for work.

(i) Enter all readings in the tabular form for 'Collimation plane' method.

(ii) Calculate Reduced levels of all staff stations.

(iii) Show usual arithmetical check.

(iv) Find gradient of line AB.

Solution :

Station	Dist. (m)	Readings			H. I.	R.L.	Remarks
		B.S.	I.S.	F.S.			
	0	2.220			410.000	407.780	ABM (stn. A)
1.	20		2.985			407.015	
2.	40		3.705			406.295	
3.	60	0.645		3.905	406.740	406.095	C.P.1
4.	80		1.770			404.970	
5.	100		2.815			403.925	
6.	120		3.200			403.540	
7.	140	1.220		3.795	404.165	402.945	C.P.2
8.	160		1.940			402.225	Last stn. (stn. B)
Σ		4.085	9.640				

Arithmetical check :

Σ B.S. $- \Sigma$ F.S. = 4.085 $-$ 9.640 = $-$ 5.555

Last R.L. $-$ First R.L. = 402.225 $-$ 407.780 = $-$ 5.555 (Both Checks tallied)

As Σ B.S. $- \Sigma$ F.S. = Last R.L. $-$ First R. L.

The gradient of AB = $\dfrac{\text{Difference between R.L. of stn. B and stn. A}}{\text{Horizontal distance}}$

= $\dfrac{402.225 - 407.780}{160} = -\dfrac{5.55}{160}$

= $\dfrac{1}{28.82}$ ($-$ve sign indicates falling gradient)

FUNDAMENTALS OF CIVIL ENGINEERING — VERTICAL MEASUREMENTS

Example 4.6 : Following staff readings were recorded while levelling on a continuously sloping ground with a dumpy level and a 4.0 m levelling staff. 0.420; 1.660; 2.880; 0.580; 1.385; 2.190; 2.995 and 3.800. The R.L. of the station where first reading was taken was 300.00 m. Rule out the page of level book and enter the above readings; determine R.L. of other staff stations by rise and fall method. Apply usual checks. **(P.U. May 93)**

Solution :

B.S.	I.S.	F.S.	Rise	Fall	R.L.	Remarks
0.420					300.000	ABM
	1.660			1.240	298.760	
0.580		2.880		1.220	297.540	CP_1
	1.385			0.805	296.735	
	2.190			0.805	295.930	
	2.995			0.805	295.125	
		3.800		0.805	294.320	Last Station
Σ 1.000		6.680	0.000	5.680		

Check : Σ B.S. $-$ Σ F.S. = 1.000 $-$ 6.680 = $-$ 5.680

Σ Rise $-$ Σ Fall = 0.000 $-$ 5.680 = $-$ 5.680

Last R.L. $-$ First R.L. = 294.320 $-$ 300.000 = $-$ 5.680

∴ The check is satisfied.

Example 4.7 : The following is the page of levelling field-book. Fill up the missing readings and complete the page. Apply usual check.

Sr. No.	B.S.	I.S.	F.S.	Collimation R.L.	Reduced level	Remark
1.	2.650			X	100.00	B.M.
2.		3.740			98.910	
3.		X			98.820	
4.	4.640		X	X	98.380	C.P. 1
5.		0.380			X	
6.	1.640		X	103.700	102.060	C.P. 2
7.		2.840			100.860	
8.	X		3.480	104.900	100.220	C.P. 3
9.			X		102.700	Last Pt.

Solution : Starting from the known data of reduced levels, the missing readings are calculated as under :

(i) Collimation R.L. will be R.L. of B.M. + B.S. = 100.00 + 2.650 = 102.650

(ii) At stn. 3, Collimation R.L. – I.S. = R.L. of point 3
∴ 102.650 – 98.820 = I.S.
∴ missing reading i.e. I.S. = 3.830 at point 3

(iii) At stn. 4, F.S. = Collimation R.L. – R.L. of C.P. 1
∴ missing foresight at pt. 4 = 102.650 – 98.380 = 4.270
New R.L. of collimation will be 98.380 + 4.640 = 103.020

(iv) At stn. 5, R.L. of stn. 5 = New R.L. of collimation – I.S.
∴ R.L. of stn. 5 = 103.020 – 0.380 = 102.640

(v) At stn. 6 F.S. = New R.L. of collimation – R.L. of C.P.2
= 103.020 – 102.060 = 0.960

(vi) At stn. 8, New R.L. of collimation = R.L. of stn. 8 + B.S.
∴ B.S. = 104.900 – 100.220 = 4.680

(vii) At stn. 9, F.S. = R.L. of collimation – R.L. of Last point
= 104.900 – 102.700 = 2.200

Sr. No.	B.S.	I.S.	F.S.	Collimation R.L.	Reduced level	Remark
1.	2.650			**102.650**	100.00	B.M.
2.		3.740			98.910	
3.		**3.830**			98.820	
4.	4.640		**4.270**	103.020	98.380	C.P. 1
5.		0.380			**102.640**	
6.	1.640		**0.960**	103.700	102.060	C.P. 2
7.		2.840			100.860	
8.	**4.680**		3.480	104.900	100.220	C.P. 3
9.			**2.200**		102.700	Last Pt.
Σ	13.610	–	10.910			

Check = Σ B.S. – Σ F.S. = 13.610 – 10.910 = + 2.700

Last R.L. – First R.L. = 102.700 – 100.00 = + 2.700

FUNDAMENTALS OF CIVIL ENGINEERING VERTICAL MEASUREMENTS

Example 4.8 : The following readings were taken with a 4 m levelling staff. The staff was held inverted at 3rd reading. Readings were 1.585, 2.630, 2.465, 3.285.

Calculate the R.L's of the staff stations. The first reading was taken on a BM of R.L. 400.000 m.

Solution : The problem is solved by collimation plane method.

Since the instrument was not shifted during the exercise, only one H.I. will be obtained.

(1)   H.I. = R.L. of B.M. + B.S. on B.M.

                             = 400.000 + 1.585

                             = **401.585 m**

(2)   R.L. of Stn. 2 = H.I. − I.S. on stn. 2

                             = 401.585 − 2.630

                             = 398.955 m

(3)   R.L. of Stn. 3 = H.I. − (− I.S. on stn. 3)

                             = H.I. + I.S. on stn. 3

Here, the I.S. is added to H.I. as the staff is held inverted at the point. Therefore, the point is above the line of sight i.e. H.I., and hence the staff reading will have to be added to get R.L. of the point above H.I. as shown in Fig. 4.14.

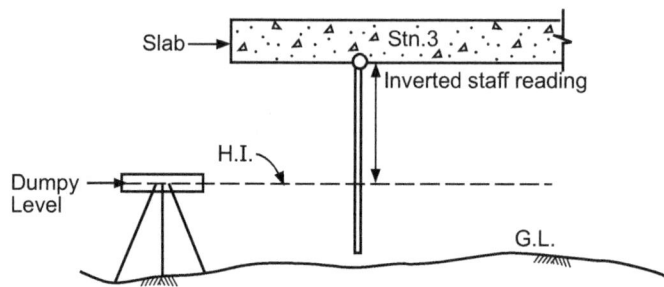

Fig. 4.14 : For staff held inverted

         R.L. of Stn. 3 = H.I. + Staff reading on Stn. 3

∴   R.L. of Stn. 3 = 401.585 + 2.465

                         = **404.050 m**

FUNDAMENTALS OF CIVIL ENGINEERING VERTICAL MEASUREMENTS

(4) R.L. of Stn. 4 = H.I. − F.S. on Stn. 4
            = 401.585 − 3.285
            = 398.300 m

The readings are entered as follows. The reading of staff held inverted is entered as negative since, it is above H.I.

Sr. No.	B.S.	I.S.	F.S.	Collimation plane or H.I.	Reduced level	Remarks
1.	1.585			401.585	400.000	B.M.
2.		2.630			398.955	
3.		− 2.465			404.050	Inverted staff
4.			3.285		398.300	Last point

Check : Σ B.S. − Σ F.S. = Last R.L. − First R.L.

∴   1.585 − 3.285 = − 1.700

   = Last R.L. − First R.L. = 398.300 − 400.00 = − 1.700

Note : The problem can also be solved by rise and fall method.

(i) Comparing the staff readings at station 2 and station 1

   2.630 − 1.585 = 1.045 (fall from station 1 to station 2)

∴   R.L. of station 2 = 400.000 − 1.045 = 398.955

(ii) Comparing staff readings at stations 2 and 3

   − 2.465 − 2.630 = − 5.095 m

∴   R.L. of station 3 = 398.955 − (− 5.095) = 404.050 m.

Therefore, there is rise of 5.095 m from station 2 to station 3.

(iii) Comparing the staff reading between station 3 and station 4

   3.285 − (− 2.465) = 5.750

∴   R.L. of station 4 = 404.050 − 5.750 = 398.300 m.

The arithmetical check is applied as usual in case of rise and fall method.

Example 4.9 : The following readings were taken with a 4 m levelling staff. The staff was held inverted at 4th reading, touching the soffit of the slab. Readings were : 1.025, 1.930, 2.525, 3.125 and 2.980. Calculate the R.L.s of the staff. The first reading was taken on a Bench Mark of R.L. 590.00 m.

Ch. 4 | 4.29

Solution : Readings will be tabulated in the usual way knowing that the fourth reading was a minus sight reading since the staff was held inverted.

	B.S.	I.S.	F.S.	H.I. or R.L. of collimation	Reduced level	Remark
	1.025			591.025	590.000	B.M.
		1.930			589.095	
		2.525			588.500	
		−3.125			594.140	Inverted staff
			2.980		588.045	Last point
Σ	1.025		2.980			

Arithmetical Check = $\sum$ B.S. − $\sum$ F.S. = 1.025 − 2.980 = − 1.855

Last R.L. − First R.L. = 588.045 − 590.000 = − 1.855

Example 4.10 : Levelling work was carried out on a continuously sloping ground using a dumpy level and 4 m levelling staff. The readings were

0.500, 1.000, 0.750, 1.000, 1.500, 0.500 and 1.500.

Rule out a page of a level field book for Rise and Fall method. Determine the Reduced levels of all the staff stns. The starting point happened to be an A.B.M. whose R.L. is 100.500 m. Apply usual arithmetic check also. **(P.U. Dec. 2003)**

Solution : The readings should be tabulated correctly properly locating the change point.

B.S.	I.S.	F.S.	Rise	Fall	R.Ls in m	Remark
0.500					100.500	A.B.M.
0.750		1.000	−	0.500	100.00	C.P.1
	1.000		−	0.250	99.750	
0.500		1.500	−	0.500	99.250	C.P.2
		1.500	−	1.000	98.250	
1.750		4.000			−2.250	
$\sum$ B.S. − $\sum$ F.S. = −2.250						

∴ $\sum$ B.S. − $\sum$ F.S. = Last R.L. − First R.L.

$\sum$ B.S − $\sum$ F.S. = 1.750 − 4.000 = − 2.250 m

Last R.L. − First R.L. 98.250 − 100.500 = − 2.250 m

Check tallies.

FUNDAMENTALS OF CIVIL ENGINEERING — VERTICAL MEASUREMENTS

Example 4.11 : During a fly levelling work the staff readings were obtained at a regular interval of 25 mtr. The readings were as under.

B.S. – 0.565, 0.990, 2.775 and 2.350.

F.S. – 1.685, 1.350, 2.055, 3.450.

The work was begun with a point whose R.L. was known to be 255.555. Enter the readings for Rise and Fall method to determine R.Ls. of all the stations. Also, find the nature and magnitude of gradient. Apply usual check. **(P.U. May 2004)**

Solution : From the data of B.S. and F.S. readings, it is observed that there are continuous change points. Readings are tabulated accordingly.

Dist.	B.S.	I.S.	F.S.	Rise	Fall	R.Ls.	Remarks
0	0.565					255.555	B.M.
25	0.990		1.685		1.120	254.435	C.P.1
50	2.775		1.350		0.360	254.075	C.P.2
75	2.350		2.055	0.720		254.795	C.P.3
100			3.450		1.100	253.695	
	6.680		8.540	0.720	2.580	– 1.860	
	– 1.860		– 1.860				

$$\text{Gradient} = \frac{\text{Last R.L.} - \text{First R.L.}}{\text{Dist.}} = -\frac{1.860}{100}$$

The check of $\sum \text{B.S.} - \sum \text{F.S.} = \sum \text{Rises} - \sum \text{Falls}$

= Last R.L. – Final R.L is obtained as – 1.860 m.

$$\text{Gradient} = \frac{1}{\frac{100}{1.860}} = \frac{1}{53.76} \text{ Falling}$$

(Since R.Ls. are continuously reducing).

Example 4.12 : During the levelling work the following readings were recorded using a dumpy level and 4 mtr. levelling staff with L.C. of 0.005 mtr. The readings were (i) 0.985, (ii) 1.215, (iii) 2.225, (iv) 2.315, (v) 2.575, (vi) 0.765, (vii) 1.880 and (viii) 2.160. Instrument was shifted after 3rd and 5th readings. The 8th reading (last reading) was taken to the bottom of the roof of the building. Enter all the readings in a level field book page and determine the R.Ls of the staff stations by H.I. method. Apply usual check. Assume R.L. of B.M. = 155.555 from where the work was started. **(P.U. May 2004)**

FUNDAMENTALS OF CIVIL ENGINEERING — VERTICAL MEASUREMENTS

B.S.	I.S.	F.S.	H.I.	R.Ls. (m)	Remarks
0.985			156.540	155.555	B.M.
	1.215			155.325	
2.315		2.225	156.630	154.315	C.P.1
0.765		2.575	154.820	154.055	C.P.2
	1.880			152.940	
		− 2.160		156.980	Bottom of roof
4.065		2.640			
	+ 1.425			+ 1.425	

Solution : The solution of the problem lies in the correct tabulation of given readings. The 1st reading will be entered in B.S. column. The instrument was shifted after 3rd reading showing that it is a change point (C.P.1). So this reading 2.225 will be entered in the F.S. column and the next reading 2.315 will be entered as B.S. reading. Similarly at 5th reading there is another change point C.P.2. The eighth reading is taken to the bottom of the roof of the building. This reading being above the line of sight, it (2.160) will be entered in the F.S. column with a negative sign. The rest of the problem will be solved by H.I. method and finally the arithmetical check should be applied to verify the correctness of calculations.

Example 4.13 : A fly levelling work was carried out, starting from a P.B.M. of R.L. 239.685 m. (Refer Fig. 4.15) and finishing work on C. Tabulate the readings shown in Fig. 4.15 and find R.L. of A, B and C. Use any method of your choice. Apply usual check.

(P.U. May 2006)

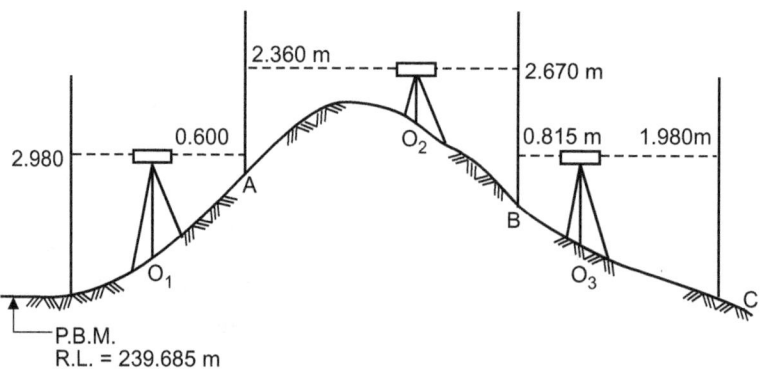

Fig. 4.15 : Fly levelling (Not to Scale)

Solution : The readings are tabulated as under :

B.S.	I.S.	F.S.	Rise	Fall	R. Ls. m	Remarks	
2.980					239.685	P.B.M.	
2.360		0.600	2.380	–	242.065	C.P.1	Stn. A
0.815		2.670	–	0.310	241.755	C.P.2	Stn. B
		1.980		1.165	240.590	C	Stn. C

Sum of B.S. = 6.155 = $\sum$ B.S. – $\sum$ F.S. = 0.905 m

Sum of F.S. = 5.250

Arithmetical check : Rises – $\sum$ falls = 2.380 – 1.475 = 0.905 m

Last R.L. – First R.L. = 240.590 – 239.685

= 0.905 m

The check tallies.

EXERCISE

1. Define the following terms :
   Level line, Datum surface, Vertical line, Reduced level, Bench mark.
2. Draw a neat sketch of a Dumpy level and name all the parts.
3. Describe the temporary adjustments of a dumpy level.
4. Explain the following terms : (a) Levelling of the instrument. (b) Focussing of the eyepiece and object glass.
5. State the difference between the temporary adjustments of a prismatic compass and a Dumpy Level.
6. Explain the following : (a) Change point, (b) Backsight reading. (c) Foresight reading. (d) Height of instrument. (e) G. T. S. Bench mark. (f) Intermediate sight.
7. Draw a neat sketch of part length of 4 m levelling staff and show on it the details of graduations. State the least count of levelling staff.
8. (a) What are the methods of reduction of levels ?

   (b) State the difference between Simple levelling and Differential levelling.
9. State how the difference between two points at a distance of half kilometre is found out.
10. State the significance of different types of bench marks.
11. What are the sources of errors in levelling ?
12. State the precautions to the errors in levelling.

FUNDAMENTALS OF CIVIL ENGINEERING VERTICAL MEASUREMENTS

13. Explain how the staff readings are entered in the page of a level field book.

14. Draw neat sketch of 3 m wooden levelling staff from 1.10 m to 1.30 m and show on it reading of 1.115 m.

15. The following readings were taken with a level and a 4.0 m staff. The instrument was shifted after 5th and 8th readings.

    2.865, 3.345, 2.935, 1.950, 0.855, 2.790, 2.640, 1.545, 0.935, 0.865, 0.190. R.L. of the starting station is 150.03 m.

    (a) Enter the readings in the form of a level book page and reduce the R.L.'s by collimation plane method.

    (b) Apply usual checks.

    Ans. Reduced levels are 149.52, 149.93, 150.915, 152.01, 152.16, 153.255, 153.325, 154.

    Arithmetical check : Σ B.S. – Σ F.S. = + 4.000.

16. The following staff readings were observed on the continuously sloping ground along the centre line of a road, with the help of a dumpy level and 4 m staff at 20 m interval. The first staff reading was taken on B.M. and the second reading was taken on the starting point of the road. Reduced level of B.M. was 350.000 m.

    0.540, 0.935, 1.245, 2.375, 3.885, 0.45, 1.635, 2.220, 3.665, 0.775, 1.555, 2.785, 3.450

    (a) Enter the readings in a page of a level book and determine the R.L. of other stations by Rise and fall method.

    (b) Find the gradient of this line.

    Ans. (a) The R.L.'s are: 349.605, 349.295, 348.165, 346.655,

    345.465, 344.880, 343.435, 342.655, 341.435, 340.770.

    (b) The Gradient is $\dfrac{349.605 - 340.770}{180} = \dfrac{8.835}{180} = \dfrac{1}{20.37}$

17. The following readings were taken with a dumpy level and a 4 m levelling staff :

    (i) 1.260, (ii) 1.435, (iii) 1.670, (iv) 0.640, (v) 1.920

    (vi) 2.56, (vii) 1.845, (viii) 2.210, (ix) 0.965 and (x) 1.325

    The instrument was shifted after 3rd and 8th readings. The R.L. of the station, where first reading was taken, was 150.000 m. Calculate the R.Ls. of other points by collimation plane method. Apply usual check.

18. The following consecutive readings were taken with a 4 m levelling staff on a continuously sloping ground on points at an interval of 20 m :

    0.525, 1.380, 2.160, 3.805, 0.460, 2.960, 3.060, 0.345, 1.925

    and 2.190. The R.L. of the last point was 639.284. Calculate:

    (a) R.L.'s of all other points by collimation method.

    (b) Gradient of the line joining the first and the last point.

    Ans. (a) The reduced levels are: 647.010, 646.155, 645.375,
    643.730, 641.230, 641.130, 639.550, 639.285.

    (b) $\sum$ B.S. $- \sum$ F.S. $= -7.725$.

    (c) Gradient of the line joining the first and the last point $= \dfrac{1}{18.12}$.

19. Following readings were observed by a dumpy level and a 4 m. levelling staff. 1.550, 1.950, 2.400, 0.850, 1.250, 1.200, 0.655. The level was shifted after the third and fifth readings. First reading was taken on B.M. 260.350 m.

    Rule-out a page of levelling field book. Enter the above readings appropriately. Find R.L. of each point and apply usual check. (**Ans.** $\sum$ B.S. $- \sum$ F.S. $= -0.705$)

UNIVERSITY QUESTIONS

1. Define levelling and state its any four types. **(Dec. 03)**
2. Draw and sketch to understand the meaning of the following terms :
   - (i) B.M. **(Dec. 03, 04; May 04, 05)**
   - (ii) I.S. **(Dec. 03)**
   - (iii) C.P. **(Dec. 03, 05; May 04, 05)**
3. Define the following terms :
   - (i) Datum. **(May 04; Dec. 04)**
   - (ii) Reduced level. **(Dec. 05)**
   - (iii) Level line. **(Dec. 04; May 04)**
   - (iv) B.S. **(Dec. 04)**
4. Write a brief note on the necessity of a change point in levelling work. Show C.P. and the aid of a sketch. **(May 04)**
5. State the use of levelling staff and draw the sketch with graduations in metric units. **(Dec. 04)**
6. Differentiate between H.I. method and Rise of fall method w.r.t. any 3 points. **(Dec. 04; May 05)**

FUNDAMENTALS OF CIVIL ENGINEERING																																			VERTICAL MEASUREMENTS

7. Define the following term :
   (i) Foresight. **(May 05)**
8. Enlist any 3 fundamental lines of a dumpy level and state their relationship. **(Dec. 05)**
9. Briefly explain the temporary adjustments of a dumpy level. **(Dec. 05)**
10. Write short note on :
    (i) Reduction of levels in respect of methods used. **(Dec. 05)**
11. Draw the figures to represent the following by assuming suitable values of R.L.
    (Dec. 03)
    (i) Till.
    (ii) Valley line.
    (iii) Uniform slope.

❏❏❏

Chapter 5

UNIT II

AREA MEASUREMENTS AND RELATED INSTRUMENTS

5.1 AREA MEASUREMENT

5.1.1 Introduction

In the topic of Area measurement, we have to see the use of mechanical planimeter to find the area of plane irregular figures. However, the initial and final readings are required to be noted. Similarly crossing of zero, the index mark has to be carefully watched. Numerical calculations are required to be done to obtain the area. To overcome this tedious procedure, an electronic digital planimeter can be used to find the area of irregular figures quickly. The planimeter works on built-in Nickel-Cadmium storage battery. Fig. 5.1 shows the different parts of a Digital planimeter 'PLACOM' manufactured by KOIZUMI SOKKI CO. of Japan. There is a rotary encoder which has replaced the integrating wheel of old mechanical planimeter. By an Electronic circuit, the pulses of rotary encoder are measured and area displayed in Digital form.

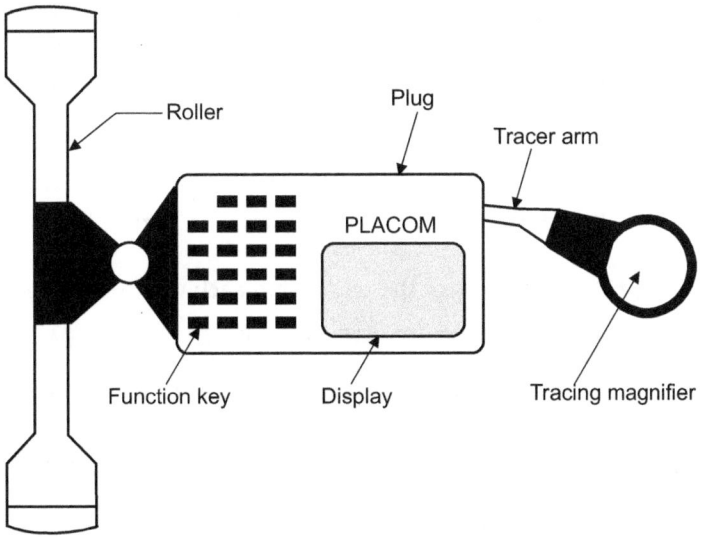

Fig. 5.1

FUNDAMENTALS OF CIVIL ENGINEERING   AREA MEASUREMENTS AND RELATED INSTRUMENTS

5.1.2 Function Keys

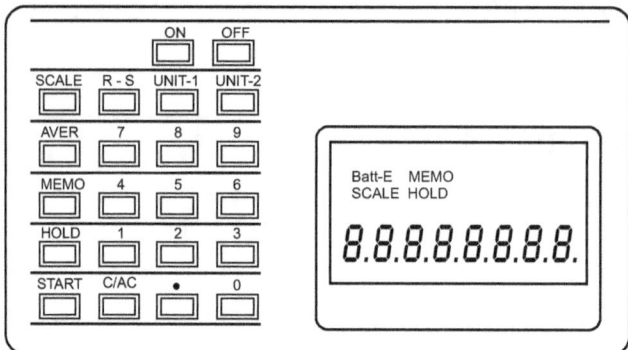

Fig. 5.2

| ON | — Power Supply ON key.

| OFF | — Power Supply OFF key.

| C/AC | — Clear and all clear key.

| START | — It is a start key for starting measurement. When the key is pressed, buzzer sounds lightly.

| HOLD | — By pressing this key, measured value is (stored) held in memory.

| MeMo | — It is a key for holding an intermediate measurement in memory.

| AVER | — It is a key for calculating average value.

| UNIT-1 | — It is a key for selecting unit system. i.e. Metric system or Foot system.

| UNIT-2 | — It is a shift key of the unit within each unit system such as $km^2 \rightarrow m^2 \rightarrow cm^2$ or acre – $Ft^2 – in^2$.

| SCALE | — Pressing of this key causes the setting of the reduced scale.

| R–S | — Pressing of this key confirms the setting of reduced scale.

| . | — Decimal point key.

| 0 | ~ | 9 | — Numerical key.

5.1.3 Measurement

Suppose an area 'P' shown in Fig. 5.3 is to be measured.

(a) **Preparation :** Paste or fix the drawing paper containing area on a drawing board. Place the roller at the position which will make a right angle with the main body. By tracing the outline of the figure, if any inconvenient movement of the roller is found, then the position of the roller is adjusted.

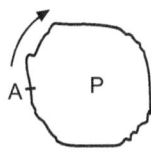

Fig. 5.3

Procedure :

(b) Press ON key to switch on the power supply.

(c) Select the unit by using 2 keys of UNIT – 1 and UNIT – 2 .

(d) Put a mark like 'A' on the outer periphery of the figure to use it as a starting point.

(e) Press START key, the buzzer sounds lightly. Confirm that display shows 0. Then trace the figure by lens (tracing point) clockwise round the circumference of the figure and close on starting point. The area of figure will be displayed on display panel.

(f) Bigger areas are subdivided into two or three parts for convenience.

(g) By the use of MEMO and AVER keys, the same area can be measured number of times and its mean value can be obtained for increased measuring accuracy.

5.1.3.1 Applications of Digital Planimeter

(i) To find the area of an irregular figure directly in digital form to the desired scale.

(ii) Averaging of the area is done to get the mean area accurately.

(iii) It is possible to find the perimeter (length) of an irregular shaped area.

In the chapters of Linear and Angular Measurements we have seen that the basic equipment for measurement of distance is either a metric chain or metallic or steel tape. Similarly, the angles of a polygon are measured indirectly by means of prismatic compass. The use of these instruments is required in the following situations :

(i) To measure the area of an irregular piece of land.

(ii) To prepare a grid for carrying out levelling on a proposed alignment of road, railway, canal or a dam.

(iii) To locate the points on a grid for preparation of a contour plan.

When the extent of work is limited and small and where much accuracy is not needed, the use of above instruments can be justified.

However, there are certain engineering works which demand high accuracy and speedy work, these instruments cannot be used; because of less accuracy and the cost of time. With the development of electronics in the last three decades, new electronic equipments have been developed for the accurate measurement of distance and angles. Hence, modern survey techniques can be employed which make use of modern electronic equipment. The distance measuring equipments are Electronic Distance Meters and Angle measuring equipment is Digital Theodolite. Similarly, Digital planimeters have been developed to measure the area of irregular figures.

5.2 NECESSITY OF ELECTRONIC DISTANCE METER AND DIGITAL THEODOLITE

There are many applications where the distances are to be known continuously or at regular intervals. It is only with the use of Electronic Distance Meter that these can be achieved at a very high speed and accuracy.

There are certain situations where the use of Electronic Distance meter and Digital Theodolite becomes a necessity. These are as listed below.

1. In a long bridge, the alignment of piers (intermediate supports) and the distance between pier to pier is to be checked.
2. In an Industrial shed, the centre to centre distance between columns and the alignment of columns is to be checked.
3. In an Industrial shed, if the final product is obtained passing from one machine to another and if the machines are installed in a straight line, the alignment of machines as well as the perpendicularity (Inclination) of rollers is to be checked.
4. If the railway line is to be located on a curved track, then the location of points on the curve is to be done.
5. If the tunnel centre line is located on a curve, then the location of those points on the curve is to be done.
6. If the verticality of a TV tower is to be checked, the use of electronic distance meter becomes necessary.
7. There are some existing structures located and spread over large area, then the location of these structures and the coordinates of those structures with respect to some origin could be obtained using Electronic Distance Meter.
8. Usually in a big project such as say Thermal Power Station, the siting of different units is done by drawing grid lines running North-South as well as East West. The location of the individual units of power station can be easily accomplished using Digital Theodolite and Electronic Distance Meter.

9. The location of centres as well as the alignment of transmission towers carrying overhead electric cables is easily done using the modern electronic equipment.
10. To prepare contour plan of a given piece of land.
11. The measurement of area of developed machine parts is quickly done using Digital Planimeter.

Like this, there are number of other situations where the use of modern electronic equipment becomes absolutely necessary to obtain accuracy as well as to save time.

We will study the parts of the Digital Theodolite and Electronic Distance Meter and the use of these equipments in the field.

5.3 ELECTRONIC DISTANCE METER

Earlier we have seen the engineering works / situations where accurate measurement of distance becomes absolutely necessary. Similarly direct measurement of distance becomes very difficult when the terrain is very rough such as valleys or steep hills. Electronic Distance meters have been developed which give an accuracy of 1 in 10^5 for ranges upto 50 km. These ED meters work on external source of power i.e. Ni-Cd battery of specified voltage.

5.3.1 Basic Principle

Suppose the distance between A and B is to be measured. A wave is transmitted from the transmitter at stn. A; with certain phase angle. There is a reflector with prisms at the other end 'B'. The wave strikes the reflector and is reflected from B and received back at the transmitter end at 'A' with different phase angle. By electronic circuitry at A, the phase difference between the transmitted wave and reflected wave is measured and converted into distance. The wave used for measurement of distance is called measuring wave.

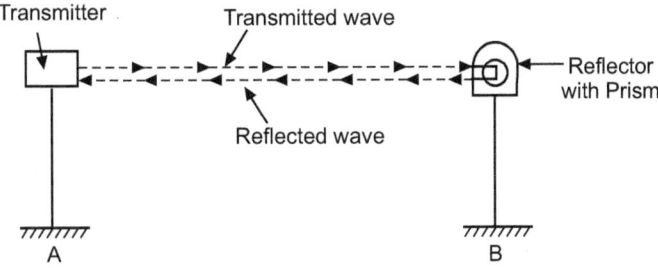

Fig. 5.4

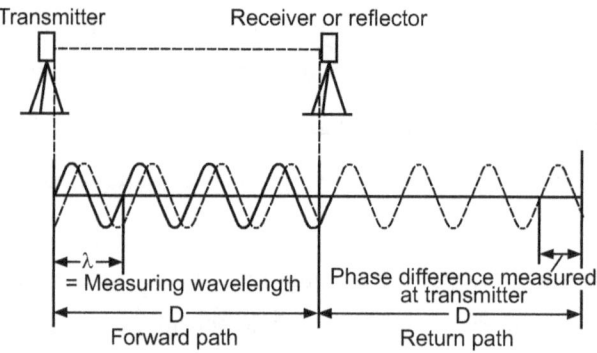

Fig. 5.5

5.3.2 Principle of Phase Comparison

Difference in phase between the transmitted and reflected waves represents the fraction of wavelength by which the double length line exceeds an integral number of complete wavelengths. Null method is used to measure the phase difference. For this an electronic circuit called as delay line is interposed so as to delay the wave till there is no phase difference between the emitted and received signals.

5.3.3 Classification of EDM Instruments

(a) Based on the Range of Measurement –

(i) **Short Range** – upto 5 kms which use infrared light wave as the signal.

(ii) **Medium Range** – upto 100 km. These instruments use micro waves.

(iii) **Long Range** – can measure distance greater than 100 km and use radio waves.

(b) Based on the precision obtainable –

(i) **Less precise** : Standard deviation of one measurement greater than ± (5 mm + 5 ppm).

(ii) **Moderately precise** : Standard deviation of one measurement = ± (5 mm + 1 ppm).

(iii) **Highly precise** : Instruments having a standard deviation of one measurement = ± (1 mm + 1 ppm).

(c) Based on Degree of integration with theodolite : The Electronic Distance meter is usually coupled with precise theodolite (least count 1").

(i) **Telescope mounted instruments** : In this case, Electronic Distance meter is mounted on the telescope of theodolite. The line of sight of Theodolite and Electronic distance meter though separate are parallel to each other.

(ii) **Electronic Tacheometers** : The Electronic Distance Meter and Digital Theodolite have coaxial optics i.e. Line of sight of each is combined into one. There is digital output of all measured data. This is also called as **Total station**, its uses are given in article 5.3.9.

5.3.4 Basic Functions Performed by EDM Instruments

   1. **Generation of measuring and carrier waves :** The measuring waves generated in the frequency range of 7.5 MHz to 500 MHz are not suitable for measuring the distance. Because when these waves travel through atmosphere, these are susceptible to changes in temperature, refraction etc. called as atmospheric interference giving rise to fading and scatter. Hence a carrier wave with a very high frequency is generated and is used in a medium for transport of measuring wave.

   2. **Modulation and Demodulation of the carrier wave :** The process of electronically superimposing the measuring wave on the carrier wave is called modulation. This occurs at the transmitter end. As the reflected wave is received at the receiver end, the reverse of modulation i.e. demodulation occurs in which the measuring wave is separated from the carrier wave.

   3. **Measurement of phase difference :** The phase difference is measured and is converted into distance.

   4. **Display results :** The result of the measurement is displayed in the digital form.

Usually for Land surveys and other constructional surveys, short range EDM instruments are used in which infrared light waves are used. The infrared light wave is transmitted in a manner similar to a visible light system (having a velocity of propagation = 299792.5 km/s). The carrier wave source is a Gallium Arsenide Infrared emitting diode. These diodes can be easily amplitude modulated at the high frequency required for EDM instruments.

5.3.5 Cube Prisms

These prisms are prepared from solid glass cubes which are cut along its diagonal, the plane making an angle 45° with the faces of the cube. The characteristic of these prism reflectors is that the incident wave and reflected wave travel along parallel paths. This is obtainable over a 20° range of angles of incidence to the normal. The range of measurement of distance of Electronic Distance Meter increases with increase in number of prisms.

5.3.6 Methods of Modulation

   (a) **Amplitude Modulation :** This is used in short range instruments where light waves are the carrier waves. In this method, the amplitude of the carrier wave is varied in direct proportion to the amplitude of the measuring wave. However the frequency of carrier wave remains constant. Thus the measuring wave information is carried by the varying amplitude of the carrier wave.

   (b) **Frequency Modulation :** This is used in Microwave instruments; wherein the frequency of the carrier wave is varied in proportion to the frequency of the measuring wave. The amplitude of carrier wave remains constant. The measuring wave information is carried by varying the frequency of the carrier wave.

5.3.7 Operating Procedure to Use EDM

Usually the EDM is mounted on theodolite. The operating instructions will vary from manufacturer to manufacturer. However the operating procedure of Red 2L EDM mounted on DT-2 theodolite is given to explain how different measurements are made.

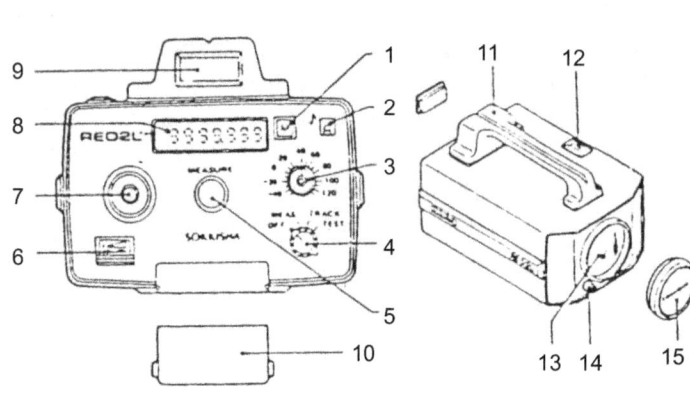

Fig. 5.6

1. ft/m switch
2. Audio switch
3. ppm dial
4. Measurement mode switch
5. Measurement start/stop bottom
6. Signal intensity meter
7. Sighting telescope
8. Display
9. Connector for keyboard SF2
10. Internal battery (BCD11)
11. Handle
12. PC and Degree/gon switch cover
13. Objective lens
14. Data output terminal
15. Objective lens cap

Fig. 5.6 shows the different parts of Electronic distance meter and are explained below : -

(a) Measurement mode and Test Switch : There are two modes of measurement of distance : -

(i) Measurement or Accurate Mode : Distance is measured accurately upto mm accuracy i.e. upto 3 decimal places. However, the time of measurement is more i.e. 6.0 sec.

(ii) Tracking Mode : Also called as Rough mode. Distance can be measured upto cm accuracy i.e. upto 2 decimal places. The time of measurement is very less i.e. 1 sec.

(iii) Test : Used to test the battery voltage of instrument and PPM correction.

(b) PPM dial : PPM is a correction factor which is to be used to account for temperature and atmospheric pressure at a place where the measurement is being done. The value of this factor can be obtained from a PPM chart supplied by the manufacturer.

(c) Signal Intensity Meter : Shows the strength of signal. The pointer should always lie in green zone, which shows adequate strength of signal.

(d) Sighting telescope : To see and bisect the reflector prism.

(e) Display Panel : Shows the measured value of sloping, horizontal or vertical distance and other parameters.

(f) ft/m switch : Selection of proper measurement unit i.e. ft or meter.

(g) Internal battery : 6 V battery which supplies power to EDM.

Fig. 5.7 shows the function key board which is fixed to the top of E.D.M. Different key functions are self-explanatory.

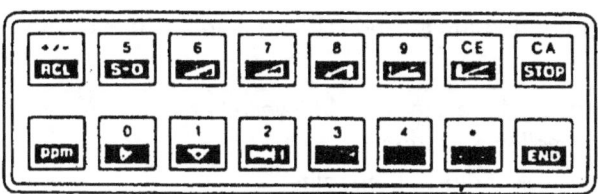

Fig. 5.7

ppm	:	Display atmospheric correction value
0	:	Enter 0/Enter zenith or vertical angle
1	:	Enter 1/Enter horizontal angle
2	:	Enter 2 / Enter setting-out data
3	:	Enter 3
4	:	Enter 4
.	:	Enter decimal point
END	:	Enter data to memory
RCL	:	Change sign (+/−) of data / Recall data
S-O	:	Enter stake-out measurement mode
6	:	Enter 6/Measure slope distance
7	:	Enter 7/Measure horizontal distance
8	:	Enter 8/Measure height difference
9	:	Enter 9/Measure E-coordinate
CE	:	Clear display / Measure N-coordinate
CA STOP	:	Stop distance measurement

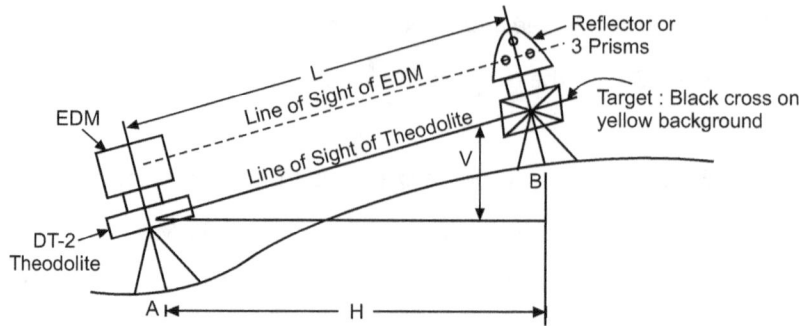

Fig. 5.8 : Showing the field use of EDM

Note : Line of sight of theodolite and EDM are parallel to each other.

5.3.8 Procedure

The theodolite and EDM are centred and levelled at station A. Similarly the reflector with target is centred and levelled at station 'B'.

1. Switch $\boxed{\text{ON}}$ power of digital theodolite.
2. Loosen upper clamp and do the indexing of telescope.
3. Bisect the centre of cross of target by upper clamp and upper fine adjustment screw of theodolite.
4. Note the reading of vertical angle displayed on Display panel.
5. Press $\boxed{5}$ to start the operation / switching on of EDM.
6. Turn knob of test switch to see that battery voltage is O.K and proper PPM correction factor is used. PPM correction factor is selected by PPM switch.
7. Select measurement mode i.e. measure or track mode.
8. If the bisection of prism of reflector is correctly done, the EDM will start measurement otherwise using the screws of EDM, correctly bisect the reflector in its centre through the sighting telescope of EDM.
9. Press key $\boxed{6}$ to obtain inclined distance L and stop the measurement by pressing $\boxed{\text{STOP}}$.
10. Press key $\boxed{0}$ to input vertical angle.
11. Input vertical angle and press $\boxed{\text{End}}$.
12. Press key $\boxed{7}$ to obtain H (horizontal distance) or key $\boxed{8}$ to obtain vertical distance.
13. Press key $\boxed{\substack{\text{CA}\\\text{STOP}}}$ to stop measurement.
14. Switch OFF the EDM.

Although the EDM may be different but the operating procedure is more or less the same.

5.3.9 Uses of Electronic Distance Measurement Electronic Distance Meter

1. To obtain the sloping distance, horizontal distance and vertical distance between two points.
2. To measure the vertical angles and horizontal angles.
3. To get the elevation of a remote object.
4. To obtain the elevations (R.Ls) of the different points with respect to certain datum or bench mark.
5. To set the points at a predetermined distance along grid lines.

Fig. 5.9

Fig. 5.9 shows EDM mounted on a digital theodolite, DT-2.

5.4 TRANSIT THEODOLITE AND DIGITAL THEODOLITE

5.4.1 Introduction

Basically, theodolite is an instrument to determine angles between two points in a horizontal plane and between two points in the vertical plane. For measuring vertical angles, the angles can be measured taking horizontal line as the datum line or zenith point as the reference point then it will be called as a zenith angle. The term "Transit theodolite" means a theodolite which can be revolved about its trunnion axis (horizontal axis) in a vertical plane.

Theodolites are classified into three types :

1. Vernier Theodolites.
2. Optical Theodolites (precise type)
3. Digital Theodolites.

In the vernier theodolites, separate verniers are provided for taking the reading of horizontal angle and vertical angle. The least count of these theodolites is usually 20" and are used for general survey and construction work. These theodolites are also called as repeating theodolites since angles can be measured by taking number of repetitions. Theodolites with different accuracies are available in the market to suit the accuracy required for a given work. However, for measuring an angle, vernier reading is required to be added to mainscale reading to obtain the total value of angle.

Precise optical theodolites are having an optical system inbuilt during manufacture which is used to read both horizontal and vertical angles precisely. They are also called as microptic theodolites since they are fitted with a micrometer for taking readings. The least count of these theodolites is usually 1" which is required in precision survey work.

These theodolites are also called as Direction theodolites since these theodolites have only one vertical axis.

5.4.2 Digital Theodolite

These theodolites are the precise type of theodolites (least count 1") in which the horizontal angles or vertical angles are directly shown on the display panel of the instrument. These require an external source of power i.e. battery of stipulated voltage while working with these instruments. A separate keyboard is provided for different operations of this theodolite. The angle measurement is done by photoelectric incremental rotary encoder which scans the motion of the telescope and registers the numerical value of either horizontal or vertical angle in degrees, minutes and seconds. The usual clamp and slow motion (fine adjustment) screws for the horizontal motion and vertical motion of the telescope are provided in other types of theodolites.

Fig. 5.10 shows the different parts of a typical digital theodolite.

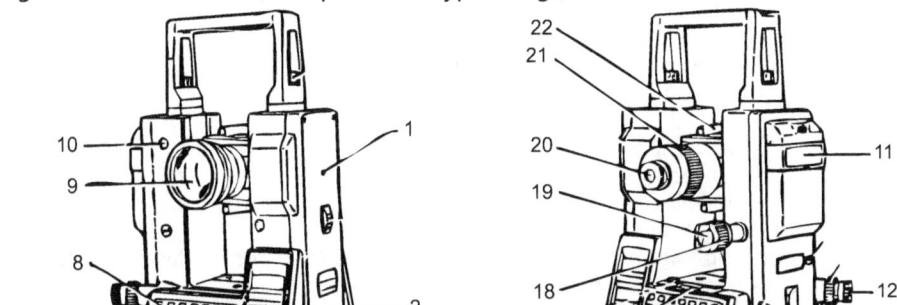

Fig. 5.10

(1) Instrument height mark (2) Display (3) Lower clamp (4) Circular level (5) Base plate (6) Levelling screw (7) Tribrach (8) Keyboard (9) Objective lens (10) EDM connector (11) Battery (12) Optical plummet eyepiece (13) Power switch (14) Horizontal clamp (15) Horizontal fine motion screw (16) Data output connector (17) Plate level (18) Vertical fine motion screw (19) Vertical clamp (20) Telescope eyepiece (21) Telescope focussing ring (22) Peep sight

5.4.3 The Essential Parts of Digital Theodolite

1. The telescope : It has eyepiece and diaphragm at one end and objective at the other end. The telescope is mounted on a spindle called as horizontal or trunnion axis. The focussing ring or screw is provided with telescope for focussing of the object.

2. Clamp screws : (i) Horizontal clamp : This is used to arrest the motion of telescope in the horizontal plane. The slow motion of telescope can be obtained by horizontal fine motion screw.

(ii) Vertical clamp : This is used to stop the motion of telescope in the vertical plane. The slow motion of telescope in vertical plane is obtained by using vertical fine motion screw.

3. Levelling head : It consists of two parallel plates i.e. a tribrach and a base plate. The tribrach carries three levelling screws. The theodolite can be levelled by the levelling screws. By means of a clamp screw, the theodolite can be fixed to tripod head.

4. Plate level : Plate bubble is provided on the instrument and is kept parallel to horizontal axis.

5. Circular level : It is provided on the top of tribrach.

6. Optical plummet : It is a small telescope to see the centering of theodolite over the station point.

7. Display window : The display of horizontal angles and vertical angles is shown in the Display window.

8. Tripod : It has adjustable legs. Theodolite is fixed on the tripod for each set up of the instrument.

FUNDAMENTALS OF CIVIL ENGINEERING   AREA MEASUREMENTS AND RELATED INSTRUMENTS

5.4.4 Special Features of a Digital Theodolite (DT-2) Uses

Manufactured by SOKKIA company of Japan are as follows :
1. Horizontal circle can be set to zero in any direction.
2. Minimum reading of 1" can be obtained.
3. The tilt angle of the vertical axis can be measured by the internal sensor and displayed. The vertical angle can be automatically compensated by the tilt sensor and the compensated angle displayed.
4. If the Digital theodolite is not functioning correctly during use, an error code will be displayed so there is a self-diagnostic function.
5. There is automatic switching off the power, 30 minutes after the last operation.
6. There is a data output connector terminal.

Key board

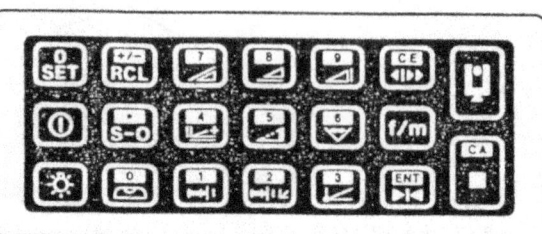

Fig. 5.11 : Key Board of Digital Theodolite

DT2 : Keys marked ■ are used in angle measurements.

DT2 + EDM : Keys marked • are used in distance measurements.

- Select theodolite mode.
- Stop measurement and transfer to basic mode.
- Stop data entry or recall.
- Set horizontal angle to zero.
- Index vertical circle when manual indexing is selected.
- Change the sign of data before entry.
- Recall data from memory.
- Enter " 7 ".
- Measure slope distance.
- Enter " 8 ".
- Measure horizontal distance.
- Enter " 9 ".
- Measure height difference.
- Clear entry.
- Select horizontal angle to left, right or by repetition (accumulation).
- This key is not used.

FUNDAMENTALS OF CIVIL ENGINEERING — AREA MEASUREMENTS AND RELATED INSTRUMENTS

- Enter decimal point.
- Measure setting-out distance.
- Enter " 4 ".
- Measure N and E-coordinates.
- Enter " 5 "
- Measure remote elevation
- Enter " 6 ".
- Measure horizontal distance between two prism points.
- Convert displayed distance to feet or metres for 5 seconds.
- Illuminate display and reticule of telescope for 30 seconds.
- Enter " 0 ".
- Display vertical axis tilt angle ON/OFF.
- Enter " 1 ".
- Enter setting-out distance.
- Enter " 2 ".
- Enter setting-out N and E-coordinates.
- Enter " 3 ".
- Enter coordinates of instrument station.
- Transfer entered data to memory.
- Hold/release horizontal angle.

Fig. 5.12 : Horizontal angle AOB

5.4.4.1 Uses/Practical Applications of Digital Theodolite

(i) To measure the horizontal angle between two stations accurately upto a precision of 1".
(ii) To measure the vertical angle between two points with an accuracy of 1".
(iii) To check the alignment of bridges, railway tracks and roads.
(iv) Digital theodolite is used in the prolongation of alignment of roads, railways etc.

FUNDAMENTALS OF CIVIL ENGINEERING   AREA MEASUREMENTS AND RELATED INSTRUMENTS

5.5 ELECTRONIC TOTAL STATION

An Electronic total station means an EDM and a Digital theodolite built as one unit. There is a data recording module (Electronic field book) to record the data and additional information. The field survey data includes the angles, distances and related information which is stored in Electronic field book. The data can be connected to an IBM compatible computer (with computer interface) which will create a suitable data base.

5.5.1 Uses/Applications of Total Station

(i) To measure horizontal angles and vertical angles.

(ii) To obtain the horizontal distance, vertical distance and inclined distance between two points.

(iii) To get the three-dimensional coordinates i.e. (x, y, z) of a point in space.

(iv) To find the length of a missing line.

(v) To find the elevation of a remote object.

(vi) To locate the points at a predetermined distance along grid lines.

5.6 G.I.S. AND G.P.S.

There are some modern techniques adopted for survey of very large areas and fixing positions of stations on a global scale. These have wide range of uses and applications in civil engineering.

5.6.1 G.I.S.

It is the abbreviation for **Geographical Information System**. It deals with **Geographic** features of an area (i.e. spatial and non-spatial features) which are very helpful for cartography (drawing the maps of the area), town planning (including regional planning, development planning and town planning schemes), resource management, etc., wherein the **Information** is a data that can be handled, understood and used with the help of computer technology.

Thus, G.I.S. is a computer-based information system used to store or represent digitally the required geographical features, analyse them and also to retrieve or manipulate the spatial and non-spatial data for planning and decision making processes.

From the data base, which needs continuous updation, we can retrieve land-uses, road networks, service lines like sewers, telephone lines, etc.; natural resources, demographic features; amenities like schools, colleges, hospitals, etc. to any required scale.

G.I.S. provides (a) conventional geographical information, (b) spatial and non-spatial information, (c) details of features like points, lines and polygons.

Drawbacks of G.I.S. are : (i) continuous updation of information is essential in digital form, (ii) error is possible if blown upto very large size, (iii) very large magnification involves diminishing of the resolution.

5.6.2 Applications of G.I.S.

(I) Resource and Geological Exploration

1. For exploration of oil fields, Digitally processed images are studied to find geological structures such as faults, fractured zones and anticlines. Surface sources of water can be detected.

2. Location of Engineering structures such as bridges, tunnels or dams can be done by studying the satellite imageries.

3. The siting of storage reservoirs can be studied.

4. The study of alternative sites for the alignment of roads and railways can be done from the aerial photographs.

(II) Environment Applications

(i) Pollution in the form of oil spills can be detected.

(ii) Thermal power plants, chemical industries, steel plants, paper and pulp mills and oil refineries, etc. use large quantities of water. The effluent from such plants poses an environmental hazard. Remote sensing can be used to monitor such areas which are polluted due to heated water discharges from such plants.

(iii) The cloud motion, precipitation, snow cover, etc. are studied from this data.

(III) Application for Land use and Land cover

Land cover means the space covered by buildings, vegetation, lakes, hills, etc. The different uses to which the land can be put to are residential purpose, industrial, agricultural purpose. Remote sensing technique is useful for preparing maps for land use and land cover. Although mapping of large areas which are inaccessible can be done rapidly, sometimes it is very difficult to differentiate images of different land use. The method is less expensive than conventional methods of land surveys. However, for mapping of small areas, the remote sensing may not be economical.

5.6.3 G.P.S.

It is an acronym for **Global Positioning System**. The primary function of G.P.S. is navigation in three dimensions. It consists of three parts of segments :

1. **Space segment**; which consists of a system of satellites.

2. **User segment**; which consists of receiver in hand or in a vehicle like ship, aeroplane, car, etc. It includes G.P.S. receivers and user community.

3. **Control segment**; which consists of ground stations, ground antenna, master control station and network of monitor stations.

A set of tracking stations is established which continuously track the satellites, compute the orbit and inject the position information about the satellite (Ephemeris) into the satellite memory on a regular basis. This information is available in a coded form in the signals transmitted by the satellites. Signals are transmitted by the satellite and the signal travel time from satellite to ground receiver antenna is observed by comparing clock readings at satellite and receiver.

Uplink data includes satellite ephemeris, position constant, clock correction factor, atmospheric data and almanac. Downlink data has coded ranging signals, position information, atmospheric data and almanac. Latitudes and longitudes are usually provided in the geodetic datum, on which G.P.S. is based.

G.P.S. satellites, also known as space vehicles, send specially coded radio signals from space. Precise positioning with 95% accuracy is possible at reference locations; providing the corrections and relative positioning data for remote receivers.

Rapid static or fast static survey can provide 4 to 10 cm accuracies with 1 km baselines and 15 minutes of recording time. Real time kinematic survey technique can provide 1 cm measurement in real time over 10 km baselines, tracking five or more satellites.

Drawbacks of G.P.S. are (i) Very costly for developing or poor countries. (ii) G.P.S. errors comprise of noise, bias and blunders for which differential G.P.S. techniques etc. are required to be used. (iii) Requires datum transformation to local user surveying system. (iv) Depends on the country, maintaining the satellite system.

5.6.4 Applications of G.P.S.

(i) To determine the positions of points on earth with reference to certain datum.

(ii) To carry out surveys for base line in triangulation survey with a reasonable accuracy.

(iii) Used in Military operations to locate the enemy positions.

(iv) It is useful in the rescue operations of ship or tracking operations of cargo ships.

5.7 USE OF LASER IN CONSTRUCTION

Laser is an acronym for **L**ight **A**mplification by the **S**timulated **E**mission of **R**adiation. It is a coherent beam having three important properties as : (a) it is almost completely unidirectional, unlike normal light which radiates or spreads in all directions, (b) it is highly monochromatic i.e. of one colour or frequency only, unlike normal light which is mostly a combination of colours, (c) it gives very intense and sharp beam as there is no destructive interference. (All rays of a laser light are in phase, giving constructive interference at all times.).

Commonly Helium-Neon gas lasers are used. Power required for laser is minimal. A constructional laser can operate all day on 12 V automobile battery without recharging.

Uses :

1. It can be used for alignment purpose, positioning, levelling with the help of laser levels in civil engineering construction.
2. It provides a quick and independent check of gradients for pipe lines, roads and railways if makes at parallel offsets can be set above the work concerned.
3. Laser plumbing is used in controlling the verticality of tall buildings.
4. For establishing a reference line-for trenching or for laying out channel offsets, levelling of ground. The reference line may be used for placing concrete, rails or tunnel lining.
5. In tunneling operation, the light shot will fall on a target board at the front end so that operator can centre its digging or boring correctly by a tunnel boring machine.
6. Used for large and complicated mechanical erection and fabrication work.
7. Used for cutting of steel plates with speed as high as 2.5 m/min.
8. Also used in opthalmic and other types of surgery.

EXERCISE

1. In what respects the digital theodolite differs from ordinary theodolite ?
2. State the special features of digital theodolite.
3. Describe briefly the different parts of digital theodolite.
4. Explain measurement of angles by digital theodolite.
5. Explain the principle of Electronic Distance meter and its different uses.
6. Write a note on classification of Electronic Distance Meters.
7. Describe amplitude modulation and frequency modulation and the instruments in which they are adopted.

8. Write short notes on : -
   (a) Measurement modes (b) Total station (c) Field application of EDM
   (d) Cube prisms.
9. Write a note on digital planimeter.
10. Explain the use of digital planimeter for measurement of area.
11. Write a note on G.I.S.
12. Explain the term "G.P.S.".
13. Explain the application of G.I.S. for
    (i) Land use and Land cover, (ii) Environmental use.

UNIVERSITY QUESTIONS

1. State and briefly explain two uses (applications) of
   (i) Total station. **(May 04, 06)**
   (ii) Laser. **(May 06)**
   (iii) G.I.S. **(Dec. 03, 04, 05; May 04, 05, 06)**
2. State any two uses of the following
   (i) Electronic theodolite. **(Dec. 03, 04, 05; May 04, 05)**
   (ii) E.D.M. **(May 04, 05; Dec. 04, 05)**
3. Briefly describe how will you use the digital planimeter to find the area of an irregular figure. **(Dec. 05)**
4. Write notes on :
   (i) E.D.M. **(Dec. 03, 04)**
   (ii) Digital planimeter. **(Dec. 03, 04; May 04)**
5. Give any two practical applications of
   (i) C.P.S. **(May 04)**
6. Write a note on 'Types of E.D.M.

UNIT III

Chapter 6

BUILDING PLANNING AND BYELAWS

(A) BUILDING PLANNING

6.1 INTRODUCTION

While planning any type of building-residential or industrial, an architect or an engineer has to pay attention to the following main considerations.

(1) Owner's requirement about the building.

(2) General scope of the proposed building.

(3) Characteristics of the building site.

(4) Rules, regulations and bye-laws prepared by various authorities.

All the necessary information is collected, carefully checked and then drawings are prepared based upon above considerations.

The building plans prepared by an architect should be consistent with the basic principles of building planning. These are (1) Aspect, (2) Prospect, (3) Privacy, (4) Grouping, (5) Roominess, (6) Furniture arrangement, (7) Circulation, (8) Sanitation, (9) Elegence, (10) Economy.

The above principles are called as factors to be considered in planning of building. They are not as the rules of mathematics but are rather flexible. The main idea in planning is to design a building in such a way that the space available can be well utilised for the desired activity taking full advantage of the environment gifts such as sun-shine, breeze, scenery etc. The above principles are applicable to all buildings in a general way. However, difference on some points are inevitable because the functions and nature of various buildings may be entirely distinct. For example, in the planning of an office building, provisions for ample lighting is an essential requirement, in case of a cinema theatre, natural lighting is secondary.

6.2 SELECTION OF SITE FOR RESIDENTIAL BUILDING

The selection of side is the most important bearing on the planning and designing 0f buildings. In practice, it is rarely possible to secure an ideal site that may fulfil all the requirements mentioned below. However, the site should be selected which will satisfy most of the following requirements.

1. Hard and firm foundation should be available at shallow depth to reduce the cost of construction.
2. Site on filled up soils, marshy, water logged area, black-cotton soil etc. should be avoided.
3. Site should be situated on an elevated place and also be levelled. It should not be in depression otherwise there will be problem of drainage, disposal of rain water and sanitation.
4. Site should satisfy the purpose and scope of the building.
5. If there is a river or nallah nearby the site should be above the highest flood level.
6. Site should not be irregular in shape or having sharp corners otherwise valuable land will be wasted.
7. Site should be situated in such an area where there is safety and security.
8. Site should be well connected by roads, service lanes.
9. As regards ownership, the site should be free from legal litigations.
10. In case of Residential Building, in addition to above, the site should be away from industrial areas, mines, congested, noisy locality, H.T. lines and free from smoke dust, insanitary conditions

    There should be availability of utility services like water-supply, electricity, gas, drainage facility etc. and also community services like post and fire protection, clearing of waste, street cleaning, and street lights etc. and amenities such as health, education, recreation, telephone, shopping centres, means of transport. etc.

    The situation of site should be such as to ensure un-obstructed natural light and air. There should be good landscape and greenery around the site for healthy living.

11. **In case of Public Building the following points should also be considered.**

    (a) The site for Administrative Buildings such as Law-courts, Town-Halls etc. should be at the focus of the main roads and should be accessible from different parts of the town.

    (b) The site for Health Centres like hospitals and Educational Buildings like schools and colleges etc. should be away from the main arterial roads and free from noise, bustle of the traffic.

(c) The site for Religious Building such as temples etc. should be at elevated place and in calm or river side and peaceful surroundings.

(d) The site for Commercial Buildings like shopping centres should be near the main business area of the town.

(e) The site for Industrial Buildings such as factories, especially those which give out obnoxious gases and fumes should be on the outskirts and on the few-ward of the town so that smoke, dust will not travel over the town to cause smoke / dust nuisance.

There should be availability of raw materials, skilled and unskilled labour at moderate rates, electric power, plentiful water for processing, easy transport of both raw and finished rates, electric power, plentiful water for processing, easy transport of both raw and finished product by road, rail, nearness to market and related industries, etc. Drainage facility should also be available for safe disposal of effluent after its treatment.

There should be favourable climate of the surrounding locality to house the labourers of the industry. There should also be availability of sufficient land not only for the present requirement but also for future expansion.

6.3 PRINCIPLES OF BUILDING PLANNING

6.3.1 Aspect

Aspect means the peculiarity of the arrangements of doors and windows in the external walls of a building which allows the occupants to enjoy the natural gifts such as sunshine and breeze.

A good aspect is desirable for :

(1) It provides comfortable conditions and cheerful atmosphere due to proper sunshine and breeze.

(2) It provides better hygienic conditions as the suns ray s are potential destroyers of organic poisons.

(3) It proves the external appearance of the building due to proper location of doors and windows.

In the aspect, consideration should be given to the placement of different rooms of the house in accordance with our activities in the house during day and night. A room which receives light and air from particular side is said to have aspect of the direction. Thus in planning the desired aspects for various rooms are as follows :

(a) Kitchen : It should have an eastern aspect. In the morning sun refreshes and purifies the air and it remains cool in the afternoon.

(b) A living room : It should have south or south east aspect. The sun is towards south in winter hence living room remains warm. The sun is towards North, overhead, or at high altitude towards south in summer and this saves the living room with southern aspect from getting unduly hot.

(c) Bed rooms : All the principle bed rooms should have west or southwest aspect for usually the brazen prevails from that direction in summer. However, a verandah, a gallery or suitable devices, should be provided on that side to protect the bed room from hot afternoon sun. Due to this protection, there will not be much heat radiations during night.

(d) Larder and store room : There will be no sun from the North side for most part of the year. Hence, larder and store room may have northern aspect.

(e) Studies, reading room and class rooms : The light from the North side is diffused and evenly distributed. Hence, the units should have North aspect.

6.3.2 Prospect

Prospect means the view one can get when one looks through the doors and windows in the external wall. It is determined by the view desired from certain rooms of the house viz. view of the garden, hills, waterfalls, and other beautiful scenery. For the sake of revilement of certain views, projecting windows are of immense value. Galleries also provide very good prospect. Prospect also means concealment of some undesirable views from certain rooms.

In the following figures, 'W' indicates projecting windows to reveal certain views. Unwanted views are concealed by blind wall faces indicated by 'B'.

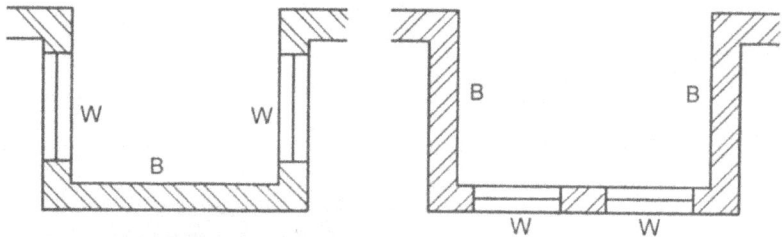

Fig. 6.1 : Face line for building

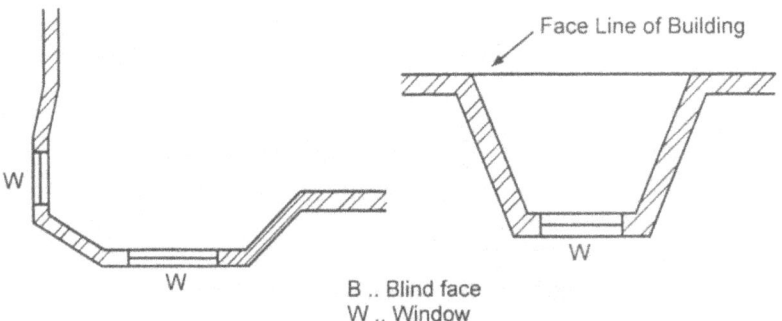

B .. Blind face
W .. Window

Fig. 6.2 : Projection windows for prospect

At certain times, the aspect and prospect considerations may be somewhat clashing and architect has to use his judgement. In general, a good layout should not be disturbed for the sake of good prospect.

6.3.3 Privacy

This is an important principle in planning the residential buildings in particular. Any accomplishment, without optimum privacy in the layout, is in vain. Privacy is of two types.

(i) The privacy of the whole building with reference to surrounding buildings and roads. This can be achieved by carefully planning the entrances, pathways and drives etc. The entrances can be screened with trees or creepers trained on lattice or grid work.

(ii) The second type is the privacy in different rooms. Namely bed rooms, bath rooms, kitchen toilets etc. This internal privacy can be achieved by :

(a) Correct positioning of doors and opening shutters. The shutters should open in such a way that the person entering the room will have the minimum view. A large portion of the details in the private room such as beds should not be visible at a glance. For better results, doors with single shutters are preferable.

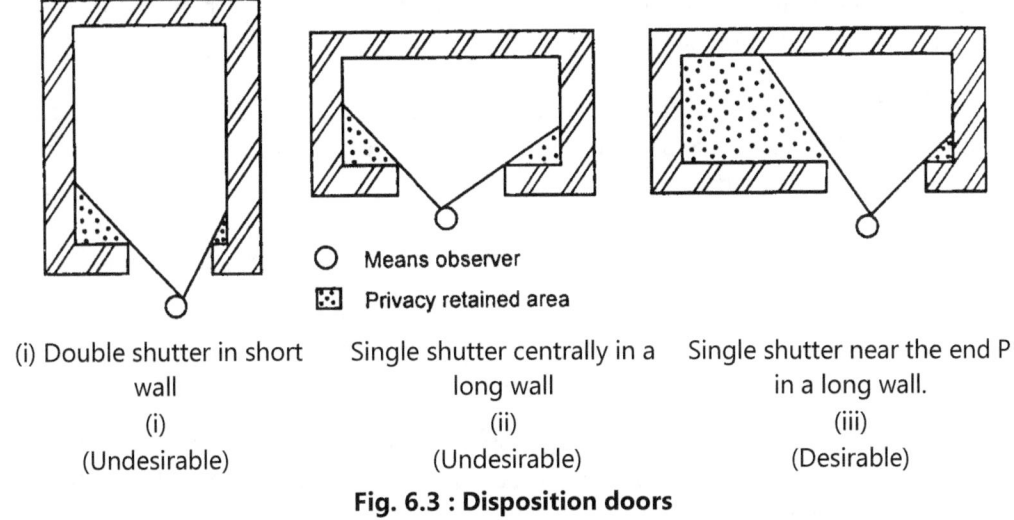

○ Means observer
▨ Privacy retained area

(i) Double shutter in short wall
(i)
(Undesirable)

Single shutter centrally in a long wall
(ii)
(Undesirable)

Single shutter near the end P in a long wall.
(iii)
(Desirable)

Fig. 6.3 : Disposition doors

(b) Provision of frosted glass instead of plain glass for windows.

(c) Provision of an independent access to services such as toilet rooms or bath rooms.

6.3.4 Grouping

Every apartment in a building has got a definite function or functions. There is some sort of sequence in them. Hence, grouping of the apartments should facilitate maintaining the sequence of their functions with least intrusion.

In a residential building :

(a) Living room should be next to verandah. It should be away from kitchen to avoid smells and smoke.

(b) Dining room should be close to the kitchen.

(c) Kitchen should be so arranged that the house wife can easily approach the entrance without invading any rooms. A window should be provided in such a way that she can easily keep a watch at the entrance of the house and also on the children playing near about there.

(d) Main bed rooms should be placed that there is an independent and separate access from each bed room to the sanitary units directly.

(e) Staircase must be approachable from maximum number of rooms.

(f) Passage areas must be minimum, well ventilated and with sufficient light.

Grouping depends upon the type of the building. Hospitals, colleges, cinema theatres, libraries or banks should be planned in such a way that occupants can move easily without causing disturbance to other units.

6.3.5 Roominess

This means the feeling of space which is usually expressed as sufficient, inadequate or more or cramping depending upon the proportion of length, breadth and height. The dimensions of the room should be arranged in such a way that maximum advantage is obtained from the minimum dimensions required for the functions expected from the room. The following observations about dimensions should be noted.

(a) If the length of the room exceeds 1.5 times the width, it will produce a cramped effect. Better proportion is L : B $\neq$ 1.2 to 1.5 : 1.

(b) **Shape :** A square room relatively appears smaller than rectangular room of the same area. It is also smaller in respect of utility as compared with rectangular shaped room.

(c) **Height :** Small rooms should not be made too high because they tend to produce a cave-like effect; such rooms appear smaller than their actual sizes.

(d) Positions of doors, windows, cupboards, lofts and their level as well as colour treatment of flooring walls, ceilings etc. are all responsible for creating the effect of space. Light colours will creates the effect of more space as compared to dark colour.

6.3.6 Furniture Requirements

The success of functional planning is revealed in turn in the plane showing detailed furniture arrangement in the various rooms. For example, the arrangement of sofas, chairs tables, carpets, television and other decorative pieces in the living room; chairs and dining table in the pieces in the dinning room cupboards and the refrigerator in kitchen, beds, easy chairs and dressing table etc. in the bed rooms.

The furniture should be arranged to give maximum area for movement, convenience regarding opening of doors, windows and cupboards. Positions of beds should give privacy, sufficient light for reading and comfortable breeze during night.

The whole set-up must be fully comfortable and it should not create any clumsy or cramped feeling.

In case of library building, hotels, schools, cinema theatres etc. the furniture arrangement plans are necessary to fix the sizes of the units with reference to number of persons to be accommodated. The sizes and shapes of machines should be taken into account in deciding the factory buildings units.

6.3.7 Circulation

Circulation in a building means 'access' or 'internal' through fares'. It is of two types.

(a) Horizontal circulation : It means access to the room on the same floor. It is achieved by proper provision of passages, corridors, halls and lobbies.

(b) Vertical circulation : It means access to the rooms on different floors. It is achieved by the provision of stairs, staircases and electric lifts.

For better circulation, the points given below should be considered in planning the building.

(1) All passages should be short, straight well lighted and well ventilated, narrow, much widening and semidard passages should be avoided.

(2) The entrances, hallways, corridors should create a sense of invitation to go from one room to the other. They are transitional places and they should be carefully planned. They should not have an old tunnel like appearance.

(3) Privacy should not be disturbed in moving from one room to another.

(4) All the sanitary services on the same floor must have an independent access from every room through a lobby. This increases the usefulness of the building.

(5) Stair should be easily accessible from entrance as well as rooms on the floor. It should have strong hand rails preferably on both sides. It should satisfy the minimum requirements regarding width, rise, tread, landing, light and ventilation.

6.3.8 Sanitation

In a broad way, the term sanitation includes considerations for ventilation light, cleanliness, and sanitary conveniences.

(a) Ventilation : It means removal of the vitiated air and supply of fresh and refreshing air to the room. It can be achieved in a natural way be providing sufficient windows and ventilators in a room, foul air produces nausea, headaches, sleepiness and thus decreases and efficiency of persons. Hence, attention must be paid to the volume of the room, the height of the room and the rate movement of air in a room.

(b) Lighting : In any building light uniform distribution is essential for good visibility. Direct and strong glare should be avoided. It is generally desirable to have predominance of light from one direction, with a smaller proportion of diffused light from another.

The upper part of the window is more effective for illuminating the far side of a room than the lower part.

Hence, vertical windows are preferable to horizontal windows of the same area. R.C.C. or steel grills should be constructed for passages and staircase so that more light is available for maximum part of the day. Cloudy days of mason form the critical time for illumination. Use of white colour for ceiling, white or light shades of colour for walls in passages and rooms improves the lighting. The artificial lighting adopted for rooms depends on their purposes, for general movements, conversation rest or recreation light should be diffused over the entire area of the room. However, for reading, writing, dressing, needlework, artwork etc. at nights concentrated lighting with relatively more illumination is desired.

(c) Cleanliness : The general cleaning and upkeep of the building is the responsibility of the occupants. However, the provisions should be made to facilitate cleaning. Dust is injurious to health. It allows the growth of bacteria and spreads the diseases. Hence,

(i) The floors should be made of non-absorbent surfaces, proper slope should be given to the floors to facilitate washing.

(ii) Interiors of the building should have a very plain treatment. Ornamental mouldings, skirtings, cornices should be often cleaned as the dust accumulate at these places.

(d) Sanitary conveniences : These include bath rooms, lavatories, latrines, urinals etc. They form the statutory requirement of a building and hence are not optional.

(i) W.C.s and bath rooms should be provided with dada so that they can be cleaned regularly.

(ii) Water carriage system is good for cleaning. Provision of overhead reservoir is necessary for continuous water supply to these units.

6.3.9 Elegance

Elegance is the effect produced by elevation and general layout of the building plan. It is always better to develop elevation before plan has been finalised to the last detail. Utility is the main consideration in preparing the plan.

Doors and windows are located on the basis of aspect and prospect considerations. However, the visualization of effects which will be produced by the elevation is always essential. The elevation depends upon the proportion of width, height, number of doors and windows and the choice of materials. Unless proper attention is paid to the elegance, a well unit plan may produce the most dull and ugly elevation. On the other hand, an elegant elevation is the external statement of the purpose of the building, its internal facts and indicates the character.

Aesthetics is the result of elegance.

6.3.10 Economy

Economy may not be a principle of planning but it is certainly a factor which affects planning. It restricts the liberaties of an architect in planning. It may also require certain commissions and alternations in the original plan.

The following general considerations should be remembered in effecting economy in planning.

(a) Economy should not have any evil effect on grouping or aspect. If need be there, to some extent prospect can be sacrificed.

(b) Strength and stability of the structure should be the main considerations. A strong and solid building may be costly in its initial cost but in the long run it may prove cheaper due to low maintenance cost.

(c) A building is an immovable property constructed to last for many generations. Comforts and convenience form the main considerations. Hence, false economy should be avoided. Scope should be kept for future expansion.

(B) BYE-LAWS

6.4 BUILDING BYE-LAWS

6.4.1 Necessity of Building Bye-Laws

A bye-law is the local law framed by a competent authority. Every locality has its own peculiarities with respect to the climatic conditions, geological conditions, i.e. availability of materials for construction, labour etc. If a building is built in a definite planned way, the construction becomes economically sound and safe. As such there must be a law or regulations on the part of the owner while building his own house. If not, the house-owner under his 'ownership' right will construct the house, which may affect the interests of others in respect of health and convenience. The landlord will take only profit into account and spend minimum amount to get the maximum benefit. The builder takes everything for granted and hopes to get away with everything. Hence, there must be restriction to limit the power of the builder or owner to deal with the property. This is done under Building Regulations which are a compressive code of Building Bye-laws.

6.4.2 Objects of Bye-Laws

1. To give guidelines to the designer, architect or engineer.
2. To prevent haphazard development.
3. To control land development and to check unauthorised construction i.e. encroachment on public and private land.
4. To limit or define the way the new structures are to be built.
5. To specify the type of materials to be used.
6. To provide open spaces, air, breeze, etc.
7. To afford safety against fire, noise and smoke etc.

The building regulations are generally uniform in character, covering the entire town, or city. The regulations are drawn by a panel of experts in different fields as Engineering, Public Health, Law, General Administration and Town planning. It is the Municipality or the Corporation which forms the building bye-laws as per the Municipal Act or Corporation Act. These bye-laws are generally passed by the Municipal councillors or corporators and then it is finally approved by the government, which then becomes a regulation to be enforced on all buildings whether constructed by the Government, Local bodies or Private persons and Agencies.

It is therefore, necessary that the planning persons must have knowledge of the building bye-laws and regulations. Only those plans are approved which comply with the requirements of building bye-laws and license for constructions is issued. We will discuss a few important bye-laws without entering into details.

6.5 IMPORTANT BYE-LAWS

6.5.1 Floor Space Index (F.S.I.) or Floor Area Ratio (F.A.R.)

The ratio of total built-up area of all floors to the plot area of the building is called Floor Space Index, abbreviated to F.S.I. It is a pure number. The F.S.I. is fixed by the local authority and is different for different areas and different buildings in the city. As such the built-up areas are governed by F.S.I. The F.S.I. therefore, checks the height of the building and as a consequence, it controls the density of population. For example, if the plot area consists of 36 squares with F.S.I. as I then the maximum buildable area will be $36 \times 1 = 36$. Now, if this area is to be utilised for multi-storeyed building, then two floors are necessary to utilise areas of 18 squares, three floors to utilise 12 squares (See Fig. 6.4), four floors to utilise 9 squares, nine floors to utilise 4 squares. (See Fig. 6.5)

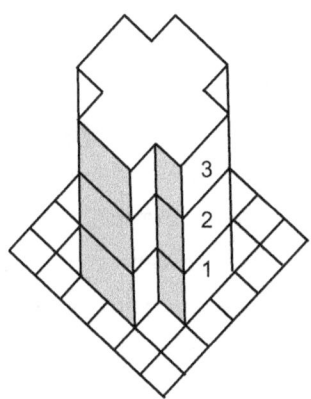   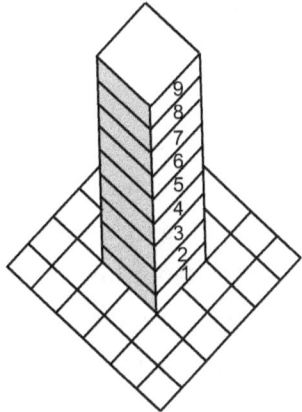

Floor space index = 1
Per floor built-up = 12 squares
(Buildable area = 12×3 = 36 squares)
Fig. 6.4

Per floor built-up area = 4 squares
(Buildable area = 4×9 = 36 squares)
Fig. 6.5

The F.S.I. is, therefore, the total area of all floors including floor. It does not include the basement area. The following is also excluded from the total area viz. staircase hall, balconies, chajjas, parking on stilt, water tanks on the roofs or terrace, garages, mezzanine floor (provided it covers not more than 40% of the area of the room and height not more than 2.6 m).

Generally, F.S.I. is fixed at I to 2 by the local authority.

In the central places of cities, for commercial + residential buildings, it is 2. In other places only for residential buildings it is 1.5, while in all suburbs and colonies it is I. But F.S.I. can be changed by the authority as and when the circumstances arise to accommodate the over-growing population. For example, in Pune and Mumbai, it can be even 3 to 5.

6.5.2 Height of Building

Tall buildings impair the value of small neighbouring houses by cutting off sun-shine, air, breeze etc. and thus, make the small houses unsuitable for inhabitation. They make the street narrow and increase the congestion of traffic and affect the air and light etc. Hence, the height of the buildings especially high-rise buildings or sky-scrapers must be controlled. It is done by means of height zoning. There are various methods of zoning which are used to control the height of high-rise buildings. In first method the height of the building is regulated according to the width of abutting road or minimum width of the rear space. [See Fig. 6.6].

Generally, 45° and 63.5° Air plane Rules are adopted. The rule states that no part of the tall building should cut the plane drawn from the edge of the road on other side or from the rear space-boundary (minimum 3 m) at an angle of 45° and 63.5° to the horizontal The ratio of height to width of the road will be 1 : 1 in case of 45° air plane rule and 2 : 1 in case of 63.5° air plane rule. Hence, the latter is very commonly used but set-back shown as 'S' [See Fig. 6.6 (b) and Fig. 6.7] is necessary as soon as the building attains permitted height. As a result of height zoning, there is considerable control in design of high-rise buildings or modern sky-scrapers.

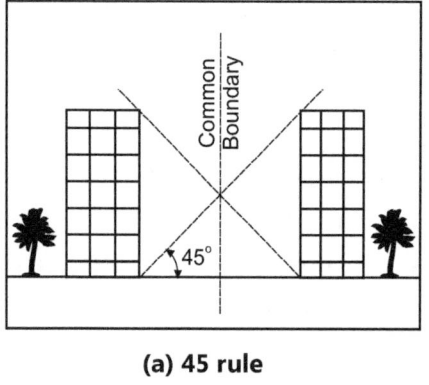
(a) 45 rule

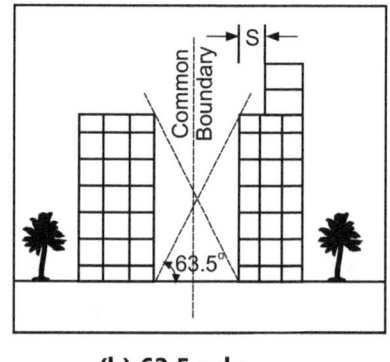
(b) 63.5 rule

Fig. 6.6

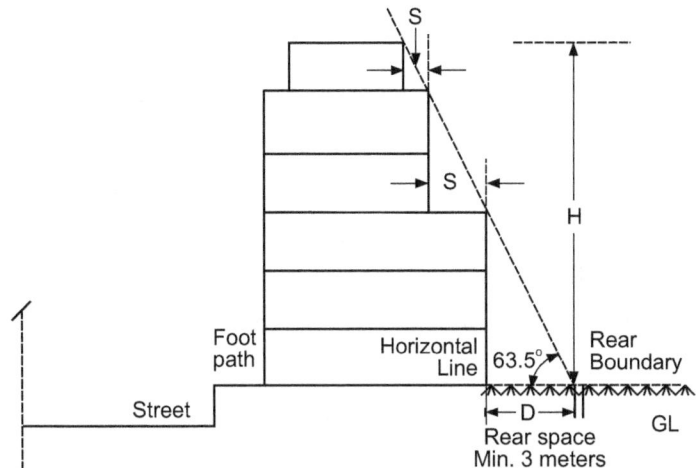

Fig. 6.6 : Rule : Height-H should never exceed D tan 63.5°

Advantages of Air-Plane Rule

1. It dose not allow the tall buildings to grow nearby building of lesser height.
2. It establishes minimum standards in terms of light, air and space, thereby creates healthy conditions.
3. It controls the set-back from roads.
4. It helps to construct the buildings with uniform height. And the harmonious grouping makes the street picture as pleasing as possible.

Table 6.1 gives a typical example of height of the building with reference to width of the roads.

Table 6.1 : Limits on Height of Buildings

Width of road	Maximum height of building
Upto 8 m	Not more than 1.5 times the width of the road.
8 m to 12 m	Not more than 12 m.
Above 12 m	Not more than width of the road and not more than 21 m.

The height of the building also depends on the vicinity of aerodromes. The height is fixed with the consultation of Civil Aviation Authority.

While planning the house you should be careful to provide the **minimum accommodate requirements as follows** :

I.S. Recommendations :

1. For proper health point of view, every habitable room should have a minimum of 9~5 sq area with at least 3.4 m width.

2. Floor area for kitchen shall not be less than 5.6 sq.m. with minimum side width of 1.8 any where.
3. The height of the habitable room shall be minimum 2.75 m. For W.C. it shall be min 2.4 m.
4. From point of view of air, light the aggregate area of door and window opening should be less than one-seventh of the floor area. Ventilators of the aggregate area at a rate of sq.m. per 10 cubic meters of space of the rooms should be provided.
5. Minimum height of plinth should be 45 cm above plot level or road level whichever is higher.

The sanitary requirements should be as follows.

(i) One water-closet of 1.2 sq.m. area.

(ii) One closed bath-room of 1.8 sq.m. area (1.5 m x 1.2 m.)

(iii) One general washing place of 2.4 sq.m. area.

6.5.3 Open Space Requirements

Certain open space should be left around the building particularly residential type. It depends on air required for the building. The open spaces shall be open to the sky and no cornice, weather shade, or roof more than 0.75 m wide shall over-hung on such open spaces. Open areas also provide facilities for parking, future expansion of road-way, good approach or access to other amenities such as water supply line or drainage line etc.

Table 6.2 : Minimum space around the building

Height of building in metres	5	6	9	12	15	18	20	24
Width of open spaces in metres	3	3.3	4	4.7	5.4	6.1	7.4	9

6.5.4 Bye-Laws for Lighting

1. For light, a clear window area in the wall abutting to the air space either directly or through an open verandah or gallery should not be less than one tenth of the floor area of the room for dry, hot climate (hot arid) and one sixth for wet, hot climate (hot humid).
2. The aggregate area of the door and window openings should not be less than one seventh of the room.
3. However, for the apartments where doors need not be closed for the sake of privacy or security, aggregate area of openings may be provided either by windows or doors.
4. This becomes a possibility in the case of living rooms and dining halls where such rooms have an open verandah or gallery.

5. In addition to the above means of light, every such room should have a ventilator of at least 0.3 sq.m. in an area near the top of each of two walls of such rooms and these ventilators should be preferably placed opposite to each other for thorough ventilation. When this is not possible, then ventilators should be placed at least in the adjoining walls.
6. Generally, the aggregate area of such ventilators is provided at the rate of 0.1 sq.m. for every 10 cubic meters of space of such rooms.

6.5.5 Set Back Distance

Building line refers to the front line upto which a building can lawfully extend. It is also called as 'set-back' or front building line. A minimum distance of this 'building line' from the centre line of the accompanying road is laid down as the limit beyond which no construction is allowed towards the road. In case of public buildings such as cinema halls and factories, the buildings attract more number of people and vehicles as such more space is required. Hence, the buildings should be set back a further distance away from the building line. The line, which accounts for this extra margin is called as 'control line'. See Fig. 6.7.

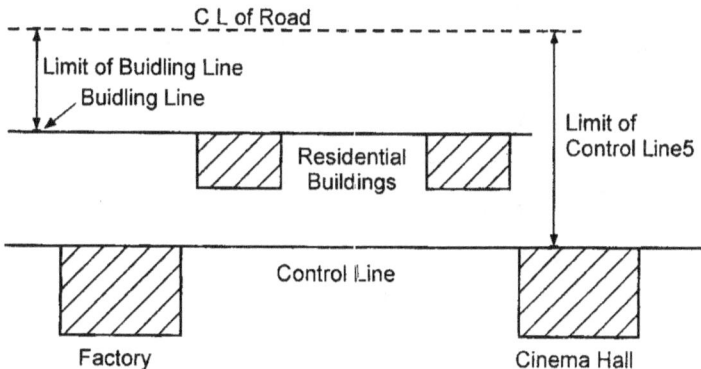

Fig. 6.7 : Building and Control lines

The limits of building and control lines are given in Table 6.3.

Table 6.3 : Building and Control Lines

Type of road	Building line	Control line
National and State Highway (N.H. and S.H.)	30 m	45 m
Major District Roads (M.D.R.)	15 m	24 m
Other Distract Road (O.D.R.)	9 m	15 m
Village Road (V.R.)	9 m	15 m

Advantages :

The set back effected by the building line has the following advantages.

1. If necessary, part of the set-back may be acquired for the purpose of widening the roads.
2. It keeps noise and dust away from the building.
3. The set-back at street corners improves visibility and provides safety to the traffic.
4. It reduces danger of fire.
5. The space of set-backs can be used as parking place or for developing a garden.
6. It helps better conditions of air, light and ventilation of the buildings.

6.5.6 Built-Up Area

The built-up area is the constructed area of the building which includes wall thickness. Therefore, built-up area is the area remaining after deducting open space area from plot area i.e. the total area purchased for the proposed building plan. See Fig. 6.8. Carpet area is the built-up area less the area occupied by walls. When open space area is restricted then the built-up area of any building is automatically restricted. According to use there are restrictions on built-up areas, as given below.

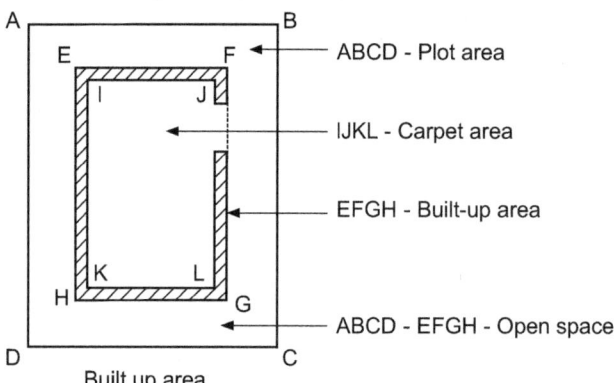

Fig. 6.8

1. In a bazaar or market area, the built-up area shall not exceed 75% of the site area, provided ample space for parking in available on the same site.
2. In an industrial area, the build-up area shall not exceed 60% of the site area.
3. In case of residential area, the built-up areas are as stated below.

Area of the plot	Permissible Built-up Area with two storeyed structures
(i) Less than 200 sq.m.	60%
(ii) 200 sq.m. to 500 sq.m.	50%
(iii) 500 sq.m. to 1000 sq.m.	40%
(iv) More than 1000 sq.m.	33.33%

6.5.7 Minimum Sizes for Different Components in a Residential Building

Requirements of individual rooms and apartments according to their sizes are discussed here along with the principles of planning and essentials of certain types of buildings from the point of view of health and standards of living and ventilation. Certain absolute minimum rules about area are fixed and are given below:

1. Every habitable room should not have an area less than 9.5 sq.m with a minimum width of 2.4 m.
2. If such a room is a kitchen, its floor area should not be less than 5.6 sq.m and preferably 9 to 10 sq.m when it is to be used for dining also.
3. A kitchen cum dining hall should not have an area smaller than 18 sq.m
4. The area of a living room of a double room tenement should not be less than 14 sq.m
5. The area of a bathroom (minimum width 1.2 m) = 1.8 sq.m.
6. Area of W.C. (minimum width 0.9 m) = 1.18 sq.m.
7. Area of store room = 3 sq.m.
8. Area of a room general = 9.5 sq.m.

6.6 CONCEPT OF ECO-FRIENDLY STRUCTURES AND INTELLIGENT BUILDING

6.6.1 Introduction

Now-a-days the construction industry and architectural group are trying to construct eco-friendly buildings using eco-friendly materials. This will preserve and protect important resources like water, land and energy. For using eco-friendly materials effectively and also economically, following factors are required to be considered for selecting proper eco-friendly materials:

1. Local availability.
2. Recyclable.
3. Performance.
4. Energy conservation.
5. Reduce pollution like air pollution, land pollution and water pollution.

6.6.2 Sources of Eco-Friendly Materials

Following are the sources of eco-friendly materials:

1. Renewable Sources:

Renewable energy is the energy generated from natural resources. As an eco-friendly construction material, wood from certified forests is a best renewable source.

2. Reuse of Waste:

From various sources like domestic, industrial, institutional, commercial etc. different types of wastes are generated. Some of these wastes can be used as an eco-friendly construction material like salvaged products, e.g. old plumbing, door frames and recycled contents of agriculture and industrial waste e.g. Bagasse Board.

6.6.3 Classifications of Eco-Friendly Materials

Eco-friendly materials are classified on the basis of construction activities or items. Following are the classifications of eco-friendly materials:

1. Excavation work
2. Timber work
3. Doors and windows
4. Tiles for flooring, skirting, dado etc
5. Roofing
6. Ceiling
7. Colours, white washing, distempering and wood finishes
8. Water-proofing and chemical additives
9. Water supply and sanitary fittings
10. Electrical works

6.6.4 Properties of Eco-Friendly Materials and Techniques

Following are the properties of eco-friendly materials and techniques:

1. Local availability
2. Renewable Source
3. Biodegradable
4. Reuse of waste product
5. Reuse/recycle
6. Aids energy efficiency in buildings
7. Reduction in air, land and water pollution
8. Durability and life span

6.6.5 Eco-Friendly Materials

Following are the eco-friendly materials:

1. Stone dust.
2. Calcium silicate boards.
3. Precast cement concrete blocks.
4. Cellular light weight concrete blocks.
5. Compressed stabilised earth blocks (CSEB).
6. Sun dried bricks.
7. Clay roofing tiles.
8. Cement paint.
9. Acrylic based chemical admixtures for water proofing, corrosion removal, rust prevention etc.
10. Epoxy resin system, adhesives and admixtures.
11. Ferro-cement panels for door and window shutters.
12. Ferro-cement roofing channels.
13. Fly-ash paver blocks.
14. Fly-ash bricks.
15. Gypsum blocks, tiles and boards.
16. Marble mosaic tiles.
17. Micro concrete roofing tiles.
18. Polymerised water proof compound.
19. Portland pozzolana cements fly ash.
20. Concrete with coal fly ash.
21. Concrete with rise husk fly ash.

22. Conventional insulation materials which are made from petrochemicals and includes: fibre glass, polyurethane, polystyrene, mineral wool etc.
23. Natural insulation materials: Flax and hemp, Sheep's wool, Cellulose, wood fibre etc.
24. Biomass roofing material : Thatch and wood tiles (Shingles and Shakes)

SOLVED EXAMPLES

Example 6.1 : A plot is having dimensions 30 m × 40 m. A building constructed on it occupies 400 m² on ground and 350 m² on the first floor. If FSI permitted is 0.8 how much area can be constructed on second floor ? **(May 2001, 4 M)**

Solution : Plot area = 30 m × 40 m

∴ $\dfrac{\text{Total build up area}}{1200} = 0.8$

∴ T.B.A. = 960 m²

∴ Area on constructed second floor = 960 – (400 + 350)

= 210 m²

Example 6.2 : For a rectangular plot 25 m × 36 m. from FSI = 1.33 and building with G +1 stray to be constructed by consuming full FSI. Front and floor margins to be left are 3 m and side margins are 2.5 m. Determine area on each floor.

Solution : Plot area = 25 m × 36 m

If perm FSI = 1.33

∴ Building area = 1.33 × 1200

= 1200 m²

Margins considered

Area of ground = [25 – (2 × 2.5)] × [36 – 2(3)]

= 600 m²

∴ Area on first floor = 600 m²

Example 6.3 : Plot corner proposed G + 1 construction with 150 sq.mtr. On each floor on plot size 14 m × 19 m. Find ground coverage and FSI proposed. If margins from all sides are 2 m and FSI = 1 are must as per Byelaws, state with reasons whether plan will be standard or not ?

Actual plot area = 14 × 19 = 266 m²

Solution : Actual ground area constructed = (14 – 4) × (19 – 4)

= 150 m²

Proposed work – FSI = $\dfrac{150 \times 2}{266}$ = 1.12

Permissible FSI = 1

∴ As proposed FSI > Permissible FSI

Plan will not be sanctioned.

Example 6.4 : A rectangular plot 20 m × 25 m has a building with two floors of built-up areas 260 m² and 200 m² respectively. Ratio of carpet to built-up areas is 0.85. Find FSI used and carpet area on each floor.

Solution : FSI = $\dfrac{\text{BU area}}{\text{Plot area}}$ = $\dfrac{260 + 200}{(20 \times 25)}$ = 0.92

Carpet area = 0.85 × 260

= 221 m² one floor

= 0.85 × 200

= 170 m² other floor

EXERCISE

[A] Principles of Planning

1. What is the necessity of planning of a building ?
2. (i) Explain "Aspect" as a principle of planning of building.
   (ii) State how "Prospect" is different from "Orientation". Explain with sketches.
   (iii) State the aspect you will provide for kitchen, bed room, factory building.
   (iv) Explain factors affecting the orientation of a building.
3. What is roominess ? State general norms for the ratio between length and width. State effect of shape of a room on roominess.
4. (i) Comment "Privacy is the important principle of planning in residential building".
   (ii) How a privacy can be provided
       (a) to one room from another room ?
       (b) from one building to another building ?
5. (a) Write short note on "Circulation" as a principle of planning.
   (b) State the considerations for better and proper circulation.
   (c) Explain the term grouping.

6. Write short note on orientation.
7. Explain the requirements of "sanitation" in building as regards
   (i) light and ventilation (ii) cleanliness (iii) sanitary apartment.

[B] Building bye-laws

8. Why building bye-laws are required ? Whether these are universal ?
9. State important building bye-laws.
10. (a) Explain terms built-up area and carpet area and FSI.
    (b) State the factors affecting FSI.
11. Make a list of factors that influence the planning of a building.
12. Distinguish between "Building line" and "Control line."
13. A building is to be constructed with G + 2 storeys and built up area on each floor is to be 600 m². A rectangular plot is purchased for this building, having width along road one third of the longer side of right angles to the road. Find the dimensions of the plot; if FSI allowed is 1.50.

    Ans. Plot area $= \dfrac{\text{Total built-up area}}{\text{FSI}} = \dfrac{600 \times 3}{1.5} = 1200 \text{ m}^2$

    $= $ (short side) (longer side) $= x \cdot 3x = 3x^2$

    $\therefore \quad x = \sqrt{\dfrac{1200}{3}} = 20 \text{ m}.$

14. A rectangular plot measures 25 × 36 m. The front and side spacing are 3 m and side set backs are 2.5 m. Permissible FSI is 1.33. G + 1 storeyed building is to be constructed to consume full F.S.I. Determine area on each storey.

    Ans. F.S.I. $= \dfrac{\text{Total built-up area}}{\text{Plot area}}$

    $\therefore \quad$ Total built-up area $= (1.33)(25 \times 36)$

    $= 1200 \text{ m}^2$

    Maximum area available in plan, on each floor leaving side margin

    $= (25 - 2 \times 2.5)(36 - 2 \times 3) = 20 \times 30 = 600 \text{ m}^2$

    $\therefore$ On each of 2 floors, construction upto 600 m² can be constructed, thereby 600 × 2 = 1200 m² area can be consumed.

UNIT IV

Chapter 7
FOUNDATION

7.1 INTRODUCTION

Introduction : The part of structure, which is above ground level is called as superstructure and the part of structure which is below ground level is called as substructure.

Foundation is the part of substructure, which receives load of superstructure and transmits it to lower and firmer strata safely without causing excessive settlement or stresses or any damage to superstructure.

It is very difficult and costly to carry out any repairs to foundation after it is constructed. Hence, it is essential to understand basic principles of foundations.

7.1.1 Definition and Purpose of Foundation

It is the part of structure below ground level, which is directly in contact with subsoil to receive load of superstructure and to transmit it to firm strata below safely.

Foundation of a building is designed to achieve following objectives :

1. It should carry loads safely. The soil strata, on which foundation is to rest, should be strong enough to safely bear the loads imposed on it.

2. Settlement of structure should be uniform and within permissible limits. Due to loads imposed on foundation, structure is likely to settle. Foundation is designed so that, settlement is as uniform as possible throughout and is within permissible limits.

3. Differential settlement should be less. If a part of foundation settles more than the other part then the difference between the two settlements is called as 'Differential settlement'. This differential settlement induces heavy stresses and cracks appear in superstructure thereby endangering safety of structure.

4. It should offer required stability to structure against uplift forces, sliding and overturning.

5. It should be strong to resist attack by harmful substances and strong undercurrents (if any) present in subsoil.

6. Construction of foundation should not cause adverse effects on adjoining structures and on environment. e.g. Vibrations during pile driving or pumping out of ground water may cause large settlement of adjoining structures.

7.1.2 Ultimate Bearing Capacity of Soil

Ultimate bearing capacity (q_u) of soil is the maximum load per unit area that soil below foundation can carry before failing in shear.

As load on soil increases, soil below foundation settles. When load is increased further, a point is reached, when the soil below is on the verge of shear failure.

7.1.3 Safe Bearing Capacity (S.B.C.)

Definition : Safe bearing capacity (SBC) is defined as the ultimate bearing capacity of soil, divided by suitable factor of safety.

In order to guard against various unknown factors such as inadequate knowledge of subsoil, loading etc. instead of adopting ultimate bearing capacity reduced bearing capacity is adopted, while designing the foundation.

Ultimate bearing capacity (q_u) when divided by suitable Factor of Safety (F.S.) gives Safe Bearing Capacity (S.B.C.).

$$\text{Safe Bearing Capacity} = \frac{\text{Ultimate Bearing Capacity } q_u}{\text{Factor of Safety (F.S.)}}$$

$$= \frac{q_u}{\text{F.S.}} = \frac{q_u}{2 \text{ to } 3}$$

Higher factor of safety is adopted, when there is uncertainty about strata, loading, ground watertable etc. Factor of safety ranges between 2 to 3. I.S. suggests factor of safety of 2.5 for shallow foundations.

7.1.3.1 Use of Code of Practice for Adoption of S.B.C.

At proposed construction site, trial pits of size 1.2 m × 1.2 m and upto sufficient depth are excavated to know the underlying strata. Depending upon strata met with, code of practice recommends Safe Bearing Capacity that can be adopted.

Following Table 7.1 gives values of Safe Bearing Capacity that can be adopted for different strata.

Table 7.1 : Safe bearing capacity of different types of soils as per BIS code

	Type of Soil / Rock	Recommended safe bearing capacity in kN/m²
1.	Broken shattered bed rock.	900
2.	(a) Soft rock. (b) Coarse compact, dry sand gravel, sand and gravel. (c) Hard or stiff clay.	450
3.	(a) Medium compact, dry sand (b) Loose gravel or sand gravel or loose coarse dry sand. (c) Medium clay which can be indented with *thumb nail*.	250
4.	(a) Fine sand, silt. (b) Moist clay, sand clay mixture which can be indented *with strong thumb pressure*.	150
5.	Soft clay, made up of ground, black cotton soil.	To be determined after proper site investigation or so.

7.2 TYPES OF FOUNDATIONS

Depending upon the ratio of depth D and width W, foundation is classified as under :

1. Shallow foundation = $\left(\dfrac{D}{W} < 1\right)$.

2. Deep foundation = $\dfrac{D}{W} > 4$

Shallow foundation is further classified according to distribution of load on soil as shown in following Fig. 7.1.

FUNDAMENTALS OF CIVIL ENGINEERING   FOUNDATION

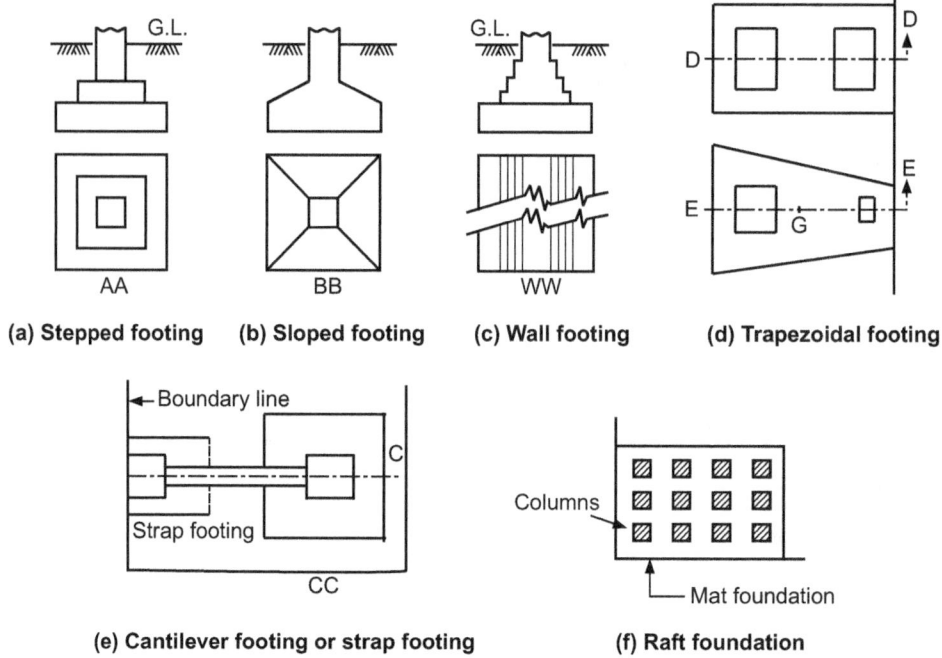

Fig. 7.1

7.2.1 Spread Footing

It is the most common type of shallow foundation used to transmit load of wall or isolated column. The base of wall of column is enlarged or spread to distribute load over a large area (to reduce intensity of load). Spread footing does not directly rest on soil. Usually about 15 to 30 cm thick lean concrete of mix (1 : 4 : 8) called as foundation concrete is first laid, as a base course to cover small pockets in foundation and to provide level surface for laying spread footing.

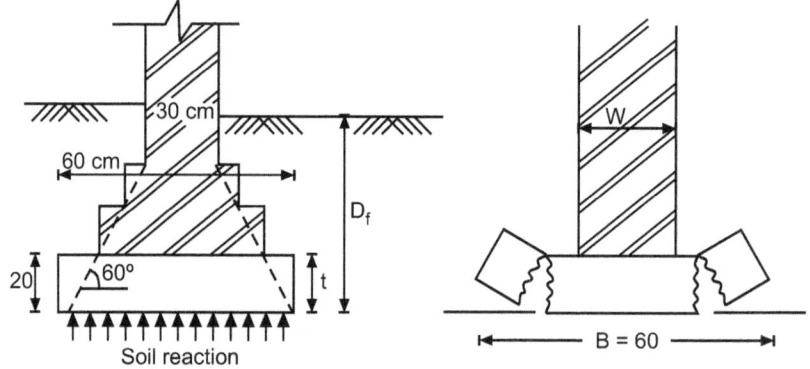

Fig. 7.2 : Stepped Foundation

Over this foundation concrete, spread footing rests. If load of wall footing is high and if there is probability of differential settlement, then instead of providing plain foundation concrete, the foundation concrete is reinforced by providing steel reinforcement.

1. If projection of footing beyond wall is excessive, the footing may crack due to soil reaction in the cantilever portion. Hence stepped foundation is provided.

2. If thickness "t" of footing is less, the wall may punch in the footing.

3. Depth of foundation (D_f) should be adequate to give necessary safe bearing capacity. Minimum depth of foundation of 90 cm is provided.

7.2.2 Isolated Column Footings

These are used to support individual columns and can be simple spread footing or stepped spread footing or sloped footing. See Fig. 7.1 (b).

7.2.3 Combined Footing

Combined footings are provided under following situations :

1. When loads on adjacent columns are very high.

2. Bearing capacity of soil is relatively less and

3. There is possibility of heavy differential settlement.

In combined footing, a common footing is provided for two or more columns. Combined footing is very rigid hence, the columns settle together and thereby eliminate possibility of differential settlement. Depending upon different loading conditions, following varieties of combined footing are provided :

(a) Rectangular Combined Footing : Refer Fig. 7.3.

This type of footing is provided :

(i) When load to be carried by the two columns is high and is nearly same.

(ii) Distance between two columns is less.

(iii) Projection of footing beyond the columns is permitted.

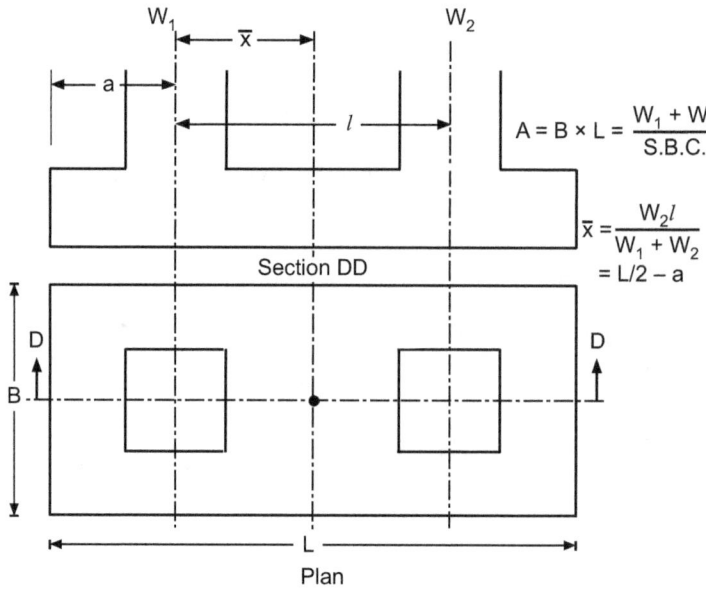

Fig. 7.3 : Combined Rectangular Footing

(b) Trapezoidal Footing : This type of combined footing is provided when,

(i) Loads to be carried by two adjacent columns are high.

(ii) *Difference between the two column loads is large* and

(iii) Bearing capacity of soil is less.

Trapezoidal footing consists of proportionately more width near heavier column and less width near lighter column as shown in Fig. 7.4.

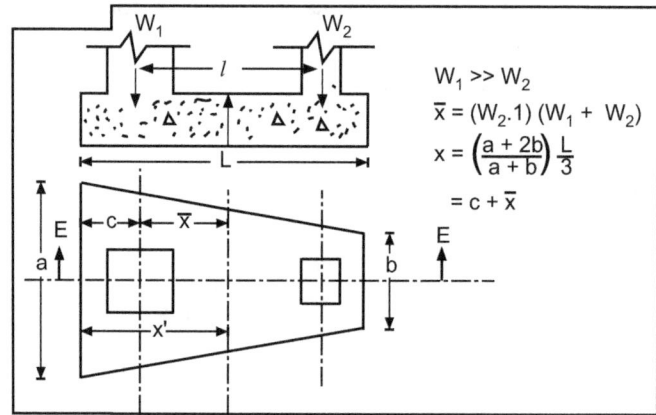

Fig. 7.4 : Trapezoidal Footing

(c) Cantilever Footing or Strap Footing : This type of footing is provided when,

(i) Column footing is not permitted to project beyond column face as in case of a column near compound wall.

(ii) When the distance between the two columns for which a combined footing is to be provided is more. In such a case, the rectangular footing is not economical.

Individual Column Footing is provided in proportion to reactions R_1 and R_2 below columns C_1 and C_2 [Refer Fig. 7.5]. Two footings are connected together rigidly by a beam. Hence the footings settle together and avoid differential settlement. Due to cantilever action, the reaction R_1 is more than cantilever load W_1.

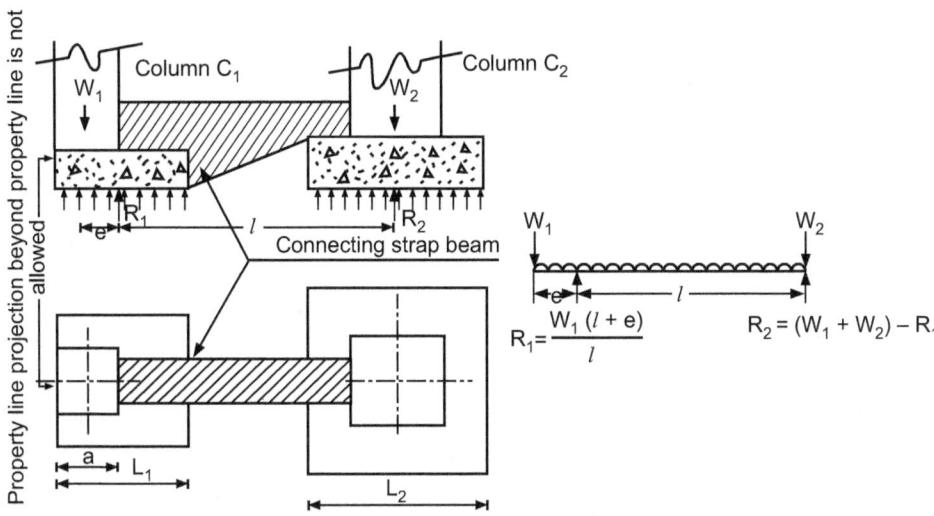

Fig. 7.5 : Cantilever Footing

Sometimes this footing is also called as pump handle footing.

(d) Mat or Raft Foundation : This type of foundation is provided when

(i) Bearing capacity of soil is low or difficult to determine or is of doubtful nature or strata is highly compressible.

(ii) Loads are heavy.

(iii) Use of spread footing would cover more than 50 % of the entire area.

(iv) It is difficult to control differential settlement.

A mat or raft foundation is a combined footing. It covers entire area beneath a structure and supports all walls through beams and columns.

Raft consists of thick, heavily reinforced inverted slab using heavy beams from column to columns. Raft tends to bridge over erratic deposits and hence eliminate differential settlement. For this reason, total settlement of 75 to 100 mm is permitted for raft foundation. In case of highly compressible strata, raft foundation is taken to such a depth that,

   Weight of excavated soil = Weight of structure and loads on structure

Such type of foundation is called as floating foundation.

Sometimes, to reduce the self-weight of thick raft, cellular foundation or reinforced basement walls serve as raft. A few types of rafts are shown below :

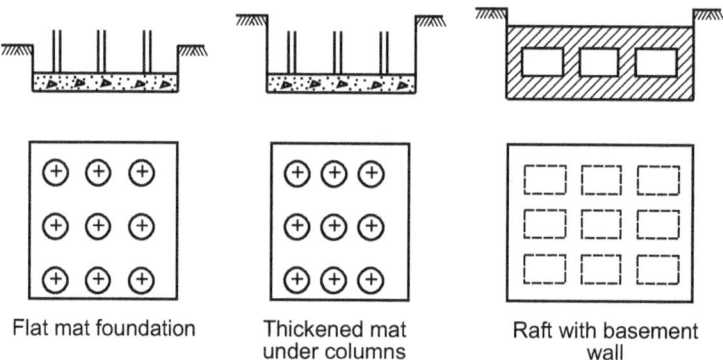

Fig. 7.6 : Mat/Raft foundation

7.2.4 Deep Foundations

These foundations carry heavy loads from structure through weak, compressible soils or fills on stronger and less compressible soils or rock at a considerable depth.

Pile foundation is a type of deep foundation and is explained below :

(1) Pile Foundations, (2) Well Foundations.

7.2.5 Pile Foundation

Pile is a long slender member that is driven on the ground or cast in situ.

Pile foundation is preferred under following situations :

(a) When open foundation is not possible or for structure such as in deep-sea, or river, or where there is heavy seepage.

(b) When open excavation upto firm strata is difficult and uneconomical or when water table is high or strata consists of expensive soils.

(c) When loads are heavy, non-uniform and there is possibility of differential settlement at shallow depth.

(d) Mat or raft foundation is uneconomical.

7.2.6 Classification of Piles

A pile is the most commonly used foundation for difficult soil conditions. They can carry loads, resist horizontal and uplift forces, or compact a loose, cohesionless deposit. A large variety of piles are available. They can be classified using the criteria listed below (see also Fig. 7.7).

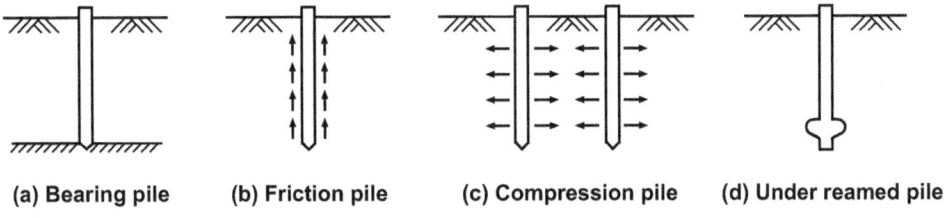

(a) Bearing pile   (b) Friction pile   (c) Compression pile   (d) Under reamed pile

Fig. 7.7 : Different types of piles

1. **Mechanism of load transfer.** A **friction pile** carries the load by mobilizing the friction along its sides. **Bearing piles** transfer the load to a stronger stratum underlying the weak zone. Of course, both components may be contributing simultaneously in resisting loads. Whether a friction or a bearing pile should be provided depends on site conditions such as the relative thickness and stiffness of soil strata and soil properties.

2. **Material of construction.** Piles may be of steel concrete or both. Because of the confining effect of soil, very little reinforcement is required for concrete piles. Wooden piles are rarely used these days as they are weak and likely to decay.

3. **Method of construction.** This can be **driven** or **bored**. Steel or precast-concrete piles are driven into the ground. Bored piles are constructed by drilling a hole into ground, lowering a cage of reinforcement, and then pouring concrete into the hole. Many techniques have been developed and a number of patented construction procedures are available.

4. **Shapes.** Piles come in a variety of shapes and sections, including circular, hollow, steel H or I sections, with enlarged base and tapered piles.

7.3 CAUSES OF FAILURE OF FOUNDATIONS

(a) Differential Settlement of Foundation : If a structure settles uniformly, then no damage is caused. However, if there is uneven settlement of foundation, then it may lead to serious cracks in superstructure. Unfortunately, it is very difficult to measure differential settlement. However, if total settlement is restricted, automatically, it reduces differential settlement.

(b) Reduction in water table level due to drying of soil or due to pumping of water from nearby structure.

The reduction in water table induces very heavy stresses on soil; which in its turn imposes heavy stresses on foundation. This leads to heavy settlement / differential settlement and thereby failure of foundation.

(c) During heavy floods, lot of soil is erroded. Removal of soil, especially in case of piers of bridges, may lead to undermining below foundation and thereby cause failure of foundation.

(d) Heavy lateral and uplift forces.

A structure may be subjected to heavy lateral forces due to wind, earth pressure of embankments. If the foundation is not designed to withstand excessive compressive and tensile stresses, then it is likely to fail.

(e) Liquification of soil due to shock waves during earthquake or vibrations caused due to pile driving or due to machines.

(f) Sliding of embankment due to shear failure of soft soil located at greater depth. The strata immediately below the structure may be firm; however, at a greater depth a soft strata may be available.

(g) Failure due to poor quality of material used in foundation or failure of foundation material to resist harmful materials present in soil below.

EXERCISE

Foundation :

1. Explain the term foundation. Why it is necessary ?
   State different function of foundation.
2. (a) Explain with the help of load settlement curve ultimate bearing capacity.
   (b) What is safe bearing capacity ?

Settlement :

3. (a) What is differential settlement ? How it is expressed ? Explain with sketch.
   (b) State allowable limits for total settlement and differential settlement as per I.S.
   (c) State causes of settlement and differential settlement.
   (d) State the maximum settlement that can be allowed for
       (i) Raft foundation (ii) Spread footing on clays.
   (e) State effects of differential settlement.
   (f) Write a short note on (i) differential settlement
       (ii) settlement of foundation.

Types of foundation :

4. (a) Explain with sketches the circumstances under which following types of foundation are adopted.
    (1) Combined footing. (2) Isolated footing. (3) Raft foundation.
    (4) Pile foundation.
   (b) Distinguish between the following :
    (1) Isolated footing and combined footing :
    (2) Bearing pile and friction pile.
    Name different types of combined footings.
    Draw sketch of (i) Cantilever footing, (ii) Trapezoidal footing when they are provided.
5. What do you understand by raft foundation ? Explain with a neat sketch. When you will adopt raft foundation ?
6. Explain the suitability of each of the following : -
   (i) Stepped footing (ii) Raft foundation (iii) Pile foundation
   (iv) Isolated RCC column footing.
   Explain the following with suitable examples : -
   (i) Choice of foundation and bearing capacity of soil.
   (ii) Bearing capacity of soil and failure of foundation.
7. State functions of foundation. State the causes of failure of foundation.
8. State the permissible amount of settlement in clayey and sandy soil.
9. Differentiate between ultimate and safe bearing capacity of soil.
10. When it is necessary to provide combined footing ?
11. What are the remedial measures adopted in case of failure of foundation ?
12. List out different types of footings and explain in one sentence their specific importance.

UNIVERSITY QUESTIONS

1. State any three functions of foundations. **(Dec. 2003)**
2. Write short note on causes of settlement. **(Dec. 2003)**
3. Explain terms : **(Dec. 2003)**
   (i) Safe bearing capacity.
   (ii) Differential settlement.

4. Differentiate between shallow foundation and deep foundation. Give two examples of each. **(May 2004)**
5. Explain four causes of failure of foundation. **(May 2006)**
6. Draw sketches of following types of foundation :
    (i) Simple strap footing. **(Dec. 2003)**
    (ii) Isolated rectangular footing. **(Dec. 2003)**
    (iii) Sloped column footing. **(May 2006)**
    (iv) Trapezoidal combined footing. **(May 2006)**

UNIT IV

Chapter 8
EARTHQUAKE

8.1 INTRODUCTION

Although we still can't predict when an earthquake will happen, we have learned much about earthquakes as well as the Earth itself from studying them. We have learned how to pinpoint the locations of earthquakes, how to accurately measure their sizes, and how to build flexible structures that can withstand the strong shaking produced by earthquakes and protect our loved ones.

Earthquakes are the Earth's natural means of releasing stress. When the Earth's plates move against each other, stress is put on the lithosphere. When this stress is great enough, the lithosphere breaks or shifts. Imagine holding a pencil horizontally. If you were to apply a force to both ends of the pencil by pushing down on them, you would see the pencil bend. After enough force was applied, the pencil would break in the middle, releasing the stress you have put on it. The Earth's crust acts in the same way. As the plates move they put forces on themselves and each other. When the force is large enough, the crust is forced to break. When the break occurs, the stress is released as energy which moves through the Earth in the form of waves, which we feel and call an earthquake.

8.2 DEFINITION

Earthquake is a **sudden shock** on the Earth's surface. It is shaking and vibration at the surface of the earth resulting from underground movement along a fault plane of or from volcanic activity.

Most earthquakes occur along a fault, a fracture in the earth's rocky outer shell where sections of rock repeatedly slide past each other. Faults occur in weak areas of the earth's rock. Faults are created by stress in the Earth's Crust. Stress is a force that changes the shape of the object. When a material is stressed, the material responds in either of the three ways :

1. It can deform elastically, which means that when the stress is removed, the material goes back to its original form/shape.

2. It can deform inelastically, which means that when the stress is removed, the material stays in its new deformed shape.

3. It can fracture or break into pieces.

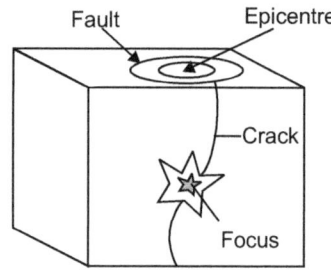

Fig. 8.1

When an earthquake occurs, the breaking of rock releases energy that travels through the earth in the form of vibrations called **seismic waves.** Different kinds of seismic waves are produced by the deformation of rock materials. A sudden slip along a fault produces both **longitudinal push-pull** and **transverse shear waves.** Seismic waves move out from the focus of an earthquake in all directions. As the waves travel away from the focus, they grow gradually weaker. For this reason, the ground generally shakes less the farther we move from the focus.

TYPES :

There are two types of Earthquake :

1. Interplate Earthquakes : Earthquakes that occur in the fault zones at plate boundaries.

2. Intraplate Earthquakes : Earthquakes take place within the interior of a plate.

Effects of earthquake : Ground shaking leads to landslides and other soil movement. These are the main damage-causing events that occur during an earthquake.

- **Primary effects** that can accompany an earthquake include property damage, loss of lives, fire and tsunami waves.

- **Secondary effects** such as economic loss, disease, and lack of food and clean water, also occur after a large earthquake.

8.3 CAUSES OF EARTHQUAKE

GROUND SHAKING :

1. Earthquake waves make the ground move, shaking buildings and structures and causing poorly designed or weak structures partially or totally collapse.

2. The ground shaking weakens soils and foundation materials under structures and causes dramatic changes in fine-grained soils.

3. During an earthquake, water-saturated sandy soil becomes like liquid mud, an effect called **liquefaction.** Liquefaction causes damage as the foundation soil beneath structures and buildings weakens.

4. Shaking may also dislodge large earth and rock masses, producing dangerous landslides, mudslides, and rock avalanches that may lead to loss of lives or further property damage.

TSUNAMI :

Tsunamis are usually made up of several oceanic waves that travel out from the slipped fault and arrive one after the other on shore. They can strike without warning, often in places very distant from the epicentre of the earthquake.

Tsunami waves are sometimes inaccurately referred to as tidal waves, but tidal forces do not cause them. Rather, tsunamis occur when a major fault under the ocean floor suddenly slips. The displaced rock pushes water above it like a giant paddle, producing powerful water waves at the ocean surface.

Tsunamis wash ashore with often disastrous effects such as severe flooding, loss of lives due to drowning and damage to property. Earthquakes can also cause water in lakes and reservoirs to oscillate, or slash back and forth.

Fig. 8.2

FIRE :

Fire is another post-earthquake threat. The amount of damage caused by post-earthquake fire depends on :

1. The types of building materials used.
2. Whether water lines are intact.
3. Whether natural gas mains have been broken.

DISEASE :

Disease Catastrophic earthquakes can create a risk of widespread disease outbreaks, especially in underdeveloped countries.

1. Lack of housing contributes to the spread of contagious diseases, such as influenza (the flu) and other viral infections. In some instances, lack of food supplies, clean water and heating can create serious health problems as well.
2. Damage to water supply lines.
3. Sewage lines.

8.4 DEFINITIONS OF THE TERMS

Focus : That point within the Earth from which originates the first motion of an earthquake and its elastic waves.

OR

It is the point on the (free) surface of the earth vertically above the place of origin (hypocenter) of an earthquake. This point is expressed by its geographical latitude and longitude.

Epicenter : That point on the Earth's surface directly above the hypocenter of an earthquake.

Isoseismal Line : A line connecting points on the Earth's surface at which earthquake intensity is the same. It is usually a closed curve around the epicenter.

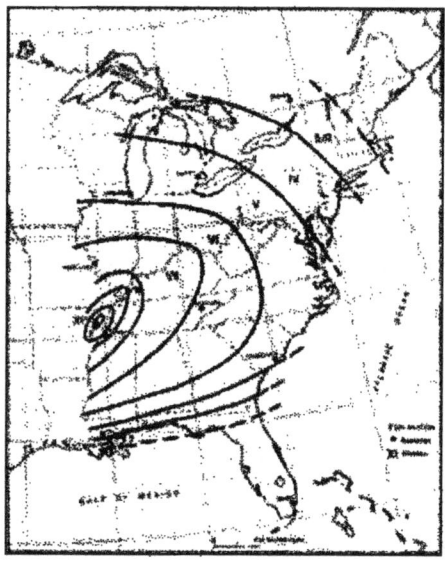

Fig. 8.3

Seismograph : An instrument that records the motions of the Earth, especially earthquakes.

Seismogram : A written record of an earthquake, recorded by a seismograph.

Hypocenter : The calculated location of the focus of an earthquake.

Intensity : A measure of the effects of an earthquake at a particular place on humans, structures and (or) the land itself. The intensity at a point depends not only upon the strength of the earthquake (magnitude) but also upon the distance from the earthquake to the point and the local geology at that point.

Magnitude : A measure of the strength of an earthquake or strain energy released by it, as determined by seismographic observations.

OR

It is the quantity to measure the size of an earthquake in terms of its energy and is independent of the place of the observation.

Richter Scale : The system used to measure the strength of an earthquake. It was developed by Charles Richter in 1935 as a means of categorizing local earthquakes. It is a collection of mathematical formulas; it is not a physical device.

OR

Magnitude is measured on the basis of ground motion recorded by an instrument and applying standard correction for the epicentral distance from recording station. It is linearly related to the logarithm of amount of energy released by an earthquake and expressed in Richter scale.

8.5 EFFECT OF EARTHQUAKE ON CIVIL STRUCTURES

Fig. 8.4 shown in itself can describe the effect caused by earthquake to civil structures.

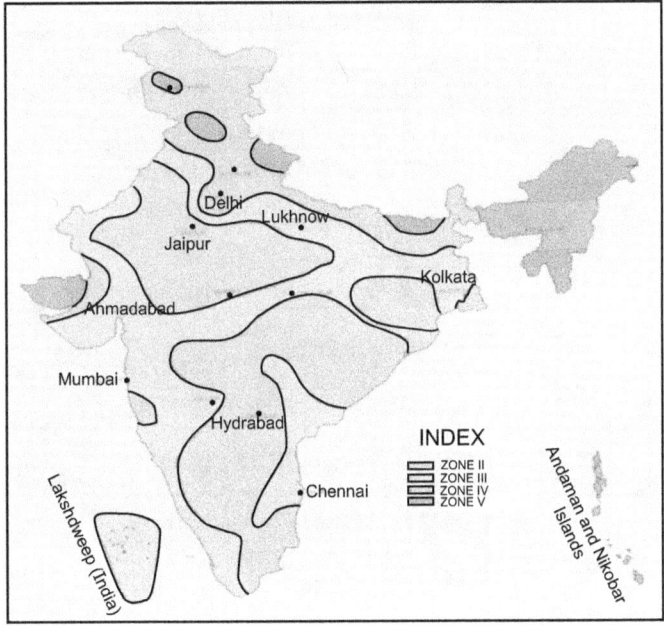

Fig. 8.4

- Due to large earthquakes total building or other civil structures can collapse.
- Other effects are :
  - Cracking of building components.
  - Dislocation of plumbing joints.
  - Damage to underground utilities.
  - Damage to pavement.
  - Seepage through dam body.
  - Collapse of Bridges.
  - Damage to electrical poles.

Table 8.1 : List of Some Significant Earthquakes in India

Date	Epicentre		Location	Magnitude
	Lat. (Deg. N)	Long. (Deg. E)		
1819 June 16	23.6	68.6	Kutch, Gujarat	8.0
1869 Jan. 10	25	93	Near Cachar, Assam	7.5
1885 May 30	34.1	74.6	Sopor, J & K	7.0
1897 June, 12	26	91	Shillong Plateau	8.7
1905 April 04	32.3	76.3	Kangra, H.P.	8.0
1918 July 08	24.5	91.0	Srimangal, Assam	7.6
1930 July 02	25.8	90.2	Dhubri, Assam	7.1
1934 Jan. 15	26.6	86.8	Bihar-Nepal Border	8.3
1941 June 26	12.4	92.5	Andaman Islands	8.1
1943 Oct. 23	26.8	94.0	Assam	7.2
1950 Aug. 15	28.5	96.7	Arunachal Pradesh – China Border	8.5
1956 July 21	23.3	70.0	Anjar, Gujarat	7.0
1967 Dec. 10	17.37	73.75	Koyna, Maharashtra	6.5
1975 Jan. 19	32.38	78.49	Kinnaur, H.P.	6.2
1988 Aug. 06	25.13	95.15	Manipur-Myanmar Border	6.6
1988 Aug. 21	26.72	86.63	Bihar-Nepal Border	6.4
1991 Oct. 20	30.75	78.86	Uttarkashi, U.P. Hills	6.6
1993 Sept. 30	18.07	76.62	Latur-Osmanabad, Maharashtra	6.3
1997 May 22	23.08	80.06	Jabalpur, M.P.	6.0
1999 Mar. 29	30.41	79.42	Chamoli Dist. U.P.	6.8
2001 Jan. 26	23.40	70.28	Bhuj, Gujarat	6.9

8.6 EARTHQUAKE ZONES

Fig. 8.5

The latest map was released by the (BIS) in 2000 and consists of four zones. Zones I and II have been merged in the new map and new regions have been included in Zone III such as the Marathwada region of Maharashtra and the Chennai area in Tamil Nadu.

Zone V is the most vulnerable to earthquakes, where historically some of the country's most powerful shock has occurred. This region included the Andaman & Nicobar Islands, all of North-Eastern India, parts of north-western Bihar, eastern sections of Uttaranchal, the Kangra Valley in Himachal Pradesh, near the Srinagar area in Jammu & Kashmir and the Rann of Kutchh in Gujarat.

EXERCISE

1. Define Earthquake.
2. What are the various causes of earthquake ?

3. Define the terms :
   (a) Focus
   (b) Epicentre
   (c) Isoseismal lines
   (d) Seismograph
   (e) Intensity
4. What are the different earthquake zones in India ?
5. Explain various effects of earthquake on civil structures.

UNIT V

Chapter 9

IRRIGATION AND WATER SUPPLY

9.1 TYPES OF DAMS

A dam is a structure constructed across a river to store water (in the reservoir) on its upstream side. The stored water may then be utilized for water supply, irrigation, hydropower generation, navigation etc. The main purpose of a dam is to make provision for the safe retention and storage of water on its upstream side.

Dams which are unique structures, are constructed of various shapes and sizes by using various types of materials such as earth, rock, stone (masonry) or concrete. They demonstrate great complexity in their load response depending upon the hydrology and geologic conditions of the site.

As failure of a dam may result in a heavy loss of human life and property, it must be designed, constructed and maintained with utmost care. Thus safety of the dam is the first and foremost consideration. The choice of the type of a dam is often governed by site conditions and availability of funds.

9.2 CLASSIFICATION OF DAMS

Dams which are of numerous types may be classified into a number of different categories based upon the purpose of classification such as its use, hydraulic design or materials of construction of the structure.

(1) Classification Based on its Use :

According to use, the dams may be classified as 'storage dams', 'diversion dams' or 'detention dams'.

  (i) **Storage dams (or weirs)** are constructed across rivers to store water in the reservoir when there is excess flow in rivers. This stored water may then be utilized during the periods of deficient supply in summer.

  (ii) **Diversion dams** are constructed to divert the whole or part of water from the river into the adjoining canal or conveyance system for carrying it to the place of use i.e. irrigation.

  (iii) **Detention dams** are primarily constructed to retard the flood flows by detaining the flood waters of river and then gradually allowing it to pass safely on the downstream side.

(2) Classification Based on the Hydraulic Design :

Based on the hydraulic design, the dams are classified as 'overflow' or 'non-overflow' dams.

(i) **Overflow dams :** As the name suggests, overflow dams are designed to pass the (flood) discharge over their crests and are therefore to be constructed of materials that will not be eroded or washed away by such discharge e.g. masonry or concrete structures (i.e. spillways).

(ii) **Non-overflow dams :** Non-overflow dams are those which do not allow the flood discharge to pass over it i.e. overlapping is not possible in case of non-overflow dams. Usually, some portion of the length of the dam is designed as an overflow (i.e. spillway) section and the remaining portion is designed as a non-overflow section. A 'composite dam' consists of an overflow masonry or concrete gravity dam joining the dikes of earth fill section.

(3) Classification on the Basis of Construction Material (Used) :

Depending upon the type of materials of construction, dams are often classified as 'Rigid dams' and 'Non-rigid dams'.

(i) **Rigid dams :** Rigid dams are those which are constructed by making use of solid rigid materials such as (stone) masonry, concrete, steel, timber etc. and are termed as 'masonry' or 'concrete gravity dams', concrete arch dams', concrete buttress dams, steel or timber dams. The Khadakwasla dam (Pune District) in Maharashtra is a stone masonry dam, whereas the Bhakra dam in Punjab is a concrete dam. Fig. 9.1, 9.2 and 9.3 indicate masonry or concrete gravity dam, concrete arch dam and concrete buttress dams respectively.

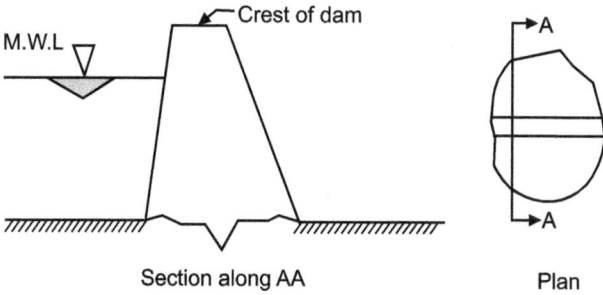

Fig. 9.1 : Masonry or Concrete Gravity Dam

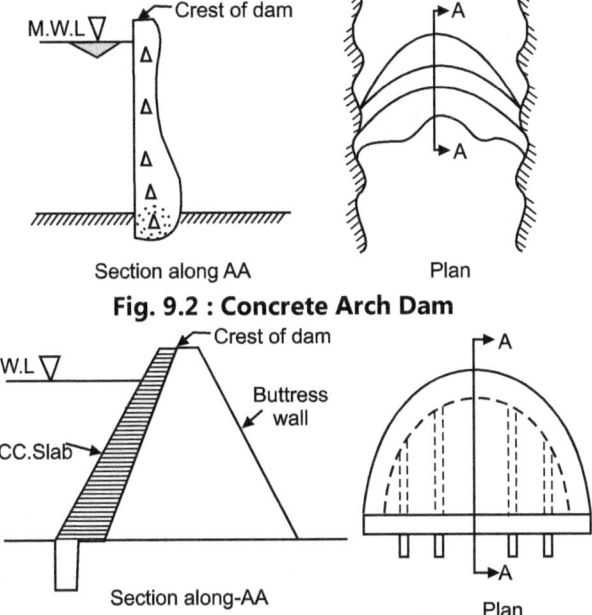

Fig. 9.2 : Concrete Arch Dam

Fig. 9.3 : Concrete Buttress Dam

(ii) **Non-rigid dams :** 'Non-rigid dams' are those which are constructed of materials such as earth or rock fill without any cementing material and are called as 'embankment dams' i.e. 'earth dams', 'rock fill dams' etc. Fig. 9.4 indicates an embankment type (either earth or rock fill) of dam. It may be noted that the embankment dams being economical account for about 84% of the dams constructed so far. Remaining 10% are gravity dams (either of masonry or concrete), 4.5% are arch type dams, 1% are buttress type dams and 0.5% are of multiple arch types.

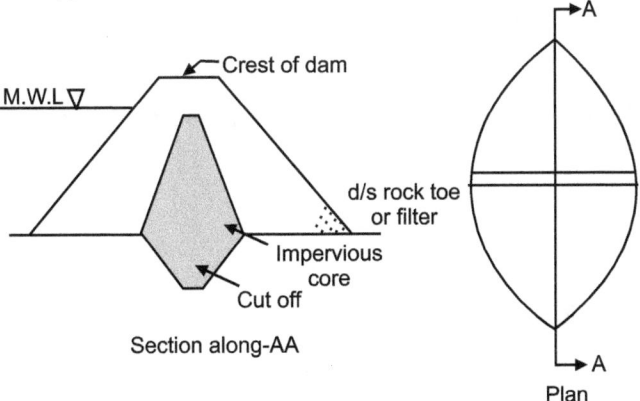

Fig. 9.4 : Embankment Type Dam (i.e. Earth or Rock Fill)

9.3 CANALS

An 'irrigation canal' is an artificial channel mostly trapezoidal in section, constructed to carry water from the reservoir, tank or direct from river to agricultural land for irrigation.

The irrigation canals may be classified in the following ways :

9.3.1 Classification of Irrigation Canals

(1) Classification based on the nature of source of supply is as follows :

(i) Permanent canal and

(ii) Inundation canal

A 'Permanent canal' is fed by a permanent source of supply. It is a well graded channel having permanent regulatory and distribution works.

The permanent canal may be either perrennial on non-perrennial depending upon its source which may be a river flowing for all the twelve months in a year (i.e. perrennial) or seasonal river (i.e. flowing for some part of the year).

An 'inundation canal' can draw its supplies during floods when the water level in the river is very high. Such canals do not require any headworks for diverting the river water into the canal. However, they are provided with canal head regulator works.

(2) Classification based on the type of soil through which they are excavated as alluvial canals and non-alluvial canals. The canals excavated through alluvial (i.e. silt deposited) soils are called as alluvial canals and those excavated through mountaneous areas are called as non-alluvial canals.

(3) Classification based on the function of canals : Irrigation canal, hydro-power canal, navigation canal etc.

(4) Classification based on the discharge carrying capacity and relative importance of the canal as

(i) Main canal

(ii) Branch canal

(iii) Major distributary

(iv) Minor distributary and

(v) Water course

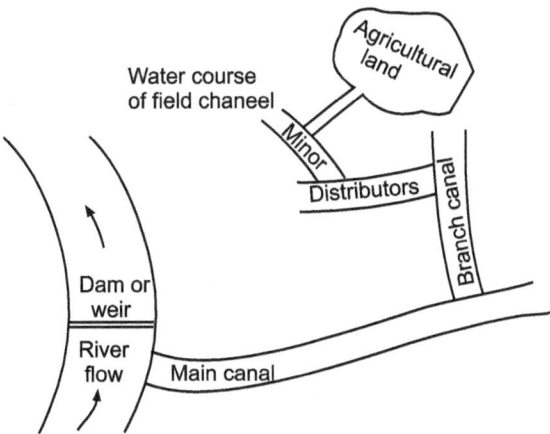

Fig. 9.5 : Typical Layout of an Irrigation Canal System

(i) **Main canal :** As the name suggests, it is the principal canal that draws large quantity of water directly from the storage reservoir or river and supplies water to its branches and distributaries. Such canals are usually not used for direct irrigation.

(ii) **Branch canals :** These are the branches of main canal which take off in either direction. These canals which carry a discharge of 5 cumecs, feed water to major and minor distributaries.

(iii) **Major distributary :** They take off from the branch canals and carry a discharge of 0.25 to 5 cubic metres per second. These distributaries supply water for direct irrigation through outlets to the field channels.

(iv) **Minor distributary (or minors) :** They take off from the branch canals or major distributaries and carry a discharge less than 0.25 m^3/sec. Minor distributaries supply water to water courses or field channels through outlets.

(v) **Water course (or field channel) :** They are small channels that carry water from the minors or distributory and supply water to the land to be irrigated. The responsibility of the irrigation department ceases at the outlet of the minors. The water courses or field channels are to be maintained in good condition by the cultivators once they are constructed.

(5) Classification Based on Financial Output : On this basis, canal will be classified into (i) Productive canal and (ii) Protective canal, the former being capable of yielding sufficient revenue after its full development at a net return of not less than the government approved rate (of about 6 %); whereas the latter one is intended to provide protection to the area from the famine. The net rate of return from such schemes will be below approved rate of 6%.

(6) Classification based on alignment :

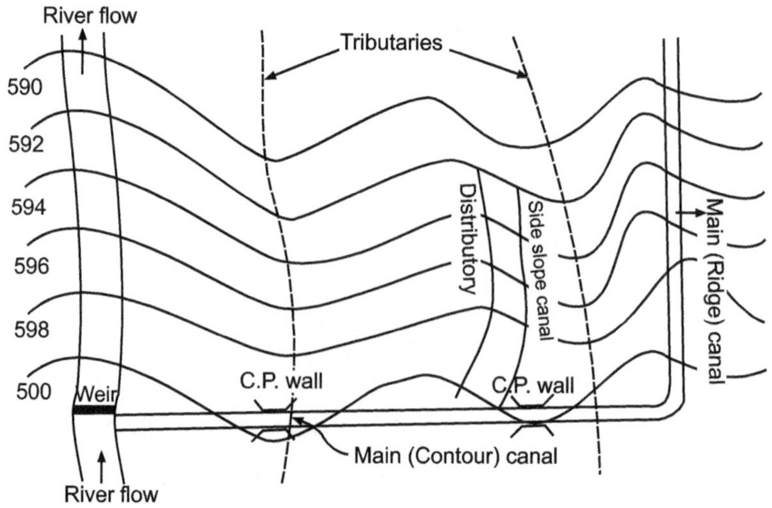

Fig. 9.6 : Definition of sketch showing Different Types of Canal Alignment

According to the alignment, the canals may be classified as follows :

(i) Ridge (or watershed) canal

(ii) Contour canal and

(iii) Side slope canal.

(i) Ridge (or Watershed) Canal : All irrigation canals are to be aligned in such a way as to command the area proposed to be irrigated with its least lengths and minimum number of cross-drainage works. Thus for canal system in plain areas, it is necessary to align the canal along the ridges or watershed (which is a line dividing the catchment area of two drainage basins). The advantage of aligning canal on watershed is that the water can flow by gravity on its either side. Moreover this also avoids crossing of any natural drains as all drains will be always flowing away from the ridges. Ridge canal also commands the maximum area to be brought under irrigation.

(ii) Contour Canal : An irrigation canal aligned practically parallel to the contour of the country is called as contour canal. However, such an alignment of canal is capable of irrigating on only one side of the country as the area on the other side is higher. As it is not economical to align the canal along a ridge in a hilly area, it will have to be aligned parallel to the contour of the area. As the natural drains will be flowing at right angles to the contour of the area, contour canals will have to cross maximum number of natural drains.

(iii) Side Slope Canal : An irrigation canal aligned approximately at right angles to the contour of the area is called as a side slope canal. Such a canal will flow parallel to the natural drain and therefore does not intercept cross drainage. Side slope canal will be neither on the ridge (i.e. watershed) nor in the valley. The side slope canal will have very steep bed slope, as the direction of the steepest slope of the ground will be always at right angles to the contour of the area.

9.3.2 General Guidelines for Alignment of a Canal

The alignment of canal in general should aim at the following :

(1) The length of canal should be minimum.

(2) The area to be commanded should be maximum.

(3) The number of cross drainage works should be less.

(4) As far as possible, canal should be aligned on watershed.

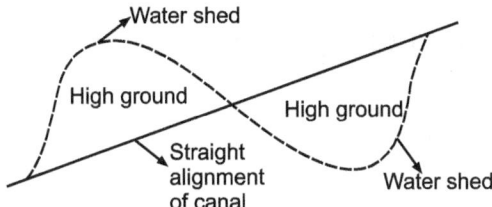

Fig. 9.7 : Typical Alignment of Canal for Sharp Turns in Watershed

(5) In case the watershed takes a sharp loop, then to save the unnecessary length, it should be aligned in straight line as shown in Fig. 9.7. However, the area enclosed between the canal and watershed, being on high ground, cannot be brought under irrigation by such a canal.

9.4 HYDRO POWER STRUCTURES

9.4.1 Introduction

The electric power generated by harnessing the natural potential of water is called as water or hydro power. The other conventional source is the 'thermal power', that generates steam by using fossil fuels (such as coal, oil or natural gas) or nuclear reactors or geo-thermal source. The contribution of hydro-power to the world's total electric power is estimated to be about 25 per cent. The most important point to be considered in the selection of a hydro-power plant is the total cost of its installation. The fuel cost of hydro-power plant once it is installed, is practically negligible (provided there is sufficient rainfall in the catchment of the storage dam) as compared to the cost of fuel required for the operation of thermal plant. Moreover the fuel is completely consumed by the thermal power plants in the process of generation of power whereas the fuel (i.e. water) required for the generation of power of hydro-plants can be re-used for irrigation purposes etc. Water turbines are required for the generation of hydro power whereas thermal power plants use steam turbines. Diesel and or gas turbines are also occassionally used for the generation of power as a standby units in case of emergencies. In most of the large power development systems, it is common practice to interconnect hydro-power and thermal plants. The advantage of such an interconnected system is that in monsoon (i.e. rainy season), most of the power can be developed by hydro-power plant, that results in fuel savings. Usually thermal power plants are operated to meet the base-load demand while hydro-power plants can be operated to satisfy the peak demands. The initial cost of installation of hydro-power plant is usually higher as compared to thermal power plant of same capacity, whereas the operating and maintenance cost of a thermal-power plant is much higher than the comparable hydro–power plant. Moreover, more expensive 'air pollution' control arrangements are also required for thermal power plants.

Some of the non-conventional sources of developing power are wind power, tidal waves power, solar energy and geothermal sources etc. which are in the development stages.

9.4.2 General Features of Hydro-Power Plants

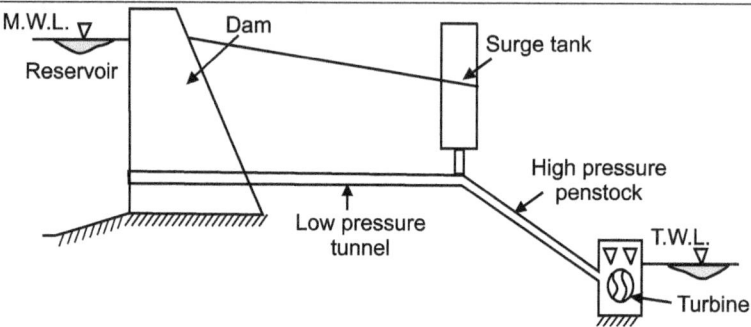

Fig. 9.8 : General Features of a Hydro-Power Plant

Fig. 9.8 shows a typical layout of a hydro-power plant. The water stored in the reservoir by the construction of a dam across a river is conveyed through the low pressure head race tunnel connected to a surge tank or chamber at the other end and then passed through the high pressure pipe i.e. penstock to the turbine. The turbine converts the hydro-power into mechanical energy which is further converted into electrical energy by the generator which is coupled to the turbine. The water after passing through the turbine joins the tail water channel on the downstream side and is then further allowed to join the parent river. The surge chamber should be located very near to the turbine so that a very short length of a pipe (i.e. penstock) in between the surge chamber and turbine will have to be designed to withstand the water hammer effects. Surge tanks serve the dual purpose of storing excess water when not required by the turbine (in case of sudden rejection of load) and also supply additional water when required by the turbine (in case of sudden opening of valve). Thus it acts as a balancing reservoir. The difference in the elevation of water in the reservoir on the upstream side of dam and the tail water is called as the gross head (H_G) over the turbine. If the flow rate to the turbine is Q (m^3/sec) and H_n is the net or effective head (obtained by deducting all the losses from the gross head) on the turbine then the hydro-power developed will be equal to $\gamma \cdot Q \cdot H_n \cdot \eta$ (watts)

where, $\quad \gamma$ = unit weight of water
where, $\quad H_n = H_{gross}$ − Losses
and $\quad \eta$ = Efficiency of water turbine
or $\quad P = \dfrac{\eta \gamma Q H_n}{1000}$ kW

Thus it can be concluded that the power developed by hydro-power plant depends upon the available discharge Q and the net head on the turbine and its efficiency.

9.4.3 Electric Power Supply and Load Demand

The electric power system should have sufficient capacity to meet the expected maximum peak load and any other additional load in the case of break down or repairs, shut down etc.

The demand for electric power is not constant but varies from hour-to-hour, day-to-day, season-to-season and year-to-year. Moreover, extra allowance for future requirements of power is also to be considered while planning any power system.

A typical daily power demand curve for a residential area is as shown in Fig. 9.9.

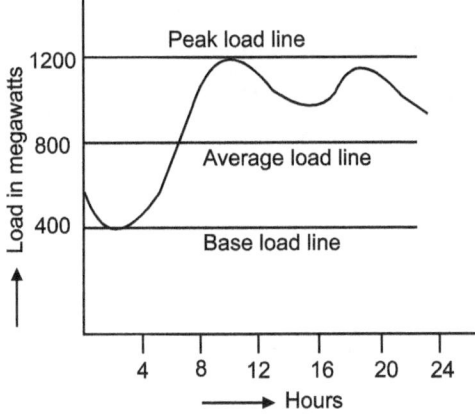

Fig. 9.9 : Daily (Power) Demand Curve for Residential Area

From the above graph, the minimum load that is continuously exceeded by the demand is known as 'base load'. The 'average load' is the mean of the demands during the period under consideration and is obtained by dividing the total area under the curve by the total time. 'Load factor' for a certain period is obtained by dividing the average load by the peak load and is usually designated as daily, weekly, monthly or annually and may vary from 40%

for residential zones to about 80% for industrial area. The unit cost of power will be small for high load factors and vice-a-versa. Approximately for one Mega-watt power generation (in our country), equipment installation cost Rs. one crore.

9.5 DEFINITIONS OF COMMON TERMS

(i) **Gross Head (H_G)** : It is defined as the difference in elevation between water levels in the reservoir (on the upstream side of the dam) and the tail race channel. Because of variable inflow rate and changing operating conditions of the power plant, the gross head may fluctuate.

(ii) **Net or Effective Head (H_n)** : It is the available head for the generation of power and is obtained by subtracting from the gross head (H_G) all losses in the system e.g. loss due to friction in pipe, entrance and exit losses and unrecovered velocity head in draft tube (applicable for reaction turbines only).

(iii) **Hydraulic Efficiency (η_H)** : It is the ratio of the net head to the gross head of the power plant i.e.
$$\eta_{Hydr} = \frac{H_{net}}{H_{gross}}$$

(iv) **Overall efficiency (η_o)** : Overall efficiency is obtained by multiplying the hydraulic efficiency by the efficiency of the turbine and generator.

(v) **Installed capacity** of the hydro power plant is the maximum power the generator can develop when acting under normal head with full flow.

(vi) The unit of electric power is the kilowatt (i.e. 1.34 H.P.)

(vii) The unit of electric energy is the power delivered per unit time i.e. per hour and is termed as kilowatts-hour (kWh).

(viii) Hydro power (P) generated = $\dfrac{\eta \cdot \gamma \cdot Q \cdot H_n}{1000}$ kW

where η = Efficiency of the water turbine
γ = Unit weight of water
Q = Discharge i.e. rate of flow in m³/sec
and H_n = Net head acting over the turbine

(ix) **Primary or firm power of the plant** : It is defined as the power which is available at all time, corresponding to the minimum available stream flow, without the storage consideration.

(x) **Surplus or secondary power** : It is the power available in excess of the primary i.e. firm power and is not available at all the times. Such a power can be sold at somewhat lower rate but without the guarantee.

9.6 TYPES OF HYDRO-POWER DEVELOPMENT

Hydro–power plants may be classified in different ways as follows :

1. **Depending upon the head (H) as**
    (i) Low head : 15 to 50 m
       (Run–of–River Type)
    (ii) Medium head : 50 to 250 m
       (Local or Remote controlled)
    (iii) High head : 250 to 300 m
       (Remote controlled type)
    (iv) Very high head : 300 m
       (Remote controlled type)

2. **Depending upon its capacity (kW) as**
    (i) Micro–hydro plant (less than 5 MW)
    (ii) Min–hydro plant (5 to 100 MW)
    (iii) High–hydro plant (101 MW to 1000 MW)
    (iv) Super–hydro-plants (above 1000 MW)

3. **Depending upon its location on the ground as**
    (i) Indoor (or underground) power plant
    (ii) Outdoor (or open surface) power plant and
    (iii) Partly indoor and partly outdoor plants

4. **Depending upon its general layout and operation procedure the hydro-plants are classified as :**
    (i) Run-of-river plants
    (ii) Diversion canal plants
    (iii) Storage plants
    (iv) Pumped storage plants

(i) **Run-of-river plant (Fig. 9.10) :** The distinguishing feature of the run-of-river plant is that it does not interfere with the normal flow of the river. Such plants have very limited storage capacity and they usually use water as it flows. Generally a weir is constructed across a river and the low head created is utilised for generation of the power. The water is not much diverted away from the main river. Some run-of-river plants have enough upstream storage known as pondage, to meet the peak demand of the same day. Due to non-uniform supply of water, its firm capacity is somewhat low and hence it can be used as a base load plant. Fig. 9.10 indicates a typical layout of a run-of-river plant. Such plants are usually located on the perennial rivers having a uniform flow throughout the year.

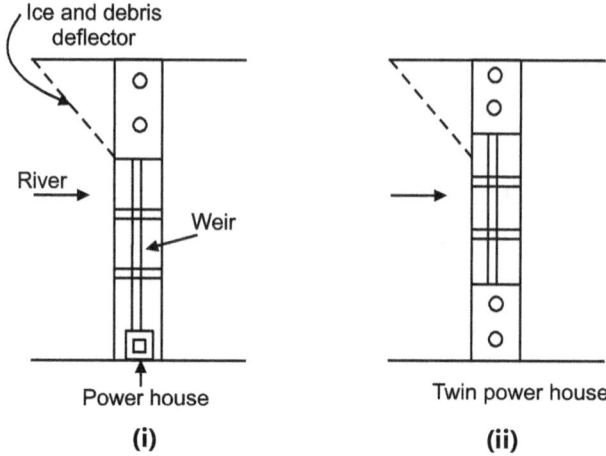

Fig. 9.10 : Run of Water Plant

(ii) Diversion canal plant (Fig. 9.11) : As the name suggests, the water from the main river impounded on the upstream side of the weir or barrage is diverted through a power canal to the power house which is constructed away from the diversion point. The water from the power house rejoins the original river further downstream. It may be either low or medium head power plant. There is no storage reservoir. The water is drawn from the 'fore bay' (a small water pool), to the power house situated on its downstream side. Fig. 9.11 shows a typical layout of such a diversion canal power plant.

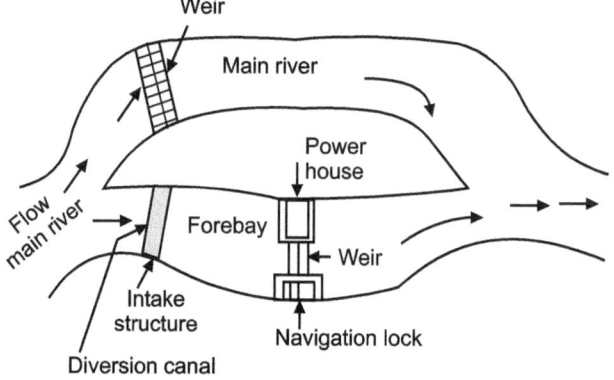

Fig. 9.11 : Diversion Canel Power Plant

(iii) Storage power plant [Fig. 9.12 (a) & (b)] : A storage power plant consists of storage dam and reservoir of sufficient capacity that permits carry over storage from the wet season to the dry season. This enables to make available firm flow far in excess of minimum natural flow in the river. It is the case of remote installation in which the main dam is separated from the power house by a considerable distance. The water is conveyed by a low pressure tunnel and penstocks (i.e. high pressure pipeline) to the turbine. This enables to increase the head over the power plant. Such plants are either medium or high head power plants. Depending upon the available run-off and demand for the power, these plants may work as base load and/or peak load power plants. Fig. 9.12 (a) and (b) show the typical layout of a storage type power plant having local and remote installations respectively.

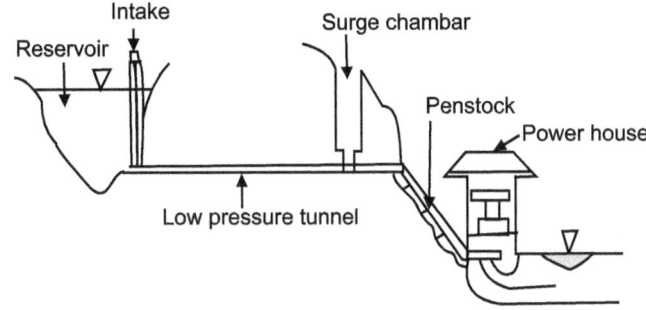

(a) Storage Plant Layout (Local Installation)

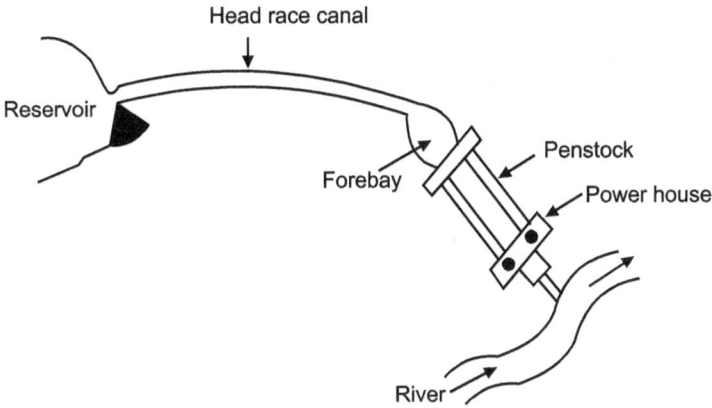

(b) Storage Plant Layout (Remote Installation)

Fig. 9.12

(iv) Pumped Storage plants [Fig. 9.13 (a) and (b)] : Sometimes the natural run-off from a river is not sufficient for the construction of a conventional hydro-electric power station. However if it is possible to create reservoirs at the head as well as tail water locations, the water may be pumped back from lower tail water side to high head water reservoir by utilising surplus power available elsewhere. Such power plants are usually used for generating energy for peak load demand and during off-peak hours, the same water is pumped back from lower level reservoir to high head reservoir for further use. Fig. 9.13 shows installation of such a pumped storage plant. Thus, such pumped storage plants assist in increasing the load factor of other existing power plants and also generate additional capacity to satisfy the peak load demands. Such pumps are usually powered with secondary power system such as run-of-river plants. The unique feature of such power plants is that very small quantity of water is required for its entire operation, once the head water and tail water reservoirs are completely filled with water. Thus the same unit is capable of working as a generating unit when water flows from high level to tail water reservoir and as a pumping unit when the water is pumped from the tail-water level to the high head reservoir. A unique reversible-pump turbine which operates at relatively high efficiency is used to operate either as a turbine or pump and thus eliminates the cost of installing separate pumping unit and pump house.

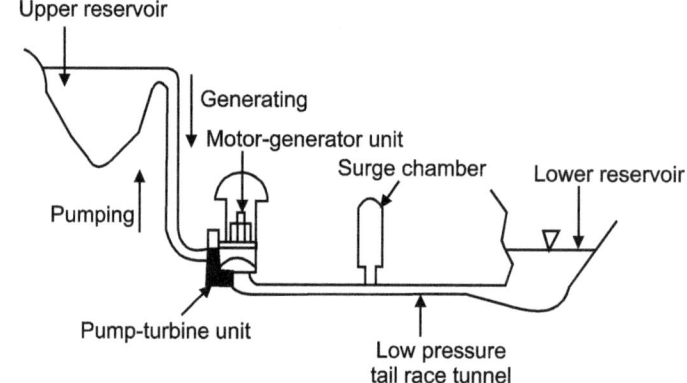

(a) Pumped Storage Plant

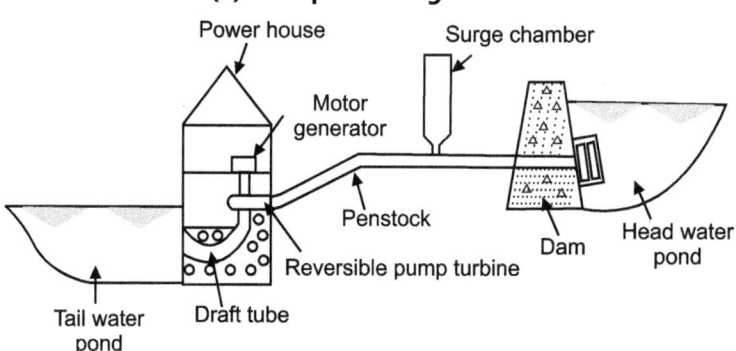

(b) Section through a Typical Pumped Storage Hydroelectric Plant

Fig. 9.13

9.7 WATER SUPPLY

9.7.1 Introduction

Water is called "Jeevan" (i.e. life) in Sanskrit. It is the basic need of all living beings. Other needs are air, food and shelter. Without water man cannot survive. In early days, water was primarily used for domestic needs like drinking, washing, bathing and cooking etc. But due to modernisation, water is also required for industrial, ornamental and sewerage purposes along with domestic needs. It is also required for parks, gardens, swimming pools etc. Water is also required for fire protection. Now-a-days, well designed and organized public water supply schemes are absolutely necessary to cater for various water requirements. Enormous quantity of water required for future industries is required to be taken into account for designing water supply schemes.

9.7.2 Necessity and Importance of Water Works

The main source of water is rainfall. When the rain falls from the clouds, it dissolves various impurities like gases and minute suspended particles present in the atmosphere. Rain water collects dust and other impurities present on the surface of the earth. Some part of rainfall evaporates and some part percolates in the earth, dissolving various soluble matters in it and ultimately joins the underground water raising its level. The balance amount of rainfall left after evaporation and percolation, flows over the surface of earth and joins nallhas, streams and rivers. This flowing water is called as runoff or surface flow. It is impure as it collects lot of matter lying on surface of earth during its flow. Also surface water contains wastes discharged by various industries. Sometimes untreated sewages are also discharged in such flowing water, causing its pollution.

Hence, water, either from surface source or from underground source, is not suitable for drinking due to various impurities present in it. Also water may contain pathogenic bacteria leading to water borne diseases like cholera, dysentery and typhoid etc. Therefore, it is necessary to treat such water and make it fit for various purposes. Water is treated in treatment units (all called as water works) which require proper design and maintenance. These treatment units reduce impurities upto acceptable standards. Civil engineers must have thorough knowledge of planning, designing, estimation and construction of various treatment units, required to make the water available of acceptable standard.

9.7.3 Uses of Water

1. Drinking, cooking and washing.
2. Bathing.
3. Swimming pools and water games.
4. Ornamental displays like fountains and cascades.

5. Watering lawns, gardens and roads.
6. For modern appliances like air conditioners, washing machines and dish washers.
7. For extinguishing fires.
8. Industrial processes and steam generation.
9. Irrigation purposes.
10. Sanitary purposes.

9.8 WATER SUPPLY SCHEMES

They essentially consist of the following phases :

1. Selection of source : The source may be surface source like river, canal, lake and reservoir or ground water source like wells and springs. The criteria in selecting the source is its reliability, minimum impurities and availability in the required quantity.

2. Collection and conveyance of raw water : The water from the source is required to be collected and conveyed to the treatment works for its purification. Depending upon the type of the source and its elevation, intake works, pump house and rising main etc. will be required. C.I. pipes are generally used. However, in case of gravity flow, open ducts or channels may be used to make the scheme economical.

3. Treatment of water : This depends upon the nature of impurities present in water, which are detected in the water testing laboratory. The usual process is sedimentation with or without coagulation, filtration and disinfection.

4. Pumping and storing water in elevated service reservoirs : The water after purification is required to be stored at higher elevation so that water is distributed to the public by gravity according to supply hours. This needs pumping of treated water, ventilation and protection during storing to avoid contamination. Additional storage of water is provided in case of breakdown of pumps. (Such additional storage is generally called as breakdown reserve.)

5. Distribution : For distribution of water, network of pipes is laid. It consists of mains, branches, distributries or feeders. Individual service connections are given from feeder lines.

The system of water supply adopted may be gravity or pumping or combination of the two, depending upon the topography of the town. Water supply to public may be intermittant (few hours in the morning and few hours in the evening) or continuous (twenty four hours).

9.8.1 Data to be Collected for Water Supply Scheme

Water is prime necessity of every individual. For supplying water to the public, water supply projects are prepared and sent to proper authority for sanction of grants required for its execution. In the design of water supply project, following data is collected :

1. **Source of raw water :** Various sources available, their reliability throughout the year, choice of the source between various alternatives available depends mainly upon the impurities present in them.

2. **Quantity of water required :** It depends upon :
    (a) **Population to be served :** This is decided by forecasting the population from census data.
    (b) **Water demands :** All types of demands like domestic public, industrial, fire etc. are sorted out.
    (c) **Design period :** Thirty years period is often considered.
    Finally total water demand per day for the city is worked out.

3. **Quality of water :** The samples of water from available sources are analysed in the laboratory to find out the various impurities present. This is essential to decide the line of treatment to be given to the raw water. This is also necessary to decide the best source out of the alternatives, if any.

4. **Survey data :** Surveys are carried out to prepare the topographical maps for intake works, rising main treatment site, location of elevated service reservoirs.

5. **Plan or Map of city or town :** The master plan containing existing roads, buildings and proposed developments along with the contours is procured, if available. If not available, plan table survey is carried out to obtain the city map. This map enables the design engineer to divide the city into various zones - low level, medium level and high level etc. and choose the position for locating distribution reservoirs with required capacity and to decide the layout of water distribution pipe network.

6. Acquisition of land and compensations to be paid to the land owners and legal complications etc.

7. Existing water supply position of the town and possibility of its expansion.

9.8.2 Components and Layout of Water Supply Schemes

Water is obtained from various sources. They are mainly classed into two categories :

(a) underground source, which consists of open well, tube well, artesian wells etc. and

(b) surface source which consists of streams, rivers, reservoirs, canals etc.

Depending upon the source of water supply the components of the water supply scheme will differ.

Following layouts are used :

1. For underground source, the components/layout involves provision of well, pump house, rising main, elevated service reservoir and water distribution pipelines. In such layout only chlorination treatment is done to supply disinfected water. It is very much suitable for village water supply schemes.

2. For surface source like river, canal etc., the components/layout consists of intake works, pumps, rising main, treatment units (like clarifiers, filters), elevated service reservoir and distribution system. This is a full fledged scheme and is used for towns and cities.

Following is the flow diagram of water supply scheme.

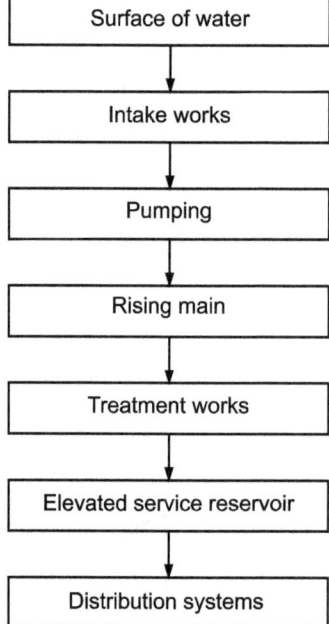

These layouts are shown in Fig. 9.14.

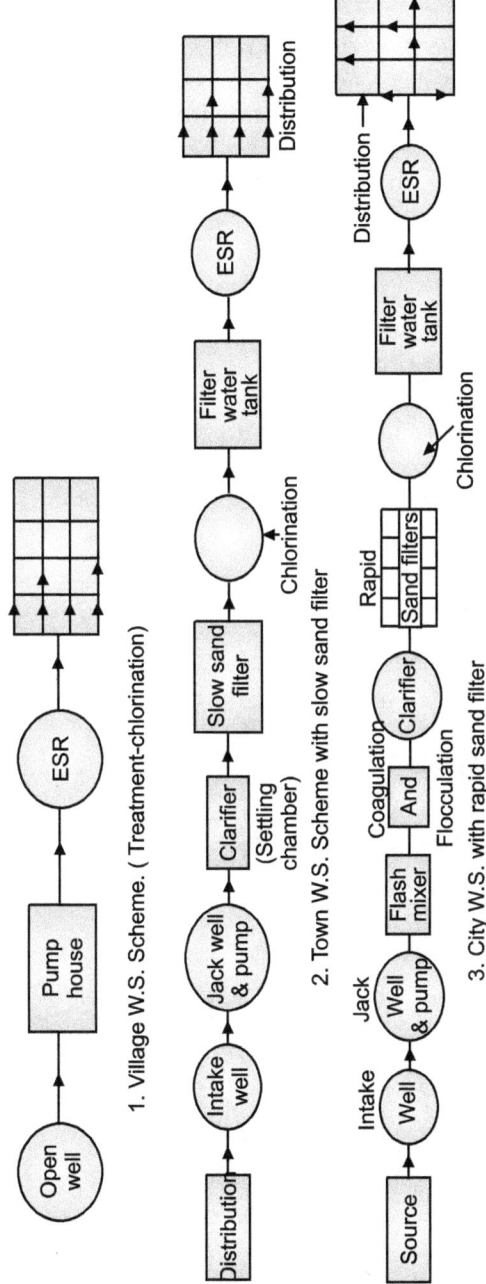

Fig. 9.14 : Layouts of water supply scheme

9.8.3 Requirements of Drinking Water

Following are the requirements of drinking water :

1. It should be colourless, good to taste, free from odour and sparkling clear.

2. It should be free from pathogenic bacteria or organisms.

3. It should be soft and free from harmful salts.

4. It should contain sufficient amount of dissolved oxygen and should be free from objectionable gases like H_2S etc.

5. It should be available in sufficient quantity at reasonable cost.

6. It should be free from radioactive matter, phenolic compounds, iodine, fluoride and chlorine.

7. It should be free from objectionable minerals like iron, manganese, arsenic and lead, and other poisonous metals.

8. It should be non-corrosive and free from scale forming compounds.

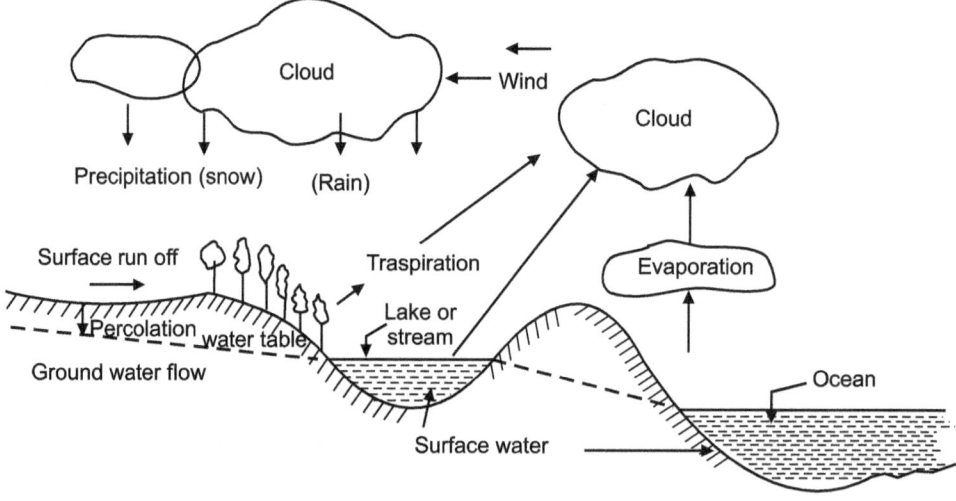

Fig. 9.15 : Water cycle

9.9 SOURCES OF WATER AND THEIR QUALITY

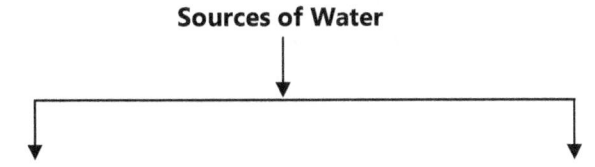

Surface source
(Useful for big cities and industrial towns)
→ Lakes
→ Rivers
→ Reservoirs (Dams)
→ Canals

Quality
1. Impurities present :
   (a) Inorganic - silt, clay etc.
   (b) Organic - Plants, dead organic materials and animals, algae and weed growth in still water.
2. Generally soft and less corrosive.
3. Contaminated due to admittance of sewage
4. Turbidity is more.
5. pH ranges between 6.5 to 7.5.
6. Hardness ranges between 30 to 150 mg/l.

Underground source
(Useful for villages and small towns)
→ Open wells
→ Tube wells
→ Infiltration wells
→ Infiltration galleries

Quality
1. Impurities present :
   Dissolved salts, minerals and gases etc.
2. Generally hard due to dissolved salts of Ca and Mg.
3. Less contaminated due to percolation through strata of soil.
4. Turbidity is less.
5. pH is more than 7.
6. Hardness ranges between 100 to 600 mg/l.

9.10 WATER TREATMENT FLOWCHART

9.10.1 Introduction

It is already seen that raw water belonging to any source may contain various impurities which are grouped as : (i) Physical impurities, (ii) Chemical impurities and (iii) Bacteriological impurities.

Physical impurities impart turbidity, taste, odour and colour to the water. Chemical impurities, depending upon their nature and extent of amount present may impart pH, alkalinity, hardness, toxicity etc. Excess amounts of some metals and dissolved gases cause corrosion to pipes, valves and fittings. Bacteriological impurities, particularly pathogenic bacteria spread water borne diseases. These impurities will be present in water in suspended, colloidal or dissolved form.

The object of water treatment is to remove or reduce these impurities upto acceptable standard, before the water is supplied to the public.

9.10.2 Treatment of Water

The complete process of removal of undesirable matter (various impurities), in order to make the water acceptable for domestic or industrial use, is commonly termed as *treatment of water* or *purification of water*. Since, treatment is a costly affair, various purification (treatment) units are constructed and maintained by Public bodies like municipality, corporations, industrial development boards or government.

9.10.3 Objectives of Treatment of Water

The following are the objectives of treatment of water :
1. To make water odour free and tasty.
2. To make it colourless.
3. To make the water safe and sparkling for drinking and domestic purposes.
4. To remove dissolved gases and turbidity of water.
5. To make it free from all objectionable impurities present in suspension, colloidal or dissolved form.
6. To remove harmful bacteria.
7. To remove hardness of water.
8. To make the water suitable for a wide variety of industrial purposes like dyeing, brewing, soft drinks, steam generation etc.

9.10.4 Various Processes and Impurities Removed

	Process	Impurities removed
1.	Screening	It is adopted to remove floating matter. It is provided at the intake point.
2.	Aeration	It removes objectionable tastes, odour and dissolved gases like CO_2 and H_2S. Dissolved oxygen is increased.
3.	Plain sedimentation	It is adopted for removing settleable suspended impurities like silt, sand etc. which are heavier than water.
4.	Sedimentation with coagulation	It is used to cause the sedimentation of colloidal and very fine suspended particles. Some bacteria are also removed.
5.	Filtration	It is the most important stage in the treatment. Colloidal and very fine particles escaped from sedimentation tank are removed. Micro-organisms are removed to a large extent.
6.	Disinfection	All remaining organisms including pathogens are destroyed.
7.	Miscellaneous (a) Softening (b) Activated carbon treatment	Hardness is removed. Matters causing taste and odour.

It should be noted that all the processes given above may not be required. Depending upon the analysis of raw water regarding its quality, suitable treatment processes are used.

9.10.5 Layout and Components of Water Treatment Plant

The layout of a typical water treatment plant is shown in Fig. 9.16.

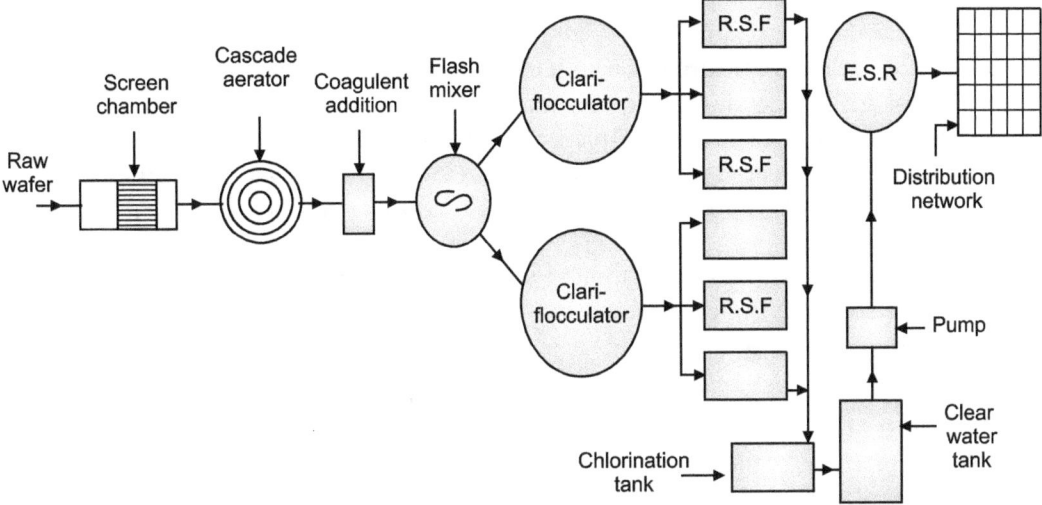

Fig. 9.16

Components of Water Treatment Plant :

A typical water treatment plant consists of the following components :

1. **Intake well, jack well and a pump house :** The raw water is admitted from the source in these wells through inlet openings fitted with coarse screen to exclude floating matter.
2. **Screen chambers :** Raw water brought through rising main is admitted in screen chamber provided with bar screens and/or fine screen to exclude remaining floating matter.
3. **Aerators :** Through aerators the water is exposed to atmospheric air to eliminate gases like H_2S, CO_2 and mineral matters like Fe, Mn.
4. **Coagulant tank :** Here the desired coagulant is added in the water.
5. **Flash mixer :** Water containing coagulant is intimately mixed in this unit.
6. **Clari-flocculator :** This is a combined unit doing the operations of flocculation and also sedimentation (often called as clarification). Water from flash mixer is admitted in the flocculation zone where with the help of moving paddles, suspended particles come together (agglomerate) and form compact settleable mass called *floc*. The water containing this floc moves to a portion of unit where sedimentation of the floc occurs.

7. **Filter beds :** These are in the form of tanks rectangular in shape. Number of such beds often called as battery of filters are provided in the big building. This building is called as filter house.

   Very fine particles and colloidal matter which have refused to settle earlier are removed through filtration.
8. **Chlorination or Disinfection unit :** Here generally chlorine is applied to filtered water to completely destroy the micro-organism escaped through filtration. This confirms the purity of water. This is the last unit of water treatment.
9. **Pumping, Elevated Service Reservoir (ESR) :** Pure water is admitted in a protected clear water tank. This water is then pumped and fed to ESR through a rising main.
10. **Distribution system :** The treated water from this overhead reservoir is fed into distribution system for consumption.

9.10.6 Carpet Area

Carpet area is the floor area of usable rooms at any floor level.

The carpet area of any floor shall be the floor area worked as per floor area and exclude the following portions of the building :

1. Sanitary accommodations
2. Verandahs
3. Corridors and passages
4. Kitchen and pantries
5. Stores in domestic buildings
6. Entrance hall and porches
7. Staircases and mumties
8. Shaft for lifts
9. Barsaties
10. Garages
11. Canteens
12. Air-conditioning ducts and air-conditioning plant rooms.

EXERCISE

1. Define the term dam and state its purpose.
2. State various methods of classification of dams.
3. Distinguish between rigid dams and non-rigid dams and their stability.
4. Define the term canal and state its purpose.
5. Give the classification of irrigation canal.
6. Explain advantages and disadvantages of irrigation.
7. Explain various methods of irrigation.
8. Write a short note on hydropower structures.
9. What are the requirements of drinking water ?
10. Explain the quality of drinking water.
11. Draw the flowchart of water treatment plant.
12. Draw the flowchart of sewage treatment plant.

UNIT VI

Chapter 10

INFRASTRUCTURE

10.1 INTRODUCTION

Infrastructure is also a branch of Civil Engineering which deals with provision of good infrastructure facilities which help to develop the rapid growth of particular area.

10.2 ROADS

The transportation of people and goods is feasible by land, water and air. The transport by land is feasible through Roadways and Railways. Both these modes of land transportation are considered as easy and economical for internal movement of people and goods. They play an important role in the economic, social and commercial development in the country.

10.3 ROAD ENGINEERING

The branch of transportation engineering which deals with the design, construction and maintenance of different types of roads is called as Road Engineering.

10.4 TYPES OF ROADS

Roads are classified into different categories as under.

1. According to location.
2. According to importance.
3. According to traffic.
4. According to tonnage.
5. According to material used.

10.4.1 Classification of Roads According to Location

According to classification, roads are classified as :

1. National Highway (NH).
2. State Highway (SH).
3. Major District Roads (MDRs).
4. Other District Roads (ODRs).
5. Village Roads.

FUNDAMENTALS OF CIVIL ENGINEERING INFRASTRUCTURE

1. **National Highway :** The main highways running through the length and breadth of the country connecting major parts, foreign highways and capital of states etc. are known as National highways. They are having the width from 7 m to 15 m considering of atleast two lane width.

2. **State Highways :** The highways linking district head quarters and important cities within the state or connecting them with National highways or with highways of the neighbouring states are known as State Highways (SHs). They are having the width varying from 7 m to 10 m.

3. **Major District Roads :** The important roads within a district serving areas of production and markets and connecting these places with each other or with the main highways are known as Major District Roads (MDRs). The width of the road varies from 5 m to 8 m.

4. **Other District Roads :** The roads serving rural areas of production and providing them with outlet to market centers, Tehsil Head Quarters, Block Development Head Quarters, Railway Stations, etc. are known as Other District Roads (ODRs).

5. **Village Roads :** The roads connecting villages or group of villages with each other or with the nearest road of higher category are known as Village Roads.

10.4.2 Classification of Roads According to Importance

According to importance of connecting holy places, stations of strategic importance, roads are classified into following categories :

1. Class I Roads.
2. Class II Roads.
3. Class III Roads.

10.4.3 Classification of Roads According to Traffic

According to intensity of traffic, roads are classified into following categories :

1. Very heavy traffic roads : Which carry above 600 vehicles per day.
2. Heavy traffic roads : Which carry 251 to 600 vehicles per day.
3. Medium traffic roads : Which carry 70 to 250 vehicles per day.
4. Light traffic roads : Which carry below 70 vehicles per day.

10.4.4 Classification of Roads According to Tonnage

According to total tonnage per day, roads are classified into following categories:

1. Very heavy traffic roads : Which carry over 1524 metric tonne per day.
2. Heavy traffic roads : Which carry 1017 to 1524 metric tonnes per day.
3. Medium traffic roads : Which carry 508 to 1016 metric tonne per day.
4. Light traffic roads : Which carry below 508 metric tonne per day.

10.4.5 Classification of Roads According to Materials Used

According to materials used the roads are classified into following categories.

1. Earthern Roads : The roads having its foundation and wearing surface consisting of one as two compacted layer of an ordinary or stabilised soil is known as earth road or **Kutcha Road.** These roads are probably provided in village areas.

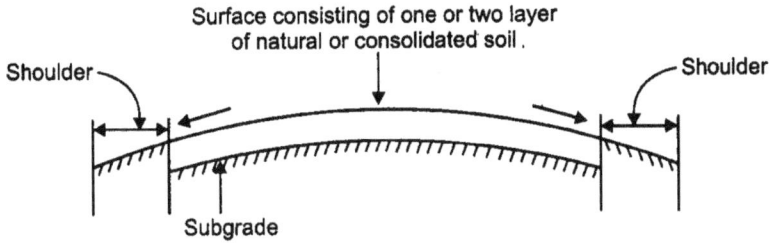

Fig. 10.1

2. Water Bound Macadam Roads : The roads having its wearing surface consisting of clean, crushed aggregates, mechanically interlocked by rolling and bound together with filter material (screening) and water laid on a prepaid base course is called as Water Bound Macadam Road.

3. Bituminous Roads : The roads having their surface consisting of bituminous material are known as bituminous roads or black top roads.

These roads are constructed of different thickness varying from a thin layer of bituminous surface dressing to about 22 cm thick layer of bituminous layer materials, according to the importance of the road. The bituminous binders used in the construction of bituminous roads are either straight run bitumen, road tar, cut back or emulsion.

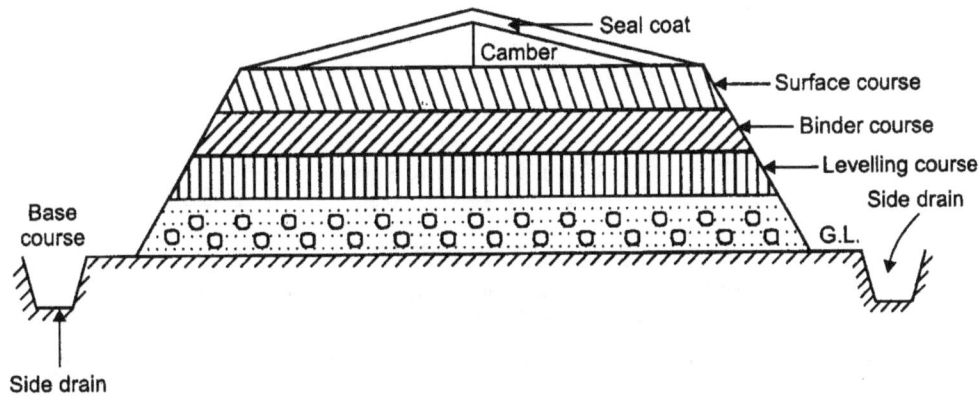

Fig. 10.2 : Section Showing Components of a Bituminous Surface

4. Cement Concrete Roads : The roads having their wearing surface consisting of cement concrete slab (Plain or Reinforcement) are called Cement Concrete Roads or simply concrete roads.

10.5 CROSS-SECTION OF ROAD IN CUTTING AS WELL AS IN EMBANKMENT

The road cross-section in embankment as well as in cutting showing important geometrics are given in Fig. 10.3 (a) and (b).

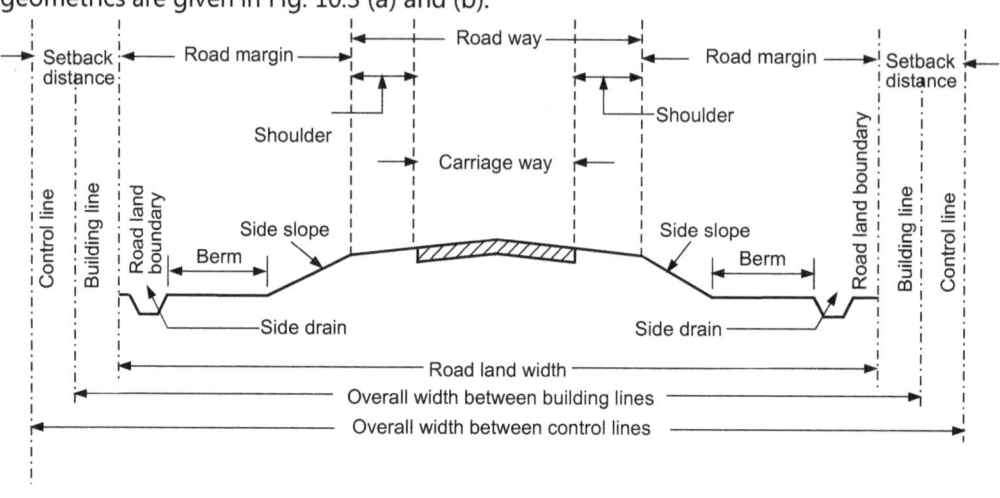

(a) A Road in Embankment

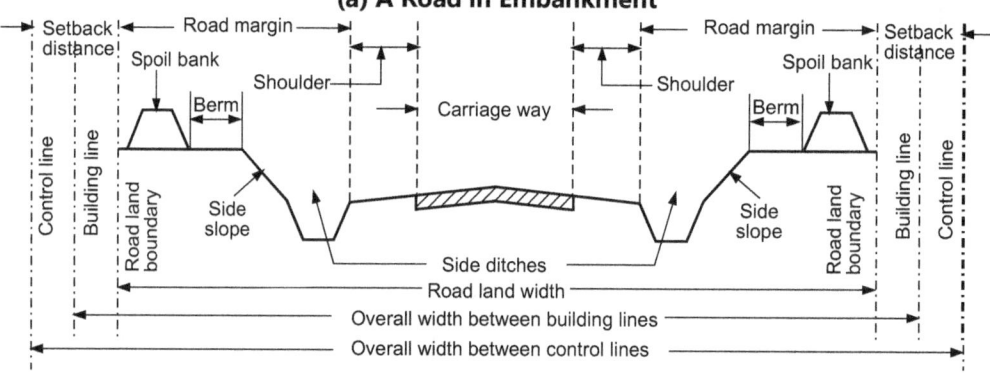

(b) A Road in Cutting

Fig. 10.3 : Road Cross-sections and Schematic Presentation of Some Important Highway Terms

These roads fall under the category of rigid pavements. These are high cost roads which remain in serviceable condition under all weathering conditions. Due to their excellent riding surface, pleasing appearance and long life under most severe traffic condition the cement concrete roads are much preferred.

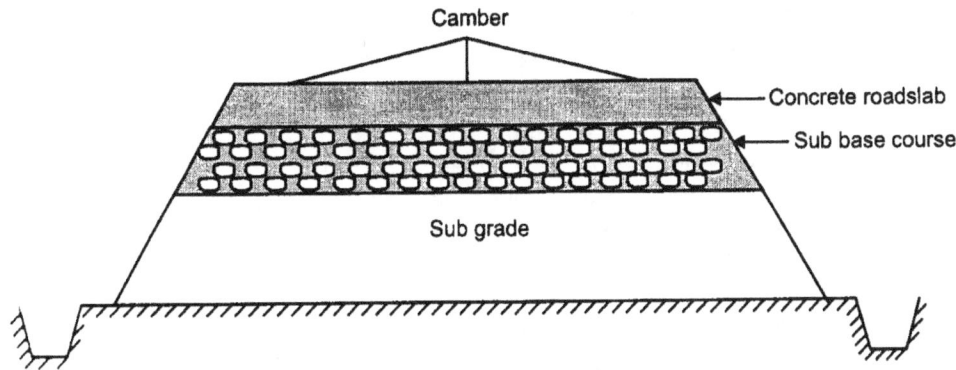

Fig. 10.4 : Section Showing Components of Concrete Road

10.5.1 Important Terms Concerning to the Road Cross-Section are Discussed Below

1. **Right of way :** The area of land acquired and reserved for construction and development of a road along its alignment is known as right of way or permanent land, and the width of right of way is called permanent land width or road land width.

   The area of land outside the right of way which is temporarily acquired for making borrow pits or spoil banks is called temporarily land.

2. **Borrow pits :** The pits dug along the alignment of a road for using their material in the construction of embankment are known as Borrow Pits.

3. **Spoil bank :** The banks constructed from surplus excavated earth on the side of road cutting, parallel to its alignment, are known as Spoil Bank.

4. **Road margin :** The portion of land width on either side of the road way of a road are known as Road Margins.

5. **Roadway width :** The top width of a highway embankment or bottom width of a highway cutting excluding the side drains is called Roadway Width or Formation Width.

6. **Carriage way :** The portion of road way constructed for movement of vehicular traffic is called Carriage Way, Pavement or Crust.

   The width of the carriage way or pavement depends on the width of traffic lane and number of lanes required.

7. **Shoulders :** The portion of a roadway between the outer edges of the pavement and edges of the top surface of embankment or inner edges of the side drains in cutting are known as Shoulders.

   The width of the shoulders varies from 0.5 to about 4 metres according to the nature of the area and type of road.

8. **Side slopes :** The slopes given to the sides of earth work of a road in embankment or in cutting for its stability are called Side Slopes.
9. **Berms :** The portion of land width left in between the toe of road embankment and the inner edges of borrow pits or the portions in between two edges of road cutting and the nearest edge of spoil bank on either side are known as Berms.
10. **Kerbs :** The boundaries between the shoulder or foot paths are known as Kerbs.
11. **Formation level :** The reduced level of the finished surface of earthwork for a road in embankment or in cutting is known as Formation Level.

10.6 CAMBER

The convexity provided to the surface of carriage way or the rise given to the center of the carriage way above its edges on straight portion of a road is called camber or cross fall.

Camber is provided on the straight reaches of a road by raising the centre of its carriage way with respect to the edges forming a crown at the given centre.

It is usually expressed in percentage of rise given to the crown of the carriage way above its edges.

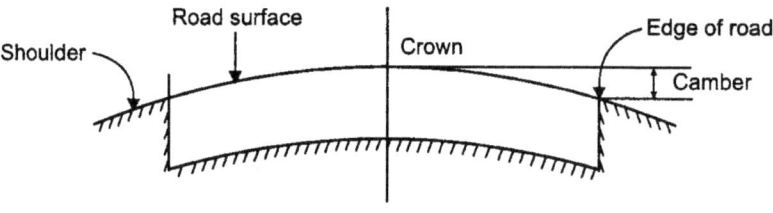

Fig. 10.5

The amount of road camber depends on the intensity of rainfall in the locality and the permeability of the road surfacing material.

10.6.1 Objects of Providing Camber

1. To drain-off water quickly from the surface of the carriage way towards the sides of a road.
2. To regulate the vehicles to their proper lanes.
3. To improve the architectural appearance of the roadway.

10.6.2 Types of Camber

The following types of camber are generally provided to the road surface :
1. Composite camber
2. Sloped or straight camber
3. Two straight line camber
4. Barrel camber.

1. **Composite camber** : It consists of two straight slopes from the edges with a parabolic or circular crown in the centre of carriage way. This type of camber can be easily constructed and maintained.
2. **Sloped or straight camber** : It consists of two straight slopes from the edges joining at the centre of carriage way.
   This type of camber is very simple and can be easily constructed and maintained.
3. **Two straight line camber** : It consists of two straight lines steeper near the edges and flatter near the crown of carriage way.
   This type of camber is considered to be the best for Indian roads because it provides more contact area of the tyres with the road surface than in other types of camber. Thus, it provides less damage to the road surface.
4. **Barrel camber** : It consists of continuous curve either elliptical or parabolic. It provides a flat road surface at the middle and steeper towards the edges.

On account of steeper edges it provides better drainage property. This camber is therefore, preferred by fast moving vehicles and is suggested for urban roads. This type of camber is difficult to construct and maintain.

Table 10.1 : Road Camber as Per Recommendations of I.R.C.

Sr. No.	Type of Road Surface	Camber
1.	High type bituminous surfacing or Cement Concrete Road.	1.7 to 2 per cent (1 in 60 to 1 in 50)
2.	Thin bituminous surfacing.	2 to 2.5 per cent (1 in 50 to 1 in 40)
3.	Water Bound Macadam, Gravel Road Surface	2.5 to 3 per cent (1 in 40 to 1 in 33)
4.	Earth Roads, Foot paths etc.	3 to 4 per cent (1 in 33 to 1 in 25)

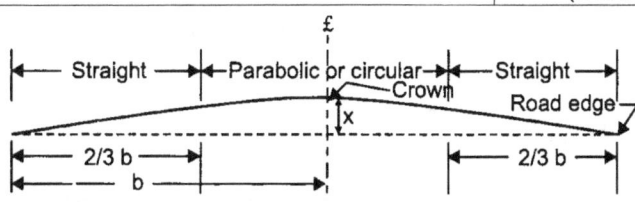

(a) Composite Camber

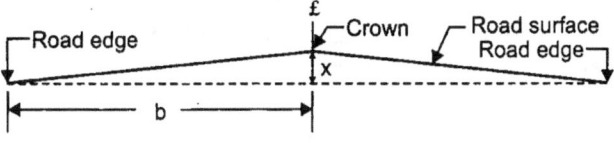

(b) Sloped or Straight Camber

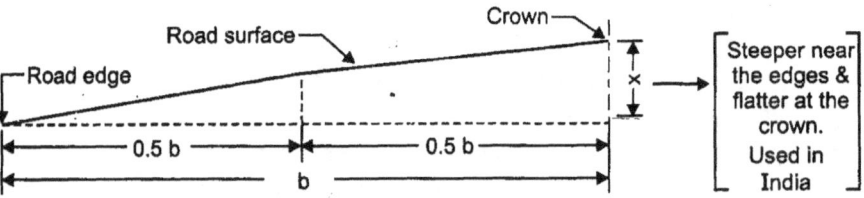

(c) Two Straight Line Camber

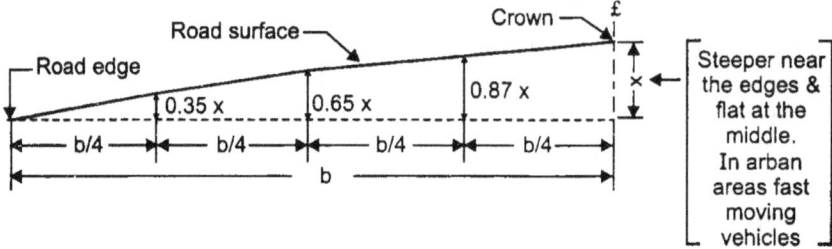

(d) Elliptical Barrel Camber

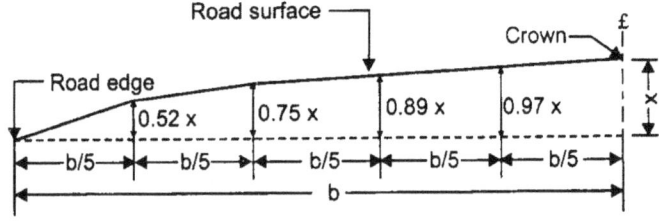

(e) Parabolic Barrel Camber

Fig. 10.6 : Types of Camber

10.7 SUPERELEVATION

The inward transverse inclination provided to the cross-section of the carriage way at horizontal curved portion of a road is called Superelevation, cant or banking.

It is expressed as the ratio of elevation of outer edge above the inner edge to the horizontal width of the carriage way or as the tangent of the angle of slope of the road surface. It is generally denoted by the letter 'e'.

From Fig. 10.7. Superelevation, $e = \dfrac{BC}{AC} = \tan \theta$

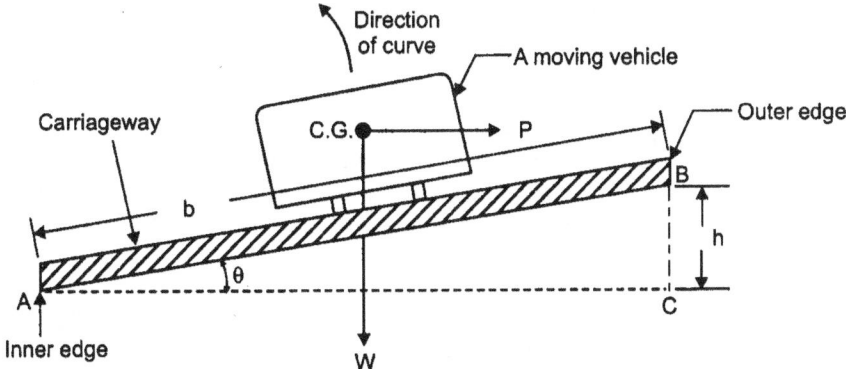

Fig. 10.7 : Carriage Way Showing Superelevation

In practice the value of e is very small. The maximum Superelevation allowed is 1 in 15 or 4°.

10.7.1 Objects of Providing Superelevation

1. To counteract the effect of centrifugal force acting on the moving vehicle to pull the same outward on a horizontal curve.
2. To help a fast moving vehicle to negotiate a curved path without overturning and skidding.
3. To ensure safety of the fast moving vehicle.
4. To prevent damaging effect on the road surface due to improper distribution of load.

10.7.2 Advantages of Providing Superelevation

1. It permits running of vehicle at high speed on a curved path or a straight path without any danger of overturning and thus results into increased volume of traffic.
2. It provides more or less even distribution of load on wheels and hence uniform stress is offered on the foundation which results into less wear on wheel tyres and springs as well as economy in maintenance cost of the road.
3. It also helps to keep the vehicles to their proper side on the pavement and thus prevents collision of vehicles moving in opposite direction on a curved portion of the road.
4. It provides drainage of the whole width of the road towards the inner side. Thus, there is no necessity of providing side drain on the outerside of the road.

10.8 GRADIENT

The rate of rise or fall provided to the formation of a road along its alignment is called as grade or gradient.

It is the longitudinal slope provided to the formation of a road along its alignment.

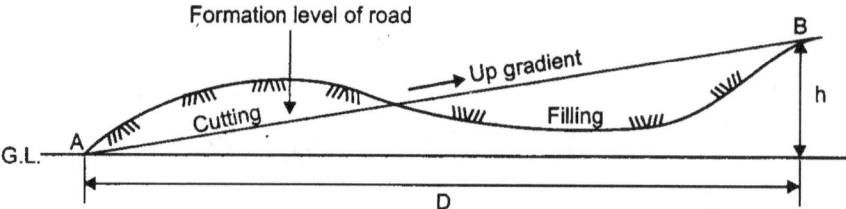

Fig. 10.8 : Alignment of a Road Showing Gradient

$$\text{Gradient} = \frac{\text{Vertical distance}}{\text{Horizontal distance}} = \frac{h}{D}$$

Or

$$\text{Gradient} = \frac{h}{D} \times 100 \text{ per cent}$$

10.8.1 Objects of Providing Gradient

1. To connect the terminal stations situated at different levels.
2. To make the earth work of the road project economical, since a perfectly level road involves more cutting and filling.
3. To provide effective drainage of rain water falling over the road surface, particularly when the pavement is provided with Kerbs.
4. To construct side drains economically with convenient depths below the ground level.
5. To reduce the maintenance cost of the road surface.

10.8.2 Factors Governing Gradient

The following are the various factors which govern the selection of gradient in the alignment of a road.

1. Nature of ground.
2. Nature of traffic.
3. Drainage required.
4. The type of road surface.
5. The total height to be covered.
6. Road and railway intersections and bridge approaches.
7. Safety required.

10.8.3 Types of Gradient

The following are the different types of Road Gradient :
1. Ruling gradient.
2. Limiting gradient.
3. Exceptional gradient.

4. Average gradient.
5. Floating gradient.
6. Minimum gradient.

1. Ruling Gradient : The gradient usually adopted while making the alignment of a road is called as Ruling Gradient.

The choice of the Ruling gradient depends on the following factors :

(a) The nature of vehicles.
(b) The type of road surface.
(c) The local topographical conditions.

2. Limiting Gradient : The gradient steeper than the ruling which may be used in restricted road lengths where the later is not feasible is called maximum or Limiting Gradient.

3. Exceptional Gradient : The gradient steeper than the limiting which may be used in short lengths of the roads only in extra ordinary situations is called as Exceptional Gradient.

4. Average Gradient : The total rise or fall between any two points along the alignment of a road divided by the horizontal distance between them is called Average Gradient.

5. Floating Gradient : The gradient on which a motor vehicle moving with a constant speed, continues to descend with the same speed without any application of power or brakes is called Floating Gradient.

6. Minimum Gradient : The minimum desirable slope essential for effective drainage of rain water from the road surface is called Minimum Gradient.

Table 10.2 : Gradients as Per Recommendations of I.R.C.

Sr. No.	Nature of the Area	Gradients		
		Ruling	Limiting	Exceptional
1.	Plain or Rolling Area	3.3 % (1 in 30)	5 % (1 in 20)	6.7 % 1 in 15
2.	Mountainous Area	5 % (1 in 20)	6 % (1 in 6.7)	7 % 1 in 143
3	Steep Area	6 % (1 in 16)	7 % 1 in 14.3	8 % 1 in 12.5

10.9 SIGHT DISTANCE

The distance along the centre line of a road at which a driver has visibility of an object, stationary or moving, at a specified height above the carriage way is known as sight distance.

10.9.1 Factors Affecting the Sight Distance

The safe sight distance depends upon the following :
1. Speed of the vehicle.
2. Efficiency of brakes of the vehicle.

3. The frictional resistance of the road surface.
4. Height of the driver's eye.
5. Slope of the road surface.
6. Eye sight of the driver.
7. Efficiency of the screen wipers during rain.
8. Weathering conditions.

10.9.2 Types of Sight Distances

The various sight distances which are considered for geometrical design of a road can be splitted up into the following types :

1. Stopping or non-passing sight distance.
2. Overtaking or passing sight distance.
3. Intermediate sight distance.
4. Lateral sight distance.

1. Stopping or non-passing sight distance : The clear distance ahead needed by a driver to bring his vehicle to a stop before meeting a stationary object on the road is called stopping or non-passing sight distance.

In case of summit curve, minimum stopping sight distance is the distance measured along the centre line of a road at which a driver whose eye sight is 1.22 m above the road surface can see the top of an object 15 cm high on the road. (See Fig. 10.9).

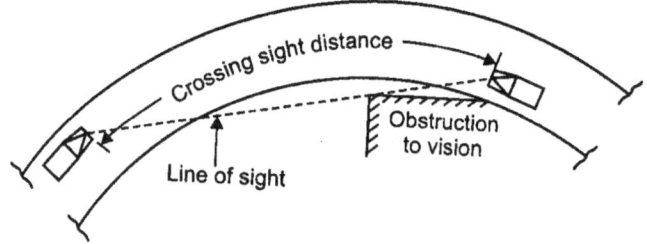

(a) Sight Distance at a Horizontal Curve

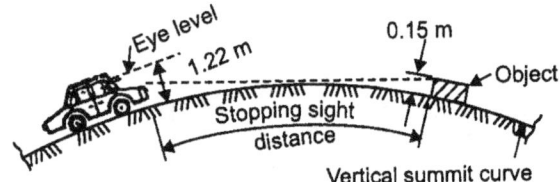

(b) Sight Distance on a Vertical Summit Curve (Stopping Sight Distance)

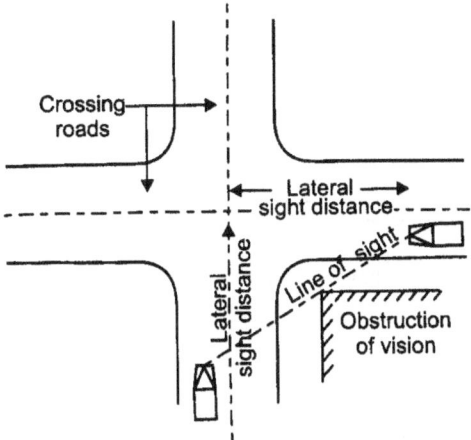

(c) Sight Distance at a Road Intersection (Lateral Sight Distance)

Fig. 10.9 : Sight Distances at Different Situations

2. Overtaking sight distance : The minimum sight distance needed by a driver on a two way road to enable him to overtake another vehicle ahead with safety against the traffic from opposite direction is called as overtaking sight distance.

The minimum overtaking sight distance depends upon the following factors :

(i) Speed of overtaking, overtaken and that of the vehicle coming from the opposite side.

(ii) Rate of acceleration of the overtaking vehicle.

(iii) Spacing between vehicles.

(iv) Skill and reaction time of the driver.

In case the driver of vehicle A running at design speed tries to overtake a slow moving vehicle B on a two lane road while the third vehicle C comes from the opposite direction, its overtaking manoeuvre is shown as below. Then the overtaking sight distance required for vehicle is A = $d_1 + d_2 + d_3$.

d_1 = The distance travelled by the overtaking vehicle A during the reaction time from A_1 to A_2.

d_2 = The distance travelled by the vehicle A from A_2 to A_3 during the actual overtaking operation.

d_3 = The distance travelled by the vehicle C coming from the opposite direction i.e. from C_1 to C_2 during the overtaking operation by vehicle A.

where,

d_1 = The distance travelled by the overtaking vehicle A during the reaction time from A_1 to A_2.

d_2 = The distance travelled by the vehicle A from A_2 to A_3 during the actual overtaking operation.

d_3 = The distance travelled by the vehicle C coming from the opposite direction i.e. from C_1 to C_2 during the overtaking operation by vehicle A.

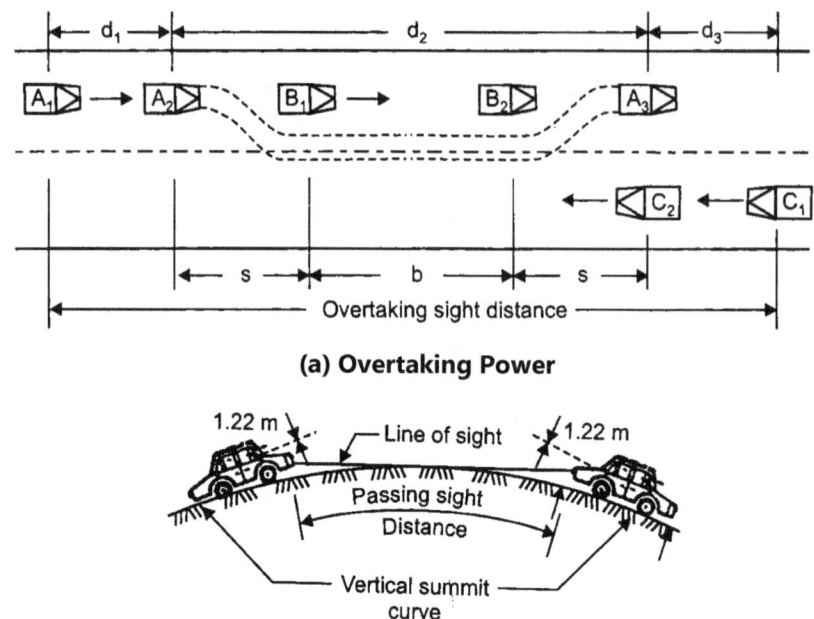

(a) Overtaking Power

(b) Measurement of Overtaking Sight Distance

Fig. 10.10 : Passing or Overtaking Sight Distance

3. Intermediate sight distance : The distance which affords reasonable opportunities to drivers to overtake the vehicle ahead with caution is known as intermediate sight distance.

This is taken as twice the safe stopping sight distance.

4. Lateral sight distance : The sight distance needed by the driver who sees another vehicle approaching the intersection, reacts and applies brakes to bring his vehicle to dead stop at the intersection without any collision or accident is called safe distance for entering into an intersection or lateral sight distance (See Fig. 10.10)

The lateral sight distances should be sufficient to satisfy the following three conditions :

(1) To enable either one or both the approaching vehicles to change their speeds to avoid collision.

(2) To bring either one or both the approaching vehicles to stop before reaching a point of collision.

(3) To enable the stopped vehicles on minor road to start, accelerate and cross the main road before the approaching vehicle, travelling at a design speed on main road, reaches the intersection.

10.10 MATERIALS USED FOR THE CONSTRUCTION OF ROADS

The materials used for the construction of road pavements are known as road materials.

The following are the different materials used for the construction of roads :

(1) Soil.

(2) Aggregates.

(3) Binders e.g. Cement and Bituminous material.

1. Soil : Soil is defined as, "sedimentary or other consolidated accumulations of solid particles produced by the physical and chemical disintegration of rocks which may or may not contain organic matter.

The soil may contain air, water, organic matter, consisting of more or less decomposed remains of plants and animal organisms, and other substances which remain dispersed throughout the mineral particles of the soil.

Functions of the soil :

   (i) To provide adequate support to the road pavement.

   (ii) To provide stability to the road pavement.

   (iii) To provide good drainage of rain water percolating through the road pavement.

2. Aggregates : The inert mineral fragments and particles forming a major portion of the road pavement are known as road aggregates.

It is the basic material for road construction. It is used for constructing pavements in cement concrete, bituminous concrete, and other bituminous constructions.

Aggregates are also used as granular base course underlying the superior pavements. These aggregates bear stresses occurring in the road structure and also resist wear due to abrasive action.

The following are the various types of Road Aggregates :

(a) Crushed stone aggregate.

(b) Gravel.

(c) Sand.

(d) Slag.

3. Binders : The materials used for binding the road aggregates in order to provide a better type of road surfacing are known as binders.

The following materials are commonly used as binders for road construction.

(i) Cement : It is used as a binding material in the concrete road pavements and also as a stabilizer for constructing stabilized earth roads.

Functions of cement in the construction of road pavement :

(a) It fills up the voids existing in the fine aggregate and makes the concrete pavement impermeable.

(b) It binds the road aggregates together into a solid mass by virtue of its setting and hardening properties when treated with water and thus provide body to the concrete pavements.

(c) It provides strength to the concrete pavements.

(ii) Bitumen : A hydrocarteneous material of either natural or pyrogenous origin, found in gaseous, liquid, semi-solid or solid in state and completely soluble in carbon disulphide is called bitumen.

The source of road bitumen is either natural asphalt or petroleum.

Bitumen is being extensively used for constructing different bituminous road pavement. It is used as a stabilizer for conducting stabilized earth roads.

10.11 RAILWAYS

The branch of Civil Engineering which deals with the design, construction and maintenance of the Railway track for safe, efficient, movement of trains is called Railway Engineering.

10.11.1 Important Technical Terms

1. Railways : A track formed of iron or steel along which the trains are driven is known as Railway.

2. Rolling Stock : The locomotives passenger coaches and goods wagons which roll or run or railway tracks constitute rolling stock.

3. Locomotive : The mechanical device which transfers chemical energy of fuel into mechanical energy in the form of motion is called locomotive.

4. Coaches or Vehicles : The passenger compartments are called coaches or vehicles.

5. Wagons : The goods compartments are called Wagons. The term is applied to goods stock.

6. Coaching Stock : All types of vehicles that run in passenger train are called coaching stock.

7. Goods Stock : Wagons used for movement of goods, heavy and bulky commodities are called Goods Stock.

10.11.2 Types of Gauges

The clear horizontal distance between the inner (running) faces of the two rails forming a track is known as gauge.

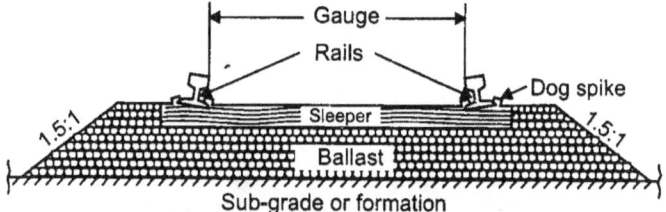

Fig. 10.11 : Section of a Railway Track Showing Gauge

The different types of Gauges are :

(1) Broad Gauge, (2) Metre Gauge, (3) Narrow Gauge

1. Broad Gauge (1676 mm) : When the clear horizontal distance between the inner faces of two parallel rails forming a track is 1676 mm. The gauge is called as Broad Gauge.

This is the standard gauge of India and is the broadest gauge in the World.

Suitability :

(i) When sufficient funds are available.

(ii) When the prospects of revenue are very bright.

2. Metre Gauge (1000 mm) : When the clear horizontal distance between the inner faces of two parallel rails forming a track is 1000 mm, the gauge is known as Metre Gauge - 1000 mm.

Suitability :

(i) When the funds available for the Railway project are inadequate.

(ii) When the prospects of revenue are not very bright.

3. Narrow Gauge : When the clear horizontal distance between the inner faces of two parallel rails forming a track is either 762 mm or 610 mm, the gauge is known as Narrow Gauge.

Suitability :

(i) When the construction of a track with wider gauge is prohibited due to the provision of sharp curves, steep gradient, narrow bridges and tunnels etc.

(ii) When the prospects of revenue are not very bright.

10.11.3 Components of a Railway Track

The following are component parts of a Railway Track.

(1) Formation or Sub-grade (2) Ballast
(3) Sleepers (4) Rails
(5) Fixtures and Fastenings

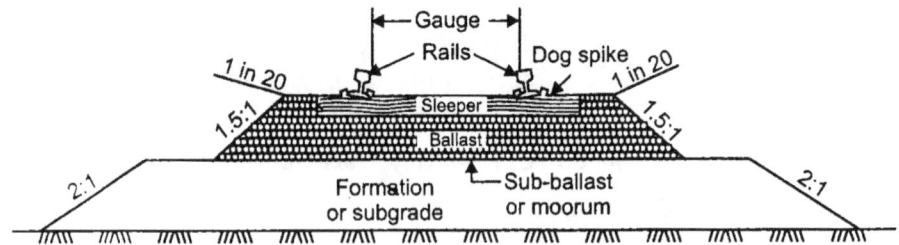

Fig. 10.12 : Section Showing Component Parts of a Permanent Way

1. Formation or Sub-grade : The prepared and finished surface of earth work on which a railway track is laid is known as formation or sub-grade.

The formation or sub-grade of a track may be constructed in embankment, cutting or at existing ground level, depending upon the topography of the area and the formation level as indicated in the finalised longitudinal section of the proposed track.

2. Ballast : The granular material spread on the formation of a Railway Track for the sleepers to rest open is called as Ballast.

3. Sleepers : The members laid transversely under the rails for supporting and fixing them to the gauge distance apart are known as sleepers.

4. Rails : The rolled steel section laid end to end in two parallel lines over sleepers to form a railway track are known as rails.

5. Fixtures and Fastenings : All the fittings which are used for linking the rails end to end and also for fixing the rails to the sleepers in a track are known as fixtures and fastenings.

The fittings which are permanently fastened in a track for making connections of rail to rail and of rail to sleepers are known as fixtures. The fixtures used in a railway track are fish plates, bearing plates, chairs etc.

The fittings which are used for securing the connection between rail to rail and rail to sleepers in a pack are known as fastenings.

The fastenings used in a railway track are spike, bolts, keys etc.

10.11.4 Advantages of Railway Engineering

1. It is suitable for transporting bulky cargo over long distances. e.g. coal, steel, timber etc.
2. Power required for railways is comparatively less because of the less inactive resistance of steel wheel on steel rails.
3. Railway provides a comfortable and safe means of communication within the reach of a common man.
4. Railway act as the biggest undertaking in the World and thus provide employment opportunities on a large scale.
5. Railway form the chief source of revenue to a country without any taxation.
6. Railway helps in promoting cultural and social ties among the people living in different parts of the country. In this way, they help in national integration.
7. During famines and calamities, Railway help in providing medical aid and other help to those affected by it.
8. Railway help in maintaining better law and order in the country.
9. In times of war, Railway help in transporting arms and ammunition from one place to other place.
10. In times of piece Railway helps in distribution of natural resources and agricultural produce.
11. Railway plays in important role in the industrialisation of the country.

Disadvantages of Railway Engineering :

1. Destination point and starting points are fixed and cannot be altered.
2. Cannot provide door to door service as the goods have to be loaded and unloaded at stations and this depend on road transport.
3. There is restriction on the path of railway line. Sharp curve and steep gradients cannot be provided, laying of track is costly.
4. Whenever the gauge changes, goods have to be unloaded and again loaded. This results in loss, breakage and theft. It also increases handling charges and delay the movement of the goods.

10.12 BRIDGES

Bridge Engineering : The branch of Civil Engineering which deals with the design, construction and maintenance of bridges is called as Bridge Engineering.

Bridge : The drainage structure which facilitates a communication route for carrying road or railway traffic across an obstruction or depression, with or without water is called as bridge.

The route of communication may be railways, roadway, cycle-track footpath, or a combination of them and the obstruction may be in the form of a river, stream, channel, valley road, or railway track.

10.12.1 Components of Bridges

A bridge is divided into following two major parts :

(1) Super structure

(2) Sub-structure.

1. Super structure : The upper part of a bridge consisting of structural system in the form of beams, girders, arches, suspension cable etc., carrying the communication route is called super structure.

This part of a bridge can be compared with roof, supported on walls and columns, in case of a single storey building, super structure of a bridge consists of beams, girders, arches, or trusses etc. over which carriage way is supported on carriage way with parapet or railing.

2. Sub-structure : The lower part of a bridge consisting of structural system in the form of abutment, piers etc. along with their foundations, which support the super-structure is called sub-structure.

This part of a bridge can be compared with walls, column and their foundations, supporting the roof in case of a single storey building.

The function of sub-structure is to support the super structure and to provide access to the traffic to the level of bridge super structure through approaches.

Sub-structure of a bridge consists of the following components :

(1) Approaches

(2) Abutments

(3) Wing walls

(4) Piers

(5) Foundation.

1. Approaches : The portion of roadways or Railway on both the ends, affected by the design and layout of a bridge are known as approaches.

The function of approaches is to enable the vehicle running on a road or railway track at normal level to approach the level of bridge floor.

2. Abutments : The end supports of a bridge super structure are termed as abutments.

The functions of the abutments are as follows :

(i) To support the super structure.

(ii) To retain the earth pressure on their back.

3. Wing walls : The walls are constructed on both sides of abutments to retain the earth banks of the river or of the bridge approaches are called as wing walls.

The functions of the wing walls are as follows :

(i) To retain the earth banks of approaches in which case they are called return wing walls.

(ii) To protect the earth banks of river from the action of water if necessary.

4. Piers : The intermediate supports of a bridge super structure are known as piers.

In very long arches, some of the intermediate supports are made of thicker section, which are known as abutment piers. Such piers are so designed as to serve the function of abutment except retaining and protecting. The earth banks of approaches.

The functions of the piers are as follows :

(i) To take and transfer the load from the bridge super structure to the sub-soil laying underneath through their foundations.

(ii) To divide the length of the bridge into a suitable number of spans.

5. Foundation : The lowermost part of the bridge sub-structure is called foundation.

All the components of a bridge sub-structure such as abutments wing walls and piers rest on foundation.

The function of the foundation is as follows :

(i) To take and transfer the load from the bridge super structure to the sub-soil laying underneath.

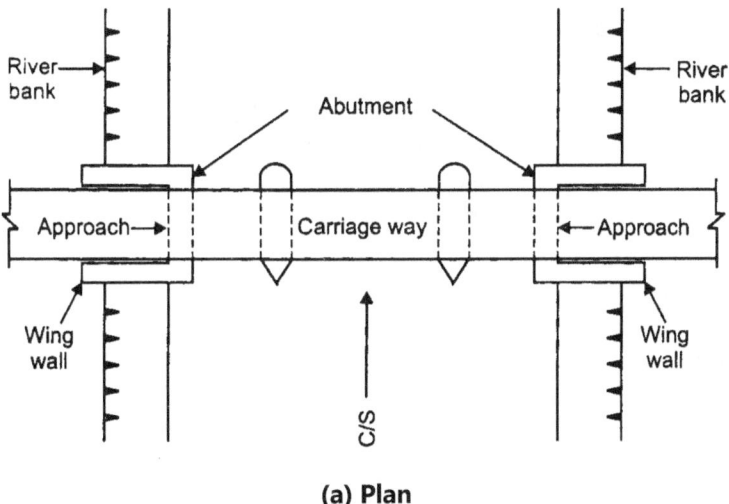

(a) **Plan**

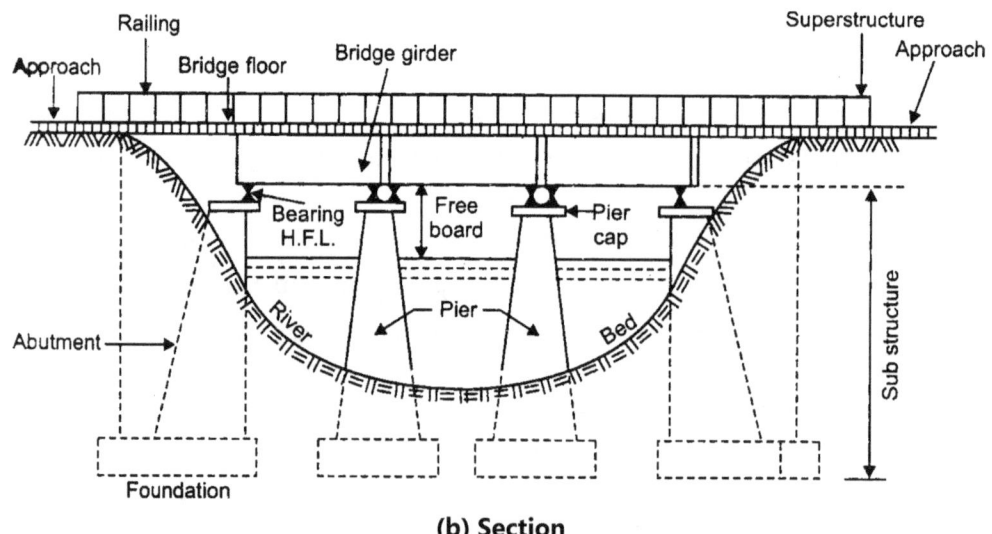

(b) Section

Fig. 10.13 : Component Parts of a Bridge

10.13 AIRWAYS

The most sophisticated and advanced mode of transport is the Air transport. Air transport is very fast and has made the world a small place. In a matter of hours, persons and things can be moved from one part of the globe to other. Tourism industry has been developed to a great extent by this mode of transport. Air-Cargo division of the most of the companies are involved in day-to-day exchange of documents and materials with their partners in the other side of globe.

Merits :

1. Very sophisticated and fast mode of transport.
2. Plays important role in war-time defence of the country.
3. Emergency supplies to remote areas can be immediately made.
4. This mode of transport can have access to areas where other modes cannot reach.
5. Earns national revenue in the form of tourism and passenger traffic.
6. A wide-spread to air transport network is a sign of development of a nation.

Demerits :

1. The system is costly. Therefore cannot be afforded by common man.
2. Investment in the setting up of infrastructure like Airports, hangers, control towers is very high.
3. The climatic factors like storms, fog, rainfall etc. also affect the routine of the air transport.

Apart from these basic modes of transport, pipe lines are used to transport (oil, water, natural gas etc.) heavy materials under or above the ground over long distances and rugged terrain, where transportation by basic modes is either not feasible or costly. Other modes like conveyor belts, escalators, cable cars and ropeways are also employed to transport men and material depending upon the situation.

10.13.1 Components of the Aircraft

Basic components of the aircraft illustrated in Fig. 10.14 are as follows :
1. Fuselage
2. Wing
3. Engines
4. Propellers (Propulsion System)
5. Three controls about   X axis – Rolling movement
                                    Y axis – Pitching movement
                                    Z axis – Yawning movement
6. Rudder
7. Elevator
8. Aileron
9. Flaps
10. Undercarriage system.

Table 10.3 describes the functions and the impact of the components of aircraft on airport design.

Table 10.3 : Aircraft components, Functions and Impact on Airport design

	Component of Aircraft	Functions	Impact on design of airport
1.	The wings	Life and support the aircraft in flight. Containers for fuel tank.	Spatial design of aircraft packing, taxiing.
2.	Fuselage	Payload, flight and engine controls.	Aircraft weight.
3.	Aileron, Flap Trim tap	Three major controls in each wing. Increase lifting force. Balance small changes in the control.	Airport traffic management to control movements for safe traffic movements.
4.	Tail assembly	Stability about lateral, vertical axes. To control climb, dives, yaws. Directional stability.	Traffic control.
5.	Landing gear (wheel)	Facilitate take off/landing.	Design of runway, taxiway.
6.	Propulsion system	Power for flight	Design of runway taxiway.

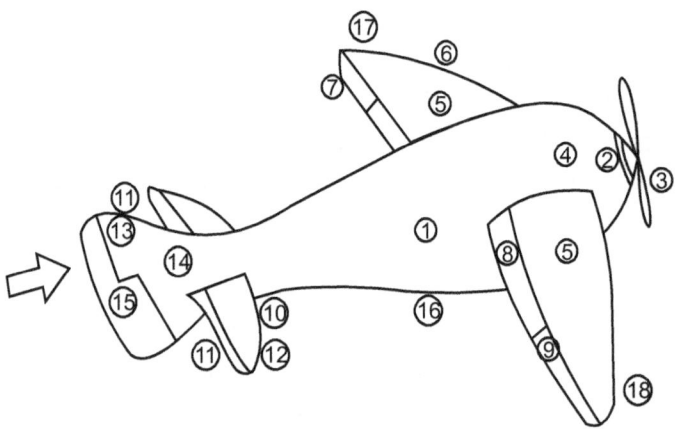

Direction of flight

1. Fuselage, 2. Nose, 3. Propeller, 4. Cockpit, 5. Wing, 6. Leading edge, 7. Trailing edge, 8. Aileron, 9. Wing flap, 10. Tail plan, 11. Elevator (Trime tab), 12. Right horizontal stabilizer, 13. Vertical stabilizer (fin), 14. Tail, 15. Rubber, 16. Landing gear (tricycle under carriage) not shown, 17. Left wing (Port wing), 18. Right wing (starboarding wing)

Fig. 10.14 : Basic components of the Aircraft

10.13.2 Aircraft Characteristics

The aircraft characteristics which dominate the airport layout and operations are as follows :

1. Aircraft size
2. Gear arrangement
3. Turning radius cockpit deflection
4. Aircraft weights
5. Propulsion
6. Speed
7. Capacity
8. Range
9. Jet blast
10. Fuel spillage
11. Take off/Landing distance requirements
12. Tyre pressure and contact area
13. Noise

10.14 RUNWAYS

They are a particular strip of the landing strip of the landing space which supports the aircraft when grounded. The runways may be paved or unpaved. The factors to be designed for efficient operations and maximization of runway utilization are priority rules for the selection of runways for landings and take offs, runway occupancy time for various aircraft types and separation of aircrafts.

10.14.1 Runway Design

10.14.1.1 Runway Length : Design Objectives

The objectives of the runway length are :

1. The runway should be long enough to allow for safe arrival and departure of aircrafts likely to be introduced in future.
2. The runway length should be compatible with the current equipments at the airport.
3. The runway length should be sufficiently long to accommodate :
   (a) The differences in the skill of pilots.
   (b) Aircraft types.
   (c) Landing and take off operational requirements.

10.14.1.2 Basic Principle of Runway Design

The basic principle of runway design is the safety of aircraft operations. It takes into account factors such as :

1. Take off and landing characteristics of the most critical aircraft.
2. Range of aircraft.
3. Altitude of the airport.
4. Runway pavement characteristics : Gradients, pavement conditions.
5. Weather characteristics and reference to standard atmosphere.

Theoretical methods of determining landing strip are founded on the basic of aerodynamics of aircraft. But experimental data of great use in the design.

10.14.1.3 Runway Length Analysis

Following are some terminologies used in analysing the landing strip requirements :

1. **Continued take off :** When the aircraft continues the take off operation with one or all of its engines in the operating condition it is called continued take off.
2. **Aborted take off :** When the aircraft is brought to the stop position within the limits of the paved runway the take off position gets aborted hence it is called aborted take off. The pilot reaction time for decision making after the engine failure is 3 seconds.
3. **Take off distance :** It is the distance travelled by the aircraft from the point of take off to the point which is 10 m above the level of the paved runway centre line.
4. **Critical take off speed :** It is the lowest speed at which pilot can maintain the control of multi engine aircraft in the case one of the engine fails.
5. **Balanced field length of the runway and one stop way :** It is the length of the runway which satisfies the length requirements of the critical take off speed (v_{tr}).

10.15 TAXIWAYS

It is a specially prepared area used for towing (taxiing) the aircraft. According to the function (purpose of aircraft manoeuvre) the taxiways are classified as :

(i) Return taxiways : They are parallel to the main runway and allow the aircraft to be towed, taxied from holding apron to the main runway.

(ii) Connecting taxiways : They work as cross over taxiways. They interlink the turn offs and return taxiways.

(iii) Branch taxiways : They connect the return taxiways to either apron, aircraft parking apron or special purpose areas.

The elements of design are the length of the taxiway, taxiing speed and number of intersections along the taxiway with individual link-length and capacity.

They are the paths on the airfield surface which are designed for taxiing of aircraft. They provide the linkage between various parts of the airfield. The speeds of aircraft on taxiways are very less than on the runways. Hence the criteria governing their longitudinal slopes, vertical curves and sight distances are not as stringent as for runways. Their geometric features are governed by FAA and ICAO specifications.

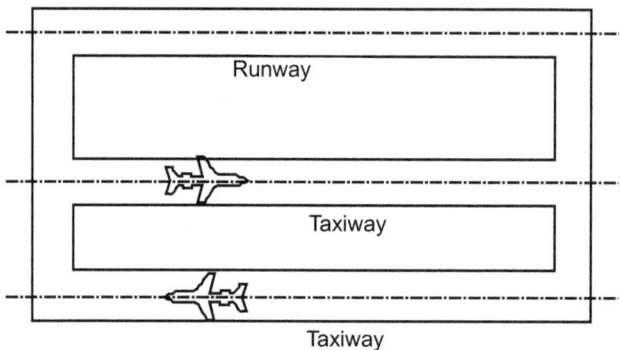

Fig. 10.15 : Runway taxiways

Each taxiway is intended to accommodate only one aircraft at a time. It has not enough space for another aircraft to pass one another. Safe taxiing of aircrafts is the objective of taxiway. Various measures taken to ensure safety wheels are passing points, markers, taxiway light. Taxiways require stronger pavement than runways due to higher loading rate due to aircraft wheels rolling over.

10.15.1 Taxiway Capacity

The runway or gate way capacity falls short of the taxiway capacity. When the taxiway crosses the runway the parameters that decide the taxiway capacity are

1. Rate of runway operations.

2. The mix of aircraft type.
3. Location (nearness or distantness) of the taxiway with reference to departure end of runway.

FAA has suggested graphical solutions for estimating taxiway capacity.

10.15.2 Design Parameters of Taxiway

The design parameters are affected by density of air-traffic, the configuration of the runway, the location of terminal building and other facilities. FAA and ICAO regulations for taxiway design are :

1. Alignment : It should be direct, straight, simple.
2. Curves : Large radii should be provided to curves as to ensure minimum taxiing speed between the range 30 to 40 kmph.
3. Intersections : Speeds are low at intersections. Clear visibility is desired.
4. Width of taxiway.
5. Pavement widening on curves should be by 5 m with 45 m flare.
6. Wing tip clearance (W) on apron taxiway : It is a function of aircraft-type. It varies from 12 m to 25 m.
7. Design of longitudinal grade for taxiways.

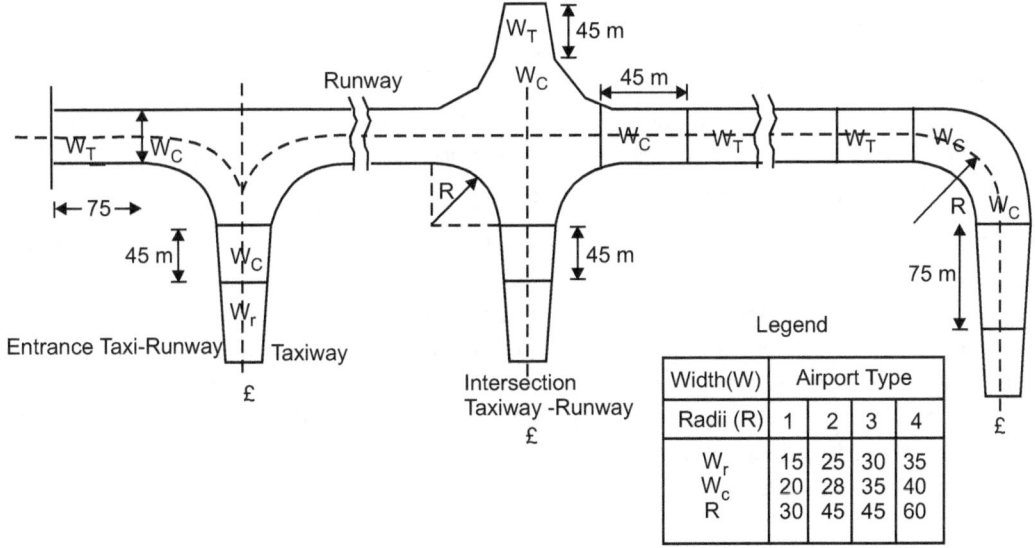

Fig. 10.16 : Typical taxi-way

The aircraft speed on the taxiways is less. The precision regarding grades depends on the density of aircraft operations. On taxiways aircraft activities are limited. Therefore, grade regulations are not stringent. In general, grades for runway and corresponding taxiway may be same. For functional airports, gradient of 1.5% is sufficient.

Taxiway vertical curves should be minimum 30 m long for each 1% grade change. However ICAO relaxation is of 27 m length.

FAA does not point out specific sight requirements for taxiways, however, where taxiways and runways intersect the analysis of intersection based on the sight distance requirements is suggested.

The gradients of the taxiways should be such that the object 3 m above taxiway should be seen over all the taxiway surface for a distance of not less than 300 m from the object. The actual sight distance requirement will depend on the airport type.

8. Transverse grade : The transverse grades for taxiway are similar to that of runways.

10.16 HANGERS-SELECTION OF SITE FOR MAINTENANCE BASE

The location for maintenance base should satisfy following requirements :

1. The maintenance base should be so located as to offer minimum distance for the movement of aircraft, service equipments and vehicles, airport personnel engaged in maintenance.
2. The length of various services such as electricity, water supply, sewerage should be minimum.
3. Operational safety to aircrafts, ground vehicles and personnel should be ensured.
4. Aircraft noise, engine noise should be below acceptable maximum limits.
5. Various stationary and mobile equipments should be planned according to their functions. Total layout should be space-economic.
6. Safety against fire and explosion hazards should be ensured.

Variety of equipments are used for aircraft maintenance with a view to reduce the maintenance time. Proper selection of the equipments influences the economics and the performance of maintenance schedule. The equipments are of stationary or mobile type. Stationary type equipments are required frequently, hence located near the place of activity. The pulled-type or self-propelled equipments many times replace the stationary equipments for want of the space at aprons or parking area. However, the stationary equipment have the advantage of reduced pollution, increased safey, reduced operational cost. The parking layout should be so planned as to maximize these advantages. Some of the stationary facilities are

1. Fuelling.
2. Direct current or one-three phase A.C. supply to aircraft system.
3. Single or three phase supply to ground equipments.

FUNDAMENTALS OF CIVIL ENGINEERING   INFRASTRUCTURE

4. Telephone communication system.

5. Information processing system required by control room and maintenance hangers.

6. Control of power sources.

These facilities are made available at loading apron parking area, engine run-up area, maintenance hangers. Adequately planned and designed structures, engineering services, power supply, fuel supply are basic elements of the stationary services.

10.16.1 Hangers and Repairs Factories

The hangers provide the scheduled maintenance, repair, check up to different aircrafts, check upto different ground equipments and assemblies. The space-requirement of the hanger depends on the aircraft-type and number and orientation of aircrafts stationed on the hanger floor.

Future trend of aircraft design in respect of seating capacity, various dimensions of the components of the aircraft is difficult to predict. Hence a right policy in planning hangers of short haul and long haul type is necessary. The types of hanger layout are :

1. Dead end hanger.

2. Direct through hanger.

3. Cantilever hanger.

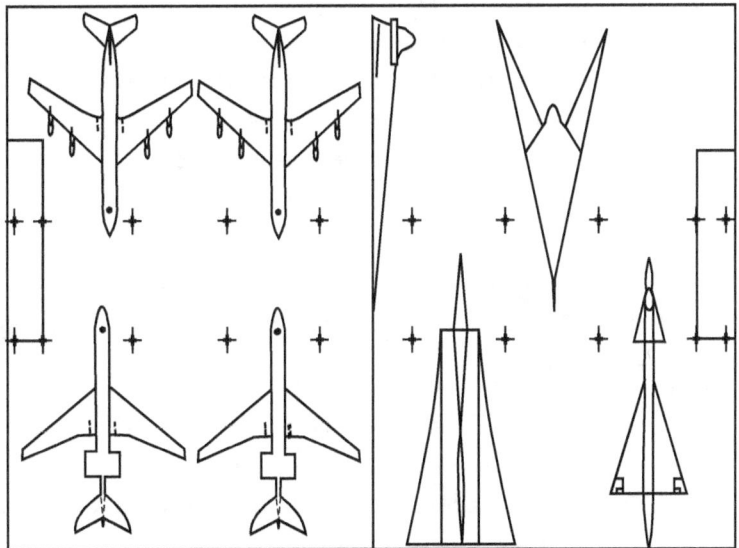

Fig. 10.17 : Layout of double-cantilever hanger (Inst. of Engrs, 1960)

10.16.1.1 The Depth of Hanger

(I) When the aircrafts are packed in single row :

The total floor area for each layout depends on the aircraft dimensions and number of aircraft parking stations. If the aircrafts are parked in single row, the depth of the hanger is found by using the formula :

$$D = L + X + Y + x_1 + x_2$$

where
- D = Depth of the hanger
- L = Length of the largest aircraft
- X = Aisle width between aircraft nose and hanger wall (3 ~ 4 m)
- Y = Aisle width between aircraft tail and hanger wall (3 m)
- x_1 = Width of foredock platform
- x_2 = Width of after dock platform

(II) When the aircraft is parked in two rows :

$$D = 2L + X + 2Y + 2x_1 + 2x_2$$

The aircraft should be provided independent exit/extrance to the hanger. The number of hanger stations (aircraft positions) is found in this way :

$$N_h = n/C$$
$$= nftk/T$$

where
- N_h = Number of hanger stations
- n = Number of based aircrafts of given type
- C = Capacity of the hanger station for a given aircraft type
- f = Annual flying hours per aircraft
- t = Relative maintenance time per aircraft i.e. hours per flying hour
- k = Yearly variation in the number of aircrafts which require scheduled maintenance
- T = Total maintenance time per year

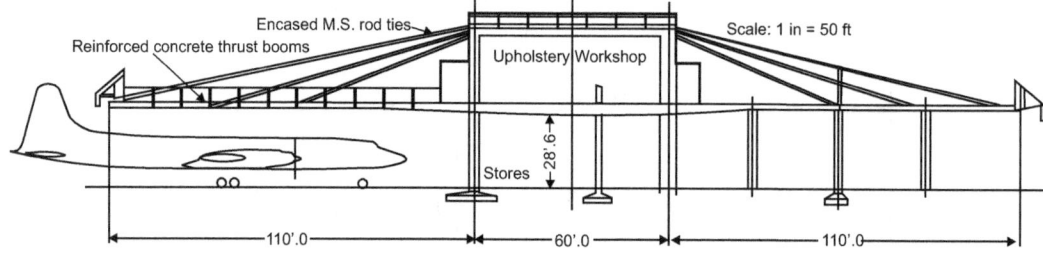

Fig. 10.18 : Cross section of B.O.A.C. wing hangers at London airport
(Source : Inst. of Engrs, 1960)

Hangers consist of long bays (300 m) with unobstructed door opening. Such openings provide flexibility, ease in aircraft manoeuvre and their arrangement for maintenance purposes. When the wing spans are uncertain the flexibility ensures maximum space utilization. Fig. 10.18 gives the layout for different aircraft-types in the double cantilever hanger. Various components to be considered for design are large span roofs, beams, portals, frames, arches, trusses, bowstrings, cylindrical shell may be used for roofs, large span doors and sport span roof to back wall.

Cantilevers :

They are provided for day-lighting and heat insulation.

Hanger doors :

Machine shop for repair and manufacture of tools and jigs used in aircraft servicing. Heat treatment, welding, vulcanizing and electroplating is done in 'hot' departments which are designed for protection against health hazard.

10.16.1.2 Hangers for Line Maintenance

Line maintenance operations are related with forepart of the aircraft. Hence wing hangers of shallow depths are designed to save the space.

EXERCISE

1. Compare Roadways and Railways.
2. Give the classification of roads according to importance.
3. Give the classification of roads according to roads.
4. What is camber in a road surface ? Illustrate it with a sketch.
5. Explain the significance of road gradients in road alignment.
6. Explain the following :
    (a) Right of way.
    (b) Camber.
    (c) Rulling gradient.
    (d) Superelevation.
    (e) Stopping sight distance.
7. Draw a neat sketch of road in embankment.
8. Define Superelevation and state the objects of providing Superelevation.
9. Explain in brief the different types of gradient.
10. What are the factors affecting the sight distance ?
11. Write a short note on stopping or non-passing sight distance.
12. What are the different materials used for the construction of roads ?

13. Enlist various advantages of Railways.
14. Define Gauge and state the various types of Gauges.
15. With neat sketch explain the component parts of a Railway Tracks.
16. Explain the necessity of Bridge.
17. With neat sketch explain the different components of a Bridge.
18. Define the following terms :
    (a) Bridge
    (b) Pier
    (c) Wing walls
    (d) Abutment.
19. Define the following terms :
    (a) Broad gauge
    (b) Gauge
    (c) Railway
    (d) Lateral sight distance.

❏❏❏

www.ingramcontent.com/pod-product-compliance
Lightning Source LLC
Chambersburg PA
CBHW081145230426

43664CB00018B/2804